Baseball
FAQ

Baseball FAQ

All That's Left to Know About America's Pastime

Tom DeMichael

Backbeat
Books

An Imprint of Hal Leonard Corporation

Published in 2015 by Backbeat Theatre & Cinema Books
An Imprint of Hal Leonard Corporation
7777 West Bluemound Road
Milwaukee, WI 53213

Trade Book Division Editorial Offices
33 Plymouth St., Montclair, NJ 07042

All images are from the author's collection.

The FAQ series was conceived by Robert Rodriguez and developed with Stuart Shea.

Printed in the United States of America

Book design by Snow Creative Services

Library of Congress Cataloging-in-Publication Data

Names: DeMichael, Tom, author.
Title: Baseball FAQ : all that's left to know about America's pastime / Tom
    DeMichael.
Description: Montclair, NJ : Backbeat Books An Imprint of Hal Leonard
    Corporation, 2015. | Series: FAQ series | Includes bibliographical references
    and index.
Identifiers: LCCN 2015042242 | ISBN 9781617136061 (Paperback)
Subjects: LCSH: Baseball—United States—Miscellanea.
Classification: LCC GV873 .D44 2015 | DDC 796.357—dc23
LC record available at http://lccn.loc.gov/2015042242

www.backbeatbooks.com

Dedicated to my dear old Daddio, who introduced me to this grand game and, soon after, watched in horror—while umpiring—when his seven-year-old son took a baseball to the back of the head.

Contents

Acknowledgments

The game of baseball has developed over the years largely because of the valuable input from people who cared enough to make it into the great American pastime. In a similar way, writing this book has been the result of valuable input from many people—some who don't even know me—who cared enough to make this the volume now in your possession.

As such, I am eternally grateful and offer my thanks to the following folks:

- Hall of Famers Rod Carew and Steve Carlton
- Outfield great Jimmy Piersall
- The Rebel—Catcher Randy Hundley
- A special tip of the cap to Cassidy Lent of the Baseball Hall of Fame, who was tireless in hitting a homer with every curveball question I threw at her
- Longtime cohorts from the dugout, Kenny Haas #25 and Bruce Carbonara
- The Society for American Baseball Research
- Jim Myers of the Arizona Diamondbacks
- Marybeth Keating, Wes Seeley, Gary Morris, and John Cerullo from Hal Leonard Publishing for their incredible patience, direction, and backing along the way
- Rob Rodriguez for his never-ending guidance and trust

and, for who they are and what they make me . . .

- Wife Paula, sons Anthony and Alex, their companions Ian and Dana, and grandson Charlie
- Tom Edinger for his constant encouragement and never-wavering friendship
- And to all the baseball fans around the world—let's play two!

Introduction

It's Much More Than Xs and Os

Yeah, yeah . . . another book on baseball.

What possibly can be written about the game that hasn't already been published?

As a former history teacher, I can tell you that names and numbers don't change. For example, Honest Abe was the sixteenth President of the United States between the years 1861 and 1865—that's the way it was and that's the way it always will be. But I also know that the way a story is told can make all the difference in the world.

So that's the strategy for this *Baseball FAQ*—telling the stories in a different way.

And why do I get the honor of undertaking such a task? Because I love the game (perhaps more than my wife, but please don't tell her—what that wonderful woman doesn't know won't hurt her). And, as a writer, I believe I can relate the myriad of baseball's matchless facets in a way that's entertaining as well as informative. Plus, I've played the game (at the lowest, lowest of levels), as well as coached kids (including my own two boys) and adults, men and women, for more than twenty-five years.

Don't think for a moment that my love affair with baseball is a private one. In 2014, nearly 75 million fans attended major league baseball in America. League reports show that in 2012, more than $54 million was spent on MINOR league baseball merchandise (not game tickets, not hot dogs, just caps, jerseys, and pennants). And consumers in 2014 America spent $619 million on baseball and softball equipment. More, the game continues to take its welcome wagon across the globe, as organized baseball is played on all six of the permanently inhabited continents. (So tell me why the game was removed from the Summer Olympics, because I just don't get it.)

Again, why am I writing this book? Consider the world of opera (stay with me, we'll get back to balls and strikes in a jiffy). As a (relatively) competent writer, I could research and assemble a competent book about arias, librettos, and divas. (Hmmm, there's a connection to baseball already.) But, as much as I appreciate the distinctiveness and difficulty that opera holds, it just doesn't float my boat. As such, a resulting book from my computer might be accurate but lifeless. (So, all my best to whoever gets the assignment for the *Opera FAQ*.)

On the other hand, I hold the game of baseball in the highest standing, both in my heart and mind. Much like a favorite song, it may be the tempo, it may be the rhythm, it may be the way the players play it. It's often hard to describe what the sport does to me, but whatever it is, it does it good.

That's not to say this book will be dry as an Arizona sandlot, or as slow and dull as a nothing-nothing tied game that goes into extra innings. As much as I love and respect the game, I also know there's room to tell the stories with a light tone and a smile. To quote former baseball player and broadcaster Joe Garagiola, "Baseball is a funny game." (Take that whichever way you choose.) After all, it's a kids' game played by very well-paid adults.

Baseball FAQ will make a valiant attempt to cover all the bases (see, I told you). You can consider it part history book, part instructional guide, part reference manual, and part bathroom buddy (hopefully, you don't run out of toilet paper or this book's in trouble). For the rabid fan (after the rabies shots), there should be some fact or anecdote you've never before heard or read. For the casual fan, there should be enough to make you a rabid fan. Perhaps it will merely help you to better watch the Little Leaguers playing down the street, or Game Seven of the World Series.

The world of baseball is vast, so an effort will be made to deliver the goods at several levels. For example, there is much enjoyment to be had by watching a Yankees home game from a choice box seat right behind home plate (unless, of course, you happen to be a Red Sox fan). But I propose there's just as much enjoyment to be had by finding a local minor league park and watching that game.

For a family of four, the Yankees game will cost you around $6,389, with $6,300 for the tickets (four from the Legends Suite, Section 023, Row 5), $35 for parking, and $54 for four hot dogs (@ $6 each), two beers (@$9 each), and two sodas (@$6 each). At those prices, you better hope Derek Jeter wiped the mustard as it dribbled down your chin. And that's no slight against the great shortstop in the Bronx—he had a great career and deserves first-year Hall of Fame induction.

But the same family of four can attend a game in Hickory, North Carolina, watching the Crawdads (a Class A affiliate for the Texas Rangers, part of the South Atlantic League), and it will cost them about $71. That's four tickets right behind home plate for $36 ($9 each in Section 109, Row 3), $3 for parking, and $32 for four hot dogs (@ $3 each), two beers (@$6 each), and two sodas (@$4 each). It's very likely the skill level won't be the same as the Yankees (and you'll have to wipe the mustard off by yourself).

But that isn't the point. The two examples demonstrate the breadth and scope in the game of baseball. It's almost guaranteed that either experience would be great entertainment for the family of four. And that family doesn't have to live in a major metropolis of over eight million people like New York City. They can enjoy a nice evening of pro baseball in a small town of forty thousand like Hickory.

It's a phenomenon that is kind of unique to baseball. Other sports, such as football, hockey, and basketball, might have structures that somewhat resemble minor league systems, but it is more likely that a top-quality player in those sports will move directly from the collegiate ranks (or even high school, like LeBron James) to a major league roster. Only baseball provides the chance to move up in the ranks as time and talents progress, thereby giving fans like us many more opportunities to enjoy the game and those players, some with names that have ranged over the years from Aaron to Zernial.

It should be pointed out that the *Baseball FAQ* is not intended to be a contest of "my sport can beat up your sport." As much as I love the game, I do not intend on launching into a campaign in an attempt to convince fans of other sports to join the ranks of baseball lifers like myself. I like watching pro football; I don't particularly enjoy watching collegiate sports like football and basketball; I don't watch hockey. Are they terrible or boring sports? Of course not.

But those other sports just don't carry the appeal or offer the magic that baseball presents to me. (So I guess I'm out of the running for penning the *Football FAQ*, but that's perfectly OK.) For me, baseball allows individual accomplishments in a total team effort, played on a field that is unlike any other in sports, in a season that—including spring training, playoffs, and the World Series—crosses almost two hundred games.

Across nearly 150 years, a half-dozen wars, and a world population that's grown from just over one billion to more than seven billion (to paraphrase James Earl Jones in *Field of Dreams*), the one constant in the world has been baseball. Many people may believe that the dog is man's best friend; I'll agree with that when Fido can get around on an inside fastball.

While I pondered writing this book, something interesting occurred to me. As much as I loved her, I didn't cry when my mom died a few years ago. And as much as I loved him, I also didn't cry when my dad just recently died. But I do shed a tear every time Roy Hobbs pauses in *The Natural* and says, "God, I love baseball."

Mom and Dad would completely understand.

Rules of the Game

Hey! Everyone Has to Play by the Rules

The Objective: Excuse Me, I Have to Go Home Now

Oh boy. This is the proverbial elephant that must be devoured. Imagine an alien has come to Earth and, wondering about our customs (and not interested in melting our brains), wants to know about our curious game of baseball. He/she/it has no point of reference, so where does one start? That's the pachyderm. So, how do we eat it? We're gonna need a bigger knife and fork.

All together, folks—"One bite at a time!"

As one might expect, the rules of the game have evolved over the last 150-plus years. By and large, that progression will be covered in the next chapters on the history of the game. For this chapter, the focus will be on the way the game is played today. Guiding our path will be the Official Baseball Rules, as defined by Major League Baseball in a document of 136 pages and ten enumerated divisions. And since it's a little dry (perhaps the elephant cooked a wee bit too long), we'll keep our trip light and breezy along the way.

So, let's put our bibs on and dig in to the rules of baseball—one delicious, sweet mouthful at a time (sorry, it's getting close to lunchtime around here).

What is the objective of the game of baseball? (Long inhale . . . pause . . . long exhale.) Two teams of nine athletes each compete on a field of play, in an effort to win by one team scoring more runs than the other; and by using equipment designed for the game, the two teams exchange the roles of offense and defense in the contest, not limited by time, but by finite units of measure called innings. (Whew.)

Runs are scored by a batter (the offense) striking a ball thrown by the pitcher, who is assisted by eight fielders (the defense). If the ball lands in fair territory safely, the batter becomes a runner, advancing to first base (or farther, depending on the type of hit). As (and if) additional hits are collected, base runners continue to advance (unless they are put out by a fielder) until they score by moving from base to base and reaching home plate safely.

The field of play has an infield of standardized measure and an outfield with minimum requirements of dimension (sounds like the start of a *Twilight Zone* episode). In other words, the infield is always a ninety-foot square (even though it's referred to as a "diamond), with a five-sided home plate at one tip of the

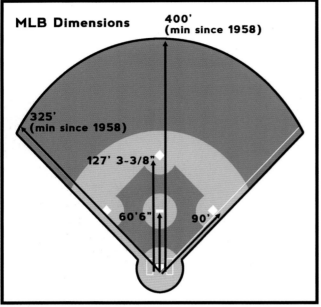

MLB Dimensions

400'
(min since 1958)

325'
(min since 1958)

127' 3-3/8"

60'6"

90'

Major league ballpark dimensions.

square—seventeen inches wide and beveled on two sides (the "roof" of the home)—made of white rubber. Bases of soft material—fifteen inches square and three to five inches thick—are located and firmly secured at the other three points of the geometric figure. They are numbered, ordinally and counterclockwise: first, second, and third.

In case anyone has ever wondered, the direct distances between home to second and first to third are each 127 feet, 3⅜ inches. Don't believe it? Just drop in the ol' right angle hypotenuse formula from Mr. Vogel's eighth-grade math class—the square root of two times one of the equal legs, or, 1.414 times 90 feet is 127.28.

Surrounding home plate is the batter's box, with rectangles of four feet wide and five feet deep, for left-handed and right-handed hitters. A catcher's box of eight feet deep extends back from the tip of home plate. The distance from home plate to the backstop is suggested (politely) to be at least sixty feet.

Halfway between home and second is the pitcher's mound, which is inside an eighteen-foot circle. In its center—and sixty feet, six inches from the tip of home plate—is the front of a rubber pitcher's plate, which is twenty-four inches wide and six inches deep. The height of the pitcher's mound is ten inches (although many hitters feel it must be two or three feet on some days).

Running from each beveled corner of home plate are foul lines (although they're actually in fair territory—go figure) that extend through the infield, into the outfield, ending at the outfield fence. Any ball struck within those white paint or chalk lines is considered "in play," while outside them is "foul" and not playable (although an out, if caught). Also outside of those lines are benches—roofed and one for each team—at a distance of at least twenty-five feet.

The outfield is the area in fair territory, backed by a wall or fence. At the foul lines, the distance from home plate must be at least 250 feet (325 feet and 400 feet to center for stadiums built after June 1, 1958). There is no official rule regarding the dimensions of bare and grassy areas, as well as the widths of warning tracks (although ten to fifteen feet is advisable).

The baseball itself is a sphere of yarn wrapped around a cork or rubber center, encased in two bone-shaped pieces of white horsehide or cowhide, sewn together with 108 red double stitches (count 'em sometime when you have nothing else to do).

The bat has to be one piece of solid wood, no more than two and sixty-one/one-hundredths of an inch in diameter at its thickest part and cannot be any more than forty-two inches long (although there is no limit to weight). For instance, the monstrous Frank Howard, at six foot eight inches tall and weighing 280 pounds, used a thirty-seven inch club in his days of the 1960s and 1970s.

Although highly out of spec, the largest wooden bat ever made was a solid cypress log in 1996, with a finished length of twelve feet, two inches long. The barrel diameter was fourteen inches, and the bat weighed 280 pounds (sounds ideal for Alfonso Soriano).

The bat handle can have tape, pine tar, or other grip assistance, for no more than eighteen inches from the knob. Any more than that can result in the bat being removed from use and possible player ejection (the next time you run into Hall of Famer George Brett, just ask him about the 1983 game against the Yanks where his home run was called back after manager Billy Martin complained about Brett's bat having too much pine tar. The Royals' third baseman exploded from his dugout like a rocket launch gone bad when umps called him on the infraction).

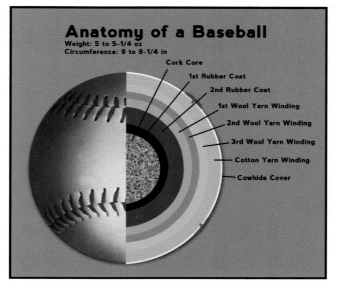

Anatomy of a ball.

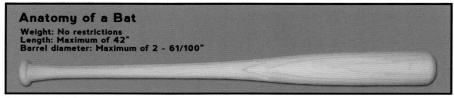

Anatomy of a bat.

The far end of the bat may be cupped or indented as much as an inch and a quarter, which makes it a bit lighter. While it's thought to be a recent development (sometimes attributed to being a Japanese invention), the cupped end dates back to a Georgia-based company that introduced the "Ok'd Cup-Bat" in the early 1940s. And, while it's not confirmed that any pro player used it, a "bat with the concaved end" was noted in an 1897 issue of the *Sporting Life* newspaper.

As one might expect, all team members have to wear uniforms with the same color, trim, and style, and they all must have numbers of at least six inches on their backs. The backs may also have the player's last name (but, if Mike Trout wants "Fish-Stick" on his uniform, then the League President has to OK it first. I doubt that's gonna happen).

The uniform sleeves cannot be ragged or split, and no uniform should have a pattern or design that looks like a baseball (duh). The team should have two uniforms—including white for home games and some other color for games on the road. Oh yeah—no commercial advertising is allowed on the uniforms.

Catchers may wear a mitt (with all four fingers enclosed as a single unit) as large as thirty-eight inches around its perimeter (that sounds big, but oversized mitts are helpful in handling the crafty knuckleball pitcher). A first baseman may use a mitt or glove (with each of the four fingers enclosed as a separate unit) no more than a foot from top to bottom. Other fielders may wear gloves no more than a foot from any finger to the heel.

The pitcher is not allowed to have a glove that is white, gray, or any color considered to be distracting (sounds like that fashionable zebra design is out). They also can't attach anything to their glove that differs in color from it.

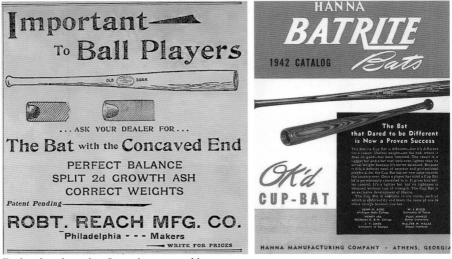

Early ad and catalog featuring cupped bat.

In terms of head protection, all players must wear helmets at bat (since 1956), while running the bases, or catching behind the plate. The same goes for base coaches and batboys or girls.

The Numbers: How Many Innings, How Many Outs?

In the simplest sense, much of the game can be explained by quantification. There are many numbers attached to the rules of baseball, such as:

One—Number of defensive players in foul territory when play begins—the catcher.

Two—Base coaches, at first and third, to direct the base running traffic (assuming there is any). Also, the minimum number of offensive players on the field at any one time—the batter and the next up, who stands or kneels in the on-deck circle. Also, it's the number of trips to the pitching mound during one inning, by a manager or coach, that results in the replacement of the pitcher.

Three—Strikes in making an out, which are legal pitches in the strike zone, or swung at and not struck by the hitter. Strikes can also be foul balls (with less than two strikes) or a foul bunt. There are also three outs in an inning (actually a half-inning, with each team's at bats resulting in three outs total a full inning).

Four—Balls in a walk, or bases on balls, which are pitches not in the strike zone nor swung at by the batter. There are also four umpires—essentially, one for each base—in a regulation MLB game.

Five—The maximum possible number of offensive players on the field at a time—bases loaded, the batter, and on-deck hitter. Also minimum number of innings required for a regulation game, should it be called before completion for weather or other reasons.

Six—Umpires in postleague games, including the World Series. Along with the base umps, one additional arbiter each is assigned to the left and right foul lines.

Seven—Inning in which a "stretch" or break is traditionally taken, often accompanied by an out-of-tune chorus of "Take Me Out to the Ball Game."

Eight—Number of defensive players in fair territory when play begins—all fielders except the catcher. Also, maximum number of warm-up pitches allowed before the start of an inning.

Nine—The number of innings in a standard game, as well as the number of offensive and defensive players listed on the starting lineup card. Nine is also the winning score in a forfeited game; the losing team is credited with zero runs.

Ten—Number of games of suspension automatically handed down if a pitcher is found to have discolored or damaged the baseball in play.

Twelve—Minimum number of regulation baseballs kept in reserve for each game, if replacements are required.

Twenty-five—Players on an active roster.

Forty—Players on a major league roster.

The Players: Who's On First?

In an attempt to be complete in presenting the rules of baseball, this section will outline the roles and actions of the players on the field. While the process may seem rudimentary at times, Mom always said, "If you do something, do it the right way." (I'm not sure if that applies to a left-hand turn.)

The battery is the two-man team of pitcher and catcher. The infield has four fielders: first baseman, second baseman, third baseman, and shortstop (who is usually positioned between second and third). The outfield has three fielders: left fielder, center fielder, and right fielder. All nine are considered to be the defense.

Infielders do not usually stay anchored to their respective bases (except the first baseman, who may straddle the bag with a runner at first, with the intention of preventing a stolen base or to pick the runner off). The infielders are normally positioned behind and away from their bases, and move to them when making a play on a runner.

Outs are recorded in the following ways:

1. Three called or swinging strikes when the batter is at the plate (Take the bat off yer shoulder! If you don't swing, you'll never hit the ball!)
2. A foul bunt with two strikes on the batter.
3. A foul ball that is tipped directly into the catcher's mitt with two strikes on the batter.
4. A batter bats out of turn in the order.
5. Any fielder who catches a fly ball, whether in fair or foul territory.
6. A ground ball that is struck and fielded in fair territory, and the fielder with the ball (either on his own or as a result of a transferring throw) touches first base before the advancing batter-runner touches the base.
7. A runner (or runners) already on base is/are forced out when, as a result of a ground ball, they are forced to run to the next base and the fielder with the ball is able to touch the base before the runner gets there. Or, if a base runner leaves a base before a fly ball is caught and the base is touched by a fielder with the ball before the runner returns safely. (Note that after many years of teaching young boys and girls the game, it cannot be overemphasized that, with less than two outs, the base runners DO NOT run on balls hit in the air until they are caught—or often, not caught—and a base runner on first MUST RUN when the ball is hit on the ground. You know, I had a full head of hair before I started coaching.)
8. On an appeal play after the fact, a base runner can be called out when it is ruled that he left the base to advance before a fly ball was caught. In such a play, the fielder moves to the base in question, and before the next pitch is made, the pitcher throws to the fielder at the base. At that point, the umpire rules safe or out.
9. Any base runner, while not touching a base, can be tagged with the ball while it is active and in play.
10. A batter or base runner is out if he interferes—whether intentional or not—with a fielder making a play on a fair ball.

11. A base runner strays more than three feet from the established baselines (real or assumed) in an attempt to avoid a tag by a fielder with the ball.

12. Note that a fielder's choice is not a way of putting out a runner, but how the official scorer views the out made. Basically, with a runner on base, a fielder receives a ground ball, and instead of throwing to first for the out on the batter-runner, he throws to another base to put out the extant runner. Hence, the label of fielder's choice—they made the decision of where to make an out.

13. A double play is recorded when two outs are made with one batted ball. For example, with a runner on first, the batter grounds to the shortstop, who throws to second base to force out the base runner and relays to first before the batter-runner reaches safely. Or, with a runner on first, a batter strikes out while the base runner—in trying to steal second base—is tagged out on a throw from the catcher to the second baseman. Or a fly ball is caught by the right fielder, who throws to first base to force out a base runner who left the base too soon and was unable to return safely.

14. Similarly, a triple play is recorded when—through a series of fortunate and well-timed actions—three outs are recorded with one batted ball. Perhaps the rarest of all defensive plays is the unassisted triple play. For example, with no outs and runners on first and second, the batter hits a hard line drive to the shortstop (out number one), who tags the runner between second and third (out number two), and runs after and tags the runner from first before he can safely return (out number three). This is how major league managers lose their hair, as well.

The Manager: Basic Strategies—for Success and Failure

The field manager is responsible for the actions of the team on a day-to-day basis. He makes decisions regarding pitching rotations, fielding assignments, batting order, in-game substitutions on offense and defense, and perhaps even individual pitches thrown. The manager is also in charge of communication (civil and, sometimes, uncivil) with umpires and the opposing team.

Despite the belief that official rules require a manager to wear a team uniform, there is no such tenet. Perhaps because of tradition (more than anything else), managers do wear uniforms—with the noted exception of legendary Philadelphia A's skipper Connie Mack. For more than fifty years, from the late 1800s into the 1950s, Mack managed more than 7,700 games while wearing a smartly tailored business suit and derby hat.

The practice of managers wearing uniforms most likely stems from their natural movement from playing on the field to managing from the dugout. Yet baseball is unique in having the field manager dressed like his players—imagine other sports having the same custom. Picture NBA coaching great Phil Jackson— silver haired and knobby kneed—directing the Bulls or Lakers from the bench. Seeing the slight figure of former NFL Bills coach Marv Levy in pads and jersey would also have been a tough image to swallow. (Yet I still wish I could stop waking up, screaming in a cold sweat, at the sight of chubby Herman Franks in a blue pinstriped Cubs uniform from the late 1970s.)

Many baseball managers are and have been former catchers—the most common position at more than 20 percent of all field positions becoming managers—perhaps because of their constant exposure to the rhythm and actions of the entire game from their position behind home plate.

Of course, the manager can't do it all by himself, so he entrusts much of the teaching and "attitude adjustment" to his coaches. There's a pitching coach (and assistant), a hitting coach (and assistant), bullpen coach (no assistant), a bench coach (who often acts as the voice of reason and second opinion during heated issues), first and third base coaches, and (very often) a strength and conditioning coach.

The smart manager keeps tabs on his players (either directly or through the chatter that runs throughout the clubhouse), knowing who's up and who's down—both on the field and off. While managing styles are wide and varied, there are those skippers who are thought of as "father figures" and those just to the right of Captain Bligh. Success can stem from both approaches, especially in setting the day-to-day lineup.

The smart manager knows when his players need a break—even if they bitch and moan about being taken out for a day. Plus, everyone knows the *Pride of the Yankees* scene where Lou Gehrig fills in for an ailing Wally Pipp and the rest was history—except the change was less dramatic, taking place in the clubhouse rather than the batter's box. The season is long, and with an occasional day off, most players remain fresh and ready for the playoff surge (if they're in such a position).

Speaking of positions, the arrangement of who shows up where in the batting order is not happenstance. There is a long-established formula, followed by most managers, to maximize the offensive production of the team. More often than not, here's how it goes:

One—The leadoff hitter has one job—to get on base. The hitter in the top spot (which is kind of silly, since—after the first inning—the position is seldom leading off any more) must be patient. He must be willing to work the count—selective in the pitches thrown, with the intent of getting on first with a walk, resulting in a high on-base percentage. He is often the fastest of base runners, hoping to steal second once he reaches first. If Hall of Famer Rickey Henderson walked to start a game, it was like giving up a double.

Two—This hitter needs to be a high-average, contact hitter—hopefully, a lefty. Why? Assume the leadoff hitter has reached first. If the two-hitter is a righty, the likelihood is high that a ground ball might start a double play—easier than if a lefty hits the open space between first and second. Also, a hit to right field by a lefty allows the base runner to move away from the ball as he heads to third base. A hit to left field by a righty puts the runner in closer proximity to the ball, reducing the chances of reaching third safely.

Three—Most often, this is the team's best overall hitter, for average and power. Assuming the previous hitter or hitters have reached base, this is a real chance for the three-hitter to drive them in and get some runs on the board. There's a lot of expectations on this hitting position, and, hopefully, it delivers.

Chicago Cubs' College of Coaches, 1960.

Four—The cleanup hitter is the "Big Bopper" (no, not the singer of "Chantilly Lace"). This is the team's best power hitter, usually forsaking average for the ability to send as many balls as possible out of the park. With the hope of having runners on base in front of Number Four, the score should start piling up.

Five, Six, Seven—In diminishing order of skill, these should be run-producing hitters, either by contact or power, adding to the run totals.

Eight—In the NL, this is usually the weakest position hitter—often pitched around to reach a hitter even worse—the pitcher. The same might be true in the AL, although the Designated Hitter takes the pitcher out of the lineup.

Nine—Yes, in the NL, this is the pitcher's spot. However, the great HOF Cardinals skipper Tony La Russa was known to occasionally hit his pitcher eighth and put his second-fastest player in the nine-hole. The same strategy is often seen in the AL, as the ninth position acts as a "second leadoff" hitter, bringing speed to the back end of the order and setting up the 3-4-5 hitters once more. Also, Cubs manager Joe Maddon began the 2015 season by routinely hitting his pitchers in the eight-spot, with a speedy player ninth. Like La Russa, he believed the arrangement would provide an additional boost to the offense. Some other managers toyed with the practice as well as the year progressed.

Like any good manager in baseball or business, delegation is an important key to success. Clear communication with his staff keeps things smooth, so it's one of the coaches, not the manager, who waves the outfield into various defensive arrangements. However, it's not unusual to see the catcher looking into the dugout before calling the pitch, since the manager, or pitching coach, often has a clear idea and plan of how to pitch effectively against the opposing team. The dugout calls the pitch, the catcher flashes the signs to the pitcher, and the man on the mound delivers.

The old adage of "Too many cooks spoil the broth" rang true for the Chicago Cubs in 1961 and 1962, when owner Philip K. Wrigley, tired of losing, created the revolutionary "Cubs Program" (unlike those for a dime that included a scorecard). Wrigley's idea was to eliminate the position of manager and replace him with what was known as "The College of Coaches."

Unfortunately, the college didn't even make it out of kindergarten—it was a complete bust. Eight coaches would rotate, from the lowest class of the minors, up to the major league club. In that way, any and all Cubs in the system would get consistent coaching and direction (on paper, it probably looked like a pretty good idea).

In lieu of a major league manager, there would be a head coach (appropriate, considering all the head cases the experiment would eventually create), who skippered the team at Wrigley Field for a period of time before rotating back to the minors. The result was anarchy, as not one of the head coaches had a winning record, and the players—and fans—suffered for it. It's no surprise the idea died a certain death, never to be seen or heard again.

Of course, a manager's job includes motivating his team, and, often, that is done at the expense of the arbiters on the field. Coaches, players, and managers are not allowed to question judgment decisions by the umps, such as ball-and-strike calls, checked swings, etc. Still, managers have been known to go chin-to-chin with the home plate umpire—not necessarily to get a judgment call changed (they can't, anyway)—but to raise the hopes and spirits of the team and fans. The expected result should be (but often isn't) a charge to victory.

Occasionally, the ranting of a skipper is just a ruse to get the desired result. Take the 1984 Dodger game, when manager Tommy Lasorda came charging out of the dugout to challenge a tag at second base. But, instead of baseball, Lasorda ranted and raved about a bad Italian restaurant he had recently visited. The umps had to stifle their laughs at the absurdity of the scene, which, to the fans and players on the bench who couldn't hear the content, was a legitimate beef by their loyal manager. Lasorda was summarily run from the game, after insisting the umps had to do it because the fans were expecting it. In fact, umpires frequently toss managers, not by their choice, but at the screaming request of the manager.

The Umpire: Kill the Who?

Since the beginning of the game in the 1800s, the Men in Blue have had the most thankless job on the field. They suffer the bile-filled ire from both teams and take abuse from the fans as well. It's been said that the best umpires are "transparent"—their actions are so smooth and accurate that they attract no attention to themselves.

Like the players they rule on, umpires must work their way up the ranks, from the lowest minors to the limited number of sixty-eight major league umpires. Their salaries range from $1,800 a month starting in the minors to an MLB starting figure of $120,000 a season. Senior umps can pull down $300,000 to $400,000 a year. Plus, the big boys receive $340 in daily per diem (yes, I know that's redundant), from which they eat and live on the road (never in the same hotels as the players). There's also four weeks of paid vacation, and the umps travel first class to game cities.

Most potential umpires get their start by attending one of three approved umpiring schools, running between four and five weeks at the very start of the year and taught by major and/or minor league umps. But, with MLB umpire turnover averaging just one a year, the chances of making it to the "bigs" are pretty slim.

Among the curricula at ump school is the reinforcement of the signals—both verbal and visual— they must use to communicate during a game. Some of them include:

Umpire signs.

- Do not pitch—the palm is held out toward the pitcher (think: Stop—Hammer time!).
- Play ball—pointing toward the pitcher or the plate.
- Strike—the right hand comes to shoulder height and makes a fist (like grabbing a pesky fly near his ear). They may also turn out, with a pointing finger or open palm (as if to shake hands with someone. Rest assured, few wish to shake hands with the ump once the game has started). On a third strike, the umpire calls it verbally and—while not officially required—often goes through a grand presentation. Some like to put their fists together, then pull them quickly apart—like ripping a cheap pair of pants in two. Others like the image of calling the pitcher's "punch out" by literally punching the air (while keeping their left up for a follow-up jab).
- Ball—officially, no signal is given, but many like to slyly flash the back of their hand down low. Verbally, "Ball four" is important, but never signaled—a pointed finger toward first base could be misunderstood as a strike and—Hoo boy!—watch the fun as everyone tries to figure out what the heck is going on.
- Foul tip—the right hand brushes the back of the left hand at shoulder height several times, followed by the standard strike call (like clearing fairy dust off the fingers. Yeah, sure).

- Foul ball (also for time out and dead ball)—both hands go up high (picture: Stick 'em up!) while clearly calling "Foul!" (or "Time" or "Dead ball.").
- Fair ball—a simple extension of the full arm into fair territory (with no verbalization. I have to timidly admit I once erred there, too eager to do my best at a college game. Both teams gave me an earful and—not surprisingly—it was the last game I umped at school. Oops—sorry).
- Ball and strike count—balls are indicated with the left hand, strikes with the right hand. Held at shoulder height, the appropriate number of fingers are pointed up.
- Out—like the strike, the right hand comes to shoulder height and makes a fist (that fly is back).
- Safe—elbows high, hands flat at the chest and swept straight out to the sides with the palms down, accompanied by a hearty "Safe!" Motioning more than once may be effective, but could also cause the ump to fly away (the wish of all managers).
- Infield fly—(Explained in the first section on baseball history). The right arm goes straight up in the air. The umpire should avoid saying, "Look! It's a bird! It's a plane!" Rather, "Infield fly—the batter is out."
- Home run—with the right arm high in the air, the index finger is rotated (think: Whoopee!)
- Balk—pointing directly at the pitcher, an ump calls, "That's a balk!" The pitcher, wanting to run and hide somewhere, has been caught.

The balk, as elusive an action as one could possibly imagine, is really not so difficult to understand. The basis of the balk call is to prevent the pitcher from any illegal action in deceiving any base runners (which is why, with bases empty, there is no balk call).

The penalty for a balk is all base runners (but not the batter) advance one base. This is not good when the game is tied in the bottom of the ninth, there are two outs, and bases are loaded for the home team. A balking pitcher sends everyone home, including the runner on third—and the visiting team has another loss in the record book.

As far as the ump (and the pitcher) are concerned, there are two acceptable pitching positions: the windup (with no one on base, the pitcher makes a full delivery) and the set or stretch (with base runners, the pitcher keeps his back or pivot foot in contact with the pitching rubber, his front or free foot in front of the other, keeps the ball with both hands together, and delivers the ball). Any other position is a no-no.

For example, if a pitcher brings his hands together in the set position and does not make a clear stop before pitching, it's a balk (deceptive motion). If he steps off the rubber by moving his free foot and not the pivot foot first, it's a balk (deceptive motion). If part of his body (such as a knee) moves toward home plate, the pitcher must deliver to home and not to a base—if he throws to catch a runner, it's a balk (deceptive motion). And, if a pitcher slips on the mound and falls backward on his patoot, it's a balk (deceptive and embarrassing motion).

In 1952, it was established that four umpires would work regular season games. These four, by the way, rotate in a clockwise manner after every game—for example, today's home plate umpire becomes tomorrow's third base ump and so on. The National League and American League maintained separate rosters of umps until 2000, when they were merged into a single group of MLB umpires.

Lena Blackburne, 1915 Chicago White Sox.

Before the game begins, MLB umps go through a ritual that has been part of the game since 1921. With the introduction of new, tightly wound white baseballs the year previous, umpires began rubbing the shine off with mud. Very simply, dirt from the playing field was mixed with water and voilà—mud.

In 1938, Lena Blackburne, a third base coach with the Philadelphia A's, wasn't very impressed with the mud recipe and thought about his hometown in Burlington County, New Jersey. Along the Delaware River, he found a unique mucky location that offered a mud more to his liking. With a pail-full in hand, he returned to the team and the umps liked it. In no time, the whole American League was using the special "baseball rubbing mud," soon followed by the National League. Today, Lena Blackburne Rubbing Mud is used by the majors and the minors, as well as many college and high school teams.

The home plate ump, also known as the umpire-in-chief (and not to be confused with the crew chief, who is usually the umpire with the most experience and is the direct report to the league office), makes the ball, strike, fair, and foul calls from home plate, and out calls at home plate.

In spite of what might seem to be a variable between home plate umps, the strike zone is clearly defined as:

- The area over home plate (including those cute little black lines that surround it).
- The upper level is the midpoint between the top of the shoulders and the top of the pants (at times in the past, it was defined as "the letters," meaning the team logo, or the armpits).
- The lower level is the point at the hollow below the kneecap (again, history regarded the broad span of the knees and tops of the shins, as well).

The strike zone is established as the batter prepares to take a swing, so it obviously varies up and down from player to player, as opposed to a fixed, invisible boundary.

A fan or two may have noticed that umpiring—at the major league level—is, and has been, a "Men-Only Club." Despite the tenets of Title IX and the fact that women have shown themselves as perfectly capable (to those with any doubt) in the world of sports officiating, the female has yet to break into the majors of baseball officiating.

Shannon Eastin made it to the NFL, and Violet Palmer, among others, made it to the NBA and WNBA, but similar success stories have eluded women who have tried to make the grade as a Female in Blue.

And, yes, they have tried. Pam Postema started in 1977 with the rookie Gulf Coast League. Recognized as one solid arbiter, she moved up the minors, reaching the Triple-A Pacific Coast League in 1983. In 1988, baseball commissioner A. Bartlett Giamatti hired Postema to ump MLB spring training games, as well as the midyear Hall of Fame Game in Cooperstown.

Postema was high profile and well regarded, appearing in sports magazines and other media, seeming to be on her way to the majors. But Giamatti died the next year, and Postema's chances quickly disappeared. When she was fired from the minors in 1989, she filed a sexual discrimination suit. It was settled out of court.

Before Postema, Bernice Gera had gone through the court system in order to umpire a minor league game in 1972. But the entire ordeal left Gera exhausted—physically, mentally, and financially—and she resigned after that one game. Since Postema, women like Ria Cortesio and Kate Sergeant have worked in the minors, but couldn't crack the major league line.

Since the start of the game in the 1800s, the umpire's word has been final. Disputes and disagreements from players and managers often resulted in their (often deserved—sometimes not) ejection. At the end of the 2008 season, with expansion at the start of the 2014 season, technology stepped in to give baseball the option of a second look, if so requested.

The addition of instant replay (following the leads of the NFL, NBA, and NHL) and manager challenges have taken the finality—and, perhaps, diluted the human element—of the umpire's decision away from the game, which is a double-edged sword. While the umpire's call is no longer the last word, they would be the first to agree that the most important thing is to get the call correct—however it's accomplished.

Umpire calls that are eligible for review include:

- Home runs and ground rule doubles
- Interference by fans
- Force plays and tags
- Fair or foul (outfield only)
- Trapped catches (outfield only)
- A batter hit by pitch
- Timing plays for the third out
- Fielders touching a base
- Runners passing runners
- General record keeping, such as ball-strike counts, outs, etc.

Each manager has one replay review in a game, although, if the challenge is upheld and the call is overturned, the requesting manager keeps the ability to challenge another call. However, the challenges are not endless—a maximum of two per manager are allowed per game. After the seventh inning—if all challenges are exhausted—the crew chief can request one on his own. Home run calls are also reviewable.

To initiate a challenge, the manager must ask the crew chief to take another look—in a timely manner. The skipper cannot, in the sixth inning, ask for a review of a call from the second inning (what kept you?). Once asked, the crew chief and one more ump will talk by headsets to Replay Command Center in New York City (sounds pretty serious to me), while an MLB umpire and a tech at the Center review all available video—at every angle—from the play.

The visual evidence must be conclusive to reverse a call. In essence, the call stands unless it's obvious upon review that it was incorrect. The Center replies to the stadium umps with the ruling, and the game continues.

One major concern for using replay was keeping it as short as possible and keeping the game moving along. A tally of instant replay use at the end of the 2014 season showed that a challenge was made in just about every other game (one challenge for every two games played), with the average length of the process taking about a minute and forty-five seconds (a manager with a beef probably took much longer in the days before replay).

How effective was replay? Out of 1,265 challenges in the 2014 season, 604 calls were overturned, so about 48 percent—almost half—were successfully disputed. Most of the questions focused on force plays and tag plays (including the everyday "out at first").

But not all of expanded replay was a rousing success. At the beginning of the season, an experimental rule was added in an attempt to reduce the number of serious injuries in the game, as a result of collisions at home plate between runner and catcher.

The rule was brought in to avoid the kind of gruesome injury that Giants catcher Buster Posey suffered in May 2011, as Marlins player Scott Cousins crashed into the receiver trying to score. Posey's left leg was broken, with severely strained ligaments in the ankle as well. The catcher was out for the rest of the year and gave MLB valuable input to developing the new rule.

Basically, it expects the catcher to block home plate, only if he has the ball. If not, the runner must be given a clear pathway to score and make a swipe tag when the ball arrives. At the same time, if the runner tries to bowl over the catcher with a bone-crunching shoulder, the ump can rule him out—regardless of whether he scores or not.

Umpires, on the field and at the Replay Center, seemed to be somewhat inconsistent in 2014 when it came to calling or not calling a "blocked plate" or "adequate pathway" for the runner, and video replays were of little help. MLB and the players union worked with umps in the off-season to clarify and further define the rule, while it remained a work in progress.

1300 AD to 1900

Now Batting . . .

How They Got to First Base

Tracing the origins of America's pastime is about as tricky as one might imagine. Suffice it to say, the roots of bat and ball games reach back much further than a storied 1845 game at Elysian Fields in Hoboken, New Jersey. Truth be told, the genesis of baseball may be centered halfway around the world and go back seven hundred years or more.

Elements of the game have been noted in 3,500-year-old pictographs on the walls of Egyptian temples, with pharaohs hitting fungoes to waiting holy men (no note was made if the balls were phare or phoul). A 1310 drawing in the British Museum clearly depicts a person in a striped uniform, bat in hand, waiting for an opponent to pitch a large ball. In 1400s' England, churchyards became ball fields, and the game of "stoolball"—a batless contest where players used their hand to slap at a thrown ball—was part of religious celebrations (without taking the concept of "the sacrifice hit" too literally).

However, baseball may take much of its influence from a Romanian game called "Oina" (Romanian experience with bats is usually confined to the vampire type, as the eastern European country is often considered the home of Vlad Tepes, a vile man believed to be the archetype for Count Dracula). Supposedly, shepherds invented the game in the first century (one hesitates to consider what they used for a ball), and it spread across the country in the fourteenth century.

Oina—sometimes called "Hoina"—uses two teams of eleven players each (no helmets or shoulder pads like other undectet-based games). With fielders covering a large rectangular field that includes nine base-like zones, oina is a short game of usually a half-hour in length. A member of the hitting team soft-tosses a ball (sized and weighted much like today's baseball) to a batter who attempts to hammer the sphere as far as possible.

The hitter then attempts to reach the base zones, while gloveless fielders can amass points by tagging or plugging the runner (hitting the poor fellow by throwing the ball at him, a rule that made it into the early days of American baseball). The game remains a national sport of Romania today, boasting that oina is "the game that unites us" (them).

This Cricket Don't Chirp

The aforementioned stoolball developed into the much more recognizable game of cricket in the British Isles somewhere around the 1500s. History records the first organized game of cricket happening in Kent, in southeast England, in 1646. Across the next one hundred years, rules and equipment would become standardized, and, perhaps not surprisingly, betting on the outcome of the game became a normal practice.

Like oina, cricket uses two teams of eleven players, with one group spread out across the field as defenders and the other batting. Like baseball, there are innings, an infield and an outfield, a pitcher (called "the bowler"), a catcher (called "the wicket keeper"), a hitter (actually two at a time, called "batsmen"), umpires, plus the obvious bat and ball. Outs can be recorded by catching a flyball. While there are a number of similarities between cricket and baseball, the games can hardly be considered interchangeable.

Widely played and enjoyed in England, there's no reason to doubt that cricket made its way to America during the disgruntled Brits' first emigration during the 1700s. However, with the American Revolution in the 1770s, it's also difficult to believe the citizens of the United States would have had anything to do with anything even remotely British in origin. Such circumstances might explain the disappearance of cricket games in America.

Curiously, a 1796 comprehensive German sports book, written by Johann Gutsmuths, outlined detailed rules for playing "das englishe Base-ball"—English base-ball, as well as a similar pastime called "das deutsche Ballspiel"—German ball game. Like many versions of bat-and-ball games from that period, there are enough resemblances to today's game that give credence to the fact that no single person (or married, for that matter) woke up one day and said, "I've got it—baseball!"

Doubleday or Cartwright?—Make Up Your Mind!

During the early nineteenth century, young Americans amused themselves with bat-and-ball games of various labels: town ball, baste ball, one old cat, goal ball, rounders, and base-ball (a label first used during the 1700s, as witnessed in Gutsmuths' book) among others. Wooden posts, stuck into the ground, took the place of bases; base runners often ran clockwise around the circuit of four or more posts (opposite of the direction we see today); outs were recorded for a ball caught on the fly—or after one bounce, too. Some took to calling this bat-and-ball version the "Massachusetts game."

Balls were often improvised as small bundles of rags and, therefore, quite soft. And that's a good thing, as an out could also be recorded by a practice known as burning, soaking, or plugging—hitting the runner with a thrown ball. (No wonder "Out" sounds like "Ouch!")

By 1833, the first organized club was formed—the Olympic Town Ball Club of Philadelphia, although town ball remained largely a game played in the New England states. As a team, the Olympics played ball into the 1880s.

In terms of baseball as we know it, one might first consider these three falsehoods: The Earth is flat; Santa Claus brings presents at Christmas; Abner Doubleday invented baseball (Actually, I still have faith in that middle one.) There are those who still believe, flying in the face of facts, that Doubleday created the game. In fact, he is memorialized in Coopers   town, with the burg's prized ballpark named after him.

In his own defense, Doubleday himself never claimed to be the maker of baseball. Truth be told, he was dead nearly fifteen years before he was saddled with the credit. So . . .

Was Doubleday a Union Army General in the Civil War? Yes.

Did Doubleday start the first cable car company in San Francisco? Yes.

Was Doubleday the architect of baseball? Foul ball!

The myth of Doubleday's supposed creation was a product of baseball itself, as a commission formed in 1905 by the National League declared Doubleday had invented the game in a cow pasture in Cooperstown, New York, in 1839. In fact, Doubleday happened to be a West Point cadet at that time.

The Mills Commission, named after a former National League president, based their decision almost solely on a newspaper story they found in the Akron, Ohio, *Beacon Journal*. The article, attributed to one Abner Graves, stated he was a former schoolmate of Doubleday in Cooperstown. He vaguely recalled seeing Doubleday scratching some diagrams for the game in the school yard dirt one day.

The commission never checked the story's sources; they didn't contact Graves at all. Perhaps not surprisingly, Graves later killed his wife and wound up in an asylum.

The Doubleday myth grew from a standing argument between British-born baseball journalist Henry Chadwick (creator of many standards in baseball records, including box scores, batting averages, and many more) and American baseball executive Albert Spalding. Chadwick claimed baseball was based on the game of rounders from his side of the pond, while Spaulding affirmed that baseball was as American as apple pie and, well, you know. Again, not surprisingly, the Mills Commission had been assembled by Spaulding, so their American-based conclusion was inevitable. And it was a lie.

Yet the myth is pervasive to this day. Don't believe it? As I write these words, I am staring at a replica of a tattered and split ball that sits over my computer. In fact, it kinda looks like a fig that has burst open. The label reads: Doubleday Baseball, Circa 1839. I know the guy wasn't part of the game I love, but the ball is an icon of what the game means to me.

The real birth of the game that we watch today was delivered by a tall, brawny New Yorker named Alexander Joy Cartwright—and even he had a great support team of bat-and-ball-wielding doctors at his side. It was September 1845.

A founding member of the Knickerbocker Base Ball Club of New York City, recognized as the first organized baseball team, Cartwright holds the honor of introducing—if not inventing—many of the rules that make up today's game. Those include: the concept of foul territory, base distances of ninety feet, innings with three outs, and an infield with home plate in one corner (rather than halfway up one baseline, like town ball). Plus, he got rid of the uncouth concept of getting

Henry Chadwick and Albert Spalding.

an out by hitting the runner with a thrown ball. Of course, the game still insisted on pitching the ball underhanded, as the concept of the wily pitcher trying to outfox the hitter (sometimes called "the striker") was a few decades away.

More than just rules, Cartwright brought a sense of standardization to what became known as "The New York Game of Base Ball." His influence began to knock the rough edges off, kind of like moving from sandlot ball to Little League. So, should you ever find yourself in New York City, on Manhattan Island near the Midtown intersection of 34th Street and Lexington Avenue, you will be roaming the land where the Knickerbockers played their early games on vacant lots.

While you're in the area, make your way across the Hudson River to Hoboken, New Jersey. Find Helmer's Restaurant at 11th Street and Washington Street, grab some good German cuisine, and appreciate the fact that you are very, very close to Elysian Fields. There, starting in fall of 1845, Cartwright and his Knickerbockers began playing baseball on a regular basis. (There's even a plaque across from Helmer's, commemorating the team's first match game in June 1846.)

Base Ball or Cannon Ball—Take Your Best Shot

The game continued, with minor evolution and variations, during the 1850s. Base Ball clubs continued to grow, mostly in the northeastern states, but the game had started to spread across the country. Large metropolitan cities like Boston, Philadelphia, and, of course, New York, boasted many clubs, but the sport had launched its movement westward.

From Detroit, Cleveland, Cincinnati, Chicago, and St, Louis, all the way to San Francisco, baseball began to take hold of the country. And not just in large cities, but more rural areas as well. Newspapers of the time began to suggest that America

New York Knickerbocker Club, 1845, Alexander Cartwright (*top center*).

should embrace baseball as a national game, much as cricket had become closely associated with Great Britain.

Curiously, the South seemed to be split on the game. Plantation owners had little interest in baseball, but townsfolk and seaport citizens seemed to enjoy the game. It has been suggested that slave masters found the task of running and being chased as some kind of role reversal for them. They were accustomed to wielding the club of control, not being the target of pursuit.

The first shots fired at Fort Sumter (triggered by a Union captain named Abner Doubleday—yes, that Doubleday) in 1861 spelled an ugly and bloody four years in American history. Yet, where it could, the game of baseball prevailed, on both sides of the conflict.

Many Union officers encouraged their soldiers to play ball, in lieu of or in addition to their normal drill routines. Along with participation, the game often drew large crowds of spectators. One Christmas Day game in 1862 drew an estimated 40,000 soldiers to watch. A Union player once observed that it was "nicer to play base than minie ball." (The minie ball was one of the first bullet-shaped ammunition loads developed just before the war.)

Mirroring the troubles the South had in securing useful resources to support their war efforts, Rebel soldiers often lacked real baseball gear and relied on inferior or improvised bats and balls. Hardware merchants were encouraged to donate anything that could help the cause.

There were many reports, most unfounded, during the war of amicable pickup games played between Union and Confederate teams. The notion that baseball could span ideological and political differences is noble and probably did occur, although probably not as often as suggested.

Prison camps on both sides of the conflict featured their share of baseball games in the unfriendly confines of their courtyards. However, after frequent contests in the war's first couple of years, the games lessened as the grind and toll

Ball game during Civil War times.

of the conflict made prisons intolerable places. Factors like disease, poor sanitation and medical care, overcrowding and extremes in summer and winter weather, and rough treatment from guards contributed to the disappearance of baseball in the detention centers of the Civil War.

While the war headed toward its conclusion in spring of 1865, the game of baseball continued to develop outside its predominance. Clubs continued their review and revision of rules, and, for the first time, admission to games was charged. Along with being America's national pastime, baseball was slowly becoming a business.

I Don't Care If I Never Get Back

Putting the war behind it, baseball reached the inevitable point of moving from being a hobby-like activity for men's social clubs to an organized sport—and gainful employment for those who excelled at it. While open expanses of parks like Elysian Fields were great spots to watch baseball, selling tickets to the game required a more manageable practice.

Enter William Cammeyer. Although not a very well-known name in baseball history, Cammeyer's claim to bat-and-ball fame came from inventive necessity. The operator of the Union Skating Club ice rink in Brooklyn, New York, Cammeyer disliked the endless cycle of being winter-wealthy and summer-sparse with income. Knowing baseball was wildly popular in the area, a simple but brilliant idea struck.

He surrounded his rink with a fence in 1862, creating a horseshoe-shaped enclosed ballpark—the first of its kind—that he called Union Grounds. Conveniently located near three trolley lines, the park had seating for 1,500 fans—paying fans—around the infield. Thousands of additional spectators could look on, gratis, from high spots beyond the outfield fence. The playing field was well manicured, and a large clubhouse easily accommodated the teams that used

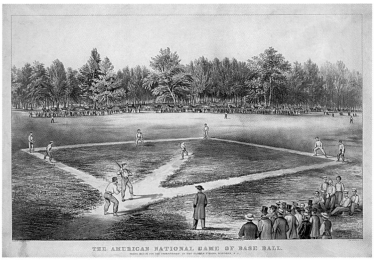

Ball game at Elysian Fields.

Union Grounds. Another unique feature was a three-story pagoda that sat in deep center field, used in the winter to illuminate the ice rink.

Ticket prices quickly rose, from ten cents, to twenty-five cents, to fifty cents. The rising costs served to keep out the riffraff and maintain baseball's respectable reputation. Union Grounds played host to many amateur matches, along with supporting pro teams like the New York Mutuals and the Brooklyn Hartfords.

But fickle fans led to uneven ticket sales, and by 1882, Union Grounds was in poor physical condition. The fence was rotting and needed replacement, as did the bleacher seats and supports. Considering those prohibitive costs, the ballpark was closed at the end of 1882 and torn down in mid-1883. However, the blueprint had been drawn for, not only baseball park structures, but operating them as income-generating sports venues.

The Game Goes Pro

As witnessed at Union Grounds, baseball was beginning to attract fans—many, many fans. Ball games featuring the New York Mutuals at Elysian Fields in Hoboken, and other teams like the Athletics in their enclosed park at 15th and Columbia in Philadelphia, were drawing tens of thousands of spectators every day.

The first real attempt at organizing the game, the National Association of Base Ball Players (NABBP), emerged in 1857 with a convention in New York City that formalized the rules of the New York game—largely formulated by the Knickerbockers. Only a few years earlier, sailmaker Harvey Ross and shoemaker John Van Horn—both ballplayers—began making baseballs in a standardized manner. The game was growing up.

Still, it had some ways to go. For one thing, the NABBP was an organization of amateur teams. Plus, the rules were still being adjusted from day to day, game to game, region to region. One 1857 contest in Albany, New York, put sixteen players on each team (no need for the outfield shift there). It's no wonder the score was 86 to 72—after just three innings.

By the late 1860s, the association suffered from the strain of trying to maintain its amateur standing, while many of the star players on the more than 400 member clubs of the NABBP were being paid under the dugout bench. It was long stated that the Cincinnati Red Stockings became the first all-professional team in 1869, but, much like the Doubleday myth, that was just a fable. Many teams were receiving a part of the ticket receipts for several years previous.

It can be easily stated that, whether or not Cincinnati was the first all-pro team, they certainly played like it that year. Taking on all comers, the Red Stockings went undefeated with a stellar record of fifty-seven wins and no losses (yes, you read that correctly—zilch, zero, zippo—no losses for the season).

Admittedly, paid players resulted in a higher quality of baseball, but also seemed to attract the baser elements of gambling. Many newspaper reporters openly speculated on the odds of upcoming contests, with clear indications of who the favorable teams were. Top-performing teams of the time included the Atlantics of Brooklyn and the Mutuals of New York.

Smelling the coffee in the concession stands, the NABBP created a category for professional teams in 1869 and regulations as to how and when they could compete against the amateur division. Two years later, the best of those pro teams broke from the NABBP and created their own alphabet soup organization: the NAPBBP, the National Association of Professional Base Ball Players (hardly a creative or original name, but remember, these were ballplayers, not masters of marketing).

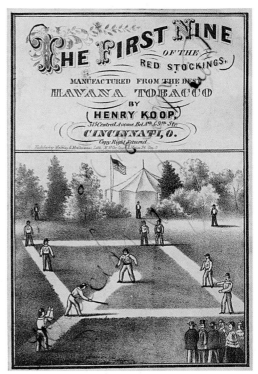

You Have to Walk Before You Can Run (and Not Just to First Base)

Simply called the National Association (NA), this first professional baseball organization didn't last but five years, for a number of reasons. For one, there was no central office to administer the many operating facets. Lacking this, there was no way to know which member teams were properly run and had a solid fan base.

Also, the Boston Red Stockings—assembled largely from the roster of Cincinnati Red Stockings—dominated

Cincinnati Red Stockings, 1869.

the season year after year. And, while wildly popular, the game attracted a number of fans who—quite frankly—were rowdy, drunken, and gamblers who tainted the desired perception of the game as family-friendly entertainment.

Recognizing the shortcomings of the NAPBBP, part owner of the NA's Chicago White Stockings William Hulbert proposed a separate National League (hooray!) for the 1876 season. It would be run as a business and only allow properly vetted metropolitan teams with respectable owners. This new league would be run by the club owners, not the players.

Eight teams comprised the National League: From the east were the Boston Red Stockings, Hartford Dark Blues, New York Mutuals, and Philadelphia Athletics. The clubs from farther west (at least as far as St. Louis) were Hulbert's Chicago White Stockings, the Cincinnati Red Stockings, Louisville Grays, and St. Louis Brown Stockings. The National League would allow no alcohol at their games, and gambling was out, too.

Hulbert went about building this new league, and his team particularly, by bringing in top-level talent. First, he hired Albert Spalding (yup, the same one from the Doubleday myth)—pitcher supreme for the Boston Red Stockings—to pitch and manage his club. Then he added stars like Cap Anson and Deacon White (both future Hall of Famers), along with hitting greats Ross Barnes and Cal McVey, among others. Guess what? The White Stockings were the champs for the National League's first year.

Grading on a Curve

Right around the time that baseball was evolving from an amateur to professional pursuit, a fourteen-year-old Brooklyn boy amused himself by tossing clamshells at the beach. Arthur Cummings marveled at the way the shells curved in a smooth arc. He wondered if a ball could be made to curve in a similar way.

It must be recalled that pitching in the early days was a very benign position in the game. Pitchers were restricted to throwing underhand only, without deception to the striker at bat. In fact, the batter was allowed to request a high or low toss from the hurler. (Imagine that today—"Mr. Kershaw . . . I'd like a straight ball, maybe 70 mph, right about . . . here, thank you very much" Yeah, sure—in your ear.)

Cummings' attempts to curve a ball were hit or miss (for him, not the batters). The teen spent nearly four years trying to develop a grip and underhand delivery that would consistently produce a curve ball. In 1867, Cummings joined the Brooklyn Excelsiors, the best of the amateur teams in the region. Despite his unimposing stature at five foot nine inches and all of 120 pounds, he became the ace of the pitching staff. In fact, Cummings was so good, he earned the nickname of "Candy," which had come to mean the best of the best.

During a game against the Harvard College squad on October 7, 1867, Cummings totally baffled his opponents with his now-mastered curve. He found that the combination of releasing the ball off his middle finger and a sharp twist of the wrist (a motion deemed illegal until 1871, but seldom taken to task) resulted in the arc he first saw come from a clamshell. Needless to say, he was ecstatic.

Candy joined the Brooklyn Stars the next year and drew the attention of everyone who followed the game. Prominent sportswriter Henry Chadwick lauded Cummings in 1871 as the most outstanding player in the country, and in 1872, the curve-balling Candy went pro with the New York Mutuals.

Cummings pitched every inning of every game for the Mutuals that year (yes, the underhand delivery of pitch after pitch would eventually take its toll on his arm). Inundated with lucrative contracts, Candy changed teams every year through 1875, pitching for Baltimore, Philadelphia, and Hartford. When the National League came calling in 1876, Cummings surprisingly stayed with Hartford, posting a record of 16 and 8 in twenty-four starts.

However, the next year would be the last for Cummings, as his switch to the Cincinnati Red Stockings found the twenty-eight-year-old with a dead arm and a dead team. His record was only 5 wins and 14

Candy Cummings, 1872.

losses. Sportswriters wrote of the pitcher giving up between 18 and 25 hits every time he took the pitcher's box.

The curve ball had greatly strained Candy's arm, plus other pitchers had figured out his secret—as had many batters. Still, Candy Cummings relished his place in baseball history, and he was posthumously elected to the Baseball Hall of Fame in 1939 as one of the first groups of nineteenth-century players.

It's a Living . . .

What exactly did it mean to be a "professional" baseball player in the 1870s? Consider the economic structure of America for the times and you'll see it was a pretty good way to make a living, just as it is today.

Generally speaking, there were no such things as the suburbs or middle class at that time, although changes would be a-comin' soon. A person basically lived in the country or in a city, and was either rich or poor (assuming some varied levels within those classes). The country had a population of about forty million people, with three-quarters of those folks living in rural areas. Urban and metropolitan regions accounted for just ten million Americans.

One out of five adults was illiterate, 45 percent of the workforce was either a farmer or a farm worker. A pound of butter was thirty-five cents, a dozen eggs cost a quarter, and a pound of coffee was also twenty-five cents. A pair of shoes cost a dollar and a man's suit was ten bucks. The average annual income in America—for a sixty-hour work week—was just under $500.

With all that established, consider the first pro ballplayers. Al Spalding, pitching and managing the Chicago White Stockings in the new National League, received $4,000 in 1876—more than eight times the income of the fans in the stands. Other players were paid anywhere from $600 to several thousand dollars a year to play ball.

Ball clubs charged men twenty-five cents to watch the game (sorry, no Skyboxes). Boys paid fifteen cents (when they weren't peeking through the knot holes in the outfield fence for nothing). Ladies, by and large, were the free guests of owners. Hungry adults could munch peanuts and drink beer (the hot dog wouldn't hit the parks until the early 1900s).

Baseball—Made for the Media

The popularity of baseball grew and grew in the second half of the nineteenth century with fans in all areas, even those without their own home teams, turning to the only available media for information—newspapers.

Using the telegraph, reporters sent stories about ball games all over the East to papers like the *New York Herald* and the *New York Times*. The Big Apple alone had a dozen papers in those days and sports became a big part of their content. Between 1878 and 1898, the coverage of sports—mostly baseball—increased seven times in American newspapers. Sportswriting pioneer Henry Chadwick quickly added box scores and stats to the accounts of the game.

Started in St. Louis as a weekly publication in 1886, *The Sporting News* soon cornered the market on baseball coverage, earning the nickname "the Bible of Baseball." In fact, it would be nearly sixty years before the magazine covered sports other than baseball. Baseball was in print everywhere.

Front page of *The Sporting News*, 1886.

A 1885 graduate of Harvard named Ernest Lawrence Thayer occasionally wrote poetry for the *San Francisco Examiner* newspaper, run by friend and former classmate William Randolph Hearst. In 1888, with inspiration purportedly drawn from a ball game in Stockton, California, Thayer wrote a poem entitled "Casey at the Bat." It was published by the *Examiner* on June 3, under Thayer's pen name of Phin. Few readers actually took note of the story.

But the power of live theater in a day before electronic media created a groundswell of notoriety for the poem, led by noted stage performer DeWolf Hopper. *Casey at the Bat* quickly became a popular item, told in schoolrooms and homes alike. Popular comic recording artist Russell Hunting produced a cylinder phonograph record of the poem in 1898.

Sheet Music, "Home Run Quick Step," 1861.

In a nutshell, the story tells of the Mudville home team, down by two runs, with two outs in the bottom of the ninth inning. Two unlikely hitters named Flynn and Blake surprisingly wind up on base, so it all points to the mighty (and perhaps overconfident) Casey to be the hero of the day. The batter takes two called strikes and the fans go crazy, seeking the umpire's skin. But Casey strikes out swinging, leaving the town of Mudville joyless.

With recorded music and radio decades away, sheet music and live concerts made an early claim to baseball. "The Baseball Polka" was written in 1858, followed by the "Live Oak Polka" two years later. "The Home Run Polka," dedicated to the "National Base Ball Club of Washington DC," appeared in 1867. "Tally One for Me," in 1877, was about scoring runs.

March king John Philip Sousa had his own amateur ball club, memorialized in the 1902 song "Three Strikes Two-Step." Many teams had their own song, including 1861's "The Home Run Quick Step" (no relation to the "Pennsylvania Quick Step," aka the Hershey Squirts), dedicated to the Mercantile Base Ball Club of Philadelphia; 1869's "The Red Stockings March"; 1894's "The New York Giants March"; 1907's "Cubs on Parade March" (apparently there was a lot of marching going on in those days).

The seminal "Take Me Out to the Ball Game" was penned in 1908, with words by Jack Norworth and music by Albert Von Tilzer—even though they never even saw the game. Other songs included "My Old Man Is Base Ball Mad" in 1909 and "The Red Sox Speed Boys" in 1912. Players also had their own tunes, such as Ty Cobb's "The King of Clubs" in 1912 and pitcher Rube Marquard's "Baseball's the Game for Me" in the same year.

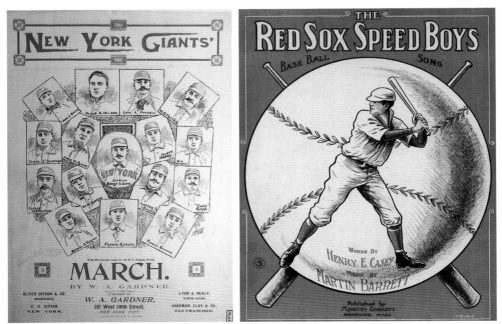

Sheet Music, "New York Giants March," 1894.   Sheet Music, "The Red Sox Speed Boys," 1912.

In a nod to today's sports bars, saloonkeepers soon found a way to add a visual element to the early available telegraph coverage of the games. In 1875, a St. Louis establishment called Massey's Billiard Hall used a blackboard to relay the local ball game scores via Western Union every half inning. Within the decade, theaters in Nashville and Augusta, Georgia, were using enormous posters with ball fields painted on them. As the scores came in, cards with players' names were moved around the poster.

The Atlanta Opera House went one better, dressing young boys in baseball uniforms and running them around the stage to demonstrate the plays as they occurred (*La bohème* it wasn't). Major newspapers took the cue and soon had large mechanized display boards outside their offices, delivering plays and scores in near-real time.

The concept continued to develop in the 1890s, as the display boards were equipped with lights, motors, and mechanical men who moved around the bases. One fan noticed the little men bowed when applauded; they could also slide, argue with an umpire, and even clap for a good play.

Tagged with magical names like "Electrascore" and "Playograph," these baseball display boards were the rage in the early 1900s. During the 1911 World Series between the New York Giants and the Philadelphia A's, more than 70,000 fans packed Herald Square in NYC to watch a game on the Playograph. Amazing, considering only fifty thousand were attending the actual game at the Polo Grounds a short distance from there.

But the days of the baseball display boards were numbered, as several new technologies would put them out of commission. In 1898, Thomas Edison shot film

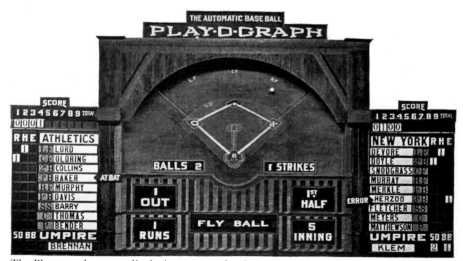

The Playograph screen displaying a somewhat inaccurate recreation of in-game progress for Game One in the 1911 World Series.

of a ball game from beyond first base, featuring a team from Newark, New Jersey, against an unidentifiable team. The rights for filming and showing in theaters of the 1910 World Series between the A's and Chicago Cubs were acquired for $500. The next year, that price went up to $3,000.

The magic of radio was slow to grab hold of baseball fans. The first broadcast of a game was a 1920 collegiate contest, but the account had to be translated into Morse code, then ditted and dahed around the world (ho-hum). The next year, station KDKA in Pittsburgh broadcast a live game between the Pirates and the Phillies. But many fans actually preferred studio re-creations of the games—complete with sound effects—for some time. Quality baseball radio was still a few years away.

A Home Run? How Crude!

One of the more curious facets from the early days of baseball was the mighty home run. Today's game has no other single event that's more thrilling or lauded as the long ball. Massive hitters enjoy (crushing, cranking, blasting—take your pick of active verb) the ball out of the park nearly as much as fans do watching it go.

However, yesterday's game held little respect for the home run. True fans of "base-ball" considered the act of clubbing the sphere over the fence (or into the crowds, as many early parks had no fences), as crude and a cheap way to score a run. As the aficionado saw it, baseball was a game of skillful and accurate hitting and clever base running (Orioles manager Earl Weaver—whose main offensive strategy in the 1960s through the 1980s was waiting for a three-run homer—would have been roundly booed eighty years earlier).

According to the 1889 *Spaulding Baseball Guide*—an annual publication issued back in the day by the game's official maker of baseballs—those who governed the game campaigned for teamwork, stressing the value of sacrifice hits that selflessly moved runners around the bases to eventually score. They looked down upon "going to the bat with the sole idea of trying to 'hit the ball out of the lot' or 'knock the stuffing out of it' in the effort to get in the coveted home run, with its costly expenditure of physical strength in the 120 yards spent in running which it involves." That was just further enforcement of the initial concept that baseball should be a game of civilized station-to-station movement, while fans politely clapped. (These guys obviously never saw a game in the Bronx.)

Chh-Chh-Chh-Changes . . .

Heading toward the end of the nineteenth century, baseball continued to evolve and morph into the game that is basically what we see today. While most of those changes were on the field, one big item off the field spelled the fates of major league players for nearly one hundred years.

Participants in baseball during the 1870s signed contracts and played for their team until each season's end. At that point, they signed with whomever they chose, which troubled the owners in the National League. As an early portent of dynasty-building desires (aka the New York Yankees), the teams were not able to establish any consistency from year to ear, and the competition between teams to sign players drove salaries up (or costs, depending on which side of the diamond one sat).

In 1879, NL teams moved to curtail the problem and began to identify a small number of players on each team as "reserved" for that team only, until they were

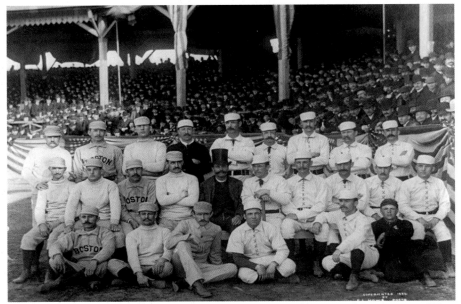

Examples of professional baseball uniforms in 1886, worn by Boston Beaneaters and New York Giants (Pitcher Old Hoss Radbourn, *back left*, indicates number of wins by his team.)

released. Although tough to enforce, it seemed this reserve clause was an effective way to build a winning team and keep down the outflow of cash.

In only eight years' time, the reserve clause was included as a standard provision in every player's contract—despite the fact that the Thirteenth Amendment had abolished slavery in America in 1865. Essentially, the team owned the ballplayer, renewing his contract for the upcoming year for the same salary as the previous year, with the player forced to perform—or not play at all. This pendulum of power would hang in the owner's favor for the next eighty-seven years.

On the field, many changes sculpted the game to improve the quality of play for the participants and the quality of entertainment for the fans. For one, consider the ballplayer's uniform. First adopted by the Knickerbockers in 1849, their standardized outfit consisted of a white flannel shirt, blue wool pants, and a straw hat (sounds like they were better dressed for a boat ride than a ball game).

By the early 1880s, the NL was toying with the idea of using different-colored uniforms, based on position. For example, the first baseman would wear a red-and-white-striped hat and shirt, and the shortstop would be found in solid maroon. It was an idea that suffered a quick (and well-deserved) death.

Hats were basically styled with rounded crowns, or pillbox shapes, both having a bill in front to block the sun. As one might surmise, a team's socks were the same color, leading many clubs to take their name from that color—the White Stockings, the Red Stockings, the Blues, the Brown Stockings (after a game on a muddy field, they were all probably brown stockings).

Gloves or mitts had been occasionally worn since the mid-1860s, but they were more suitable to keep hands warm than safe. The first leather gloves resembled driving gloves, with none of the size, webbing, or padding we see today.

The mid-1880s saw widespread use of fingerless mitts to protect the hand. In 1889, the catcher was permitted to wear a padded mitt—first patented by Phillies receiver Harry Decker. Two years later, he added laces to the back of the mitt to make wearing

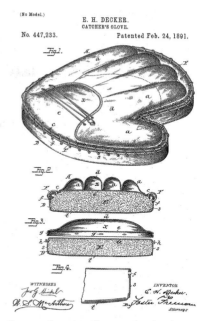

Patent drawing for catcher's glove, 1891.

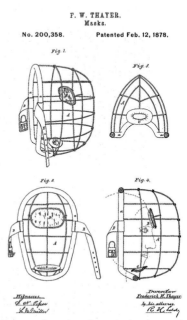

Patent drawing for catcher's mask, 1878.

No. 755,209.   PATENTED MAR. 22, 1904.
J. E. BENNETT.
BASE BALL CATCHER.
APPLICATION FILED FEB. 18, 1903.

NO MODEL.   4 SHEETS—SHEET 1.

Fig. 1.

Witnesses   *Inventor*
H. J. Boden,   James Edward Bennett
B. F. Gray.   By Joseph W. Towse
                                         atty

Clever? Yes. Practical? No.

it easier. A catcher also found wearing a chest protector eased the pain of foul balls and missed catches. Deacon White is credited with an air-filled, canvas-and-rubber bladder in the early 1880s—padding soon replaced the air filling.

Catchers wore a rubber mouth guard—much like boxers wore—starting in the early 1870s. A Harvard College player named Fred Thayer adapted a fencing mask to protect the catcher's face, receiving a patent for his catcher's mask in 1878. Improvements continued through the 1880s.

Much of the concern for the catcher's safety stemmed from rule changes on the pitcher's side. At first, the catcher saved his hide by standing a good distance back from the batting area. But in 1883, the pitcher was finally allowed to deliver the ball from above the waist. The next year, all pitching restrictions were lifted. These changes prompted the receiver to move closer toward the hitter, and closer to danger. As such, the position needed more protective equipment.

The bat—more likely a war club in those days—could be as long as forty-two inches, with a barrel no thicker than two and a half inches. As much as eighteen inches of the handle could be wrapped with twine to improve the batter's grip. As a throwback to the days of cricket, one side of the bat could be flat—an advantage for the hitter that was abolished in 1893. In 1895, the maximum barrel thickness was increased to two and three-quarter inches.

The almighty strike was finally defined in 1887 as a pitch above the knees, below the shoulders and over the plate, while batters were no longer allowed to request a high or low pitch. An additional provision in 1894 made the foul ball (other than a tipped ball) a strike as well.

A called ball—considered an unfair pitch—originally earned the pitcher a warning in 1863. Following that, three more unfair balls got the striker a free pass to first base. The number of these called balls for a walk continued to vacillate, in increments from as many as nine to, finally, four in 1889. Around the same time, in 1887, a batter hit by the pitch was awarded first base—assuming he made an attempt to avoid being struck.

The pitching distance has always been a great source of conjecture (and a lot of pitching). The pitching box—five-and-a-half feet long by four feet wide—had been located fifty feet (from the front of the box) to home base. In 1893, it was increased to sixty feet, six inches, although there is no evidence at all to support the somewhat logical assumption that sloppy penmanship led to a "zero inches" indication being read as "six inches."

Rules of the day required the pitcher to keep his back foot in contact with the box, putting him about fifty-five feet from the plate. When the distance was increased, the box was also eliminated and replaced with a rubber slab that was twelve inches by four inches.

Unfortunately, there's no notation as to why the slab wasn't centered exactly halfway between the plate and second base (a distance of about sixty-three feet, seven inches). It may have been to allow the third baseman a clear throw to first base, but there's no real info to validate that theory. Two years later, the pitching slab was increased to a size of twenty-four inches by six inches—a dimension that remains to today.

The pesky "infield fly rule" took shape after several variations, all based on the fact that infielders were getting a little sneaky. They attempted to get easy outs by intentionally dropping infield pop-ups, forcing base runners to leave the safety of the bags and be tagged out. In 1895, the infield fly rule was called with only one out and runners on first and second, or first, second, and third. In 1901, it was once more changed to apply with less than two outs.

1901 to 1950

A Solid Single . . .

A Little Healthy Competition Is a Good Thing

With the owners of the National League firmly holding the reins of professional baseball, some of the players naturally tried to break off into their own renegade organizations. Among them were the American Association, the Union Association, and, appropriately enough, the Players Association. By and large, they were ineffective and lasted only a year or two each during the 1880s.

The NL, however, was having some problems. It had added four more teams, for a total of twelve. But bad teams and bad attendance saw the demise of clubs in Baltimore, Cleveland, Louisville, and Washington. At the open of the twentieth century, major league baseball was played by the Boston Beaneaters (good thing they played outdoors), Brooklyn Superbas (Latin for "proud"), Chicago Orphans, New York Giants, Philadelphia Phillies, Pittsburgh Pirates, and St. Louis Cardinals. Their season included as many as 139 games.

A man named Ban Johnson, the commissioner of the minor Western League, believed there was enough reason to expand the game by starting up another professional organization in 1902. Called the American League, it reclaimed discarded NL teams in Baltimore (Orioles), Cleveland (Broncos), and Washington (Senators). The AL added the Boston Americans, Chicago White Sox, Detroit Tigers, Philadelphia Athletics, and St. Louis Browns. Johnson became the league's first president.

The National League tried to turn a blind eye that year to these young whippersnappers, but began bleeding some of their best players. Sixty percent of the 1901 AL rosters was comprised of NL players, including future Hall of

AL President Ban Johnson.

Famers like second sacker Napoleon Lajoie, pitchers Cy Young and Eddie Plank, among many others.

The Orioles were sold in 1902 and moved to New York for the upcoming season, where they were called the Highlanders. Ten years later, they moved to the Bronx, where they were no longer on high ground. The club changed its name to the New York Yankees.

It was clear to the National League that the American League was a for-real thing, so they made nice with the new league in 1903. Both leagues agreed to honor players' contracts and the reserve clause, so they would stay out of each other's cupboards. What's more, they fancied ending each season with the top team from each league vying for a grand championship. They would call it "The World Series." In its initial contest, the Series featured the AL Boston Pilgrims (formerly the Americans) beating the NL Pittsburgh Pirates, winning five of a proposed nine-game set.

Unfortunately, the Series would not be played in 1904. Owner of the NL-winning New York Giants, John T. Brush, felt the AL repeat winner, the Boston Pilgrims, was not worthy of his major league team. What's more, fiery Giants manager John McGraw had a personal bone to pick with AL president Ban Johnson, calling him crooked. The two (not-so) Giant leaders took their ball and went home.

The fans and other club owners—even the Giant players—were downright furious at the petulant behavior. Brush smelled the coffee and assembled a formal proposal in the off-season for an annual World Series, commencing with the 1905 season, to determine the top team in professional baseball. And, for the time being, everyone was happy.

This Georgia Peach Was Rotten

Most of the first two decades in the twentieth century were very good for baseball. Outstanding pitchers like the Giants' Christy Mathewson and the Senators' Walter Johnson—the Big Train—dominated the leagues. Other standouts from the era included Napoleon Lajoie, a second baseman who dominated the American League and finished with a .338 lifetime average, with more than 3,200 hits and nearly 1,600 RBI.

Perhaps the first real slugger of the twentieth century came from Wahoo, Nebraska. Sam Crawford, who was known as "Wahoo Sam," made the art of the triple his personal project. In a nineteen-year career, Wahoo Sam hit 309 triples and drove in more than 1,500 runs. Crawford also had an amazing total of 16 home runs in 1901—amazing, because twelve of them were inside-the-park round-trippers. He played fifteen of his years, patrolling right field, for the Detroit Tigers. Playing next to Crawford was the biggest and best player of the times, and he clearly was a study in contrast.

There can be no question that Tyrus Raymond Cobb—the Georgia Peach—was a great, great—repeat, great—ballplayer. His numbers speak for themselves, at the plate, on the bases, and in the field. But whatever demons that tormented Ty Cobb and led him to act as he did left his teammates hating him as much as the fans.

Sam Crawford, 1913 Detroit Tigers.

The center fielder for the Detroit Tigers (as well as two seasons at the end of his career with the Athletics) amassed some amazing offensive numbers in the days before the home run became a valuable tool. In his career, Cobb achieved nearly 4,200 hits, scored more than 2,200 runs, drove in over 1,900 runs (with the notation, once more, that he hit less than 120 round-trippers), and stole nearly 900 bases. He walked more than 1,200 times, while striking out less than 360 times. Cobb finished his career with a stellar .366 batting average.

One would think that impressive stats would lead to happy camper, but Cobb was far from it. His aggressive and reckless approach to the game left a sour taste in the mouths of his opponents and teammates alike. In his defense, he began his career while his mother answered manslaughter charges that she had shot his beloved father dead. Although she was acquitted, it left Cobb sad and withdrawn, near physical and mental exhaustion in 1906.

Despite Cobb's disdain for segregation in baseball, as he stated later in life, he seemed to have racial issues at some level. In 1908, he was charged with assaulting a black motorist in an early occurrence of road rage; in 1909, Cobb was indicted for assault with intent to kill, following a knife attack on a black hotel security guard in Cleveland (Cobb pled guilty to a lesser charge and settled a civil suit out of court). In 1924, he beat a black ticket taker in Philadelphia's Shibe Park.

Long accused of keeping his spikes filed sharp, Cobb did cut an A's third baseman in 1909. But Cobb sent a letter to Ban Johnson, suggesting that player's spikes be routinely inspected by the umpires and stating that he "never spiked a man willingly."

In 1912, Cobb endured endless heckling and jeering from a New York fan named Claude Lueker, who made crude and disparaging remarks about the Tiger's mother and accusing Cobb of being half-black. Goaded by his own teammates, Cobb jumped into the stands and beat Lueker mercilessly. While the bum in the bleachers may have earned the attack, there was a mitigating factor—

he had no hands, having lost them in an industrial accident.

The AL was not at all amused and immediately suspended Cobb for the incident. Then a funny thing happened. His Tiger teammates, despite their immense dislike for Cobb, went on strike in support of their center fielder. After one day, Ban Johnson was forced to reduce the suspension to ten days.

There can be no question that Cobb was almost invincible against pitchers, working hard to find and exploit any weakness they might have. When a hurler might have the fortune to hold the upper hand against Ty, he would dutifully study his opponent (decades before videotape made that an easy task) to reverse the advantage. Soon after, Cobb would have solved the mystery, gaining superiority once again against American League pitchers.

While Cobb continued to achieve great success on the field, the Tigers around him did not. By 1921, Cobb was named player-manager of the Detroit team. In spite of several seasons with winning records, Cobb's magic did not rub off on the Tigers. He surprisingly left the team in 1926, amid unfounded suspicions of fixing a 1919 game against Cleveland. The Georgia Peach quietly returned for two seasons with the

Ty Cobb, 1914 Detroit Tigers.

Philadelphia Athletics, hitting .357 and .323 in his final two years in the game.

Perhaps in an example of "what goes around, comes around," Cobb's life after the game was pretty miserable. Twice-divorced and with five children who wanted little to do with him, Cobb made a lot of money through investments in cotton and Coca-Cola. In 1939, he won election to the first class in Baseball's Hall of Fame, collecting more votes than even Babe Ruth.

But Cobb's health began to fail, due in part to his alcoholism. He befriended sportswriter Al Stump to pen an autobiography, a process colorfully outlined in the 1994 movie *Cobb* (covered elsewhere in this book). Subsequent investigation showed that Stump fabricated much of the sensationalist content of the book and other articles he wrote about Cobb.

Legendary stories about Ty Cobb persisted even after his death in 1961. One myth—not true—was that, as a despicable player, Cobb's funeral resulted in the attendance of only a few members of the baseball community. In reality, the Cobb family arranged a quick and private service, specifically requesting that players and management from the sport stay away.

A complex and confusing personality? Yes. A man disliked by many? Yes. One of baseball's greatest ballplayers? Absolutely, yes.

Give 'Em the Heater, Mr. President

The tradition of having the President of the United States throw out the first pitch on opening day dates back to 1910, although it wasn't the first time the commander in chief found himself amused by the game of baseball.

It is suggested that George Washington, the Father of Our you-know-what, enjoyed tossing a ball around with his troops. They probably amused themselves with rounders, the game brought over from England. Second Prez John Adams admitted that as a boy, he played "bat and ball." On the other hand, Thomas Jefferson believed that ball games were too violent (he obviously never saw a Montreal Expos game).

Honest Abe Lincoln—probably more suited for the role of umpire than player—was known to enjoy town ball and even watched the evolving game of baseball from behind the White House while in office. His successor, Andrew Johnson, may not have been a top-notch government administrator, but he knew his baseball and even gave employees time off to watch a series between the Washington Nationals, Philadelphia A's, and the Brooklyn Atlantics in the late 1860s.

President Grover Cleveland hosted the 1885 Chicago White Stockings at the White House, where ballplayers like Cap Anson and Mike "King" Kelly shook the man's hand with such vigor and strength that he avoided shaking hands again when they left. Yet Cleveland avoided watching the game, wondering aloud, "What do you imagine the American people would think of me if I wasted my time going to the ball game?" (Probably that he was a regular guy who liked baseball, that's all.)

Benjamin Harrison finally gave in, attending several ball games in the nation's capital in the summer of 1892. When Harrison was defeated by William McKinley later that year, the president-elect was invited to throw out the first pitch of the 1893 season for the Washington Senators. A grand presidential box was built, draped with bunting, as dozens of Congressmen attended. But McKinley left them all waiting; he was a no-show, and the Senators lost the opener as well.

Roughrider Teddy Roosevelt—an early proponent of exercise and fitness—scoffed at baseball as a "mollycoddle" game. Even though he was honored with a golden season pass from the National Association of Professional Base Ball Leagues in 1907, ol' TR never used it.

But the man to follow Roosevelt into the White House—William Howard Taft—loved the game, recognizing it as "the national pastime." Unfortunately, the team in Washington, recently purchased by Clark Griffith, was not a winner. Baseball writer Charles Dryden, noting the Senators' loss of one hundred games in 1909, joked, "Washington—First in War, first in peace, and last in the American League."

President of the American League Ban Johnson invited Taft to toss out the first pitch for the Senators' 1910 season. With an awkward toss to starter Walter Johnson—who initially refused the honor—Taft began a tradition in Washington that every president (except Jimmy Carter) has enjoyed. The game was a good one, as well, with Johnson pitching a one-hitter and Washington defeating the Philadelphia A's, 3 to 0.

While Taft enjoys the historic honor of the first president to toss out the first pitch, he does not own claim to a tradition that many folks like to lay at his feet. The president attended a game in Pittsburgh, and, in between the top and bottom of the seventh inning, he supposedly stood up to stretch his legs. The crowd respectfully joined Taft, and, according to legend, the seventh-inning stretch was born.

President William Howard Taft (holding derby) at opening day, 1910.

Cute story, but unfounded. Actually, evidence points to the practice being a local custom in Cincinnati. Red Stockings player Harry Wright noted the activity in a letter to a friend in 1869, where he watched as fans stood and stretched during the seventh inning—several decades before Taft supposedly rose for greatness.

Pete Was Pretty Neat

Another Grover Cleveland—this one in baseball, not the Oval Office—was Grover Cleveland Alexander. Known as "Pete," Alexander may just have been the most dominant pitcher in the National League during the teens and Roaring Twenties. Splitting his time between the Phillies (less than eight seasons), the Cubs (nine seasons), and the Cardinals (four seasons), he won 373 games, with single-season records between 1915 and 1917 of 31–10, 33–12, and 30–13 as examples of his impact on the game.

Born in 1887, he was named for the US President who sat in the White House at the time. As a farm boy from Nebraska, Alexander shucked a lot of corn, which strengthened his arm for future pitching prowess. By age twenty-two, he was playing minor league ball and caught the eye of the Philadelphia Phillies.

The lanky right-hander brought his side-armed delivery to the majors, where his rookie 1911 season dropped a lot of jaws. His record was an incredible 28 and 13, pitching nearly 370 innings and finishing with an ERA of 2.57.

Proving it was no fluke, Pete spent the next six years with the Phillies, posting ERAs under 2.00 in three of them, pitching more than three hundred innings in each of them, and earning 61 shutouts. But the team feared he might be drafted into World War I and traded Alexander to the Cubs after the 1917 season.

The Phillies' hunch turned out to be right, as Alexander went 2 and 1 pitching for Chicago, with a 1.73 ERA, before heading overseas. When he returned, Pete—like many—wasn't the same man. The battle experiences left him deaf in one ear,

Grover Cleveland Alexander, 1915 Philadelphia Phillies.

he was abusing alcohol and, possibly from a minor league beaning years before, suddenly subject to epileptic seizures.

He was able to return to the Cubs and pitch, albeit not as the dominating pitcher he'd been before the war. Still, Alexander was able to win more than twenty games twice and keep his ERA around 3.00 (twice below 2.00). But the Cubs believed Pete's drinking was a real problem and traded him to the St. Louis Cardinals in the middle of the 1926 season.

It was a good move, both for Alexander and the Cards, as they took on the Yankees in the Series that year. Pete tossed two complete games for wins, and saved game seven to lead St. Louis to the world championship. The next year, he went 21–10, with a 2.52 ERA.

With age and substance abuse taking their toll, Alexander pitched two more seasons for the Cards. He returned to the Phillies for a final and very ineffective three-loss tour before being released in early 1930.

But Alexander had made his mark on the game, earning induction into Cooperstown in 1938. Poor health and alcoholism led to his passing in 1950, leaving fans to wonder what might have been without Pete's tragic circumstances.

By the Way—He Pitched, Too

Volumes and volumes have been written about baseball's greatest of all time—Babe Ruth. Kudos fly as fast and as far as a Bambino homer about Ruth's prowess as a feared hitter, but much less has been said about his days as a pitcher in the beginning of his career. His accomplishments and talents as a hurler only serve to solidify his legacy as baseball's best ever.

Only a nineteen-year-old pup in 1914, Ruth signed a minor league contract with the Baltimore Orioles, only to be sold to the Boston Red Sox in July of that same year. His first game at Fenway Park resulted in a win, as Ruth went seven innings to come out on top of the 4–3 victory. But he struggled and was sent down to the minor league Providence Grays until the last week of the season, where he pitched against the Yankees, earning a complete game win and stroking a double for his first major league hit.

Ruth spent his first full season with the Red Sox in 1915, where he went 18 and 8, with sixteen complete games and an ERA of 2.44. Along the way, he batted .315, with 4 homers and 20 RBI, to give a clue as to what the future would hold.

The next year of 1916 saw the Babe deliver an incredible season on the mound, as he went 23 and 12 in more than 320 innings, with a sparkling 1.75 ERA, nine shutouts, and twenty-three complete games. Making it to the World Series against the Brooklyn Dodgers, the Red Sox took it all, with Ruth pitching all fourteen innings in game two and getting a 2–1 win.

Proving that his pitching was no fluke, Ruth's 1917 season was a repeat of excellence. He earned a 24 and 13 record, with a 2.01 ERA, and an amazing 35 complete games out of 38 starts. But his hitting couldn't be ignored, as his average for the year was .325, with 6 doubles, 3 triples, 2 homers, and 14 RBI.

The media had noted the Babe's hitting talents way back to his rookie year, and he wanted to play every day—sitting between pitching starts didn't make him a happy camper. In 1918, he got his wish by playing first base and the outfield, quickly becoming the number four cleanup hitter. Even though his pitching starts were cut in half, Ruth still assembled a record of 13 and 7, with a 2.22 ERA and eighteen complete games (out of nineteen starts). At the plate, he hit .300, led the league with eleven home runs (remember, it was still the Dead Ball days), and drove in 66 runs.

Double duty for Ruth that year led the Red Sox back to the World Series, where they met the Chicago Cubs. The Babe was 2 and 0, with one complete game and one shutout, and a 1.06 ERA. More, he pitched 29-2/3 consecutive scoreless innings (including the Series in 1916), a record that stood until the 1960s. Boston won the Series, four games to two.

In 1919, the shift to everyday offense continued, with the Babe playing more than 110 games in the outfield, while pitching in just seventeen games. Still, he had a 9 and 5 record, with twelve complete games and a 2.97 ERA. His work around the plate (home, not dinner) was stellar—a .322 average, with league-leading stats of 103 runs scored, 29 homers (incredible, considering the dead ball), 113 RBI, and an OPS of 1.114.

Ruth was not oblivious to his own talents, and made sure Red Sox owner Harry Frazee knew it. The Babe wanted more money before the 1920 season started, while he didn't pay much attention to the team's rules on curfew. Frazee figured the Bambino's excessive lifestyle would lead to an early retirement from the game—or more.

The Red Sox owner jumped at the chance to sell Babe Ruth to the New York Yankees in 1920. His team had finished in sixth place, despite the Babe's contributions in 1919, so Frazee was happy to unload his pitcher/outfielder for the large sum of $125,000. Yankees owner Jacob Rupert was happy to pay it.

In his fifteen seasons with the Yankees, Ruth would only pitch in five games—and won all five. As a pitcher, Ruth had a lifetime record of 94 and 46, with an ERA of 2.28. There's no question that had he continued his days on the mound, he would have amassed Hall of

Babe Ruth, 1919 Boston Red Sox.

Fame stats (although it wasn't even built until after his retirement in 1935). His greatness in the batter's box only sealed the deal.

The Dead-Ball Era Was Gone—But so Was Ray Chapman

Yet the Babe's move to the Yankees and blossoming as a full-time hitter was also fortuitous, considering the timing of some rule changes that occurred. Those, along with some other factors, brought the twenty-year period known as the Dead-Ball Era (1901 to 1921, or so) to an end.

The foul strike rule, brought into the National League in 1901 and the American League in 1903, finally made some foul balls hit by batters count as strikes. Up to then, some hitters could foul off pitch after pitch with no penalty, until they got something they could lay into for a base hit. The foul strike rule gave pitchers an advantage and decreased run production.

Offensive production in the Dead-Ball Era was measurably down, from before and after those two decades. Total bases, averaging around twelve and a half per game as 1900 rang in, quickly dropped to between nine and eleven per game. Only in 1920 and later did they return to the range of twelve and a half (the years of Ruth, Gehrig, and other sluggers pushed the total bases per game average to fourteen and fifteen). Likewise, runs-per-game dropped from five and six to three and a half to four in a similar period.

The return to aggressive offensive production began when major league baseball changed the center of official balls from rubber to cork in 1911, as well as changing the type of yarn winding in 1919. Also, at the end of the 1920 season, doctored pitches—spitballs, scuffed and cut balls—were outlawed, along with a ruling that required soiled baseballs to be replaced, rather than kept in use during the game.

The death of Indians shortstop Ray Chapman, struck in the head with a scuffed ball on a dark day thrown by Yankees submarine-delivery pitcher Carl Mays, only served to reinforce the need for clean and often-changed baseballs. (Ruth, playing right field that day, heard the sickening impact that fractured Chapman's skull more than nearly three hundred feet away.)

Carl Mays was much like Ty Cobb—equally disliked by teammates and fans. He claimed there was no evil intent in the fateful pitch; Chapman was known to naturally stand close to the plate. Following the incident, players around the league suggested that Mays be banned from the game, while some newspapers demanded that the game begin using batting helmets

Ray Chapman, 1919 Cleveland Indians.

(not necessarily a new concept, although protective headgear didn't become common until the early 1950s and an official major league mandate for the 1956 season).

Ballpark dimensions must also shoulder some of the blame for the loss in run production during the Dead-Ball Era. New ball teams meant finding space to play, with existing outdoor facilities often adapted for baseball. In the years before 1900, the average left field distance had been around 330 feet. By 1910, that average increased to over 350 feet. Likewise, right field distances averaged around 300 feet in the same time period, with an increase to 325 to 330 in the first decades of the twentieth century. Curiously, center field was always deep, averaging 420 to 450 feet before, during, and after the Dead-Ball Era. (That average wouldn't drop below 410 feet until the late 1960s.)

The curtain for the Dead-Ball Era came down at the start of the Roaring Twenties, helped by the offensive juggernaut named Babe Ruth. Despite his prowess as a power hitter, Ruth never struck out more than he walked in any of his full seasons. In fact, he never struck out more than one hundred times a year (take that, Adam Dunn). He did, however, walk more than one hundred times a year in thirteen seasons.

It was only fitting that Babe Ruth be one of the first five members chosen for the Hall of Fame, joining Ty Cobb, Walter Johnson, Christy Mathewson, and Honus Wagner as the Class of '36. The construction of the actual facility in Cooperstown was completed in 1939, allowing their official induction.

The Beast of Baseball

Baseball gained great momentum in the twenties and thirties, with the New York Yankees capturing everyone's attention by winning eight World Series in those two decades. Other prominent teams of the time included the New York Giants, St. Louis Cardinals, Philadelphia Athletics, and the Chicago Cubs.

The game boasted hitting stars like first baseman Lou Gehrig, second baseman Rogers Hornsby, catcher Mickey Cochrane, and outfielders like Mel Ott and Al Simmons. On the mound, pitchers like Dizzy Dean, Lefty Grove, Carl Hubbell, and Charlie Root excelled.

One young player, a farm boy from Maryland, had fans taking notice of his prodigious power and overall baseball prowess. Jimmie Foxx, with massive arms and a thick neck, first made the majors in 1924. The Philadelphia Athletics bought his contract from a minor league team in July of that year—despite the fact that Foxx was a high school junior of only sixteen years of age.

Originally a catcher, Foxx spent time at first and third base for the A's by the time he was twenty. By 1929, he was pretty much established as the Philadelphia full-time first sacker, helping the team win the first of its two consecutive World Series championships. His tape-measure home runs led to fearsome nicknames like "The Beast" and "Double-X."

Generous and good-hearted, Foxx was liked and admired by teammates and fans alike. His seasons of 1932 and 1933 saw home run totals of 58 and 48, respectively, and RBI totals of 169 and 163. With batting averages of .364 and .356,

Jimmie Foxx, 1938 Boston Red Sox.

Foxx was a shoo-in for Most Valuable Player honors in both years (as well as nailing the Triple Crown in 1933). These were numbers usually reserved for Yankee players named Ruth and Gehrig.

By 1936, Foxx found favor with the Boston Red Sox, where he had been traded in the off-season. His performance didn't disappoint his new fans, as he hit .338, with 41 homers and 143 RBI. Yet the Red Sox still finished sixth that year.

In the next season, doubts began to cloud Foxx' future, as he hit .285, with 36 home runs and 127 RBI (still a great season, but not like his previous years). But Jimmie silenced the critics in the following year of 1938. His average returned to .349, as he slammed 50 homers and drove in 175 runs. The outstanding numbers earned Foxx his third MVP award.

The next few years saw a gradual decline in production, although he still averaged 30 home runs and 110 RBI, with an average of near .300 or above through 1941. By June 1942, Foxx was sold to the Chicago Cubs, where he hit only .205 in seventy games. He retired at the year's end, but joined the war-strapped Philadelphia Phillies team in 1945 for eighty-nine games.

Life after baseball for Jimmie Foxx was not good. A beaning in 1934 had created serious sinus issues, and he drank heavily to ease the pain. Divorce and poor real estate investments left him close to broke. At times during the 1950s, Foxx coached and managed minor league and college teams, as well as selling cars and driving a coal truck.

Nearing the sixties, Foxx gave the game one more shot as hitting coach for the Minneapolis Millers, a Triple-A minor league team for the Red Sox, but that only lasted for a year. Still dealing with alcohol abuse, Foxx relocated to Florida and took part-time jobs where he could.

He passed away in 1967, only fifty-nine years old. But, with a lifetime batting average of .325, and 534 home runs and more than 1,900 RBI, Foxx had been enshrined in Cooperstown in 1951, alongside peers like Ruth, Gehrig, and other contemporaries who achieved greatness in the game.

Stars like Foxx sustained the country's hunger for the game of baseball. It had also matured to the point where it made sense to pit the best against the best—baseball's all-stars. But the genesis of the midsummer classic was based on other influences than just sports.

The City of Chicago, incorporated in 1833, announced a World's Fair to commemorate their centennial in 1933, calling it "A Century of Progress." Mayor Edward J. Kelly approached the *Chicago Tribune* newspaper, seeking a sports event to include in the celebration. Sports editor Arch Ward was charged with coming up with an idea.

Knowing that July 6 happened to be an off day for both American and National Leagues in baseball, Ward suggested bringing the best players from both leagues together for an exhibition game—something that had never been done before, even though the concept had appeared in *Baseball* magazine nearly twenty years earlier.

Despite some initial hedging from some players and owners, everyone came on board for the game. The *Trib* assured that they would underwrite any financial losses, and their readers would vote for the team members. It would be a one-time special event.

The All-Star Game was played at Chicago's Comiskey Park, with more than 47,000 fans in atten-

1937 All-Star game: (*L-R*) Lou Gehrig, Joe Cronin, Bill Dickey, Joe DiMaggio, Charlie Gehringer, Jimmie Foxx, and Hank Greenberg.

dance. The game's biggest names—Ruth, Gehrig, Foxx, Simmons, Grove, Hubbell, Frisch, and others—came out to see which league was best. Appropriately, the Bambino stroked a two-run homer in the third inning—the first in All-Star history.

When nine innings were complete, the AL came out on top with a score of 4 to 2. What's more, it was such a success, it was decided to make the All-Star Game an annual event. The following year of 1934 saw the game held at the Polo Grounds in New York, with one of the most amazing pitching demonstrations ever seen.

Starting for the National League, Giants pitcher Carl Hubbell faced the best of the American League. The game started with a single and a walk, then Hubbell went to work with his screwball. First, Babe Ruth took a called third strike. Then Yankee teammate Lou Gehrig struck out. Jimmie Foxx followed with a K to end the inning.

The second started with both Al Simmons and Joe Cronin whiffing. Hubbell had struck out five of the ALs best hitters consecutively, even though the American League went on to win, 9 to 7. But the more than 48,000 fans in the horseshoe-shaped park knew they had witnessed something very special.

Baseball While the Battles Raged

In the decades when all baseball games were played during the day, the following witticism showed up in business offices in any city that had a major league team: "All requests for leave of absence, on account of grandmother's funeral, sore throat, housecleaning, lame back, turning of the ringer, headaches, brain storm, cousin's wedding, general ailments or other legitimate excuses, must be made out and handed to the boss not later than 10 a.m. on the morning of the game."

All that changed on May 24, 1935, when night baseball came to play. Not that baseball under the lights was a novel idea—several semipro games had been tried way back into the 1880s, and portable lighting systems had been used in several

Cincinnati, Crosley Field, May 24, 1935: First major league night game.

minor league games in the 1920s. The Des Moines Demons, a Class AA minor league team, hosted the Wichita Aviators under a permanent lighting setup on May 2, 1930. The introduction of nighttime games was a big boon to attendance in the minors.

Yet Baseball Commissioner Kennesaw Mountain Landis was not impressed (ever see a picture of Landis smiling? Me, neither). Point blank, he told Larry MacPhail (general manager of the trendsetting Cincinnati Reds), "Young man . . . not in my lifetime or yours will you ever see a baseball game played at night in the majors." (Landis probably voted for FDR's opponent every four years, too.) The Reds defeated the Philadelphia Phillies that first night by a score of 2 to 1. The aforementioned President of the United States threw a ceremonial switch in Washington, D.C., as lights flashed to life in Crosley Field.

The Reds hosted seven more night games that year, with other teams watching closely. Within the next six years, eleven of the sixteen major league teams installed lights for their stadia. By the end of the 1940s, everyone was on the "baseball under the lights" bandwagon.

Except the Chicago Cubs. That's not to say they didn't have good intentions. In 1935, Cubs owner Philip K. Wrigley called night baseball "a passing fad" (the same was said for television and the Beatles). But the executive must have tempered his opinion, as he began stockpiling steel under the bleachers at Wrigley Field. His plan was to have lights installed in time for the 1942 season.

Unfortunately, despots named Hitler and Tojo upset those plans with the sneak attack on Pearl Harbor in December 1941, throwing the country into World War II. Wrigley donated his 165-ton load of steel and thirty-five thousand feet of copper wire for the war effort the next day. The Cubs owner made three separate applications with the War Department to erect lights on wooden structures, but was turned down every time.

Wrigley Field would eventually get its lights—more than forty years later—with a rain-shortened first-night game on August 8, 1988. Their opponents were the Phillies, and the skies opened up in the fourth inning, forcing an actual and complete first-night game the next night—August 9—against the Mets.

The war put a crimp in more than just building supplies. The conflicts in the European and Pacific theaters pulled more than twelve million Americans into the ranks of the military between 1941 and 1945. As might be expected, those rosters included many major

Baseball commissioner Judge Kenesaw Mountain Landis.

league ballplayers, with Commissioner Landis wondering if the game should even continue at all as the world war persisted.

The month after Pearl Harbor, the commissioner wrote a letter to FDR suggesting that baseball should cease with the country at war. The president responded the next day, sending what is remembered as "the Green Light Letter." Roosevelt insisted that baseball was necessary during dire times, as those working on the home front would appreciate the recreation. He also encouraged more night games, giving those on the day shift the chance to see baseball.

Real American Heroes

While the games continued on the home front, many ballplayers found themselves changing uniforms, trading their baseball jerseys for military khakis. Over forty-five hundred pro players—more than five hundred major leaguers and four thousand minor leaguers—joined the military during World War II. Some of the bigger names to serve were pitcher Warren Spahn, slugger Hank Greenberg, pitcher Johnny Vander Meer, power-hitting Johnny Mize, catcher Mickey Cochrane, all-around stars Stan Musial and Enos Slaughter, among others.

Two major leaguers—Senators outfielder Elmer Gedeon and A's catcher Harry O'Neill—didn't come home. Fearing the negative impact on American morale that losing a superstar player in battle might have, military commanders kept many big-name players stateside. For example, Joe DiMaggio, who had thrilled fans with his record-setting fifty-six-game hitting streak in 1941, was stationed in California, New Jersey, and Hawaii. He continued to thrill fans, playing service

Pirates' Vince DiMaggio working during wartime, 1943.

games for recovering injured soldiers.

Still, Indians pitcher Bob Feller—already a three-time twenty-game winner before signing up with Uncle Sam's team—served in the Navy aboard the battleship USS *Alabama*. Feller saw action in both the Atlantic and Pacific theaters.

Ted Williams, hitting an astounding .406 in the 1941 season, joined the Navy in 1942. Williams trained as a pilot and gunner, but still played exhibition games at military camps in Indiana and Florida. While never seeing action in World War II, Williams was recalled to active duty as a Marine pilot during the Korean War. He flew nearly forty combat missions before an ear infection earned him a medical discharge.

Even though Feller and Williams played the game at Hall of Fame levels, one can only wonder what their stats would have been had they not lost prime time during their military service. Using simple projections, their outstanding careers become that much more outstanding.

For instance, Feller served three years during the Second World War—years smack-dab in the midst of a great career. Assuming he would have performed at the same level during those three years, Feller would have amassed: 81 more starts, with 46 more complete games, 44 additional wins (giving him a total of 310), and 430 more strikeouts, which would have pushed his lifetime total over 3,000.

Similarly, the great Ted Williams lost about four and three-quarters seasons to both wars. Once more, simple math shows that—with those seasons included—Williams would have played more than 2,800 games in his career, totaling more than 3,300 hits, 2,500 walks, 2,300 RBI, and 650 home runs. That last number would have put him only second to Babe Ruth at that time and, based on current numbers, sixth all-time.

With Eyelashes Like That, She Must Have a Great Batting Average

With ballplayers holding bayonets instead of bats, baseball clubs were hard pressed to field teams in order to abide by FDR's Green Light Letter. As such, wartime baseball saw players like the St. Louis Browns' Pete Gray—an outfielder with only one arm. There was also the Boston Red Sox' Bert Shepard—having lost part of one leg during the war, he made one appearance as a pitcher in 1945. The Reds' Joe Nuxhall, all of fifteen years of age, pitched in a relief role in 1944.

There's little doubt that these players would not have made their major league debuts at those points if America had not been at war. The minors saw more than forty leagues dwindle down to only eighteen. Somehow, the game needed to provide quality players to entertain the home front crowds.

Cover of AAGPBL's Racine Belles 1947 Yearbook.

Chicago Cubs owner Philip K. Wrigley charged a committee of his management to deliver a list of ideas, so that his ballpark could remain busy if attendance dropped from a lack of good players. The group responded with the suggestion of a girls' softball team, and the All-American Girls Softball League began in the spring of 1943. The name was changed to the All-American Girls Baseball League in mid-season, then the All-American Girls Professional Ball League (AAGPBL) at the end of the year.

Wrigley kicked in one hundred grand of his own money to get the league going, with an initial group of four teams, geographically close to honor wartime travel restrictions. Confined to the states of Wisconsin, Illinois, and Indiana, the teams were: the Racine Belles, the Kenosha Comets, the Rockford Peaches, and the South Bend Blue Sox.

Much of the AAGPBL's birth was well noted (albeit, adapted and enhanced with cinematic license) for the 1992 feature film *A League of Their Own* (covered elsewhere in this book). But the game originally began as a hybrid of softball—with a twelve-inch ball, shortened base paths, and underhanded pitching—and baseball—with a raised pitcher's mound, leadoffs, and base stealing.

The best women players were taken from softball teams in the US and Canada, as well as recruited from high schools, church groups, and company teams. As depicted in the film, the final tryouts for 280 women took place in Chicago's Wrigley Field. Sixty players were selected in the end, split into four rosters of fifteen. A manager, a business manager, and lady chaperone completed the lineup for each team.

The players received weekly salaries of anywhere between forty-five and eighty-five dollars. The women signed professional contracts, prohibiting them from working anywhere else during the season and, more, agreeing to high moral standards and strict rules of conduct. Beauty experts from the Helena Rubinstein cosmetics company worked on poise and proper appearance with the women during the evening hours after workouts.

Logo for All-American Girls Professional Ball League.

The AAGPBL designed a one-piece uniform—a short-skirted tunic, similar to figure skating and tennis outfits—but it was obvious the uniform was intended for the eye and not the base paths. No matter; stolen bases led to cuts and bruises, as well as high laundry bills.

The 1943 season was 108 games, with a 5-game series between the Kenosha and Racine teams for the championship. The Belles swept the Comets in three games, becoming the first World Champs in the AAGPBL.

The experiment was successful enough for Wrigley to add two more teams—in Milwaukee and Minneapolis—for the 1944 season. But there were still problems. Getting women to play in major league parks was a great triumph, but also hindered a huge attraction in baseball. With major league distances to the fences, women couldn't hit the home runs that so many fans liked to see.

Wrigley quickly lost interest in the endeavor and sold the league for reorganization under a Board of Directors. With a big advertising and public relations push in 1945, as well as plenty of media coverage, AAGPBL attendance reached more than 450,000 for the 1945 season. Even as the war ended that year, the AAGPBL added more teams and developed a minor league system, as well.

By 1948, the women's league had adopted overhand pitching and a total of ten teams drew more than 900,000 fans for the season. But while the AAGPBL played a vital role during the war, it was obvious that it could not match up against men playing major league baseball. Attendance began to fall and the minors folded.

Former major league players like pitcher Guy Bush, and future Hall of Famers Max Carey and Jimmie Foxx were enticed to manage teams in the AAGPBL, but the damage was beyond repair. In 1954, the final season for the league wound up with only five teams, with the Kalamazoo Lassies winning the last championship.

And Here's to You, Jackie Robinson

As outlined elsewhere in this book, Major League Baseball remained an exclusive, whites-only organization under an unwritten "gentlemen's agreement" that dated back to just a few years after the end of the Civil War. Black players remained segregated from the game for eighty years, until the color line was finally broken.

Commissioner Landis did little to encourage integration, although he did intervene in an ugly racially based incident in 1938. During a WGN radio interview before a game between the Chicago White Sox and the New York Yankees, Bronx outfielder Jake Powell stated he spent part of his off-season as a police officer. Powell further claimed that he stayed in shape by beating up blacks—although he used a crude racial epithet instead.

Powell was not only a bigot, but a liar as well—he was never employed as a cop. In the ensuing outrage, the commissioner suspended Powell for ten days, although many had called for him to be banned for life. No matter; only after Landis died in 1944 was there any positive movement toward abolishing the color line in baseball, even though it's clear that the club owners had just as much say in the matter over the years as the commissioner had.

Landis' successor, Happy Chandler, believed the time for integration in the game had come, with World War II as the catalyst. Referring to blacks, he

Jackie Robinson, 1950 Los Angeles Dodgers.

reasoned, "If they can fight and die on Okinawa, Guadalcanal (and) in the South Pacific, they can play ball in America."

Brooklyn Dodgers general manager Branch Rickey, who had shown his innovative ways in baseball by creating a modernized system of farm clubs in the 1920s, wanted to win games very much. While they had won the 1941 NL pennant, the Dodgers were getting old and—like all the other teams—would soon be picked apart by the military draft board.

Rickey believed that omitting black players made his quest for a winning team that much more difficult and resolved to get the ball rolling (so to speak). Even though the Negro Leagues had star players like Satchel Paige, James "Cool Papa" Bell, Josh Gibson, and others, Rickey knew the first black player in the major leagues would have to be very special—not just with baseball skills, but with patience and restraint.

Jack Roosevelt Robinson was a four-sport letterman from UCLA, leaving college to play semipro football in Hawaii. Joining the US Army in 1942, Robinson stayed stateside, where he was commissioned as a second lieutenant and quickly showed his mettle and integrity. Ordered to move to the back of a segregated bus at a Texas-training camp, he refused and was arrested for insubordination in 1944. Brought up for court-martial, Robinson's impeccable reputation placed a spotlight on the injustice, and he was acquitted of the charges.

Robinson was discharged in 1945 and began playing baseball for the Kansas City Monarchs of the Negro Leagues. Alongside teammates like Satchel Paige and Double Duty Radcliffe, Robinson hit a robust .414. While in Chicago with the Monarchs, Robinson was approached by a Brooklyn Dodgers scout named Clyde Sukeforth. Branch Rickey wanted to see Robinson in his New York office.

The three-hour meeting took place on August 28, 1945, where Rickey made clear his intentions. He believed Robinson was the man to break the color barrier—not just because of his baseball skills, but because he had the guts and determination to stay focused and not respond to the terrible things he would hear—from fans and other ballplayers. Robinson was up to the challenge.

Joining the Montreal Royals, a Dodger farm team in the International League, in spring of 1946, Robinson made a strong first impression. He hit .346 for the season, leading the Royals to the Junior World Series championship and setting the stage for the upcoming season with the Brooklyn Dodgers.

Robinson's major league debut came on April 15, 1947, with the Dodgers beating the Boston Braves, 5 to 3. He played first base and went 0 for 3, with a sacrifice hit, as well as reaching base on an error and scoring the running run.

As Robinson and Rickey knew, the attitudes were cold and the atmosphere would be tense as the season progressed. Outfielder Dixie Walker, born in Georgia and the Dodgers' most popular player, didn't want Robinson—or any black player—on the team. He went so far as to write GM Rickey a letter, asking to be traded. In later years, Walker admitted to starting a petition among Dodgers players, opposing the addition of Robinson (Walker also admitted extreme regret over the incident).

Yet Walker held no outright animosity toward Robinson. Owning a hardware store in Birmingham, Alabama, Walker knew his Southern customers would refuse to patronize the business if he was known to associate with any blacks. Later, Robinson described Walker as a very fair person.

Less can be said for the manager of opponent Philadelphia Phillies, Ben Chapman. Granted, trash talking in sports is a given, but Chapman—by his own admission—said terrible things to Robinson (as well as Italian Joe DiMaggio and Jewish Hank Greenberg, among others). And, where DiMaggio or Greenberg could give it back, Jackie knew he had to remain silent. It should be noted that Chapman, like Walker, seemed to mellow and change his racist attitudes as he grew older.

Dodger shortstop and team captain Pee Wee Reese allegedly came to Robinson's side—literally—in a road game against the Cincinnati Reds in May of that first year. As fans showered Robinson with racial slurs, some say Reese stopped the game and walked to his teammate at first base. He placed a comforting arm around Jackie's shoulders, which quickly quieted the crowd. Eyewitness accounts vary somewhat, but seem to verify the basics of the event.

In 2005, a bronze statue commemorating the scene was erected outside the stadium of the minor league Brooklyn Cyclones. Unfortunately, proving that some things never change, the statue was vandalized with vile racial slurs and Nazi swastikas in 2013.

As for Robinson, his first season in the majors resulted in the Dodgers winning ninety-four games and the NL pennant as well. The first baseman hit .297 in 151 games, with 29 stolen bases and an OBP of .383. It was good enough to earn the Rookie of the Year Award for Jackie.

In 1949, Robinson won the NL MVP Award, putting together a great season with a .342 average, 37 stolen bases, and 124 RBI. He played his entire ten-year career with the Dodgers, retiring in 1956 at age thirty-seven. He was enshrined in the Hall of Fame in 1962. In 1997, baseball honored Jackie Robinson's role in the game's history by permanently retiring his jersey number of 42 for all major league teams.

And even though many fans and players never came around (witness the aforementioned statue defacing), Robinson delivered a moving and definitive performance in his ten years to many more. He also paved the way for more black players, including the Indians' Larry Doby, the Giants' Monte Irvin, and the White Sox' Minnie Minoso among the first for other teams.

Stan the Man

Names of the greatest of the great in the game get thrown around like a ball in so many pepper games, with predictables like Ruth, Aaron, Mays, Williams, and Mantle usually as givens. Sadly, some names inevitably get lost in the shuffle—Stan Musial might be one that, while sometimes overlooked, stands right up there with the rest.

The town of Donora, Pennsylvania, has spawned several ballplayers of repute, least of whom were Ken Griffey and his son, Ken Griffey Jr. But Musial also hailed from Donora. Named Stanley, he quickly earned the common Polish nickname of Stashu (my suburban Chicagoland neighborhood had several while I was growing up).

An outstanding amateur ballplayer as a teen, Musial signed a deal with the St. Louis Cardinals as a sixteen-year-old but impressed few, both as a pitcher and as a

1960 Topps card, Stan Musial, St. Louis Cardinals.

hitter. But as he matured, his ample skills became apparent, and in 1941, Musial joined the Cards for what would be a grand and impressive twenty-two-year career. Excluding the year of 1945, where he served in the Navy at the end of World War II, Musial put up consistent numbers that would lead to an easy election to the Hall of Fame in 1969.

Stan the Man topped a batting average of .300 or more an amazing seventeen times, including hitting .365 in 1946 and .376 in 1948. The twenty-time All-Star won the NL MVP award three times—1943, 1946, and 1948. During the 1940s, he helped the Cards reach the World Series four times, winning three championships.

An outfielder and first baseman, Musial was steady in his defense. But his bat work was stellar, including both contact and power. He finished his career after the 1963 season, posting a lifetime 3,630 hits—fourth behind only Rose, Cobb, and Aaron. He had a .331 lifetime average, with 725 doubles, 475 homers, and more than 1,950 RBI. Even more amazing was his 1,599 walks to only 696 strikeouts.

For many years after retiring, Musial appeared at the annual induction ceremonies at Cooperstown. With little or no prodding, he would whip out his harmonica and lead everyone in "Take Me Out to the Ball Game." A true baseball superstar, Musial had a full life, passing away in 2013 at the age of ninety-two.

4

1951 to 1970

Rounding Second . . .

Westward Expansion–California, Here They Come

A s far as major league baseball was concerned, it had been a national pastime that included only the eastern half of the country—at least until the early 1950s. Certainly, minor league teams existed from coast to coast, but just as radio and television moved westward from their eastern roots, so did the major league game.

As interest and attendance dwindled in some markets, club owners looked to cut their losses, even if it meant packing up their tents and moving elsewhere. In Boston, supporting two major league teams became difficult, so the NL Braves—even though they won the 1948 pennant—moved to Milwaukee in 1953. The exodus had started.

The following year, St. Louis also felt the strain of trying to shoulder two major league franchises. The AL Browns had lasted for over fifty years, even under owner Bill Veeck's 1951 stunt of sending three-foot-seven-inch Eddie Gaedel up to the plate as a pinch hitter (he walked on four pitches). Veeck unsuccessfully tried to

Major League Expansion - 1953 to Present

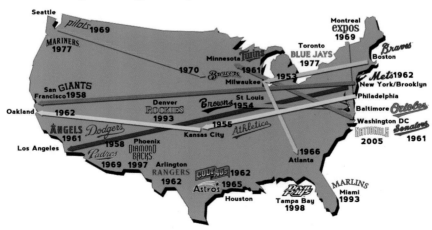

The confusing spaghetti bowl of MLB expansion.

move the failing club to Los Angeles, then sold the Browns to a group of Baltimore investors. The Baltimore Orioles returned to town, having left for New York City fifty years before.

Guess what? Philadelphia couldn't handle two teams either. The AL Athletics were constantly at bottom of the division, decades after manager Connie Mack had assembled powerful teams behind pitcher Lefty Grove, infielder Jimmie Foxx, and outfielder Al Simmons. The team was sold and moved to Kansas City in 1955 (only to relocate once more thirteen years later, this time to Oakland, California).

Despite its girth, the Big Apple of New York City had three major league teams—something had to give. In 1958, Dodgers owner Walter O'Malley packed up the team that had occupied Ebbets Field in Brooklyn and took the long-offered advice of Horace Greeley—they went west. Los Angeles greeted the Dodgers as the first major league team in California.

Similarly, the New York Giants followed that same year, having won the World Series in 1954, but seeing poor attendance at the Polo Grounds since then. The north-central California city of San Francisco welcomed the team, who made their home in Candlestick Park.

The activity quieted down for a few years, but the Washington Senators moved to Minneapolis in 1961, becoming the Twins. At the same time, baseball added teams for the first time in sixty years. The nation's capital got one back, keeping the name of the Senators.

Los Angeles, proving it could support a winning team (the Dodgers took it all in 1959), received its second club in three years. The Angels started the 1961 season without a permanent stadium, playing their games in Wrigley Field. No, not that one; Cubs owner Phil Wrigley had built the Los Angeles stadium to house his minor league team in the 1920s. (The Angels would share the new Chavez Ravine

Wrigley Field, in Los Angeles.

home of the Dodgers for several years, finally landing in their own Anaheim stadium in 1966.)

Expansion continued for baseball in 1962, this time for the National League. New York got the Mets (actually, the Metropolitans), who immediately became the punch line for almost every sports joke in the country. Casey Stengel, who had deftly delivered the Yankees to multiple World Series in the 1950s, became the on-camera clown and manager for the new New York team, who lost 120 games that first year. Playing their first two seasons in the old Polo Grounds, the Mets moved from Brooklyn to Queens and Shea Stadium in 1964.

The Deep South finally got its own team to root for, as the Houston Colt .45s sweltered under the Texas sun in Colts Stadium for their first three years. In 1965, they changed their name to the Astros and moved into the world's first domed sports stadium, the Astrodome—touted as the Eighth Wonder of the World.

The wonder of the Astrodome is how it survived its first few years. The playing field was originally Bermuda grass, which created humidity problems, and, as a result, rain occasionally fell inside the massive structure. When the clear roof panels had to be painted to reduce glare, the grass lacked the essential ingredient of sunlight and died within months. The rest of the season was played on dirt painted green. The next year, artificial AstroTurf was born.

Baseball now had twenty teams, but they weren't done with their relocating yet. In 1966, the South rose once more as Atlanta acquired the Milwaukee Braves franchise, after poor attendance in the Wisconsin brew town.

Another round of expansion in 1969 brought the total of pro teams to twenty-four, as well as splitting the leagues, each into East and West divisions. San Diego got the Padres and the game went international, as Canada's Montreal got the Expos. In the AL, Kansas City had baseball once again with the Royals and the Pacific Northwest got the Seattle Pilots.

But after only one year, the Pilots' owners couldn't afford to keep the team going and were unable to get a domed stadium built. The club was sold to a Milwaukee-based group—including future baseball commissioner Bud Selig. The Pilots moved to Milwaukee, where they were named the Brewers (since the Braves now roamed Atlanta).

The Senators, after eleven seasons in Washington, had nothing to show but their one above-500 finish in 1969. The Orioles, only forty miles away, had a winning club that ate into the Senators' fan base. The Dallas–Fort Worth Metroplex stepped up and purchased the team, renaming it the Texas Rangers.

It might not be too surprising to know that Seattle got another shot at the majors when more expansion in 1977 added the Mariners. This time, the Kingdome was open and ready for business, so Seattle had its domed stadium. Canada got its second team, as the Blue Jays flew into Toronto. Major League Baseball now had twenty-six teams.

Things quieted down for more than fifteen years, until 1993. Then things got noisy for a while. Two more teams were added, with the National League receiving the Florida Marlins in Miami and the Colorado Rockies in the mile-high city of Denver. There were now twenty-eight major league teams, with seven clubs in each division.

Geography alone demanded that something be done about the arrangement of clubs in their divisions. How could the Milwaukee Brewers be in the AL East when the White Sox, directly to the south, were in the AL West? How could teams like the Braves of Atlanta and the Reds of Cincinnati be in the NL West? The year of 1994 saw a major realignment.

When the smoke cleared, the two divisions in each league became three: the East, the Central, and the West. In the infinite wisdom of the game that is sometimes baffling, both the AL and NL East and Central divisions had five teams, and the West divisions had only four. But then, there was no even way to split the fourteen teams in each league three ways.

The added divisions would allow for another tier of playoffs in the fall. Of course, that didn't matter, since a labor dispute between owners and players led to a strike that canceled the end of the 1994 season. What's more, that strike did something that world wars and even an earthquake couldn't do—stopped the World Series from being played (detailed elsewhere in this book).

Fast-forward to 1998, when expansion and realignment continued. Each league received a new team: Phoenix and the NL got the Arizona Diamondbacks, while St. Petersburg and the AL got the Tampa Bay Devil Rays. The NL and AL each had fifteen teams, which meant that within each league, one team would be left out of the daily schedule (obviously, you can't match up fifteen teams evenly). Interleague play (started the season before) would have to be an everyday occurrence (cutting into the novelty and attraction of it), or a lot of teams would have a lot of off days.

The simplest solution was to move one team from one league to another. The winner (or loser, based on your viewpoint) was the Brewers team, which moved from the AL East to the NL Central. Who knew hitting a ball with a bat could be so complicated?

At first, interleague play pitted teams from each division in their league against the corresponding division in the opposing league. In 2002, the format was changed for competing games in all divisions.

The final chapters in the saga of relocation came in the twenty-first century. In 2005, the Montreal Expos found themselves with a flaky domed stadium (left over from the 1976 Summer Olympics) and poor attendance. In fact, the Expos had begun splitting home games between Montreal and San Juan, Puerto Rico, back in 2003. Mercifully, the Expos were moved to Washington, D.C., where they took the Nationals name (the Texas Rangers, previously the Senators, still held the rights to the Senators name).

In 2013, the Houston Astros were sold, with the stipulation that they move to the AL West. The move was highly unpopular with many Astros fans, but as interleague play had been under way for more than fifteen years, it was not a problem for interleague play to now occur on an everyday basis.

Moving forward, it's difficult to predict when and where the next baseball expansion will happen. Some experts suggest the following cities as prime candidates for major league franchises: Salt Lake City, Utah; Portland, Oregon; Oklahoma City, Oklahoma; Memphis and/or Nashville, Tennessee; Las Vegas, Nevada; Norfolk, Virginia; and Austin, Texas.

Oh, Henry!

Getting back to the timeline of baseball's evolution, the 1950s were dominated by the New York Yankees, who continued to set the standard for everyone else to aspire to. Joe DiMaggio—the Yankee Clipper—saw his career come to an end, one that spanned those of fellow Yank Lou Gehrig in the thirties and the up-and-coming phenom known as Mickey Mantle.

Despite losing three seasons to military service—at the height of his skills—DiMaggio still put together some amazing numbers. His hitting streak of fifty-six consecutive games in 1941 (which, after being blanked in a July game against the Indians, stretched for another sixteen games) is a record that most likely will never be broken. As a center fielder, DiMaggio was fast and sure—even with eye-popping Yankee Stadium dimensions of 490 feet to straightaway center field.

In thirteen seasons, Joltin' Joe hit for a .325 lifetime average, with 361 homers (he lost many to Yankee Stadium's left-center field power alley of nearly 460 feet) and more than 1,500 RBI. He also had nearly 800 walks, compared to only 369 strikeouts. Numbers like that made DiMaggio a shoo-in for the Hall of Fame in 1955.

Elsewhere in the game, Jackie Robinson's breaking of the color line had paved the way for great black ballplayers. From the late 1940s into the 1950s, team after team added black players like outfielder Sam Jethroe with the Braves in 1950 and infielder Ernie Banks with the Cubs in 1953. The last team to integrate was the Boston Red Sox, with infielder Pumpsie Green joining in 1959. Of course, one of the greatest ever was Henry Aaron.

He arrived in the majors with the Milwaukee Braves in 1954, having been coached out of using an awkward cross-handed grip (as a righty, he had his left hand on top of the right—opposite of what is considered standard). Aaron would stay for an incredible twenty-three-year career.

The outfielder appeared in twenty-one-straight All-Star Games, even though he had to endure the racial taunts that Jackie Robinson and others encountered. As a minor leaguer in the Deep South, Aaron and other blacks were forced to eat and sleep in other accommodations, always inferior, apart from their white teammates. On the field, Henry showed the same restraint that Robinson had demonstrated,

Joe DiMaggio, 1941 New York Yankees—obviously before he met Marilyn!

Hank Aaron, 1963 Milwaukee Braves.

turning a deaf ear to rude and insulting comments.

Henry showed stamina and consistency in his major league career, leading to the amazing accomplishment in 1974 of surpassing Babe Ruth's coveted lifetime home run record of 714 home runs. Getting to such a glorious achievement was something less than pleasant.

As Aaron neared the record during the 1973 season, ignorant and irrational letters poured in, wishing nothing but failure and—in some cases—death for the hitter. At one point, the hate mail reached three thousand letters a day. The FBI got involved, and Aaron traveled with Secret Service agents. The season ended with the slugger at 713 home runs, one behind Ruth.

The 1974 season opened with Henry homering in his very first at bat, tying the Babe. Four days later, on April 8, Aaron faced Dodgers pitcher Al Downing and, in the fourth inning, stroked a home run to become the all-time champion. (Another player has since hit more in his career, but used steroids and other illegal performance-enhancing drugs to reach those numbers.)

All told, Henry Aaron had a career that easily put him among the top of the offensive stats in the history of the game. His more than 3,700 hits firmly placed him in third place, only trailing Ty Cobb and Pete Rose. With nearly 2,300 runs batted in, Aaron holds the all-time record, surpassing Ruth himself. He also is the all-time leader in total bases with 6,856, far above Stan Musial and Willie Mays. With a .305 lifetime batting average, Aaron entered the Hall of Fame in 1982.

Aaron also excelled in the postseason, hitting .362 with 4 doubles, 6 homers, and 16 RBI in two World Series appearances and one Division Championship Series with the Milwaukee and Atlanta Braves.

Willie Mays, a contemporary of Aaron's, was also considered among the best of all time. Known as "The Say, Hey Kid," Mays was a true "five-tool" player—he could hit, hit with power, run, field, and throw. In fact, many experts tag Mays as the best all-around player in the history of the game. If he wasn't, he was dang close.

A great hitter and fielder in semipro and Negro League games, Mays was first scouted by the Dodgers in 1950. But they passed, noting the youngster couldn't hit a curveball (who can, at eighteen years of age?). On the other hand, the New

York Giants didn't pass on the kid, signing him for a $4,000 bonus and a monthly salary of $250.

Playing for a Giants minor league team in Minnesota to start 1951, Mays tore up the place. He was hitting .477, but hesitated when Giants manager Leo Durocher called him up to the major league team in May. His fears were unfounded, as Mays won the NL Rookie of the Year Award with a .276 average, 20 homers, and 68 RBI.

However, military service essentially took Mays away until the 1954 season. Upon his return, all he did was hit .345, with 41 home runs, 110 RBI, 195 base hits, which led to his winning the MVP Award. Even better, Mays and the Giants got to the World Series against the Cleveland Indians.

Patrolling center field in the cavernous Polo Grounds, Mays

Willie Mays, 1961 San Francisco Giants (with former Dodgers catcher Roy Campanella).

punched his ticket for immortality in the eighth inning of Game One. Indians batter Vic Wertz—already boasting a triple and two singles for the day—cranked a pitch deep into center field, seemingly way over Mays' head, with two runners on base.

With his back to the diamond, the outfielder ran at top speed, literally running under the ball, and made the catch directly over his head. Perhaps more amazing was Mays' presence of mind to quickly turn and throw the ball back to the infield, allowing one runner to advance only one base, while the other stayed at first. The Giants would sweep the Indians in four games to become World Champs that year.

Mays had an absolute cannon for a throwing arm, along with the ability to catch almost everything hit in his area. Even so, his style of making the "basket catch" flew in the face of all proper methods of outfield defense. Receiving the ball with his hands held waist-high and the glove turned upward, Mays defied two basics: keep the ball above your head for the catch and keep your hands ready to throw. But with his unique talents, Willie could write his own rules.

The Giants moved to San Francisco in 1958 and in the next few years, added black and Latin stars like first baseman/outfielder Orlando Cepeda, first baseman/outfielder Willie McCovey, and pitcher Juan Marichal. The Giants finished first in the NL in 1962, losing the Series to the Yankees in seven games, and during the 1960s, they also finished second five times.

Mays also had an impressive decade, averaging 164 hits, a .300 batting average, 35 home runs and 100 RBI. He won his second MVP Award in 1965, hitting .317, with 52 homers and 117 RBI. The only part of Mays' game that suffered was his speed on the bases, as injuries made him less of a base-stealing threat.

As happens with all ballplayers, great and not, age catches up and slows them down. Willie Mays was no exception, and, at age forty-one, he found himself traded to the New York Mets in 1972. Even though he was back in the city where it all started, Mays was no longer the All-Star player he had been. In less than two seasons with the Mets, he totaled only 14 homers and less than 100 hits.

Mays retired after the 1973 season, with stats that matched or surpassed those of many all-time top players. He had nearly 3,300 hits, 660 home runs (third only to Aaron and Ruth at the time), more than 1,900 RBI and 300 stolen bases, and a .302 lifetime average. Willie was an easy first-ballot choice for the Hall of Fame in 1979.

The M&M Boys

Perhaps to the dismay of many baseball fans, the 1960s began in the same way the 1950s had gone—the Bronx Bombers dominated the game. Between 1950 and 1959, the Yankees finished first eight times and won the World Series six times. They did it with an obvious balance of great pitching and greater hitting.

The Yanks had deep pitching, with hurlers like Ed Lopat (winner of 21 games in 1951), Allie Reynolds (winner of 20 games in 1952), Vic Raschi (three straight seasons of 20 or more wins), Whitey Ford (Hall of Famer who won 236 games in his entire career wearing Yankee pinstripes), and Don Larsen (pitcher of the only perfect game in World Series history, Game Five of the 1956 Fall Classic).

Star position players included catcher and outfielder Yogi Berra (three-time MVP and Hall of Famer, hitting nearly 360 home runs and driving in more than 1,400 runs), shortstop Phil "Scooter" Rizzuto (Hall of Famer and aggressive on-the-field leader), first baseman Bill "Moose" Skowron (five-time All-Star), and catcher/outfielder Elston Howard (nine-time All-Star and 1963 MVP winner).

The greatest Yankee from that era was Mickey Charles Mantle. Coming from the mining town of Commerce in the northeast corner of Oklahoma, Mantle was first spotted as a sixteen-year-old, switch-hitting shortstop playing semipro ball in 1948. A Yankee agent signed the youngster to a bonus of $1,100 and a monthly salary of $400, with an assignment to a Class D team in Independence, Kansas.

Mantle soon demonstrated his lethal combination of speed and power for the Yankees at spring training. When legend Joe DiMaggio prepared to retire from center field at the end of the 1951 season, "The Mick," at nineteen years of age, was anointed as his successor. After a strong start, Mantle slumped and was sent down to the minors in the middle of the season.

The move destroyed Mantle's confidence, and he called his father. Mutt Mantle, who had played his share of semipro ball, drove to see his son and, instead of sympathizing with Mickey, called him a coward. His dad started packing his son's things, aiming to take Mickey back to Commerce and a life as a miner. Through a flood of tears, Mickey vowed to give baseball one more shot.

And he certainly did. In forty games with the Yankees' minor league team in Kansas City, Mantle hit .361 with 11 homers and 60 RBI. Back with the big team, Mickey hit .284, with 6 homers and 20 RBI, helping the Yankees win the AL pennant.

In the second game against cross-town rivals the New York Giants, right fielder Mantle barely avoided a collision with Joe DiMaggio in center field. In doing so, Mickey caught his spikes on a drain cover. Something popped and he immediately fell to the outfield grass with a severe sprain to his right knee. (Subsequent research suggests that Mantle suffered a torn anterior cruciate ligament that day and played the rest of his amazing career with it never being repaired.) Carried off on a stretcher, Mantle spent the night with his dad, who had come to town to see his son play in the World Series.

Mickey Mantle, 1961 New York Yankees.

Mickey couldn't walk the next morning, and when Mutt tried to help his son to his feet, the elder Mantle collapsed. Mutt was dying from Hodgkin's disease, but hadn't revealed the malady to his son. Early in the next season, Mantle's dad succumbed to the disease.

Early on, Mantle's prodigious power was evident. During a 1951 spring training exhibition game at USC, Mantle hit a ball left-handed that left the ballpark and landed somewhere near an adjoining football field. The estimated distance was a mind-boggling 656 feet. Another homer hit by Mantle that day, this one right-handed, landed on top of a three-story building more than 500 feet away. Mick would also produce titanic shots at Washington's Griffith Stadium in April 1953 (565 feet) and Detroit's Tiger Stadium in September 1960 (643 feet).

In May 1963, Mantle hit a left-handed homer that struck the upper façade of Yankee Stadium, prompting speculation that it nearly left the entire park—a feat that was never accomplished, before or since. Projected distances, established with eyewitnesses, math, and computers, range between 630 and 735 feet. (No matter the disparity—that sucker was hit, and hit hard.) Mickey admitted it was probably the hardest ball he'd ever hit.

Through the 1950s, Mantle continued to astound fans of the game. In 1956, he won the first of three Most Valuable Player Awards, and took the coveted Triple Crown. He hit .353, while blasting 52 homers, driving in 130 runs, and scoring 132 runs (with an untreated torn ACL? Yikes). The following year, Mantle repeated his feats, winning his second MVP with a .365 average, 34 homers and 94 RBI, and an incredible on-base percentage of .512. (Double yikes. No wonder he was intentionally walked 23 times that year.)

Seeking to improve their impressive lineup, the Yankees added a left-handed power hitter named Roger Maris in 1960. The soft-spoken outfielder had shown flashes of power and superior defensive skills in three seasons with the Cleveland Indians and KC Athletics, so the Yanks figured Maris to be a perfect complement to Mantle.

They were right, as Mantle and Maris were a feared duo in the 1960 season. Slowed by his nagging injuries, Mickey hit just .275, but still cranked forty home runs and drove in ninety-four runs. He would up being in the running once again for the MVP Award, only to finish second to Maris, who had a solid average of .275, with 39 home runs and 112 RBI.

But the Yankees suffered a tough loss in the World Series, going seven games against the Pittsburgh Pirates. The NL team took a 9 to 7 lead into the ninth inning of the deciding game, with the Yankees fighting back to tie it in the top of the inning. With Ralph Terry in relief, hoping to take the tie into extra innings, the Yankees could only watch when second baseman (and future Hall of Famer) Bill Mazeroski drove a home run into the left field stands to win the championship for the Bucs.

The 1961 season would be a thrill for baseball fans, and a nightmare for both Mantle and Maris. The game had featured a 154-game season since 1920, based on each of the eight teams playing their opponents seven times. But expansion (one team each in the National and American Leagues) required increasing the season to 162 games—18 games against each opponent. (For the AL, that started in 1961. The NL followed suit in 1962.)

The New York Yankees came out of the blocks running. By July 1, their record was 45 wins and 27 losses, and, what's more, it was clear that their two sluggers—Mantle and Maris—would be making an assault on the holiest of baseball records—Babe Ruth's single-season home run total of 60.

Moving quickly, former sport writer (and old pal of the Bambino) baseball commissioner Ford Frick announced that the record of 60 homers could only be broken if someone achieved it within the first 154 games of a season. Anything outside that would place an asterisk next to the new record (an attempt to somehow cheapen the accomplishment). No matter, Mantle and Maris were both on pace to make history.

The newspapers tried their best to paint a vicious

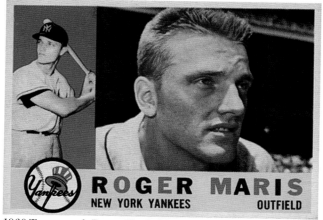
1960 Topps card, Roger Maris, New York Yankees.

Maris at bat, Mantle on deck, 1961.

rivalry between the two teammates, but Mantle and Maris wouldn't bite—they were goods friends and supported each other's efforts. All they cared about was helping the Yankees win. The media was always in Mantle's corner, believing him to be an authentic Yankee, while Maris was an outsider. Mickey's smile and "Aw, shucks" attitude played well; Roger was aloof and thought to be not worthy of the Bambino's throne.

By the first week of September, Mantle trailed Maris, 53 to 56 homers, with eighteen games remaining. The pressure of the chase wore thin on both; Mickey was worn and missed four games with a serious cold; Roger found his hair falling out in bunches and he couldn't sleep. By the middle of September, Mantle faced the reality that he wouldn't break Ruth's record, hitting his 54th and final home run on the 23rd.

A few days later, Mickey visited a doctor named Jacobson, who injected his right hip with a vitamin shot. (It should be noted that the doctor was well known to administer strong amphetamines, and his medical license was revoked in 1975.) The result was a seriously infected wound and an abscess that left an open wound down to the bone. Mick was hospitalized, still pulling for his teammate to break Ruth's record.

Maris tied the Babe on September 26, hitting a home run off the Orioles' Jack Fisher. On October 1—Game 163, since the Yanks had tied the Orioles in a game back in April—Maris set his record in the fourth inning, homering on his second at bat against Boston's Tracy Ballard. Roger didn't even want to play that day; his teammates had to talk him into it.

Much of the media's emphasis was placed on Maris playing 7 more games than Ruth did (Maris played in 161 games that year). However, they didn't mention that

Roger's record-tying home run was hit in his 684th plate appearance, while Ruth's came in his 687th plate appearance—actually, three more than Maris. No matter how it's sliced, both home run records were monumental.

Maris' single-season record of 61 home runs lasted for thirty-seven years (Babe Ruth's lasted for thirty-three). The Cardinals' Mark McGwire hit his 62nd home run on September 8, 1998, and he wound the season up with 70. Cubs outfielder Sammy Sosa hit 66 that same year, but McGwire has since admitted to using steroids, and, according to MLB drug testing results from 2003, Sosa came up positive for a performance-enhancing drug.

Just the Koufax, Ma'am . . .

It might seem that all things baseball between the 1920s and the middle of the 1960s started and ended with the Yankees—but they didn't. Plenty of teams had plenty of fine players—along with the aforementioned Hank Aaron, Milwaukee had slugging third baseman Eddie Mathews and pitchers like Warren Spahn (both Hall of Famers).

The Cincinnati Reds had a fine Rookie of the Year in 1956 named Frank Robinson. A solid and intense outfielder, Robinson hit 25 or more home runs in nine of his ten seasons with the Reds and drove in 90 or more runs six times. Named the NL Most Valuable Player in 1961, Robinson was traded to the American League and the Baltimore Orioles in 1966, where he immediately won the AL MVP Award—and the Triple Crown—by hitting .316, slugging 49 homers, and driving in 122 runs.

Frank Robinson, 1975 Cleveland Indians.

Robinson played until 1976, the last two years as player/manager for the Cleveland Indians, becoming baseball's first black manager. A twelve-time All-Star, Frank assembled a career record of 586 home runs (at that point, fourth all-time), along with 2,943 hits, more than 1,800 RBI, over 200 stolen bases, and a .294 lifetime average. He was also the only player ever to win the MVP Award in both leagues. Robinson was an easy choice for the Hall of Fame in 1982.

The Dodgers, moving westward from Brooklyn to Los Angeles in 1958, won the World Series in 1959 (having already won while in New York in 1955), as well as taking it all in 1963 and 1965. They, too, had a strong hitting lineup, including catcher Roy Campanella, first baseman Gil Hodges, and outfielders Duke Snider and Tommy Davis. Speedy shortstop Maury Wills stole a then-record 104 bases in 1962, with nearly 600 for his career.

What really added to the Dodgers' edge was their pitching, especially from Don Newcombe (winner of the Cy Young and MVP Awards in 1956) and hard-throwing, brushback specialist Don Drysdale. The latter was never afraid to claim the inside part of the plate, hitting more than 150 batters in his fourteen years with the Dodgers.

A power pitcher, yet possessing great control, Drysdale struck out more than two hundred batters six times, totaling nearly

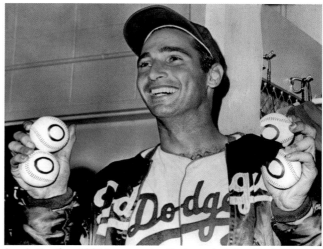

Sandy Koufax, 1965 Los Angeles Dodgers (celebrating his fourth no-hitter).

2,500 Ks in his career, while walking only 855. As an eight-time All-Star, he also was feared as a hitter, stroking 29 homers and driving in 113 runs in his career—great offensive numbers for a pitcher. In 1965, Drysdale hit .300, with 7 homers and 19 RBI. Winning more than two hundred games in his career, Drysdale had a 2.95 earned run average, receiving the Cy Young Award in 1962. He entered the Hall of Fame in 1984.

Opposing teams hated facing Drysdale, but also realized he wouldn't be their only problem during their LA visit. Left-handed Sandy Koufax was perhaps the most feared pitcher in the early to mid-1960s. His dominance on the mound was without question. Pirate Willie Stargell once compared trying to hit Koufax with trying to "drink coffee with a fork."

Signed with the Brooklyn Dodgers in 1954, he joined the major league team the next year. But Koufax was largely ineffective through the 1950s, with an ERA near or over 4.00 and records near or under .500 during that same period. He was wild, yet showed signs of amazing talent, striking out eighteen in one 1959 game.

Much like the black players that came before him, the Jewish Koufax endured mean-spirited and threatening comments in his career. But also like his predecessors, he silenced many with his skill and determination to succeed.

Struck with an epiphany, he once said, "I became a good pitcher when I stopped trying to make them miss the ball and started trying to make them hit it." Koufax backed off his power-pitching approach, incorporating off-speed pitches and a devastating curveball. In 1961, he had a record of 18 and 13, with 269 strikeouts in 255.2 innings pitched.

Losing nearly half of 1962 to a circulation problem in his arm, Koufax still went 14 and 7, with a 2.54 ERA. The next four seasons were nothing short of incredible. Between 1963 and 1966, his record was a combined 97 wins and 27 losses, for a .782 winning percentage. He had strikeouts of 306, 223, 382 (at the time, a modern-day record), and 317, with only a total of 259 walks in that same period. His ERAs during those four years were 1.88, 1.74, 2.04, and 1.73 (was there even a reason for opponents to show up at the park on the days that Sandy was pitching?).

Koufax won both MVP and Cy Young Awards in 1963, as well as receiving Cy Youngs in 1965 and 1966. He threw four no-hitters—including a perfect game in 1965—and seemed to be unstoppable. Yet the end was very near.

Called "The Man with the Golden Arm," Koufax stunned fans and the entire sports world after the 1966 season, suddenly announcing his retirement. His gilded appendage was arthritic, and Koufax just couldn't take the pain any more. Only aged thirty, his twelve-year career was over. But his accomplishments assured him entry to Cooperstown, as he entered in 1972 as the Hall's youngest member.

Long Divisions and Hitting Specialists

Dominating pitchers like Drysdale and Koufax weren't unique to either league during the mid-1960s. Minnesota's Jim Kaat (later with the Phillies, the White Sox, the Yanks, and the Cardinals), turned in several solid seasons during the decade, including a stunning 25 and 13 record in 1966. His year also included nineteen complete games and over three hundred innings pitched. Six of his seasons in the sixties featured earned run averages under or just over 3.00, and he won eight of his sixteen career Gold Glove Awards.

Playing his entire career with the St. Louis Cardinals, right-hander Bob Gibson was feared and respected simultaneously (somewhat rare in baseball, much more rare in organized crime). Between 1963 and 1970, Gibby won at last eighteen or more games seven times, with ERAs essentially at or under 3.00. Twice winning the Cy Young Award, he added the NL Most Valuable Player to one of them in 1968, finishing the year with a microscopic 1.12 ERA. Gibson completed his seventeen-year career with more than 250 wins, 3,100 strikeouts, and 250 complete games, entering the Hall of Fame in 1982.

Bob Gibson, 1967, St. Louis Cardinals.

High-kicking Juan Marichal played most of his sixteen-year career with the San Francisco Giants. His 191 wins in the decade easily outdistanced Gibson's impressive 164 wins in the same period. Seven of those years had Marichal posting ERAs of 2.75 or less. Did he have stamina? You bet, as he showed in a 1963 game, where he pitched a sixteen-inning, complete game, 1–0 victory over the Milwaukee Braves.

A dark point in Marichal's career came in a 1965 game against the Dodgers. Marichal and Koufax—the game's starters—were pitching tight and inside, dusting off batters on both teams. In the third inning, the Dodger lefty came close to Marichal when the Giant was at the plate. When Dodger catcher Johnny Roseboro threw the ball back to his pitcher, he unfortunately came very close to Marichal's ear intentionally.

The incident incensed the Giants pitcher, and he slammed his bat into Roseboro's head

Johnny Roseboro grabs Juan Marichal as Sandy Koufax tries to break it up, 1965.

(years before catchers wore protective skullcaps), resulting in a two-inch gash over the catcher's left eye. Benches emptied, with a brawl between the teams. When order was restored, Marichal was ejected (and subsequently fined $1,750 with a nine-game suspension).

The pitcher wound up with more than 240 wins in his sixteen-year career, as well as more than 240 complete games. He had over 2,300 strikeouts, against only 709 walks, and had been a nine-time All-Star. There was no question that he had Hall of Fame stats, but Marichal was not elected in his first two years of eligibility.

He knew why—the Roseboro incident had not been forgotten. Marichal reached out to the retired catcher and invited him to his charity golf tourney in the Dominican Republic. During a news conference there, Marichal offered his sincere apologies to Roseboro, and they were accepted.

The pitcher reached the Hall the following year and thanked Roseboro for his support during his acceptance speech. When Roseboro passed away in 2002, Marichal was asked to deliver the eulogy.

Other pitchers who dominated the 1960s include the Tigers/Phillies/Pirates' Jim Bunning (eight seasons with 17 or more wins, five season with an ERA under 2.80, joined the Hall of Fame in 1996), Hoyt Wilhelm (twenty-one years with nine teams as one of the game's first top-notch relief pitchers, five-time All-Star, elected to the Hall of Fame in 1985), and Denny McLain (last pitcher in the majors to win 30 or more games in one season—31 in 1968, winning the Cy Young and AL Most Valuable Player Awards, flowed up with a 24 and 9 season the next year, along with a second Cy Young Award).

The superiority of pitching over hitting reached its peak in 1968. The crop of bona fide pitchers, combined with a strike zone that had been enlarged in 1963 (by commissioner Ford Frick to further save the legacy of his old pal Babe Ruth), led to a weakened offense in both leagues. Average runs per game in 1968 were only 6.7, down from 9.1 only seven years previous. The mighty Yankees turned in a team average of .214 (no, really). The AL batting average was an anemic .230, with the NL a bit better at .243 (but still poor).

While the National League managed to have four hitters finish above .300, the American League and Boston's Carl Yastrzemski were hard pressed to hit .300 (he hit .301 for the year, making it by going .378 in the final month of September). Only one slugger hit more than 40 homers (the Senators' Frank Howard), and only three drove in more than 100 runs.

Fans have always liked to watch runs being scored in baseball, so something had to be done. MLB owners talked about changes like three-ball walks or adding a designated hitter, but decided to move more cautiously by changing the strike zone back to what it was before 1963 (Commissioner Ford Frick had retired in 1965, replaced by former Army General William D. Eckert). At that time, it was enlarged from the batter's armpits and the top of the knees to the top of the shoulders and the knees. Returning to the smaller zone would reduce the pitcher's advantage and give the batter more hittable pitches.

The other major change was lowering the height of the pitcher's mound, from fifteen inches to ten inches. Several teams had been suspected of keeping the mound at even higher levels, clearly giving their pitchers an advantage as they towered over batters (as well as the opponent pitchers . . . hmmmm? Sounds even to me). A lower mound would level the playing field (literally) and give the batters a more direct shot at the ball.

The end of the 1960s wasn't all pitchers and batters, as defense was still a key component of the game. One player in particular set the bar at a high point to which others might reach—Brooks Robinson.

Brooks Robinson, 1967 Baltimore Orioles.

With the nickname of "The Human Vacuum Cleaner," it might be assumed that Robinson sucked at third base, and he did—in a good way, as nearly every baseball hit in his direction wound up drawn into his mitt. At times, he appeared to be part acrobat and part tomcat, pouncing on the ball and—sometimes at impossible angles—making a sure throw to first.

Joining the Baltimore Orioles in 1955, Brooks came to the majors with a label of "all-field, no-hit." While he didn't tear the cover off the ball like teammates Boog Powell and Frank Robinson, Brooks Robinson proved to be no easy touch at the plate. In his twenty-three-season career—all with Baltimore—he hit at or over .285 seven times, drove in 80 or more runs eight times, and slugged 18 or more home runs eight times. In 1964, he hit .317, with 194 hits, 28 homers, and 118 RBI—good enough to win the AL MVP Award.

In all, Robinson was a fifteen-time All-Star and earned sixteen consecutive Gold Glove Awards at third base. He led the Orioles to a World Series title over the Dodgers in 1966 and additional Fall Classic appearances in 1969, 1970, and 1971. His election to Cooperstown was a no-brainer in 1983.

As outlined previously, baseball made a major expansion for the 1969 season, not only adding four new teams (the San Diego Padres, Montreal Expos, Kansas City Royals, and Seattle Pilots), but breaking the National and American Leagues each into Eastern and Western Divisions. The reasons were clear: With separate divisions, another level of postseason play would be added (meaning more income for the game and its owners), and, with added geographical regions (including outside the US for the first time), baseball would continue its reign as the National Pastime.

The concern over low run scoring didn't go away, so one of the most divisive decisions in baseball happened in 1973. The pitcher—not including anomalies like Babe Ruth—was always considered the weak link in the game's batting order. To increase run production, it was proposed to replace the pitcher in the batting order (not necessarily the ninth spot) with a "designated hitter."

The DH—as it was called—had one job: Go to the batter's box four or times a game—no fielding, no pitching. He would take his cuts, run the bases if needed, then return to the bench until his next turn in the order.

The DH was not necessarily a new idea. Connie Mack, legendary manager of the Philadelphia A's, originally proposed the idea in 1906 as an alternative to the game's weak-hitting pitchers. In the late 1920s, John Heydler, then-president of the National League, wanted to add a designated hitter as a way to speed the game up. In both cases, the concept never took hold.

In 1973, the American League resented the fact that since 1965, it had scored over 2,300 runs less than the National League had scored. The AL needed some way to correct the disparity, and, although the NL wanted no part of the designated hitter (of course, their league was scoring runs . . .), they did agree to let the American League use the rule if it could get OKed. The vote among the AL owners wasn't unanimous, but eight out of twelve teams voted to try the DH rule for three years (that was forty-two years ago, as of this writing).

On April 6, 1973, the Yankees' Ron Blomberg—a young outfielder/first baseman whose tender legs kept him from ascending to the throne once held by Mickey Mantle—became the game's first DH. He walked against Boston's Luis Tiant and continued to mostly DH for the Yankees for three seasons, along with a quarter of a season with the White Sox before retiring in 1978. Hardly a Hall of Famer, Blomberg (and his bat) still hold their spots in Cooperstown.

The National League did consider the DH rule in 1977, but wound up with a vote of six yeas, four nays, and two abstaining. With seven votes needed to put the designated hitter in the NL, the election fell one short and the topic has never been voted upon since.

RON BLOMBERG

1972 Topps card, Ron Blomberg, New York Yankees—Baseball's first DH.

Many managers dislike the DH rule, feeling it limits their options in terms of pinch-hitting and pitching strategy in later innings. For the most part, players have embraced the DH as a means to extend their careers and, in the cases of people like Paul Molitor and Frank Thomas, have found their way to the Hall of Fame, largely as designated hitters.

Still, the fact remains that one league uses the DH and the other doesn't. With interleague play as a regular practice across the season, it's somewhat confusing since AL pitchers must hit when playing in the NL team's park, and, conversely, the NL pitchers don't bat when they visit the AL parks. The same is true for all postseason play, which some folks believe has diluted the significance of the World Series.

The quality of designated hitters won't always be at the level of David Ortiz or Frank Thomas, yet there seems to be no clear decision for either the full adoption or complete demise of the DH.

Arguing Against Reserved Seating

Cardinals center fielder Curt Flood played the game very well, starting in the late 1950s. He won eight consecutive Gold Gloves for his defense and appeared in three All-Star games. Flood hit over .300 six times, twice delivering 200 or more hits. But baseball remembers Curt Flood more for what he accomplished off the field.

As pointed out previously in this chapter, players' contracts had included the reserve clause for nearly one hundred years, essentially making them indentured servants for their team. They either signed their contracts every year or they didn't play. Even though several players had tried to sue baseball in the 1940s and 1950s—claiming the reserve clause violated antitrust laws concerning interstate trade and commerce in America—no one had ever been able to

Curt Flood, 1969 St. Louis Cardinals.

successfully challenge the ownership's right to do what they would
with players.

That is, until 1969, when the St.
Louis team traded Flood, along
with Tim McCarver, Byron Brown,
and Joe Hoerner, to the
Philadelphia Phillies for Dick
Allen, Jerry Johnson, and Cookie
Rojas. Enjoying life in St. Louis,
Flood refused to accept the deal
and, with the guidance of his
lawyer and the executive director
of his union, the Major League
Baseball Players Association
(MLBPA), Marvin Miller, sued
Major League Baseball for viola-
tion of antitrust laws.

Knowing that, win or lose,
Flood would stand little chance of
returning to baseball (what club
owner would want this "trouble-
maker" on their team?), the outfielder proceeded with the suit,
with the knowledge that others
might benefit from the results.

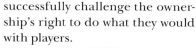

Copy of 1969 letter from Commissioner Bowie Kuhn
to Curt Flood.

They did, although he lost his own effort: first in federal court in 1970, then in
appeals in 1971, and finally, the US Supreme Court found in favor of the club
owners, by a vote of 5 to 3, in 1972. The courts held that baseball was exempt from
federal and state antitrust laws.

But Flood lost his battle in order to win the war. His suit raised consciousness
surrounding the owners' unfair advantage, and when a new contract—the Basic
Agreement—was created in 1970, it included something brand new. Players with
grievances could ask for independent arbitration, never before allowed.

Curt Flood's challenge opened a small but important hole in the club owners'
dam, with subsequent events eventually breaking through completely. In 1973, the
MLBPA added a clause in their agreement known as the "10/5 Rule"—also called
the "Curt Flood Rule." It stated that a player with ten years of major league experience, including five years with their present team, had the right to veto any trade.

In 1974, Jim "Catfish" Hunter left the A's, as an arbitrator found that owner
Charlie Finley had violated his contract. Hunter joined the Yankees the next year
as a free agent. In 1975, Dodgers pitcher Andy Messersmith and Orioles pitcher
Dave McNally became free agents after playing the season without signing their
contracts. Free agency in the game would soon become a common means of player
movement and successful team building.

Finally, in 1998, the US Congress passed the Curt Flood Act. The legislation stated that baseball was not exempt from antitrust laws, just like other professional sports like football and basketball.

Clemente and Tom Terrific

On the field, fans marveled at the Pittsburgh Pirate outfielder named Roberto Clemente. He was strong, he was fast, he should have had an "S" on his chest. The Puerto Rican star commanded respect for his efforts, on and off the field.

In his eighteen seasons with the Bucs, starting with the 1955 campaign as a twenty-year-old, Clemente was a presence in right field. An eventual twelve-time All-Star, his powerful and accurate throwing arm was partly due to his success as a javelin thrower at his Puerto Rico high school.

News of the teenaged star drew the attention of major league scouts, and the Brooklyn Dodgers signed Clemente in 1954, if only to keep the New York Giants from locking up the future phenom. But the Pirates drafted Clemente when the chance came up after the season.

Making the big league club out of spring training, Clemente was soon a fan favorite, displaying his rocket arm and ability to make good hits out of bad pitches. In his first two seasons, he had 18 and 17 assists, respectively, strong numbers from the outfield. He would finish his career with more than 260 assists (more than any other right fielder ever), as few tried to take an extra base on Clemente.

In postseason play, Roberto twice helped the Pirates to win the World Series, in 1960 and 1971 (where he won Series MVP, hitting .414). Along with League Championships, Clemente hit .318, with 3 homers and 14 RBI in five postseason appearances.

Between 1955 and 1972, Clemente had 190 or more hits six times, hit above .300 thirteen times, and earned twelve consecutive Gold Gloves. In 1966, he won the NL MVP, with a .317 average, 29 home runs, and 119 runs batted in, along with 202 hits and 105 runs scored. In his last at bat of the 1972 season, Clemente collected hit number 3,000.

After the season, Clemente returned to his home in Puerto Rico as usual. Just before Christmas, Managua, the capital of the Central American country of Nicaragua, was wracked by a strong earthquake. Clemente, anxious to lend a hand, organized a relief effort and boarded one of the rescue planes on New Year's Eve, bound for the ravaged area. Soon after takeoff, the plane reported mechanical problems and crashed into the Atlantic Ocean before it could return safely to Puerto Rico. Clemente was gone.

Despite rules that required players to wait five years before Hall of Fame eligibility, a special election selected Roberto Clemente to join Cooperstown posthumously the following year—making him the first Latin American to be so honored. There was never any doubt about his qualifications.

Elsewhere in the game during the 1960s came the Miracle Mets. The butt of many a joke since their creation in 1962, the Mets had never had a winning season in their first seven years. Then came 1969.

Everyone picked the Chicago Cubs to go all the way in '69. On August 16, they were in first place, up by nine games and a healthy thirty-one games over .500. The rest of the season is pointed to as a complete collapse, with the team playing all home games during the day as the suggested main reason for their fall from grace. (Forty-six years later, the memory is still fresh. So, with tear ducts tapped of all lachrymal fluid, I will avoid any further details.)

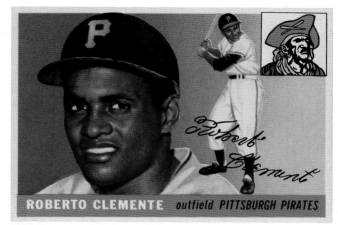

ROBERTO CLEMENTE outfield PITTSBURGH PIRATES

1955 Topps card, Roberto Clemente, Pittsburgh Pirates.

On August 13, the Mets were ten games behind the Cubs. But, truth be told, it must be noted that the Mets' success was no miracle—they played great baseball down the stretch and finished from that date with a crushing record of 38 wins and only 11 losses. They deserved to win.

The team really didn't do it with hitting, as the team average was only .241. Their top RBI producer (Tommie Agee) drove in 76 runs. Only one player (the same Agee) hit more than 20 homers (the next highest was Art Shamsky with 14). Only Cleon Jones hit over .300 (a robust .340). As a team, the Mets only stole 66 bases all season.

No, the triumph of the Mets' season was largely due to the lefty-righty combo of starting pitchers Jerry Koosman and Tom Seaver. Between them, they won 42 games, while losing only 16 (for good measure, the Mets also had a twenty-two-year-old pitcher named Nolan Ryan, who went 6 and 3 that year).

Seaver, known as "Tom Terrific," really was. At the age of twenty-four, he went 25 and 7, with a measly 2.24 ERA and more than 200 Ks. It goes without saying that Seaver deserved—and won—the Cy Young Award that year (the first of three, all with the Mets).

In a twenty-year career—played with the Mets, Reds, White Sox, and

Tom Seaver, 1969 New York Mets.

a final year with the Red Sox—Tom Seaver won 311 games, had an ERA of 2.86 and more than 3,600 strikeouts. A twelve-time All-Star, he was elected to the Hall of Fame in 1992 with the highest-ever percentage of 98.8 percent of the vote.

Known as a smart, thinking-man's pitcher—with solid tree-trunk-like legs to provide much of the drive in his delivery—Seaver guided the Mets to a dominating World Series win against the Baltimore Orioles in 1969. They would return, with Seaver once more leading the way, in 1973. Unfortunately, they ran into a buzz saw known as the Oakland Athletics.

5

1971 to 2000

Heading for Home . . .

The Dynasties of the Seventies—the Mustache Gang

The A's, having come over from Kansas City in 1968, were a huge success in the early 1970s—because of (and in spite of) their quirky and complex owner named Charlie O. Finley. The man was part innovator, part slave driver, and part (a very large part) egomaniac. Above all, he was a super—no—a super-duper salesman, capable of selling the proverbial refrigerator to an Eskimo, complete with icemaker. But there's no doubt that Finley loved the game. He just had a peculiar way of showing it.

A multimillionaire in the insurance business, Finley bought the Kansas City A's in 1960. He made an immediate impression on the ball club and fans by bringing in Frank Lane as the general manager, then reversing several of Lane's transactions. The GM lasted less than a year of his eight-year arrangement with Finley. Similarly, field manager Joe Gordon stuck around for only sixty games before being fired and replaced—mid-game—by right fielder Hank Bauer (while the fans saw it orchestrated that way, the hiring had actually been arranged beforehand).

The owner showed no fear in trying new, innovative—albeit, goofy—ways to attract fans. He hosted greased pig competitions, installed a mechanical rabbit named Harvey behind home plate (who would rise up to supply the ump with new baseballs), had an arrangement of compressed air jets called Little Blowhard to keep home plate clean, and used a Yellow Cab to ferry bullpen pitchers to the mound. (Consider his loony alternate idea of installing an elevator directly under the mound, where the relief pitcher would rise up majestically to take his place at the rubber. Never happened.)

Beyond the right field fence, a sheep—complete with shepherd—grazed to celebrate an Athletics home run by ringing a bell. The idea

A's owner Charlie Finley.

stuck for four years, until an errant homer hit one of the sheep in the head and killed it. From then on, there never was another ewe.

Finley also shocked everyone by creating new team uniforms—sleeveless, colored bright yellow with green undershirt and trim. In a game where home togs were only white and road togs were only gray, the Kansas City uniforms were blasphemous. Finley didn't care, as he kept the brightly hued uniform in home or road games for years to come—where the times actually caught up with his radical idea.

Within a few years, Finley was anxious to move the team out of KC (something he boldly promised the public he would never do) and made a deal to relocate the A's to Louisville. He overlooked one small detail—Finley neglected to tell the American League what he intended to do, and they swiftly put the kibosh on the arrangement.

The owner's egocentric ways also alienated the KC media, which was not a very smart move. With his front-office meddling, the media compared Finley to folks like the miserly Ebenezer Scrooge and the evil, quick-to-behead queen from *Alice in Wonderland.* On the field, Finley's A's lost ninety or more games in five of the seven years they were in Kansas City.

By the end of the 1967 season, the lease at the KC Municipal Stadium was up and Finley got league approval to move the Athletics to Oakland. In the meantime, the owner and GM Hank Peters spent several million dollars in building a minor league system of players that would soon produce fruit—by the bushel basket.

In 1962, Cuban-born shortstop Bert Campaneris signed with the A's for a bonus of $500. In 1964, the club spent $650,000 to sign eighty players. Among them were pitcher Jim "Catfish" Hunter, John "Blue Moon" Odom (both nicknames were created as marketing ploys by Finley), and outfielder Joe Rudi.

The MLB had its first amateur draft in 1965. The first player picked—going to the last-place A's—was standout Arizona State University outfielder Rick Monday. Three other players from that year were Monday's third base teammate Sal Bando, along with pitcher Rollie Fingers and catcher Gene Tenace. The '66 draft took another ASU star named Reggie Jackson. In 1967, pitcher Vida Blue was a second-round pick for the A's.

The move to Oakland paid immediate dividends in 1968, as the club finished two games over .500—a first for the Finley-owned team. Their records improved in 1969 and 1970, where they finished in second place both years. The table was set for an exciting decade of the 1970s for the team.

Yet Finley couldn't leave well enough alone. In 1969, Jackson started the season by cranking home runs at a pace rivaling the record years of Maris and Ruth. The twenty-three-year-old slugger's tempo lightened, and he finished the year with 47 round-trippers, while drawing big crowds for Oakland. The next year, Finley gave Jackson a tough time in awarding him his new contract—despite the fans Jackson had put in the seats—and Reggie ended up having a bad year at the plate. Jackson was eventually benched for a while, and he wound up far off his previous year's stats.

Similarly, Vida Blue had an amazing year in 1971, going 24 and 8, with a microscopic ERA of 1.82 and fanning 301 batters. The pitcher won the Cy Young Award and the AL's Most Valuable Player trophy. Once more, Finley and Blue went head-to-head when contract time came the following spring, and the bad experience led Blue to a subpar season of 6 and 10, with only 111 Ks.

With Dick Williams managing the team—the fourth skipper, by the way, in the three years since relocating to Oakland—the product on the field was top-notch and almost unstoppable. In 1971, the A's won 101 games behind Blue's great season, and Hunter's twenty-one wins, as well. But they were swept in three straight ALCS games by the Baltimore Orioles.

In 1972, Finley tweaked his team by trading Rick Monday to the Cubs for left-handed starter Ken Holtzman, who won nineteen games for the A's that year. But the acquisition of former thirty-game winner Denny McClain wasn't as successful, and he was traded to Atlanta before mid-season after a weak 5 and 5 record, with a bloated 6.04 ERA. The owner had also introduced a rotation of white, bright yellow, and Kelly green pullover jerseys, hailing back to his days in KC. Finley added white spiked shoes to boot. (Insert groan here).

Finley also offered the players exactly the kind of bonus opportunity one would expect from an eccentric owner like him. When Jackson arrived at spring training sporting a full beard,

Reggie Jackson, 1972 Oakland A's.

the A's owner agreed to give $300 to every player who followed suit by growing facial hair. The team became known as "The Mustache Gang," with reliever Rollie Fingers drawing special attention with his waxed, handlebar mustache. While most of baseball remained clean-shaven, another Finley-led promotion would gain acceptance in the game.

The A's took their division with 93 victories, then defeated the Tigers in the ALCS series. But the Oakland team would have to face the Cincinnati Reds—the fearsome Big Red Machine—in the World Series without their most dynamic player, as Reggie Jackson had torn his hamstring in the playoffs. After the first four games, the A's were up 3 wins to 1, each contest having been just one-run wins for both teams.

The Reds charged back in the next two games and won them both. Again, the decisive seventh game was a close one, with the A's winning by a 3 to 2 score. They had their first world championship in forty-two years. All through the celebration, Finley was as prominent as the players. He also went overboard in designing and purchasing World Series rings for his players and staff, spending more than $1,500 on each ring—an exorbitant amount in 1972.

The club did a repeat performance in 1973, with its owner once more making some adjustments. Catcher Dave Duncan, often unhappy with how Finley treated

1973 Oakland A's in their dugout.

the team, was traded for catcher Ray Fosse. Setup pitcher Bob Locker went to the Cubs for fleet center fielder Bill North.

Gene Tenace, now at first, stroked 24 homers, and Sal Bando added 29. Reggie Jackson hit .293, with 32 home runs and 117 RBI, good enough to win the AL MVP award. Pitchers Ken Holtzman and Catfish Hunter each won twenty-one games, and Vida Blue won twenty. The A's won ninety-four games, then beat the Orioles to win the ACLS.

The World Series was coast-to-coast, as the A's were pitted against the aforementioned New York Mets. Once more, Finley became a bigger story than his team winning the world championship, this time involving a substitute second baseman named Mike Andrews.

The A's lost Game Two in twelve innings by a score of 10 to 7, but not wholly because Andrews made two errors in the late innings (the A's made three more in the game, hardly World Series–caliber play). After the game, Finley pressed a contrite and exhausted Andrews to sign a letter stating the second baseman was injured (an outright falsehood) so that his spot on the roster could be filled by young Manny Trillo, known as a fine fielder.

Angry A's players responded by wearing Andrews' number—17—on their uniforms in protest of Finley's actions. Baseball Commissioner Bowie Kuhn, even more angry, ordered that Andrews be immediately returned to the roster. In spite of the enormous distraction, the Oakland team won their second consecutive World Series in seven games.

However, the fallout from the controversy included Finley's outright lies to the media about the circumstances and manager Dick Williams' resignation, despite winning two world championships with the A's. The commissioner fined Finley $7,000 for his indiscretions. And Mike Andrews never played in the majors again.

As mentioned previously, the Basic Agreement in 1973 allowed for independent arbitration in salary disputes. That meant that Finley would have to open up his checkbook for his World Series winners, and he didn't like that. He headed the negotiations in nine arbitration hearings (instead of leaving it to the GM, which is standard) and ended up losing five of them.

For the 1974 season, Alvin Dark was named manager and the team wanted a three-peat. As the season went, Joe Rudi and Sal Bando each hit 22 homers and combined to drive in more than 200 runs. Jackson and Tenace had 29 and 26 home runs, respectively, and shortstop Bert Campaneris hit a robust .290. The front three starters of Hunter, Blue, and Holtzman won a total of sixty-one games and closer Rollie Fingers went 9 and 5 with 18 saves.

To no one's surprise, Finley again jerked baseball's chain by signing Herb Washington, a world-class track sprinter who'd never played a day of organized ball, to be the "designated pinch runner" for the team. He never had an at bat or plate appearance, but scored 29 runs and stole 29 bases for the A's in 1974.

Unfortunately, Washington was also caught stealing 16 times, proving that a speedy runner is not the same thing as a base runner in the game. He was released early in the next season and never appeared for any other team.

The team won ninety games in 1974, once again hooking up with the Orioles for the ALCS, which the A's took in four games. Oakland matched up against the LA Dodgers, who won 102 games in the regular season. Despite that, the A's beat the Dodgers in five games and had their third straight World Series championship.

The Oakland A's won their division in 1975, even though Hunter left the team and signed with the Yankees. But their postseason play was short-lived, as they lost to the Boston Red Sox in three games. The dynasty was done, with Finley breaking up the team and the A's quickly sinking to the bottom of their division by the second half of the 1970s. For example, they lost a stunning 108 games in 1977. In 1980, Finley sold his beloved Oakland team to the Walter Haas family, who also controlled the Levi Strauss clothing company, for more than $12 million.

Back in 1973, Finley had found an eleven-year-old A's fan in the Oakland parking lot and thought he looked like a young Hank Aaron. The kid started hanging around the clubhouse and front offices, as Finley took a liking to him. He stuck around until the end of the decade, then joined the Navy after realizing he would never make it as a major league ballplayer. Becoming a young man, Stanley Burrell—who Finley had nicknamed "Hammer" because of his resemblance to Hammerin' Hank—hit the big time as a premier star in rap music named MC Hammer.

Dynasties of the Seventies—The Big Red Machine

Just as the A's were a team of high-strung and emotional players, as was their owner, the previously mentioned Cincinnati Reds were just the opposite. There was more than one meaning to their moniker of "The Big Red Machine." For the most part, they were cold, methodical, and efficient. And, like the A's, they dominated their league in the early 1970s.

Claims to coining the nickname are split between their hard-nosed and scrappy Pete Rose and sportswriter Bob Hunter. Rose owned a red 1934 Ford at the time and said it was his Little Red Machine and his Reds team was the Big Red Machine. Hunter, writing in Los Angeles, pointed out that the Big Red Machine was invading when they played the Dodgers in 1969.

The Reds made their mark with massive hitting, slick fielding, and so-so pitching. During the decade of the 1970s, the team finished in first place six times and second place three times. They won ninety-eight or more games five times. They competed in the Fall Classic four times. To put it bluntly, they were damn good.

Managed by the first-time skipper George "Sparky" Anderson, the 1970 Reds were young and powerful. Catcher Johnny Bench, who reinvented the concept of catching from both a defensive and offensive view, cranked 45 homers, with 148 RBI and a .293 average at age twenty-two, good enough win the first of two NL MVP awards. In his seventeen-year career—all with the Reds—Bench was a ten-time Gold Glover, a fifteen-time All-Star, and entered the Hall of Fame in 1989.

At third base, Tony Perez had his own MVP-type of year (yet not as good as Bench's). The Cuban star hit .317, drove in 129 runs with 40 homers and a massive OPS of .990. (Perez would join Bench in the Hall of Fame in 2000.) Big Lee May handled first base, along with hitting 34 home runs and driving in 94 runs. Outfielders Bobby Tolan and Pete Rose hit identical .316 averages, with Rose collecting 205 safeties.

On the mound, only Jim Merritt won twenty games, but relievers Wayne Granger and Clay Carroll combined for 51 saves. The team won 102 games and

1970 Cincinnati Reds team picture.

swept the Pirates to win the ALCS. But they came up against the Baltimore Orioles, who won the World Series in five games.

The Reds finished fourth in 1971, but returned to first place in 1972 by winning ninety-five games. Much of the team was the same, with a few valuable additions. Joe Morgan, who had handled second base in Houston for nine seasons, came to the Reds with blazing speed and a solid glove.

Morgan, known for his left-handed batting stance that included flapping his back arm like a chicken (actually an intentional habit designed to keep his elbow out and away from his body), stole 58 bases and scored a league-high 122 runs. The ten-time All-Star and five-time Gold Glove winner was elected to Cooperstown in 1990.

Once more, Bench was money in the bank with 40 homers and 125 RBI, and Perez, having moved to first base, added 21 home runs and 90 RBI. Rose hit his usual .300-plus average, and shortstop Davey Concepción was solid with the glove. The pitching staff was adequate, with Gary Nolan posting a 1.99 ERA and lefty Tom Hall going 10 and 1 in relief. Postseason play saw the Big Red Machine roll over the Pirates again, but break down in seven games against the A's, as noted before.

In 1973, the Reds won ninety-nine games. Bench and Perez drove in their usual 100-plus RBI, Rose had a typical year of 230 hits, and the pitching carried them along. But, despite their winning ways, they lost the NLCS to the Mets in five games.

The Reds finished 4 games behind the Dodgers in their division (the Reds and Braves were both in the NL West—don't ask why) in 1974, but won an astounding 108 games in 1975. Again most of the usual suspects were in place, but added the potent bat of outfielder George Foster, who hit .300, with 23 homers and 74 RBI. Also on hand was young Ken Griffey (Sr., not Jr)., who hit .305 and patrolled right field.

Yes, Bench, Perez, and Rose did their customary great job, and Joe Morgan won the NL MVP award with a .327 average, 94 RBI, 132 walks, and 67 steals. The pitching staff was good, with relievers Rawly Eastwick and Will McEnaney combining for a record of 10 and 5, with 37 saves.

The Reds, to no one's surprise, bested the Pirates in three straight, then tangled in one of the greatest World Series ever with the Boston Red Sox. Many fans recall the nail-biting Game Six as an example of how great the game can really be.

The Red Sox were down to the Reds, three games to two, and found themselves on the short end of a 6–3 score in their part of the eighth inning. With two outs, pinch hitter Bernie Carbo stroked a three-run homer off Rawly Eastwick to tie the game. Boston fans went wild, but the best was still to come.

In the bottom of the twelfth inning, Red Sox catcher Carlton Fisk golfed Pat Darcy's second pitch toward Fenway Park's Green Monster. Fisk slowly moved down the baseline, using his arms to wave as much body English into the ball as possible so that it might stay fair. It did and the jubilant hitter rounded the bases with a walk-off home run. There would be a Game Seven for the Reds and Red Sox.

Tied 3 to 3 in the top of the ninth, two walks and a single by Joe Morgan led the Reds to their first World Series championship since 1940. Like the Oakland A's, the question was: could the Reds repeat their success?

The answer was: yes, as the 1976 Reds team won 102 games in the regular season, as the team batting average was a healthy .280. Bench had an off year, but Joe Morgan won his second straight NL MVP award by hitting .320, with 27 home runs and 111 RBI, a .444 on-base percentage, and 60 steals. George Foster also picked up the slack by hitting .306, along with 29 homers and 121 RBI. In fact, the outfield of Foster, Cesar Geronimo, and Ken Griffey all hit over .300 and combined to steal 71 bases.

As many as six starters were spread out, each starting at least twenty games. Closer Rawly Eastwick went 11 and 5, with a stingy 2.09 ERA and 26 saves. The Philadelphia Phillies were toast for the Reds, going down in three straight. The New York Yankees, having won ninety-seven games in the regular season, were also no match for the Reds. The Big Red Machine steamrolled the Yanks in four straight to sweep the World Series and gave them the second World Championship in as many years.

The rest of the 1970s was a mixed bag for the Big Red Machine. They finished second in 1977 and 1978 and lost a few of their important cogs. By 1979, even though superstar pitcher Tom Seaver had joined the club, Tony Perez had moved on to the Expos. Likewise, Pete Rose and Rawly Eastwick took their gear to the Phillies. The Reds won their division, but were swept by the Pirates in three straight, leaving the Big Red Machine in pieces.

Dynasties of the Seventies—The Bronx Zoo

In New York City in the mid-1970s, the Yankees basically picked up where the Oakland A's had left off—winning on the field and whirling in turmoil in the clubhouse. A shipbuilding magnate named George Steinbrenner had purchased the team from CBS in 1973, setting off years of excitement (and controversy) for the Bronx Bombers.

When Charlie Finley (yes, again) violated Catfish Hunter's contract, leaving him a free agent in 1974, Steinbrenner swooped in and signed the pitcher to an unprecedented five-year contract for $3.2 million with the Yankees. The groundwork for unrestricted free agency had been laid.

Steinbrenner also brought in the feisty and argumentative Billy Martin to manage the team (Martin would leave and come back to the Yankees a total of five times, with a sixth go-round under preparation when Martin was killed in a car accident in 1989). It was no secret that Martin and Steinbrenner had a love-hate relationship. But it was also no secret that Martin knew how to manage winning teams and that was the bottom line for the Yankees owner.

The manager's first full year with the team—1976—saw the Yankees win ninety-seven games and the AL East. On the field, the Yankees were captained by catcher Thurman Munson, who hit .302, with 17 homers and 105 RBI. A solid fielding infield was anchored by Chris Chambliss at first and Graig Nettles at third. The pair combined for nearly 190 runs batted in and 61 homers. The outfield had the speedy Mickey Rivers in center, who stole 43 bases and hit .312. Left fielder Roy White chipped in 31 steals and a .286 average.

The Yanks' top three starting pitchers—Hunter, Ed Figueroa, and Dock Ellis—teamed up for 53 wins, and all had ERAs under 3.50. The bullpen had closer Sparky Lyle, who, along with "Dirty" Dick Tidrow, saved a combined thirty-three games. The team took the KC Royals in five games, but lost—as previously noted—four straight World Series games to the Reds.

Royals' George Brett grapples with Yankees' Graig Nettles, an example of the volatile 1977 Bronx lineup.

Martin and Steinbrenner hated to lose and took steps to improve the team in 1977. The position of shortstop was strengthened by trading for sure-handed Bucky Dent from the White Sox. On the mound, the Yankees obtained Mike Torrez, and, having been part of the winning Big Red Machine from the year before, Don Gullett signed on as a free agent. They also brought in a young left-hander named Ron Guidry.

Without question, the biggest addition (and biggest presence, on and off the field) was outfielder Reggie Jackson. His reputation as a superstar was established with the A's, as was his propensity to argue with authority when he thought he'd been wronged. His arrival would bring plenty of fireworks for baseball fans everywhere—on the field, in the dugout, and in the clubhouse.

Jackson was a college star at Arizona State, where he originally attended on a football scholarship. Wanting to play both football and baseball, Jackson switched completely to the diamond game in his sophomore year. Playing for an amateur team run by the Orioles, the young man set several hitting records and was offered $50,000 to join Baltimore. But Jackson wanted to stay in college, so he passed. In 1966, he was drafted by the Kansas City Athletics.

Ironically, after his outstanding years with the A's, Jackson was traded to the Orioles in 1976, but became a free agent at the end of the year. He quickly signed a five-year, multimillion-dollar deal with the Yankees. Reggie had a big swing, hit big home runs, and made big strikeouts (his career total of nearly 2,600 is the all-time record).

Jackson's arrival in the Big Apple was quickly polarizing, as he was quoted in a major magazine as being "the straw that stirs the drink," although he claimed he was misquoted. Barely two months into the season, Martin had already twice benched Reggie—mainly to show who was the boss. In June, Martin pulled Jackson from right field in mid-game when the manager thought Reggie had dogged his effort to catch an easy fly ball hit by the Red Sox slugger Jim Rice. In the dugout, Martin screamed at Jackson, then physically went after him. Billy had to be held back by two Yankee coaches.

In Jackson's twenty-one-year career (he spent five years with the California Angels and a final year with the A's after his tenure with the Yanks), the fourteen-time All-Star slugger hit 563 home runs and drove in more than 1,700 runs. Pretty fast in his younger years, he ended up with 228 stolen bases and a lifetime slugging percentage of .490. He was elected to Cooperstown in 1993.

The 1977 Yankees, in spite of all the drama, won an even one hundred games. There was plenty of run production, as Munson, Nettles, and Jackson each drove in more than 100 runs. Nettles stroked 37 home runs and Reggie added 32. The four main starters—Figueroa, Torrez, Guidry, and Gullett—combined for 60 wins, while the bullpen team of Lyle and Tidrow went a total of 24 and 9, with 31 saves.

Again, the Yankees bested the Royals in five games to win the AL pennant. It was on to face the LA Dodgers for the world championship. It would be a memorable series and one where Jackson was tagged with an appropriate nickname—and he certainly earned it.

A reporter asked Yankees catcher Thurman Munson a question about the Series, and he deferred to his slugging teammate, suggesting, "Go ask 'Mr. October.'" There may have been sarcasm in the statement, but there was also truth.

After five games, the Yankees had a 3–2 lead against a very good LA team—filled with players like the swift second baseman Davey Lopes, power hitting Steve Garvey, Ron Cey, Reggie Smith, and Dusty Baker, and tough pitchers like Burt Hooton, Don Sutton, and Tommy John. Hooton, famous for his baffling "knuckle-curve," started Game Six in Yankee Stadium.

With the Yankees down 3 to 2 in bottom of the fourth, Munson singled to left.

The Reggie Bar, an example of how far a player's marketing value can go.

Up came Reggie—first pitch, Boom! Two-run homer. The next inning, Reggie at the plate—first pitch, Boom! Another two-run homer. Leading off the bottom of the eighth, Reggie comes up—first pitch, Boom! His third home run of the night. Three pitches—three balls blasted out of the yard. Even Garvey was amazed at the display, later admitting he acknowledged the feat by quietly clapping in his mitt for Jackson.

Down 8 to 3, the Dodgers tried to mount a rally in the ninth inning, but they could only muster 1 run, and the Yankees—bad blood, Reggie benchings, and all—were World Champs.

The Yanks had a slow start in 1978, although left-hander Ron Guidry had a year that no one would forget. At the end of the season, Guidry had a fantastic record of 25 wins and only 3 losses, with a miserly ERA of 1.74, 9 shutouts, and 248 strikeouts. It easily earned the pitcher the Cy Young Award. The team also benefitted with solid hitting from left fielder "Sweet" Lou Piniella, plus a reliable closer in Rich "Goose" Gossage.

To all appearances (especially Steinbrenner's), Billy Martin had lost control of the Yankees. Jackson had grudgingly been moved to the designated hitter spot and, in July, incurred Martin's wrath by missing multiple bunt signs. Martin suspended the slugger for five games, then stuck his foot in his mouth by calling both Reggie and George "liars" in a press report. Martin resigned before being fired.

If that wasn't goofy enough, Steinbrenner—just five days later—announced that the Yankees manager for the 1979 season would be . . . Billy Martin. Bob Lemon, who had replaced Billy, would finish the year, then move into the front office. (Makes one think that Yankee Stadium was awash in seltzer bottles and whoopee cushions—who could possibly take anything seriously?)

Somehow, the team won one hundred games, after a victorious one-game playoff with the Boston Red Sox. Light-hitting Bucky Dent cranked a home run over the Green Monster in Fenway, which put the Yanks ahead in the seventh. Once more, Jackson came through, hitting a home run in the eighth, which made the difference when the Red Sox replied with two runs in their half of the inning. The 5 to 4 New York lead held up, and, after beating the Royals in four games for the ALCS, the Yankees found themselves in a rematch against the Dodgers in the World Series.

Once again, the series went six games, with the Yanks earning their second consecutive world championship. Jackson, as usual, had a tremendous series, hitting .391, with 2 homers and 8 RBI. But Bucky Dent (apparently not-so-light-hitting) won Series MVP honors with a .417 average, 10 hits, and 7 RBI. Thurman Munson also hit a robust .320.

The Yankees' run of success in the 1970s came to an end in 1979, with a tragic event overshadowing any drama on the field. Lemon continued to manage for the first sixty or so games, then Martin returned to the helm. But Billy couldn't right the team, and they finished in fourth place. Once more, Steinbrenner fired Martin.

More notable was the loss of catcher and Yankee captain Thurman Munson, who was killed while flying his private plane on an off day in August. While the tragedy pulled the team together emotionally, it also made digging out of a mediocre 58 and 49 record, fifteen games out of first place at the time of the accident, a difficult task.

Since then, the New York Yankees have done just fine, appearing in postseason play a generous nineteen times since their World Series win in 1978. Along the way, they have won five more World Championships, behind such impressive players as shortstop Derek Jeter, reliever Mariano Rivera, first baseman Don Mattingly, base-stealing outfielder Rickey Henderson, along with outfielders Dave Winfield and Bernie Williams.

A Lull in the Action

The decade of the 1980s for baseball was about as far away from the previous ten-year period as one could imagine. Where the seventies had repeat World Series winners like the A's, the Reds, the Yankees, and the Pirates, the eighties had nine different teams taking home the Commissioner's Trophy as the best in baseball. The closest thing to a dynasty in the 1980s was the St. Louis team, as the Cardinals appeared in three World Series, winning the 1982 matchup against the AL Milwaukee Brewers. Home runs were down, stolen bases were up, and the shadows of labor problems and recreational drugs darkened the game.

The power outage of the 1980s was the worst in baseball since the 1940s, when World War II took many of the game's best hitters overseas. The sixties and seventies had plenty of thumpers, like Aaron, Mantle, Mays, McCovey, Bench, Stargell, Jackson, Killebrew, and others, all hitting 40 or more homers repeatedly (not to mention Mantle, Mays, Maris, and Foster cranking more than 50).

It's difficult to identify the exact reason for the reduction of long balls in the decade, as hitters launched 40 or more homers a mere thirteen times between 1980 and 1989. As will soon be revealed, part of the reason might be due to a philosophical change—for some teams—in how to score runs. Still, the number of runs scored overall was higher in the 1980s than the 1970s, although the addition of two teams to the AL (Mariners and Blue Jays) must also be considered. Suffice it to say, the reduction in homers did not equate to lower scores in the eighties.

One pitcher in particular made run scoring a challenge in a career that spanned four decades. Nolan Ryan—the Ryan Express—was only nineteen years old when he made his debut with the 1966 New York Mets. His skills on the mound would take him on a twenty-seven-year journey, also pitching for the Angels, Astros, and Rangers.

Nolan Ryan, 1981 Houston Astros.

While not a beefy pitcher, he made his mark with a blazing fastball. When he added a nasty curve ball to his arsenal when he joined the Angels, Ryan was downright devastating. As a record-setter, he is first in no-hitters with 7, first in strikeouts with 5,714, first in single-season strikeouts with 383, among other records (like first in walks with 2,795 and wild pitches with 277). Ryan also had twenty-four years with 100 or more strikeouts and collected 300 or more Ks in six different seasons.

A good example of Ryan's ability to totally dominate a game came in July 1973, as he pitched the second of his seven no-hitters, this one against the Detroit Tigers. Having struck out seventeen batters, Ryan faced Tiger first baseman Norm Cash—AL batting champ in 1961—with two outs in the bottom of the ninth. As Cash stepped into the box, home plate umpire Ron Luciano stopped the hitter before the first pitch.

Cash had gone into the dugout and, instead of a bat, had come out with a table leg in his hands. Luciano quickly noted it was not allowed and Cash couldn't use it. "Why not?" said the Tiger, "I won't hit him anyway." Cash quickly popped out with a regulation bat, and Ryan had the no-no.

At age forty-four, Ryan became the oldest pitcher ever to throw a no-hitter and finished his career at age forty-six. He won a total of 324 games, and, despite his dominance, Ryan never won the Cy Young Award and played in only eight All-Star games. Still, his impact in the 1960s through the 1990s made Nolan Ryan an easy first-ballot inductee to the Hall of Fame in 1999.

Mike Schmidt, 1981 Philadelphia Phillies.

Somewhat unique to the period was the crop of top-notch third basemen. Certainly, players like the Dodgers/Cubs' Ron Cey, the Braves/Cardinals' Bob Horner, Rangers/Reds' Buddy Bell, and the Brewers' Paul Molitor (pre-DH) made for a solid bunch of "hot corner" he-men. Beyond those, however, were three exceptional players.

For many fans and experts, the Phillies' Mike Schmidt was the best third baseman ever. In his eighteen-year career, Schmidt combined solid fielding with great and timely power hitting to anchor the Philadelphia team. Retiring in 1989, Schmidt totaled 548 home runs, with nearly 1,600 RBI (having driven in 100 or more runs nine times). He also had more than 400 doubles, 174 stolen bases, and an impressive lifetime OPS of .908. The twelve-time All-Star won three NL MVP awards, along with ten Gold Gloves. Deservingly, Schmidt entered Cooperstown in 1995.

In the American League, very few players could match up with the Kansas City Royals' George Brett. The left-handed third baseman thrilled fans in 1980 by finishing the season with a .390 average—the highest since Ted Williams batted .406 in 1941. While not a true power hitter, Brett still hit 20 or more home runs in eight seasons, and drove in 90 or more runs in six seasons. He also hit

George Brett, 1982 Kansas City Royals.

Wade Boggs, 1990 Boston Red Sox.

665 doubles and finished his twenty-one-year career with more than 3,100 hits and a .305 lifetime average. The thirteen-time All-Star won the AL MVP award in 1980 and joined the Hall of Fame in 1999.

Wade Boggs took his position at third for the Red Sox in 1982, making an immediate impression with a .349 average in 104 games that year. It was only the start of something big, as Boggs played eleven seasons for Boston, then moved to the dreaded rival New York Yankees in 1993. He finished his eighteen-year career spending two seasons with the AL expansion Tampa Bay Devil Rays.

Boggs, who indulged a pregame superstition of always eating chicken (which certainly led to a few "fowl balls" during the game), as well as always taking batting practice at 5:17, was a twelve-time All-Star. He finished with 3,010 hits and a .328 lifetime average. Boggs hit .330 or more nine times and had 1,412 walks, nearly doubling his strikeout total. He won the Silver Slugger trophy nine times and the Gold Glove twice. He was elected to the Hall of Fame in 2005.

While speed has always been an essential element of the game, it seemed to take on a new life in the 1980s. Despite the reduction of home runs in the decade, it was speed on the base paths that led to increased run scoring. While all of baseball didn't embrace the "point-to-point" philosophy of stealing bases to score, many teams did.

In the American League, it was one name—Rickey Henderson. Splitting his time between the A's and the Yankees, the swift outfielder stole 75 or more bases seven times in the 1980s, including breaking the century mark three times. In 1982, Henderson set the single-season record with 130 steals. He finished his long, twenty-five-year career with the all-time record of 1,406 thefts. Henderson also set all-time records in runs scored with nearly 2,300 and unintentional walks with more than 2,100.

A rarity for a speedster, Henderson also hit nearly 300 home runs in his career, almost all from the unlikely source of the leadoff spot. The ten-time All-Star won the AL MVP award in 1990 and played for nine different teams in both leagues. Rickey gained easy access to the Hall of Fame in 2009.

Rickey Henderson, 1988 New York Yankees.

The aforementioned Cardinals built their winning teams around speed and switch-hitting. Three of the eight regular starting lineup in 1982 batted both left- and right-handed. As an example of the lessened emphasis on power, the Cards won it all that year by hitting only 67 home runs and stealing 200 bases.

Furthermore, by 1985, they were led by speed demon Vince Coleman, who led the National League in stolen bases for six straight years between 1985 and 1990. He also had three consecutive years of 100 or more steals in that period. Coleman's speed on the base paths unseated the fast man from Montreal, Tim Raines, who had four straight league-leading seasons of 71, 78, 90, and 75, respectively.

The decade was also witness to many unusual events, not least of which was the emergence of Kirk Gibson as the epitome of the wounded warrior, coming to the rescue to save his team from defeat. It was certainly one of the most dramatic moments in the history of baseball.

The outfielder had spent his first nine seasons with the Detroit Tigers, helping to lead them to the 1984 World Series over the San Diego Padres. In 1988, he signed on as a free

Kirk Gibson celebrates his game-winning homer in Game One of the 1988 World Series.

agent with the Los Angeles Dodgers, once more helping a team to reach the post season. In fact, his .290 average, along with 25 homers and 75 RBI, earned him the NL MVP for the year.

Facing the Oakland A's in Game One of the World Series, Gibson was unable to start. Injuring both knees in the NLCS against the Mets left the outfielder barely able to stand, and he stayed in the clubhouse with ice packs on both legs. It was an exciting game, and in the bottom of the ninth, the A's had a 4 to 3 lead.

A's manager Tony La Russa brought in his lights-out closer, Dennis Eckersley, to finish the game. The pitcher quickly retired Mike Scioscia and Jeff Hamilton, then walked Mike Davis. Meanwhile, Gibson had been hitting balls off a tee in under the stadium and told Dodgers manager Tommy Lasorda that, if needed, he could pinch hit.

It was needed, so Gibson hobbled his way up the dugout steps and took his place in the batter's box as the Dodgers fans went bananas. The batter quickly fouled off Eckersley's first two pitches, nearly falling over after each one. Gibson then fouled a third pitch weakly down the first base line. The count eventually ran full on the hitter.

Eckersley's next pitch was a strike, a slider low and a bit outside, and Gibson somehow stroked the pitch—almost one-handed—into the right field seats. As the stadium erupted, Gibson rounded the bases, pulling his clenched fists away from each other in a victorious gesture. The pain in his knees made the trip difficult, but the beauty of the moment left Gibson numb.

Eckersley had not given up a home run in nearly two months. The Dodgers' win seemed to take all of the starch out of the cocky A's, and, while Oakland managed a win in Game Three, LA won the Series in five games.

The 1980s ended with one of the strangest occurrences ever seen in baseball. The 1989 World Series pitted the Oakland A's against their neighbors across the Bay, the San Francisco Giants. The geographic proximity of the two teams couldn't have been more coincidental.

Oakland won the first two games in their stadium, moving to Candlestick Park for Game Three. About twenty minutes before the first pitch—5:04 p.m.—the ballplayers were just leaving their clubhouses, the fans were still filing in, and radio and TV announcers were broadcasting their pregame shows.

At that point, the one thing that everyone in California fears, but seldom talks about, happened. The Bay Area was rocked with an earthquake, a near-seven on the Richter scale. It was the biggest since the disastrous 1906 San Francisco earthquake. In the small town of Gilroy, California—almost one hundred miles from San Francisco—no one noticed that a geologist predicted a World Series earthquake several days previous.

It rolled through the stadium, with players moving out to safety in the center of the field, then frantically scanning the seats for their families. Massive lights on standards that surround the park swayed a dozen feet or more. On the ABC-TV telecast, announcer Al Michaels was cut off in mid-sentence, as he said, "We're having an earth . . . " The broadcast image went to snow, as power was cut and transmission lines failed (Michaels would later admit that he believed he and his colleagues were about to be pitched out of their booth to the deck below).

Curiously, many fans stayed in their seats, as the stadium suffered little damage. A group of them began to sing, "We will, we will—Rock you!" Another fashioned a sign that read, "If you think that's something, wait until the Giants come to bat." To the dismay of some of the crowd, Commissioner Fay Vincent, safe in the stands, ordered the game postponed for an indefinite period.

Definition of irony: Giants fan holds sign moments before an earthquake shook the 1989 World Series.

In the aftermath, sixty-three people were killed and the earthquake caused more than $6 billion in damage. Vincent pushed the resumption of the World Series back five days, then another five when power and broadcast support were yet to be fixed. In the meantime, he readied ballparks in Chicago, New York, and other areas to be prepared, just in case the Series needed to be moved.

The World Series did resume on October 27, but many players later admitted that it was difficult to get pumped up after what they had experienced. The A's won the next two games in Candlestick Park, sweeping the Giants. Oakland's manager, Tony La Russa, asked that champagne not be served, feeling it would be improper. Both teams knew they'd been in a very unique World Series, where the outcome was secondary to those affected by the earthquake.

The Best of Times, the Worst of Times

Earthquakes notwithstanding, the 1990s in baseball had plenty of excitement, as well as its share of rocky moments. In opposition to the previous decade, stolen bases were down and home runs were up—way up, and out. A showdown between two big boppers—later to be viewed as a tainted contest—renewed everyone's interest in the game after a serious labor dispute shut down the game. And, like the 1970s, only a few teams dominated the postseason.

In 1990, the Atlanta Braves finished last in their NL East division, having won only sixty-five games. Likewise, the Minnesota Twins finished last in the AL West, winning seventy-seven games. But in 1991, what happened with those two teams had never before happened in the history of the game.

The Twins and Braves went from worst to first in 1991, facing each other in the World Series. For the Atlanta team, it would be the first of five Fall Classics in the decade. For the Twins, they won ninety-five games, then beat the Toronto Blue Jays in five games to win the AL pennant.

Led by manager Tom Kelly, the Twins had a balanced team of power, a bit of speed, great pitching, and solid fielding. First baseman Kent Hrbek hit .284, with 20 homers and 89 RBI. Always smiling center fielder Kirby Puckett matched that RBI total, while hitting .319. Outfielder Shane Mack and catcher Brian Harper also hit over .300 for the season. Switch-hitting designated hitter Chili Davis had a great year, with 29 home runs and 93 runs batted in.

Top three starters—Jack Morris, Kevin Tapani, and Scott Erickson—each pitched more than two hundred innings and led the staff with a combined total of 54 wins. Sharp closer Rick Aguilera had 42 saves and a stingy 2.35 ERA.

The 1991 Series had several unique aspects. In all seven games, the home team was the winner—the Twins won the first two in the Metrodome. (I was there for the first game. Loud was clearly an understatement.) Moving to Fulton County Stadium, Atlanta won the next three. Back in Minneapolis, the Twins took the last two. Also, three of the seven games went into extra innings, adding even more excitement.

The Braves team that lost would just not go away in the 1990s. Their top pitchers—Tom Glavine, John Smoltz, and Steve Avery—were all under twenty-five when they first made the postseason in 1991. Still, they combined to win fifty-two games that year.

The infield had Sid Bream and Brian Hunter platooning at first, who totaled 23 homers and 95 runs batted in. At third, switch-hitting Terry Pendleton had nearly 190 hits for a .319 average. Right fielder David Justice stroked 21 home runs with 87 RBI, and in center, Ron Gant slammed 32 homers, drove in 105 runs, and stole 34 bases, as well.

The Braves returned to the World Series the next year after winning ninety-eight games in the regular season, bringing mostly the same team as the 1991 version. They added speedster Otis Nixon in center, who hit near .300 with 41 stolen bases. A young outfielder named Deion Sanders hit .304 in less than one hundred games. A two-sport star, Sanders—nicknamed "Neon Deion"—crossed town to play cornerback and return specialist for the football Falcons.

Another impressive 1992 occurrence was the Toronto Blue Jays becoming the first non-American team to make it to the World Series. They made the trip worthwhile, as they defeated Atlanta in six games to become World Champions.

The year also welcomed a new commissioner. After Bowie Kuhn, Peter Ueberroth served one four-year term in the mid-1980s and was replaced by Bart Giamatti (father of actor Paul Giamatti). Less than three years into his term, Giamatti had a heart attack and died in 1989. His deputy, Fay Vincent, took over the position.

In 1990, Vincent made no friends with the owners after they had locked out the ballplayers in spring training over a labor dispute. The commissioner intervened and negotiated a new Basic Agreement. But the team owners saw Vincent as a meddler, and he resigned following a vote of "no confidence" from them in 1992.

Curiously, Vincent's replacement would be one of the team executives who forced him out. Bud Selig, owner and president of the Milwaukee Brewers, was named Executive Council Chairman of major league baseball until 1998, when he was officially appointed commissioner. As an owner, it was easy to see whose interests would ultimately be served, although it must be said that Selig made a good effort to represent all of baseball during his service.

With a total tenure of twenty-two years, Selig held the position only two years short of Kennesaw Mountain Landis, baseball's longest-serving commissioner. Selig retired in January 2015, with Rob Manfred assuming command of the game.

In 1993, the Braves liked the taste of success and, wanting to keep that, signed free agent Greg Maddux—the Cy Young Award winner from the previous year—to join an already impressive starting pitching staff. Maddux brought his A-game, winning twenty games with a 2.36 ERA and grabbing the second of what would be four consecutive Cy Young Awards.

Known with equal respect as "Mad Dog" and "The Professor," Maddux established himself as one of the very top pitchers to ever play the game. In his twenty-three-year career, he spent eleven with the Braves and ten—in two spells—with the Chicago Cubs. Maddux also made brief stops with the Dodgers and Padres.

The slightly-built right-hander proved that winning wasn't always based on a blazing fastball. He meticulously studied video of his opponent hitters and used a sub-90-mph cut fastball—with nasty, almost magical, movement—to keep them off the base paths. Still, he ended up with over 3,300 strikeouts, allowing less than 1,000 walks.

Maddux finished his career with 355 wins, a 3.16 lifetime ERA, and more than five thousand innings pitched. A skilled fielder as well, he won eighteen Gold Gloves and appeared in eight All-Star games. He was an easy first-round selection to the Hall of Fame in 2014.

Maddux' addition to the Braves helped the team win 104 games in 1993. Yet they lost the NLCS to the Philadelphia Phillies in six games. The Phils would meet the Blue Jays in their second straight trip to the World Series.

In Game Six, the Blue Jays were up three games to two, but the Phillies appeared to be headed toward a Game Seven, as they led 6 to 5 in the bottom of the ninth. Facing the Philadelphia closer, "Wild Thing" Mitch Williams, Jays' right fielder Joe Carter hit a game-winning 3-run homer, Ecstatic, Carter cranked his arms and legs as he rounded the base paths, ending the Series in true dramatic fashion.

Greg Maddux, 1994 Atlanta Braves.

In 1994—well, that year is addressed in another chapter.

With things in baseball back to quasi-normalcy in 1995, the focus returned to the game on the field. The Dodgers signed Hideo Nomo, a star in the Japanese Pacific League and the first Nippon player to play major league ball since 1965. He finished the season with a 13 and 6 record and 236 strikeouts, the most Ks in the NL.

Despite the work stoppage between 1994 and 1995, a long-standing record was able to be broken, with a new one to replace it. Shortstop Cal Ripken Jr., having won the Rookie of the Year award in 1982 with the Orioles, began playing every game on June 5 of that year. Fourteen seasons later, Ripken continued play-

Cal Ripken Jr., 1993 Baltimore Orioles.

ing, nearing the consecutive games record of 2,130, set by the Iron Man, Yankee great Lou Gehrig.

On September 5, a large banner outside the right field wall of Camden Yards in Baltimore unfurled, revealing "2131" and Ripken had the new record for endurance in playing every day (even more astounding when one considers he was playing the challenging and active position of shortstop). A grateful Ripken

Frank Thomas, 1993 Chicago White Sox.

ran a victory lap around the perimeter of the field that night, shaking many fans' hands and acknowledging their support.

Ripken kept right on playing for another solid three seasons, finally sitting on September 20, 1998. His final tally was 2632 consecutive games—the equivalent of more than sixteen full seasons. Along the way, Ripken established himself as a capable fielder and great hitter. He ended his twenty-one years with 3,184 hits, including more than 600 doubles, 431 homers, and nearly 1,700 RBI. A two-time AL MVP, he played in nineteen All-Star games and earned eight Silver Slugger Awards. Cal Ripken entered Cooperstown in 2007.

As far as the postseason was concerned, the Braves—once more—returned to the World Series. They faced the Cleveland Indians, having won their first pennant in more than thirty years. This time around, the Braves won the World Championship that had eluded them, as they beat the Indians in six games.

Among the many stars in the game was a giant slugger, appropriately nicknamed "The Big Hurt." Frank Thomas, at six-foot-five and 275, was all natural, without a speck of pharmaceutical help. A college tight end, Thomas earned his nickname by putting a "big hurt" on the poor innocent baseballs that met his bat.

Playing sixteen of his nineteen years for the Chicago White Sox, Thomas moved from first base to the role of designated hitter, becoming one of the first dominant run-producers at that position. Seattle's Edgar Martinez and Milwaukee/Toronto's Paul Molitor made similar impacts.

Thomas won two consecutive AL MVP awards in 1993 and 1994. In most of his first ten seasons, Thomas put up numbers that matched the best of Ted Williams. For his career, he drove in more than 100 runs ten times, stroked 30 or more home runs nine times (40 or more four times), and hit .300 or more nine times. With a lifetime average of .301, Thomas entered the Hall of Fame in 2014.

Yet Thomas was not able to make much of a contribution to the White Sox' memorable 2005 season. Separate fractures of his left ankle and foot kept Thomas on the DL for much of the pennant-winning year—their first since 1959—that the Sox enjoyed under fiery manager Ozzie Guillen. A firm believer in "small ball" (where speed and contact hitting take precedence over the long ball), the skipper looked to leadoff hitter Scott Podsednik for excellence on the base paths. The outfielder responded with 59 stolen bases.

But the White Sox still delivered plenty of power, as first baseman Paul Konerko stroked 40 homers and drove in 100 runs. Other sluggers included right fielder Jermaine Dye (31 home runs), DH Carl Everett (23 home runs), and third baseman Joe Crede (22 home runs).

The starting pitching was strong, with lefty Mark Buehrle going 16 and 8, twenty-five-year-old Jon Garland going 18 and 10, Jose Contreras going 15 and 7, and Freddy Garcia going 14 and 8. Relief was led by Neal Cotts, with a 4–0 record and a 1.94 ERA. Dustin Hermanson closed with 34 saves.

In the postseason, Chicago swept the Red Sox in three games for the Division Championship and took four out of five from the Angels to win the AL pennant. The White Sox played lights out against the Houston Astros, sweeping all four games to win their first World Series since 1917.

In the last four years of the 1990s, suffice it to say the Braves returned to the World Series twice—and lost both times. The Yankees, having been absent from the postseason for the last fifteen years, made up for lost time by showing up in three of those last four years, They won all three Series, two by four-game sweep.

The bump in the pattern was 1997, with wild card entry Florida Marlins—only in the game since 1993—meeting up against the Cleveland Indians for the World Series. The Marlins—sometimes referred to as "The Fighting Fish" (hopefully, as little as possible)—had finished second in the NL East, then defeated the Giants in the NLDS as a wild card entry, and beat the Braves in the NLCS to make the finals.

Led by veteran manager Jim Leyland, the Marlins made it with solid hitting from players like Moises Alou, Bobby Bonilla, and Edgar Renteria, along with strong pitching from Kevin Brown, Alex Fernandez, and Al Leiter. Closer Robb Nen had 35 saves in the regular season.

On the other hand, the Indians were thumpers, with power hitters Jim Thome, Manny Ramirez, Matt Williams, and David Justice combining for 131 homers and 396 RBI. Pitching was not the Indians' strong suit, as starters Charles Nagy, Orel Hershiser, Chad Ogea, Bartolo Colon, and Jared Wright combined for a chubby ERA of 4.75.

Still, it was a spirited and exciting Series, going a full seven games. Game Three was a slugfest, as the Marlins came out on top, 14 to 11. The deciding seventh game went eleven innings, with the Marlins winning 3 to 2 for the World Championship.

The decade should be noted for the emergence of the one-inning closer and a decided increase in saves. Although the stat dated back to the early 1950s, Chicago baseball writer Jerome Holtzman was credited with creating a formula for it, and "the save" became an official stat in 1969.

Through the 1960s and 1970s, individual save totals from pitchers may have averaged in the mid-twenties to mid-thirties each year. Teams seldom had a defined "closer," and those who did often pitched them for two innings or so. In the early eighties, specialists like Bruce Sutter, Willie Hernandez, and Dan Quisenberry started to become ninth-inning-only pitchers, and save numbers quickly moved into the forties. The closer, as it became defined, had one job: Get the last three outs and preserve the win for his team.

With that philosophy widely adopted by the 1990s, it was not unusual to see save seasons of fifty-plus. Specialists like Bobby Thigpen and Trevor Hoffman made closing a coveted role for their teams.

The trend continued into the 2000s, as the Yankees' Mariano Rivera and Dodgers' Eric Gagne posted totals into the fifties. In 2008, Angels closer Francisco

Kerry Wood, 2012 Chicago Cubs.

Rodriguez (K-Rod to his friends) set the all-time record with 62 saves in a single season.

On several occasions, successful starting pitchers made the transition to successful closers. John Smoltz of the Braves won a Cy Young Award in 1996, going 24 and 8, with a 2.94 ERA as a starter. In the early 2000s, he moved into the closer role, earning 55, 45, and 44 saves in 2002, 2003, and 2004, He returned to start in 2005, having several winning seasons before retiring in 2009. He entered the Hall of Fame in 2015.

Dennis Eckersley was a starter for Cleveland, Boston, and the Chicago Cubs for the first twelve years of his career. He then moved to Oakland, where he became a dominant closer for nine years—saving more than three hundred games and winning both the Cy Young Award and MVP in 1992. Eckersley was inducted to Cooperstown in 20014.

Kerry Wood won NL Rookie of the Year honors in 1998 as a twenty-one-year-old starting pitcher. Blessed with a blazing fastball, as well as a knee-buckling curve and slider pitches, Wood struck out an MLB record-tying twenty batters in only his fifth big-league start. In all, he struck out 233 in 166.2 innings in 1998.

Yet he didn't even pitch the next year. He needed Tommy John surgery on his pitching elbow. First performed in 1974 on pitcher Tommy John (hence the label), a torn ligament in the elbow is repaired by harvesting similar tissue from another part of the body and using it for replacement. The procedure is considered to be 70 to 80 percent effective, and, such as in Wood's case, players can return after a year or so of tough rehab.

Which he did, although Kerry seemed plagued with injuries in the years to follow—strained triceps, torn shoulder rotator cuff, and upper back strain, among others. Still, he battled through them, winning more than seventy games in his first nine years as a Cub. In 2008, Wood moved to the closer role, saving 34, striking out 84 in 66.1 innings, and being selected as an All-Star—his second mid-season trip.

After stints with Cleveland and the Yanks, Kerry Wood returned to the Cubs in 2011 as a reliever. With ten appearances in 2012, he decided to retire in May. As fans wildly stood and applauded, Kerry was met at the edge of the Cub dugout by a hug from his young son. Not every ballplayer gets to finish their career on their own terms, but Wood did.

6

2001 to Beyond

On to the Next At Bat . . .

Baseball in the Twenty-First Century—The National Pastime Becomes International

T he global impact of baseball can be viewed in several different ways—although the "World" in World Series took more than ninety years to actually expand beyond the borders of the United States. In 1993 and 1994, the Toronto Blue Jays became the first non-American team to vie for—and win—the World Championship.

Canada first entered the majors in 1969, with the Montreal Expos—long a minor league city—joining the National League in the second expansion of that decade. Originally called the Royals, they first appeared in the minors in 1896.

For many years, spring training had looked to locations that offered good weather early in the year—in the country and outside the US borders. Countries like Mexico, the Dominican Republic, and Cuba (pre-Castro) have hosted major league teams before the seasons started.

With more teams in the game (seeing that the MLB expanded from sixteen to thirty teams in less than forty years), clubs found they needed to tap previously unexplored areas for new talent. Hundreds of ballplayers have come from the Dominican Republic since the early 1950s, including the Alou brothers—Jesus, Felipe, and Matty—along with Robinson Cano, Vladimir Guerrero, Pedro Martinez, David Ortiz, Manny Ramirez, and Sammy Sosa, among many others.

Entering the 2000s, emphasis was placed on the addition of players from Asia—not just Japan, but South Korea and Taiwan as well—along with Cubans who dared to escape the island for the promise of big league ball.

While the San Francisco Giants had brought Masanori Murakami from Japan to

Masanori Murakami, 1965 San Francisco Giants.

pitch in the MLB back in 1964, it was largely regarded as an exchange program between the two global major league organizations. Murakami posted a fine MLB record of 5–1, with 100 Ks in less than ninety innings—mostly in the 1965 season—when the pitcher returned to Japan.

Thirty years later, in 1995, pitcher Hideo Nomo—with four great seasons in Japan under his belt—joined the LA Dodgers as a free agent. In spite of his previous Japanese action, he was still considered a newbie in America and won the Rookie of the Year Award. In a twelve-year career, he struck out two hundred or more batters in four different seasons.

Along with Ichiro Suzuki—outlined in another chapter—another Japanese player to make his mark in America was outfielder/DH Hideki Matsui. Known in his homeland as Godzilla, he hit more than 20 homers five times in the US, drove in more than 100 runs four times, and hit .290 or better four times.

Brought to the Red Sox with great fanfare in 2007, pitcher Daisuke Matsuzaka (Dice-K) won thirty-three games in his first two seasons in the majors. Injuries kept his impact minimized in the remainder of his eight-year MLB career, and he returned to continue pitching in Japan after the 2014 season. Other Asian players who have made it to America include South Koreans outfielder Shin-Soo Choo and pitcher Hyun-jin Ryu, along with Taiwanese pitcher Wei-Yin Chen.

Cuban players tell harrowing stories of braving huge waves in tiny boats, in their journey from communist Cuba to America and baseball freedom. While the first Cuban defection happened more than fifty years ago at the height of tensions between America and the Caribbean nation, a large number of Cubans have come to the states in the last twenty years.

One unique story is that of pitching brothers Livan and Orlando Hernandez. When Livan defected first (through Mexico), he joined the Marlins. Brother Orlando was left behind and banned from Cuban baseball for his brother's actions. Two years later, Orlando escaped in a small watercraft and got stranded on a deserted island before the US Coast Guard found him. He soon joined the Yankees. Both brothers were quickly part of World Series championships and enjoyed substantial careers before retiring.

Other Cubans who have had successful years in the MLB include pitchers Danys Baez and Jose Contreras, and shortstops Yuniesky Betancourt, Yunel Escobar, and Alexei Ramirez. Lefty relief pitcher and three-time All-Star Aroldis Chapman has stunned opposing batters by consistently throwing fastballs of 100 mph and higher—once hitting an amazing 106 mph. Several other Cuban standouts have recently made impressive offensive impacts.

Livan and Orlando Hernandez.

In only a few seasons in the majors, out-fielder Yoenis Cespedes has hit at least 20 homers and driven in 80 or more RBI every time. Despite his reckless style, outfielder Yasiel Puig has been an offensive juggernaut for the Dodgers, while flashing great defensive skills as well. In his first two years in the MLB, Puig has shown speed and power, as well as a combined .305 average.

Making an explosive entry into the game, Jose Abreu had one of the greatest rookie seasons for any player in 2014. The White Sox first baseman posted an amazing slashline of .317/36/107, along with 35 doubles. He earned All-Star and Silver Slugger honors, as well as easily winning Rookie of the Year.

Jose Abreu, 2014 Chicago White Sox.

Some Things Are More Important Than Baseball

Just like a number of Mondays during the baseball season, many teams were enjoying an off day on September 10, 2001. Sunday night's games included the first-place Yankees beating the Boston Red Sox by a 7–2 score, the Mets losing to the Marlins in Florida 4–2, and the Pittsburgh Pirates losing to the Reds 5–3. On Tuesday, September 11, the teams were scheduled to resume play.

But a terrorist attack, not unlike the surprise 1941 bombing of Pearl Harbor, sent those cities—and all of America—into a silent daze. Passenger planes were used like kamikaze bombers on the cities of New York and Washington, D.C., with heroic passengers diverting a fourth plane into an isolated field about sixty-five miles from Pittsburgh. The events that morning killed more than three thousand people. Suddenly, baseball had no meaning at all.

Almost immediately, Commissioner Bud Selig canceled all scheduled Tuesday games. With a countrywide grounding of all air flights, teams like the Mets had to return to their hometown by bus. It was a trip unlike any minor league bus ride they had ever taken. Many of those players, as did many Yankees, traveled to ground zero and various locations around the city to offer support and comfort to emergency workers and those affected by the incident.

By the day's end, Selig announced baseball was being canceled until further notice. Yankee Stadium was the site of a huge memorial service, while the parking lot of Shea Stadium became a distribution point for relief goods. Dozens of players went to hospitals and meeting centers for those awaiting word about their missing loved ones.

About a week later, on September 17, the games resumed—but they were different in a number of ways. Like much of America's public sites, ballparks were heavy with heightened security forces. Bomb squads with dynamite-sniffing dogs

President George Bush tosses the first pitch in Game Three of the 2001 World Series.

were everywhere. The seventh-inning stretch tradition of singing "Take Me Out to the Ball Game" was changed or amended with the singing of "God Bless America."

The resulting 2001 World Series found the Yanks going up against a tough Arizona D'Backs club, led by pitchers Curt Schilling and Randy Johnson—who respectively won twenty-two and twenty-one games in the regular season. First baseman Mark Grace was, as usual, right around the .300 mark, and left fielder Luis Gonzales had cranked 57 homers and driven in 142 runs, while batting .325.

The Yanks had their normally impressive team, with first baseman Tino Martinez delivering a slashline of .280/34/113 and shortstop Derek Jeter hitting .311. Pitcher Roger Clemens went 20–3, Mike Mussina won seventeen games, and left-hander Andy Pettitte won fifteen. Mariano Rivera closed with 50 saves.

The Arizona team arrived in New York with two wins under its belt already. Yankee Stadium was covered by more than one thousand city police officers, as well as Secret Service snipers perched on nearby rooftops. President George W. Bush flashed a confident thumbs up to the crowd and threw out the first pitch (tossing full from the rubber, he cut the heart of the plate with a changeup—it was a very nice pitch).

While the Yankees won the next three games in New York, their return to Phoenix saw them lose the final two games. Still, New York was a winner in the country's eyes, having quickly recovered from 9/11 with strong and solid resolve.

A Tall, Left-Handed Drink of Water

Randy Johnson was a twenty-four-year-old rookie with the Montreal Expos in 1988, but he wasn't easy to miss. With a lanky build and six-foot-ten-inches in height, everyone knew when he was pitching—especially the opposing batters. With 35 wild pitches and 41 hit batsmen in his first five seasons, no one wanted to dig in at the plate. Plus, a collision with teammate Tim Raines earned Johnson his nickname of "The Big Unit."

A trade in 1989 sent Johnson to the Mariners, where he found some control. He struck out 1,175 batters and won seventy-one games in his first five seasons with Seattle (including 308 Ks in 1993). In 1995, Johnson had a sterling record of 18–2, with a 2.48 ERA and 294 Ks, a performance that earned him his first Cy Young Award.

The 1993 All-Star Game had a quick and humorous confrontation between the pitcher and Phillies left-handed hitter John Kruk. Johnson's first pitch sailed wildly over Kruk's head, with the hitter nervously stepping out of the box and reconsidering his chosen line of work. A second pitch—fast-ball—creased the center of the plate for the first strike. A breaking pitch followed, with Kruk weakly swinging while simultaneously moving out of the box. The next pitch was the same, with the same flailing result from the hitter for a strikeout. Kruk left relieved, and Johnson showed an uncharacteristic smile as he left the mound.

A trade in 1998 led to a half-season with the Houston Astros. Johnson then signed as a free agent with the D'Backs, where he had four straight seasons of more than 300 strikeouts (an amazing

Randy Johnson, 1993 Seattle Mariners.

total of 1,412 in that period, as well as 81 wins). His pitching resulted in four con-secutive Cy Young Awards, although injuries the following year kept him mostly on the DL.

The D'Backs traded Johnson to the Yankees before the 2005 season. While he won seventeen games each year, his strikeout count was down substantially, and, two years later, the Yanks traded him back to Arizona. Back problems and surgery limited the pitcher to only 15 wins and 40 starts in the two seasons with the D'Backs. As a free agent, Johnson signed with the Giants, but a rotator cuff injury held him to just a half-season of work, and he retired after the 2009 season.

In his twenty-two-year career, Johnson won 303 games, with a 3.29 earned run average. More importantly, his 4,875 strikeouts landed him in second place in all-time Ks, behind Nolan Ryan. The Big Unit was a shoo-in for the Hall of Fame, being elected in 2015 with an overwhelming 97 percent of the vote.

This Prince Albert Doesn't Come in a Can

Among the many fine ballplayers to come from the baseball Mecca known as the Dominican Republic, Albert Pujols has impacted the game like few others in the twenty-first century. Debuting with the St. Louis Cardinals in 2001, there was little that Pujols couldn't do. He played third, first, and outfield positions in his first two seasons—winning Rookie of the Year, Silver Slugger, and All-Star honors in his first.

Settling in at first base, Pujols led the Cards to seven postseason appearances, including three World Series. Although he seemed destined to be a lifetime

Albert Pujols, 2010 St. Louis Cardinals.

fixture in St. Louis (much like Stan Musial, a player he was often compared to), Albert became a free agent after the 2011 season.

Crossing into the American League, he signed an incredible contract with the LA Angels, calling for $240 million over a ten-year period. It would make him a free agent once more in 2022, at the age of forty-one—although his deal calls for a ten-year, $10 million personal services agreement with the Halos after he retires. Plus, he receives four season tickets for each year of the contract and a hotel suite on road trips (Prince Albert, indeed).

But there can be no doubting his talents, although injuries hampered his production in 2013. Otherwise, going into the 2015 season, Pujols had 2,519 hits (561 doubles—hitting more than 50 on three different occasions), hit 520 home runs (40 or more six times), and drove in more than 1,600 RBI (except for his injury season of 2013, he has driven in 99 or more runs in every season played).

His lifetime average is .317, with an incredible OPS (on-base plus slugging) percentage of .991. On the field, he has earned two Gold Glove Awards, along with three MVPs, six Silver Sluggers, and selected an All-Star eight times. Even if he didn't play another game, Pujols would be close to a first-year entrant for Cooperstown.

Now Batting, Number Two—Der-eck Gee-tah!

From the beginning days of the modern game, all eyes have looked to New York as the "majorest" of major league cities (I'm still convinced that ESPN believes there's only two major league teams worth covering—the Yankees and their rivals, the Red Sox). More directly, the Yankee team has always had a star—larger than life—for fans everywhere to follow and idolize. Of course, there was Ruth, then DiMaggio, then Mantle, and then Reggie Jackson (even though he also starred with the A's, the Orioles, and the Angels).

The latest of those iconic players has been Derek Jeter. There can be no doubt that, just like the four previously noted Yanks, Jeter will wind up in Cooperstown now that his playing days are over—most likely in 2020, his first year of eligibility.

Pulled from the mold of tall, two-hundred-pound shortstops—like Cal Ripken Jr.—Jeter grew up in Michigan, but was always a Yankees fan. After winning several High School Player of the Year honors, his dream of playing in the Bronx came true as the Yanks drafted him in 1992.

By 1996, he was their starting shortstop and, with a slashline of .314/10/78, Jeter won the AL Rookie of Year Award. It was the start of a twenty-year career, including five World Series championships with the team. Playing in thirty-three postseason series (including playoffs, as well as the Fall Classic), Jeter hit .308, with 20 homers and 61 RBI. He was the MVP in the 2000 Series, as well as the 2000 All-Star Game.

Jeter was honored by being named captain of the Yankees team in 2003—joining the ranks of previous field leaders like Babe Ruth, Lou Gehrig, Thurman Munson, and Don Mattingly. Similar to Reggie Jackson's moniker of "Mr. October," Jeter earned the nickname of "Mr. November" when he hit a game-winning, extra-inning homer in 2001 on November 1. The Series start had been delayed by the terrorist attacks on 9/11.

Derek Jeter, 2008 New York Yankees.

A broken ankle and subsequent complications limited Jeter to just seventeen games in 2013, and the thirty-eight-year-old realized retirement was near. With a final season in 2014, Jeter ended up with career stats of more than 3,400 hits, more than 1,900 runs scored, more than 250 homers and 350 steals. He was a twelve-time All-Star, a five-time Gold Glover, and won five Silver Slugger Awards.

Kershaw, and Goldschmidt, and Trout—Oh My!

As far as tomorrow's stars are concerned, it's anyone's guess. History has shown that strong starts don't necessarily equate to strong careers with strong finishes. For every Johnson and Jeter, there have been many Rookies of the Year that showed great promise, then disappeared faster than a toupee in a tornado (two that come to mind are outfielder Joe Charboneau in 1980 and pitcher Mark Fidrych in 1976).

In the current group of players who have established themselves as superstar-caliber, three stand out above the rest—pitcher Clayton Kershaw, first baseman Paul Goldschmidt, and outfielder Mike Trout.

A starting pitcher with the Dodgers since 2008, Clayton Kershaw has dominated hitters since 2010. In that period, he's struck out two hundred or more batters in every year, averaged a 2.26 ERA and 220 innings pitched, and twice won twenty-one games. The four-time All-Star has earned Cy Young Awards in 2011, 2013, and 2014, as well as the NL MVP Award in 2014.

Goldschmidt is a big guy with big talent. Playing for the D'Backs, he has played two full seasons (a third was cut short by a broken hand) with impressive stats. Goldschmidt has averaged 29 homers and 106 RBI, with a .292 batting percentage.

Mike Trout, 2014 Los Angeles Angels.

He's already a two-time All-Star, with a Gold Glove and Silver Slugger as well.

Trout is a three-time All-Star and winner of three Silver Sluggers in his first three full seasons, instantly making an impact with the LA Angels. Despite his linebacker appearance, Trout has speed to accompany his power. In just three short years, through the 2014 season, he's averaged 32 homers, 101 RBI, 34 stolen bases, and a .305 batting percentage. He won Rookie of the Year honors in 2012 (as a twenty-year-old) and the AL MVP Award in 2014.

Looking Back to the Future in the Business of Baseball

Fans may see the game on the field, but few have any real idea of what it takes to make that game happen on a daily basis. Of course, there are the concessions vendors who get the beer cold and the red hots hot, and the grounds crew members who prep the field. But what goes on in the front office? Whatever it is, it has changed drastically—from what used to be a simple business model, to as sophisticated as any twenty-first-century company could be.

Historically speaking, a ball club was usually owned by a major business magnate or wealthy family in the city where the team played. Reporting to the owner was a general manager, who handled almost every facet of operation—baseball and nonbaseball in nature. Under the GM was an assistant, with departments for finance, public relations, and other areas—usually a carbon copy of how the owner's other ventures were put together.

As the game entered the 2000s, roles and the structure of the front office have changed substantially. It's not unlike the way the abacus of long ago became the adding machine, then gave way to a handheld calculator, and finally a complex computer—capable of performing any computation its user could think of.

In many cases, the single owner has given way to the conglomerate of business partnerships, complete with boards of directors and multiple stockholders. Why? Think of it this way—the average ticket to a major league game in 1965 cost about two dollars—today, the average price is just about twenty-eight dollars. In other words (in case it wasn't obvious), the cost of doing business has become much more expensive and complex, making it prohibitive for any one person to own and run a ball club.

The GM may still remain, but, more likely, there is a clear division of responsibility. Many teams have two leaders—a president of baseball operations and a president of business operations. Quite obviously, one oversees all things baseball, the other oversees all things business. In some cases, like the Arizona D'Backs, there is a chief baseball officer (the great HOF manager Tony La Russa currently holds that spot).

Baseball ops can include the coaching staff, scouting (local, regional, advance, and international), player development, minor league operations and spring training operations (both are entire and separate substructures unto themselves), tracking and analysis of team stats and performance (home and visitors), the medical staff (including strength and conditioning, athletic trainers, orthopedics, sports psychologists, and even dentists), as well as team equipment and clubhouse management (someone has to wash those uniforms!).

Enough cannot be said about the traveling secretary—bearing in mind that half of a team's season is spent away from the home field. When the players are on the road, how do they get to a city? Where will they stay when they get there? What about their clothes and gear? Who hands out the per diem meal money? The traveling secretary is part travel agent, part concierge, part event planner, part road manager, and part mommy. God bless the traveling secretary.

In the business portion of the club, one finds departments like finance and accounting (there's payroll, purchasing, accounts payable, and business analysis), human resources (hiring and staffing, risk management, insurance and benefits, and labor relations), legal counsel (making sure those big contracts are signed and on the up-and-up), information technology (keeping computer systems running right so everyone can crunch the numbers—baseball and biz), marketing and advertising (selling and branding the team), community relations (being a good neighbor in the city and surrounding area), and media, communications, and public relations (working with broadcasters, journalists, photographers, and digital/social media).

There's also the folks that sell the tickets—not just behind the box office Will Call cage, but skybox and luxury suites, corporate partnerships and group sales (there's much opportunity in attracting large companies and small church groups to come see the game), season tickets and individual sales, and guest services, too.

Then you've got the stadium operation people—tour and special events coordinators, landscapers, turf and groundskeeping crew, maintenance—cleanup, plumbing, electrical, mechanical and HVAC—the security staff, and don't forget warehouse and receiving.

Of course, there are game day personnel—concessions (food, drinks, and current scorecards/programs) and merchandise vendors (plus chefs, cooks, and servers in the premium suites, too), as well as video and graphics specialists (there's a lot of stats and images to be programmed into those big video boards), cable/TV/radio announcers, camera people, and engineers, on-field promotions and all those interns (remembering there has to be somebody to shoot the T-shirts into the crowds).

Missed anyone? How about interpreters (Latin and Asian ballplayers, you know), the receptionist, organist, and public address announcer—"Have your pencils and scorecards ready for today's lineups." Oh, yeah—what about the mascot in that hot suit? In all, a major league club may have as many as 250 people or more on the payroll—not counting who's in the dugout and on the field.

One may find his fill of college grads and MBAs on the business side, while the baseball side taps into the wealth of experienced talent known as "the ex-ballplayer" (many of whom have college degrees, as well). Who else knows the inner workings of what happens—getting scouted, getting signed, getting to the majors? Those who have actually gone through the process. A quick peek at the front-office personnel in the thirty major league teams reveals at least fifty former MLB players—not counting the dozens who are active as scouts, coaches, and instructors.

While a large percentage holds some version of the nebulous (and possibly superfluous) title "Special Assistant to (the GM, the President, the Organization, etc.)," a fair number are in top executive positions. Along with the previously mentioned Tony La Russa as Chief Baseball Officer, other MLB veterans are titled VP of Baseball Operations, Assistant GM, VP of Player Personnel, Executive VP, Senior VP, and Senior Advisor, among others.

What's more, these aren't just "ham 'n' eggers"—at least twenty are members of the Baseball Hall of Fame. Certainly, the clubs look to their credentials, notoriety, and fame as instant credibility factors, but their experience is often tapped where an MBA might fear to tread.

The front offices of MLB clubs have long been all-white and all-male. Efforts for diversity have begun to break down those walls—albeit slowly—as blacks, females, Hispanics, and Asians have started to occupy key positions, both in club front offices and in MLB headquarters.

Another change in how baseball does business concerns the way top-level players are compensated. As previously noted, up to 1975, players played for whatever the owners wanted to pay them. With the advent of free agency (and subsequent adjustments to the Collective Bargaining Agreement), players now negotiate for the best possible deal (with their agents greedily rubbing their hands together).

At first, heavy hitters and top tossers received deals that paid large annual amounts for one or more years of playing for a club. By 1990 or so, multiyear contracts were the norm, with signing bonuses and additional perks (private suites on the road, flights and accommodations for family members to join the player during the season, etc.) included. Still, some clubs refused to commit to any more than three years, hedging against unforeseen future injury or ineffectiveness.

By 2000, long-term contracts for big dollars were the rule for the game's superstars. Agreements with annual guarantees of $12 million to $16 million were the norm, with durations of four to six years. In 2001, Alex Rodriguez drastically upped the ante by signing a ten-year deal for more than $250 million.

Recently, the trend has morphed from rewarding established stars to giving budding stars long-term contracts. Players—many barely twenty-five or twenty-six years of age—have been signed to deals of eight to ten years, or more. Witness the bank-busting deal that Marlins player Giancarlo Stanton signed in 2014, paying him an eye-popping $325 million for thirteen years.

The reasoning is clear—teams are betting on the future, with the hopes of avoiding subsequent free-agency negotiations that could be much more costly for them. Yet some clubs are building in options on their side for one or more years, allowing them to extend the deal—if the player does what he's expected to do.

Similarly, established players are receiving long-term deals that—in most cases—will extend past their effective years. Clubs will sign a player at thirty years old to a ten-year deal, knowing he'll be hard pressed to produce hits, runs, homers, strikeouts, etc., at the age of forty. Paying for reduced production for two or three years at the end of the deal is considered the "cost of doing business" by signing a top-name star.

Beyond 2015—Will You Still Glove Me Tomorrow?

Quite frankly, the game of baseball is facing issues that could affect its very existence. In the 1940s and 1950s, baseball truly was the great American pastime, as it dominated the media, as well as conversations at the water cooler and in schoolyards alike. But what's happened in the sixty years since then?

How about . . . NFL football, NBA basketball, NHL hockey, youth soccer, cable TV, home computers, handheld video games, Facebook, Twitter, Instagrams, selfies, and whatever is next to come down the pike. So it's clear, baseball has a lot to compete with—if it wants to survive.

Most likely, that job starts at the top, and maybe there's good news there. Following twenty-two years as the leader of baseball business (although not officially named commissioner for six years), Bud Selig stepped down in 2015.

Selig's tenure at the top spearheaded many changes in the game, including interleague play, revenue sharing, drug testing, the combining of the NL and AL administrations into his office, and several major labor agreements (although the World Series was canceled for the first time ever, when players struck under his watch).

Another Selig effort was overseeing expansion, which meant more teams, more games, more postseason activity (which, while translating to a bigger fan experience, also meant more ticket sales, more concessions, more media coverage, etc. As an ex-club owner, the commissioner certainly didn't forget his roots).

The new commissioner, Rob Manfred, started with the main baseball office as an independent legal counsel in the late 1980s, then joined the staff to become the chief of labor relations. He became baseball's COO in 2013. Now, as the top dog, Manfred is keenly aware of what's in store for him and that the future of baseball is in his hands.

Manfred knows the game has to recapture the interest of kids everywhere, both in playing baseball and watching it as a fan. His office is working on a number of programs to involve kids and young adults, especially those in urban areas. One such activity, RBI—Reviving Baseball in Inner Cities, started under commissioner Peter Ueberroth in 1989—is getting a close look. Another is the Baseball Tomorrow Fund, which helps to build ball fields in areas that are economically challenged.

At the major league level, the game has begun to address the issue of time. While some "old school" fans (and players) like the current pace of the game, it's been noted that the average contest length has steadily increased over the years.

In 1950, the average ball game took about two hours and twenty minutes (of course, before major TV coverage started that requires commercial breaks of two and three minutes each). By 1970, that figure had increased to just a few minutes over two and a half hours. By the end of the 2014 season, average games were taking three hours and seven minutes.

It's agreed that something needs to be done, although a long-standing directive in the Official Rule Book (8.04, to be exact) has always insisted that, with the bases empty, the pitcher must throw the darn ball within twelve seconds. Obviously, it's a rule that's never been enforced.

Starting in the 2015 season, significant changes in the pace of the game included batters having to keep one foot in the box during an at bat (how many times have we endured the stepping out, hands rubbing dirt, batting gloves adjusted, helmet reseated, etc.? Just hit the ball, will ya!). Dawdlers will receive a warning, then a series of blows to the wallet—up to $500.

Other changes include a time limit to changing pitchers, making a swift return to action after a media break, and managers being able to challenge replays without leaving the dugout.

And that brings up the elephant in the ball field known as "instant replay." While its details are outlined in another chapter, it has met with mixed responses since becoming fully operational in 2014.

Purists insist that umpires, while as fallible as anyone, should remain the be-all and end-all in on-field decisions. Why? Because that's the way it's always been. But many folks, including the umps themselves, know that getting the call correct is what really matters. The umpires' video command center in New York City now makes that a reality.

It's said that "one picture is worth a thousand words." With video replay in baseball, five hundred of those words are "Safe!" and the other five hundred are "Out!" But some suggest that replay is only the start—why not have a laser-based strike zone? Ball or strike, no argument. Checked swing, no argument. But why stop there? Today's technology would make adding sensors and data collectors easy, to the bat, the ball, mitts and gloves, bases—you name it.

But if that were to happen, before long the game would look like RoboCop facing off against a T-800 cyborg. Pitches would reach speeds of 200 mph, and homers would need landing approvals from air traffic controllers.

Put simply, the game of baseball—while needing to change and adapt for today's fan—can't afford to lose sight of the how and why of how it got here.

Houses of the Holy

I Don't Care if I Never Get Back . . .

Have Your Pencils and Scorecards Ready

For many baseball fans (yours truly included), stepping out onto the concourse of a major league baseball stadium often feels like it should be accompanied by dipping one's hand into a font of holy water and making the sign of the cross. There's no intention of blasphemy here, only an observation of the reverent feelings that can sometimes happen. The combination of what has historically occurred in the park, combined with the anticipation of what is about to occur in the next three hours or so, makes the experience a memorable one.

The function of the ballpark is wide-ranging. For the teams, it's a facility where they work. For the fan, it's an outlet for entertainment. For the club owner (and the municipality in which it resides), it's a revenue generator. For the structure's architects, it's a challenge of blending functional necessity with allure and comfort.

The evolution of early ballparks is covered elsewhere in this book, so much of this chapter will—in some sort of geographic manner—look at stadia of today, as well as some of the more historic facilities that no longer stand.

Today's Ballparks

That title might be a misnomer. Today's ballparks include thirty parks that have been built within the last 105 years—quite a large span of time and hardly representative of "today." Yet, with parks that opened just a few years ago, to those that opened all the way back when William Howard Taft was America's president, the expectations for adequate baseball facilities are pretty broad.

What, then, does a "modern" ballpark require? At the very least, it should have:

- A minimum of ten or more acres of fairly flat land, on which to build the stadium.
- A playing field, as directed by the official rules of the sport, to support a game of major league baseball (with consideration to drainage, irrigation, maintenance, and equipment storage, along with safe and functional lighting for nighttime games, and a bullpen area in which home and visiting pitchers can warm up).

- Adequate facilities for two teams to dress, shower, and keep their personal items safe, as well as conference, training, and workout areas for their continued development.
- Business offices for administrative, sales, marketing, public relations, and other support functions for the team.
- Sufficient seating—at various price points—to accommodate anywhere from 30,000 to 50,000 fans.
- Food, beverage, and merchandise preparation areas and concession stands for sales and consumption.
- An information delivery system for spectators, including scoreboard, large-format video screens, public address gear, music, and game-related data.
- Ample parking, as well as close proximity and access for public mass transportation.
- Where deemed necessary for the efficient completion of the game in adverse weather conditions, a permanent or retractable roof or structure.

To make sure this happens, all it takes is to spend anywhere from $500 million to $1.5 billion, plenty of meetings (and paperwork) with various city, county, and even state officials, and an army of lawyers and accounting experts. (Excited or discouraged yet?)

The Northwest Territory

Only one stadium occupies this portion of the country, as the Seattle-Tacoma area (often called Sea-Tac) supports Safeco Field, the home of the Seattle Mariners. Opened in 1999 and built on twenty acres of land directly south of the old Kingdome stadium, the park features a retractable ten-acre roof that moves in three sections, from behind right field toward home plate. The roof fully covers the field, but does not completely enclose the park, and, as such, the fans can still enjoy the feeling of watching a ball game in an open-air atmosphere.

Safeco Field has a capacity of 47,116 fans, with the largest video screen in the majors—a high-def LED image of more than eleven thousand square feet (fifty-six feet high by more than two hundred feet wide. What a Kiss Cam!). The playing field uses a custom blend of four Kentucky bluegrasses and two rye grasses, designed to be hearty in the damp and cool climate of the Northwest.

The design group known as NBBJ was the architect of Safeco Field, winning awards for combining a nostalgic look with modern necessities. The brick façade is reminiscent of Brooklyn's Ebbets Field, while the park—located near the industrial Port of Seattle area—provides cover for railroad tracks that pass directly east of the stadium.

The naming rights for the park were purchased by Safeco Insurance, which is based in Seattle. The company paid $40 million for a twenty-year deal to have their name attached to the ball field.

Safeco has long been regarded as a pitcher's park, considering its low elevation above sea level and original fence distances. (Higher air pressure means higher drag, but, contrary to popular beliefs, high humidity will actually help a baseball in flight, not lessen it. It's scientific—you could look it up!)

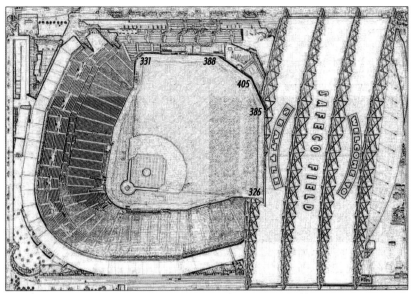

Seattle Mariners, Safeco Field (Roof cutaway), Seattle, Washington.

Still, that didn't seem to affect Alex Rodriguez and Ken Griffey Jr. in the park's first year of existence. Respectively, they hit 42 and 48 home runs, and drove in 111 and 134 runs. Safeco has kept its low-runs reputation since, although recent slight adjustments in fences and walls might help hitters in the future.

Go West, Young Man . . .

Oh, the parks you'll see in the west and southwestern parts of the country. Starting in Northern California and moving south, one first encounters a stadium with a status that comes close to Safeco Field.

The San Francisco Giants play their home games in AT&T Park—even though the poor facility might suffer from an identity crisis. Opened in 2000 as Pacific Bell (or Pac Bell) Park, it was renamed SBC Park in 2003 when telecom company SBC Communications acquired Pacific Bell. Then, three years later, SBC merged with AT&T, and the park finally became known as AT&T Park (until the next merger, divesture, IPO, or other money-making machination in big business).

The park resembles Safeco in its reputation as a pitcher-friendly ballpark, although it has a Jekyll-Hyde sort of personality. During the days, hitters fare much better at AT&T, but when the sun goes down, so does the long ball count. Located on the west side of San Francisco Bay, the stadium is often a victim of swirling winds and fog, much like its predecessor, Candlestick Park.

AT&T Park was designed by HOK Sport Venue Event, long-known as a leader in stadium architecture. They split off into a separate group called Populous in 2008, and only recently has HOK decided to return to designing sports facilities. For AT&T Park, which cost $345 million to build, they drew from classic open-air parks like Wrigley Field and Fenway Park for inspiration.

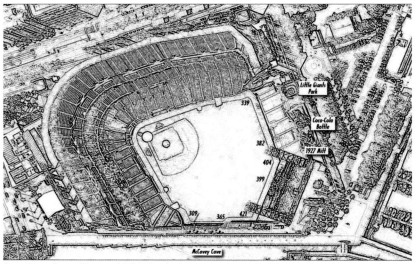

San Francisco Giants, AT&T Park, San Francisco, California.

Overlooking the fans entering the park's main gates is a nine-foot statute of Giants great Willie Mays. Inside, the park holds 41,503 people and two baseball teams that are bound to have a challenging time in navigating the angular and asymmetrical outfield.

The left field foul line is 339 feet, with a right field line of a cozy 309 feet, but that's where the fun ends. Deep right center field is a cavernous 421 feet, after a bump in the right field power alley of 365 feet. The left field power alley quickly extends to 382 feet before meeting the center field wall at 404 feet (in other words, plenty of room for the company's summer picnic).

Beyond the twenty-four-foot-tall right field wall (the height was determined by the number worn by the Say, Hey Kid) is McCovey Cove. The waters of San Francisco Bay are named after the Giants Hall of Famer Willie McCovey and are easily reached by a home run that leaves the park there. At the end of the 2014 season, sixty-eight balls had made it into the Cove, with many recovered by fans who patrolled the area in kayaks and rowboats.

AT&T Park is also unique with its eighty-foot-long wooden replica of the classic Coca-Cola bottle beyond left field, equipped with four curved slides for kids. For the littlest Giants is Little Giants Park, a fifty-by-fifty-foot replica of AT&T Park. There's also a ten-ton, twenty-six-foot-tall ultra-realistic sculpture of a 1927-style, four-fingered fielder's mitt.

And, occasionally, baseball is played at AT&T Park.

Across the bay, just east of San Leandro Bay, is the home of the Oakland A's. The O.co Coliseum, formerly Oakland-Alameda County Coliseum, was built in 1966 for $25.5 million, from a design by the architectural firm of Skidmore, Owings, and Merrill. For many years, the stadium has also been home to the Oakland Raiders football team.

With a $200 million facelift in the mid-1990s, the Coliseum still has a symmetrical footprint, reminiscent of many ballparks built in the late 1960s and early 1970s. The renovation replaced center field bleachers with a four-level upper deck, while the field remained at 330 feet down the lines and 400 feet to straightaway center.

The center field addition, called Mount Davis in honor of Oakland Raiders owner Al Davis, caused some dissension among baseball fans. The four-level structure enclosed the park and eliminated the once-enjoyable view of the Oakland Hills in the distance, disappointing many who preferred their baseball with a more open stadium.

The stadium could still be considered cozy, with seating for 35,067. Yet, with some of the largest foul areas surrounding the diamond, field-level fans may seem somewhat removed from the action. Like its neighbor across the waters—and for many of the same reasons, as well as the ample foul territory—the O.co Coliseum is a friendly venue for pitchers.

Like most ballparks, the O.co Coliseum has its share of hot dogs and beer. Food fans can take advantage of what is considered to be a superior variety of BBQ, including a tasty steak sandwich and pork ribs. Others prefer the assortment of grilled Polish and Italian sausages, along with bratwurst, before returning to their seats for the game with their beloved A's.

Hopping onto Route 101, one can head south nearly four hundred miles before reaching the heralded crown jewel in Chavez Ravine known as Dodger Stadium. Opened in 1962, the park was literally carved into side of the Elysian Hills, an area directly north of downtown Los Angeles.

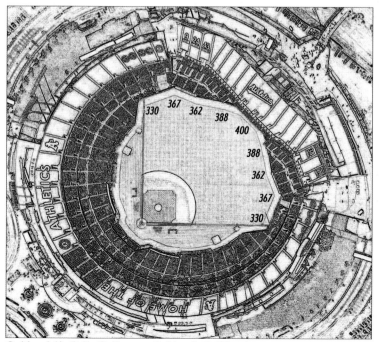

Oakland A's O.Co Coliseum, Oakland, California.

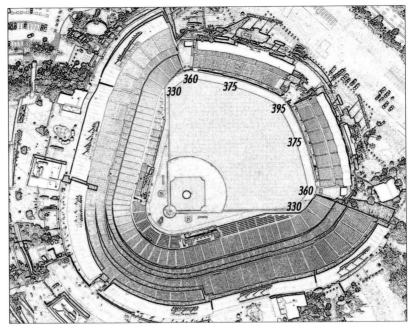

Los Angeles Dodgers, Dodger's Stadium, Los Angeles, California.

Club owner Walter O'Malley worked with architect and civil engineer Emil Praeger to design the baseball-only stadium. Praeger's credentials were impressive, including designing the Tappan Zee Bridge in New York and supervising 1950s renovations to the White House. Under his direction, bulldozers moved more than eight million cubic yards of dirt and stone to accommodate the new stadium.

More than fifty years later, Dodger Stadium is the third-oldest MLB park. With seating for 56,000 fans (some famous for showing up late and leaving early), the park has the largest capacity in the major leagues. Among its unique features are the six seating tiers that have their entrances at their own level, allowing easy access for fans.

Synonymous with the stadium and the Dodgers themselves is broadcaster Vin Scully. Going into the 2015 season, the veteran's voice covered the team for sixty-five continuous years on radio and television—easily the longest tenure of any broadcaster with one team. At age eighty-seven, he continues to do play-by-play for all Dodger home games, as well as road games in California and Arizona. The press box at Dodger Stadium is named for Vin Scully, and he was elected to the broadcaster's wing of baseball's Hall of Fame in 1982.

The stadium and its surrounding area feature more than two hundred species of plants and trees, all tended to by a certified arborist—a first for major league baseball. The landscape sports varieties of cacti and ferns, as well as palm trees, all native to the climate of Southern California. Plus, the stadium is kept looking clean by getting a fresh coat of paint during every off-season.

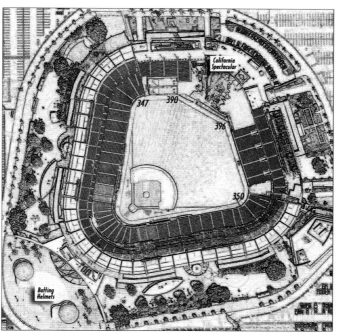

Los Angeles Angels of Anaheim, Angel Stadium of Anaheim, Anaheim, California

   Pitchers tend to love Dodger Stadium, as the ball doesn't seem to carry well when it's hit. Despite the relatively short distance of 330 feet down each foul line, the outfield quickly expands to allow fielders plenty of space to track down fly balls.

   Travelling twenty-five miles southeast from LA brings one to Angel Stadium of Anaheim, home of . . . well, the Anaheim Angels (officially, the Los Angeles Angels of Anaheim, but why waste the ink? Wait a minute . . . Oh, well).

   Called Anaheim Stadium when first opened in 1966, the park was designed by architects Noble W. Herzberg and Associates. The original owner of the then-Los Angeles Angels was the "singing cowboy" of movies and music, Gene Autry, who had the park built on 160 acres of farmland, just down the road from Disneyland.

   With seats for just a bit more than 43,000 fans, the stadium quickly earned the nickname of the "Big A." The appellation was mostly due to the giant 230-foot, 240-ton steel letter "A"—a scoreboard topped with an angelic halo—that was erected just beyond left-center field.

   By 1980, the stadium was expanded to accommodate the Los Angeles Rams football team, who would share the stadium with the now-named California Angels. With the outfield enclosed with additional seating—raising the capacity to 65,000—the Big A was relocated outside in the main parking lot, just off the 57 Freeway.

   Fifteen years later, the Rams moved to St. Louis, and a major renovation was planned to return the stadium back to a baseball-only facility. The Disney Company purchased the team in 1996, called them the Anaheim Angels, and

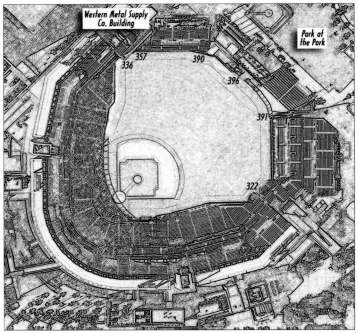

San Diego Padres, Petco Park, San Diego, California

footed a large portion of the $118 million facelift budget. The 20,000 outfield seats added for the Rams were pulled, returning the partially open-air grandstand and bleacher seating.

Disney engineers, rich with design experience from Disneyland, incorporated theme park–like features in the renovations. At the main entrance, two enormous red Angels batting helmets—estimated to be size 649-1/2—greeted those coming into the park. Another such area was left-center field, where faux rocks, a waterfall, and ninety-foot geysers, along with real trees, made up a unique batter's eye known as the California Spectacular.

At the same time, naming rights for the stadium were sold, and the park was called Edison International Field. Although the deal was for twenty years, Edison canceled the agreement in 2003, and the park earned its current name.

Moving south from Anaheim, just a few miles from the border of the Baja Peninsula in Mexico, is the city of San Diego. Taking a cue from many newer ballparks that have been located in the busy downtown area, PETCO Park is home to the San Diego Padres. Just outside the left field foul line, across East Harbor Drive, is the water of San Diego Bay.

Architects at Populous worked closely with Heritage Architecture and Planning to preserve the long-standing Western Metal Supply Company building, a historic landmark built in 1909. Together, the designers incorporated the red brick structure into the park's left field area, and it became the actual foul pole. The building houses the Padres Team Store, as well as a restaurant and other fan attractions.

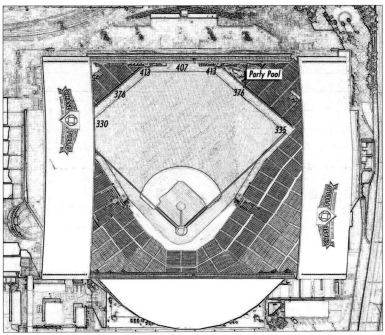

Arizona D'Backs, Chase Field, Phoenix, Arizona

Construction on PETCO Park, originally budgeted at $300 million, began in 2000 and quickly ran into a work stoppage when the money apparently ran out. After a delay of more than a year, the local city council approved the dollars needed to complete the project. The stadium was ready for the 2004 season, with a final cost of $474 million and a seating capacity for 42,500 fans.

PETCO Park quickly acquired a reputation as a somewhat cavernous pitcher's park, with home runs becoming a rare commodity for both home and visiting teams. By 2012, it was decided to spend $25 million to move the left and right field fences in by ten feet, with the right field fence also lowered by three feet (the park is still regarded by many players and Sabermetricians as pitcher-friendly).

The changes seemed to make some difference. Total homers at PETCO had averaged 126 per year since the first season in 2004. After the fences were moved, the total shot up to 146 in 2013. However, that number dropped to a mere 101 in the following season.

A club promotion before the 2014 season offered two season tickets to any fan who could hit a homer (only one swing each) at PETCO (no word if Padres players were allowed to compete, but it's not likely). With over one thousand eager hitters taking a crack at the prize, no one made it over the fence.

A left turn onto US 8 and one is easterly bound, through Yuma, Arizona, across the Sonora Desert, and into Phoenix. With average monthly summer temps at ninety-plus degrees ("but it's a dry heat," my dear Granny's fanny!), the prospect of playing baseball became an indoor-only proposition for the city's first MLB team in 1998.

Cooler heads prevailed (literally), and Phoenix' team, the Arizona D'Backs, usually play all their day games under the protective roof of Chase Field. Night games vary, depending on temps and dust storms and such. Either way, massive air conditioning units can drop the park temperature by more than thirty degrees from the sweltering heat outside.

Formerly called the Diamondbacks when it all started in 1998, the stadium was then known as the Bank One Ballpark, which quickly condensed down to "the BOB." Local architect firm Ellerbe Becket designed the stadium—the first American park in baseball to have a retractable roof (9 million pounds in weight), as well as real grass (Bull's Eye Bermuda, no doubt). The construction costs amounted to more than $350 million.

Holding 48,569 people, Chase Field is recognized as one of the top-five hitter-friendly parks in the game. Despite a center field that extends well beyond four hundred feet from home plate, baseballs fly over the fences 12 percent more often than the average park.

Some of those spheres—called "splash balls"—have landed in the Ramtrucks. Com Party Pool, located beyond the right-center field, 415 feet from home plate (in fact, fifty by the end of the 2014 season). The 8,500-gallon pool and spa can accommodate up to thirty-five people, and the facility can be rented for fun and frolicking during D'Backs home games (an occasional reminder that baseball is being played would be a nice touch).

When Bank One merged with JPMorgan/Chase Bank in 2005, the naming rights moved over to Chase for the 2006 season. The BOB was dropped, and Chase Field has been the name hanging on the shingle ever since.

Plains Speaking

With pack mules loaded with provisions like hardtack and pemmican (that's OK, we'll stop somewhere along the way), we make our way north, around and past the Rockies for almost nine hundred miles before coming to Denver, Colorado. At an altitude of more than five thousand feet, the air is thin, and breathing can be a bit harder than usual, but there's still enough atmosphere to play baseball.

After playing two seasons in Mile-High Stadium, the Colorado Rockies moved into their own park, called Coors Field, in 1995. Built on a seventy-six-acre site for $300 million, the north downtown stadium was designed by HOK Sports. In an unusual move, the Coors Brewing Company purchased the naming rights for a total of $15 million—with an open-ended arrangement that has an indefinite time limit.

During excavation before the actual construction began, a large number of dinosaur fossils were uncovered, leading to suggestions that the facility be named "Jurassic Park." Instead, a large purple dinosaur mascot named Dinger became a fixture at Rockies home games (no word as to whether he has any DNA connections to other certain purple dinosaurs found in pop culture).

Speaking of dingers, Mother Nature offered a hand in the early days of Coors Field and home runs hit there. As Denver is known as the Mile-High City, you can be sure there is a reason for that—and you would be correct to assume that the town (and Coors Field) sits some 5,280 feet (or so) above sea level. Because of the increased altitude, science became involved with the park, more than in any other MLB stadium.

At the risk of turning this into a yawn-inducing science class, suffice it to say that the higher the altitude, the lower the density of the air. And the lower the air density, the farther a struck baseball can travel. The numbers show that the difference is 5 percent. In other words, a batted baseball that travels 375 feet at AT&T Park (sea level, you see) will travel another 19 feet or so at Coors Field. The result could be a warning track out at AT&T Park becoming a round-tripper at Coors Field.

Right along with that, it was discovered that in the first seven seasons at Coors Field, an average of 3.20 home runs were hit per game. On the road, Rockies games averaged 1.93 per game—quite a disparity. As such, in 2002, Coors Field began storing game baseballs in a special humidor (perhaps along with a fine cigar or two), set to seventy degrees Fahrenheit and 50 percent humidity.

The results were pretty immediate. The next nine seasons at Coors Field showed baseballs flying out of the park at a rate of 2.39 per game, while Rockies away games stayed essentially the same at 1.86 per game. With the playing field (or playing atmosphere) evened somewhat, hitters were now a bit disappointed to make the trip to Coors Field, but pitchers no longer feared a ballooning ERA.

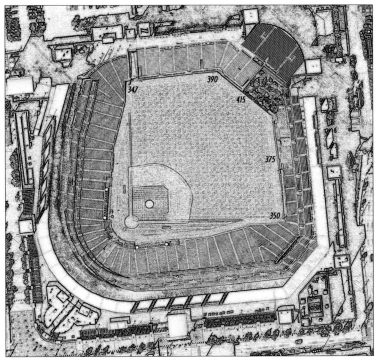

Colorado Rockies, Coors Field, Denver, Colorado.

Kansas City Royals, Kauffman Stadium, Kansas City, Missouri

Back on the road, it's a six-hundred-mile drive east on US 70 to Kansas City, home of the Royals and Kauffman Stadium, sometimes called "The K." More than forty years old, the park has undergone a number of facelifts and it still stands, ready to offer a great game of baseball to its fans.

When Charlie Finley packed up the Kansas City A's and moved them to Oakland after the 1967 season, the city was left without a major league team. Fortunately, local businessman Ewing Kauffman was on hand to bring an expansion club right back into Kansas City in 1969. The Royals played their first four seasons in Municipal Stadium, longtime home of the Negro League's KC Monarchs.

Kauffman and his GM, Cedric Tallis, worked with HNTB Architects to design a baseball-only stadium that borrowed the best features from parks like Dodger and Anaheim Stadium. At the same time, the football-only Arrowhead Stadium was built next door for the Chiefs in the NFL. The entire project cost $70 million.

Royals Stadium opened in 1973, with seating for 40,625 fans and some of the more unique features for the time. Beyond the center and right field walls was a stunning display of waterfalls and fountains surrounding a twelve-story crown-capped scoreboard. As was customary for the time, grass was passed over for artificial turf.

The odd sod lasted until replaced by the real thing in 1995. Also around that time, in 1993, Ewing Kauffman was honored by having the stadium renamed for him. In 2004, it was decided to move the outfield fences back by ten feet (other than the foul poles), creating a more spacious playing field. Yet the ballpark remains a neutral park, favoring neither batters nor pitchers.

Five years later, a major, $250 million renovation project was designed by Populous, bringing Kauffman Stadium into the twenty-first century. The scoreboard was entirely rebuilt—with HDTV capabilities—and seating was reduced to 38,177, for a more intimate fan visit.

The area beyond the outfield walls was totally built up, becoming the appropriately named "Outfield Experience." The carnival-like area features a kids-friendly miniature infield called "the Little K," as well as pitching mound, batting cage, base running, miniature golf, a playground, carousel, and live entertainment. A seven-thousand-square-foot Royals Hall of Fame displays the team's heritage and best players.

Midwest Americana

A trip of less than seven hours north and one arrives in the Twin Cities of Minneapolis and St. Paul. In the northwest section of the Minneapolis downtown area, just west of the mighty Mississippi River, is one of the newer stadiums in baseball—Target Field, where the Twins play their home games.

Opened in time for the 2010 season, Target Field—a baseball-only stadium for 39,025 fans—put the Twins back out in the open air, following twenty-eight years in the enclosed Metrodome. Retailer Target Corporation paid an undisclosed amount to hold the naming rights for the stadium for twenty-five years, designed and built by Populous at a cost of almost $550 million.

The architects passed over the use of red brick for Kasota limestone as an exterior material, using more than one hundred thousand square feet, mined locally from nearby Mankato. A retractable roof was considered, but no one wanted to pay the estimated additional cost of $100 million. Target Field was also designed to be as ecologically friendly as possible, even using captured rainwater to clean seating areas in order to save potable water.

With a Minnesota climate that can put some games into subfreezing temps, Target Field is able to keep the playing surface warmed to mid-sixty degrees with a five-zone in-ground system. More than three hundred radiant heaters keep fans at every seating level out of the chill. The festive left field roof deck offers a gas-fed fire pit.

Center field has a high-def widescreen video screen, along with an illuminated replica of the vintage 1961 logo showing two cartoon ballplayers—named Minnie and Paul—shaking hands across the Mississippi River. Entrance gates are numbered in honor of great Twins players like Harmon Killebrew (3), Tony Oliva (6), Kent Hrbek (14), Rod Carew (29), and Kirby Puckett (34).

With only a few years of experience and data, it's difficult to accurately characterize the park factors at Target Field. Initial observations believe the stadium

Minnesota Twins, Target Field, Minneapolis, Minnesota

is fairly neutral, as hitters and pitchers share equal ground in its playability. The field has seen an average of 138 home runs across its first five years of existence.

Just about 350 miles southeast across Wisconsin—known as the Badger State, as well as the home of some of the greatest (or grate-est) cheeses in the world—is the city of Milwaukee and Miller Park. The stadium is home to baseball's Brewers ball club.

After more than forty years of playing home games in Milwaukee County Stadium—both as an American and National League team—the Brewers moved into the 43,000-seat, baseball-only park in 2001. Designed by HKS Architects and built by Clark Construction, Miller Park cost more than $300 million and was located on land beyond center field of the old County Stadium. The Miller Brewing Company, a longtime member of Milwaukee's community, paid $40 million for the naming rights, which run until 2020.

The most notable feature of the stadium is the five-panel, fan-shaped retractable roof. Weighing in at a hefty 12,000 tons, the covering can open or close in ten minutes. Like other cities in the upper Midwest, Milwaukee's climate can vary, from wet and cold to hot and humid, so a retractable roof was considered a must from the very start of planning.

The club strives to give everyone a memorable experience (as do all thirty teams), offering special events and other fan-friendly encounters. In the midst

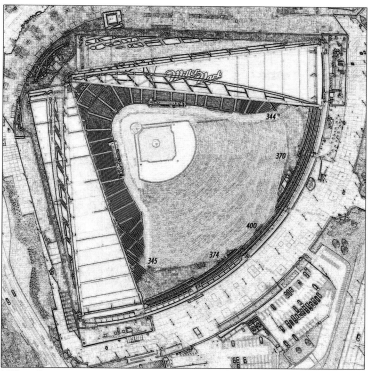

Milwaukee Brewers, Miller Field, Milwaukee, Wisconsin

of every sixth inning, the well-known Famous Racing Sausages run against each other on a warning track course, from the third base dugout, behind home plate, and crossing the finish line near the first base dugout.

The three originals—Bratwurst, Polish Sausage, and Italian Sausage—eventually found themselves in a crowded field, as Hot Dog and Chorizo have joined the "track meat" over the years. And if the fans happen to be vegetarians, they can always enjoy the antics of mascot Bernie Brewer. The costumed character perches high in the left field bleachers and, after every Brewer home run, makes a thrilling slide down onto an oversized home plate. But wait—there's more! Barrelman, the walking beer keg, also patrols the aisles.

Over the years, Miller Park has become a lifeboat of sorts for other teams and their scheduled games. Early in the 2007 season, the Cleveland Indians found themselves in an Ohio snowstorm, and they brought their three-game series with the Angels to warm and covered Miller Park. The next year, Hurricane Ike forced a scheduled two-game series between the Houston Astros and Chicago Cubs to be relocated to the Milwaukee stadium. Cubs pitcher Carlos Zambrano pitched a no-hitter in the first contest, and Cub hurler Ted Lilly took a no-hitter into the seventh inning on the following day at Miller Park.

In spite of the pitching success on those two particular days, Miller Park is considered to be somewhat of a hitter's park. Since its opening in 2001, it has

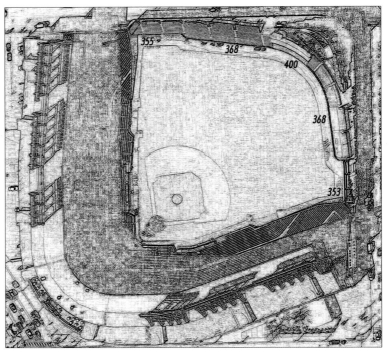

Chicago Cubs, Wrigley Field, Chicago, Illinois

routinely favored long balls and run scoring more than dominant pitching, although its average park factor in runs scored has only been 1.014 since then. However, home runs have been hit at Miller Park at a mean of 17 percent more than the average ballpark.

If one avoids rush-hour traffic, the trip from Milwaukee south along Lake Michigan into Chicago should take about ninety minutes. On the city's North Side is a ballpark full of memories and heritage, having just celebrated its one hundredth year of existence—Wrigley Field.

Built in 1914 at a cost of $250,000 for the Chicago Whales of the short-lived Federal League, the park belonged to local restaurateur Charles Weeghman. The owner hired local architect Zachary Taylor Davis to design the 14,000-seat stadium, built on the former site of a theological seminary. When the Federal League folded after the 1915 season, Weeghman purchased the Chicago Cubs franchise and moved them into the beautiful stadium he had built for the Whales.

In 1919, chewing gum magnate William Wrigley Jr. bought the club from Weeghman and renamed Weeghman Park as Cubs Park. In 1926, he named the park after himself, and Wrigley Field has been the name on the marquee ever since. In that same year, a second tier was added to the grandstands, increasing the park's capacity to 40,000.

A decade later, bleacher seating was added from the left field foul pole to the right field foul pole, actually reducing the park's capacity a bit to around 38,000. At the same time, a large, hand-operated scoreboard was placed high above the center field seats, and Japanese creeper ivy was planted along the outfield wall (by a young twenty-three-year-old man named Bill Veeck).

Wrigley Field has remained essentially the same for the last seventy-seven years, with the addition of an angled chain-link fence along the top of the ten-foot-high outfield wall in 1972. Intended to keep frisky fans from hopping down onto the playing field, the fence—referred to as "the basket"—is considered a home run for any ball that lands in it on the fly.

Following spirited negotiations with local apartment building owners (whose rooftops provide unique views of Cubs games—for a price, shared by the owners and the ball club) and the city of Chicago, Wrigley Field underwent more than $500 million of renovations following its centennial anniversary in 2014.

Current capacity is just over 41,000, and, despite the protesting of the rooftop owners, a large Jumbotron video screen—the last MLB park to add one—and additional outfield signage are only part of the changes. Expanded and upgraded clubhouses, batting tunnels—badly needed—as well as an open-air plaza and new hotel just outside the park, bring Wrigley Field into the present day, while preserving a long-standing landmark. In fact, the scoreboard and ivy remain the same.

In spite of its notorious reputation as a hitter's delight when the wind is blowing out, Wrigley Field basically rates as a neutral ballpark. In the last ten years, the home run park factor at "The Friendly Confines" has averaged only 7 percent above the typical stadium.

Only a half-hour on the Kennedy and Dan Ryan Expressways brings one to the Cubs' South Side rivals—the Chicago White Sox, who play their games in US Cellular Field, "The Cell." Built in 1991 by HOK Sport and first named for its eighty-one-year-old predecessor, Comiskey Park, the stadium cost $160 million and seated 44,300 fans. In 2003, telecom company US Cellular paid $68 million for a twenty-year naming rights agreement (for many Chicagoans, it will always be Comiskey Park).

Bringing favorite features from the old stadium, like arched windows on the exterior walls and a colorful exploding scoreboard, pleased many White Sox fans. The frighteningly sloped and treacherous upper-deck grandstands didn't please many White Sox fans (including this author and some family members).

Inside of ten years, renovations began to remedy the vertigo-inducing upper deck, including the removal of more than 6,000 seats. Also, distances to the foul poles were reduced by twelve to seventeen feet, and a center field party deck was added. All the changes, priced at $100 million, were well appreciated when the Sox won the World Series in 2005.

As is often the case, the new park was built on the parking lot of the old park, with the old park replacing the lost parking. In the case of Comiskey/US Cellular, the previous home plate site, along with foul lines, are located in their original places as part of the new lot. Also, several statues are found around the stadium, honoring White Sox greats like Minnie Minoso, Carlton Fisk, Frank Thomas, and, the latest addition, recently retired Paul Konerko.

Perhaps to the dismay of Cubs fans, US Cellular Field rates as a much more hitter-happy park than its North Side counterpart. In fact, baseball guru Bill James rates the park at the same offensive level as the homer-friendly launching pad

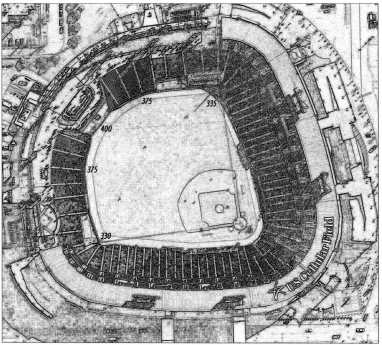

Chicago White Sox, US Cellular Field, Chicago, Illinois

known as Coors Field. Data from the last ten years show that the home run park factor of US Cellular Field is nearly 30 percent higher than the average MLB ballpark.

It's a straight shot of about three hundred miles southwest down I-57, across the Mississippi River, to St. Louis and Busch Stadium. Opened in 2006, the baseball-only park is home to the Cardinals. A far cry from its cookie-cutter predecessor, the new park followed the current tradition of building ballparks in what's called "retro-classic" appearance, using quaint, time-tested materials like red brick for the exterior.

Designed by Populous, Busch Stadium seats 46,861 in open-air fashion and was built overlapping the site of the old stadium, directly north of the new park. The construction cost a total of $365 million, taking just over two years to complete. The park is named for the beer-brewing Anheuser-Busch Company in a naming agreement that runs through 2025.

The current stadium is sometimes called Busch III. When August Busch purchased the team in 1953, he renamed Sportsman's Park as Busch Stadium. When that venue closed in 1966, the new park was called Busch Memorial Stadium.

The massive St. Louis Gateway Arch looms beyond the center field seats. An impressive Cardinals Hall of Fame Museum, as well as the Ballpark Village—a combination of retail, restaurant, and residential space—occupies the area behind the left field grandstands.

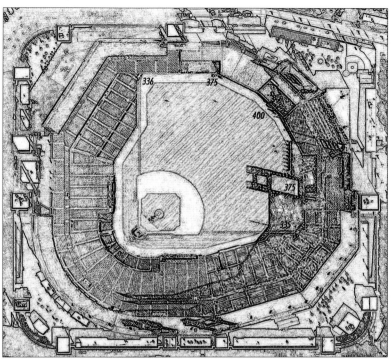

St. Louis Cardinals, Busch Stadium, St. Louis, Missouri

Despite the retro-classic design, the playing field is symmetrical, with matching dimensions of 335 feet down the foul lines (left field actually adds one foot), 375 feet to the power alleys, and 400 feet to straightaway center. The folks in the Cards' front office, along with HOK, wanted the new Busch Stadium to play neutral, but apparently they missed the mark.

The first nine seasons resulted in evidence showing that Busch Stadium sits in the bottom ten parks for offense, making it a pitcher's park. The club wanted a home run park factor of 100; they got 17 percent less than that. Of course, those numbers meant little to Albert Pujols, who still averaged more than 40 homers a year at the new park before leaving for the Angels.

Deep Fried in the Deep South

It's a long haul from St. Louis, all the way south to Arlington, Texas—650 miles— so pack a lunch. In the midst of what's called the Metroplex—halfway between Dallas and Fort Worth—is the home of the Texas Rangers (the ball team, not the cops). Just southwest of the Six Flags Over Texas theme park sits Globe Life Park in Arlington.

One of nine MLB stadiums opened in the 1990s, Globe Life seats 48,114 at five different levels in an open-air arrangement, designed by David M. Schwarz Architectural Services, with HKS Inc. as the architect of record. Built for a cost of

$191 million, the park is situated about a quarter-mile southeast of where the old stadium—Arlington Stadium—stood. That property is now part of the parking facilities of the Six Flags theme park.

Fans better double-check their tickets to make sure they have the right name on them, as Globe Life has undergone several changes since it opened in 1994. Originally called The Ballpark in Arlington, it was changed to Ameriquest Field in Arlington in 2004 (a $75 million deal that quickly soured), then to Rangers Park in Arlington in 2007. In 2014, Globe Life Insurance inked a ten-year contract for an undisclosed amount to paint their name outside the park.

Seating at Globe Life makes the game an intimate one for the fans, as their location around the infield can be as close as only forty-five feet. A high-def video screen, at more than five thousand square feet, overlooks the playing surface from the right field stands. Other great amenities include the Texas Rangers Hall of Fame and a youth ballpark with seating for 650 fans.

Pitchers had better beware when plying their craft at Globe Life Park. Next to Coors Field, the Texas stadium is considered to be the most hitter-friendly facility in the game. With an old-style asymmetrical field, the generous dimensions (404 and 407 to center, for example) still can't keep baseballs from flying out like airplanes at nearby Love Field.

Since 2001, the stadium's park factor for home runs has been 15 percent over the average park. In that same time period, home and opponent thumpers at

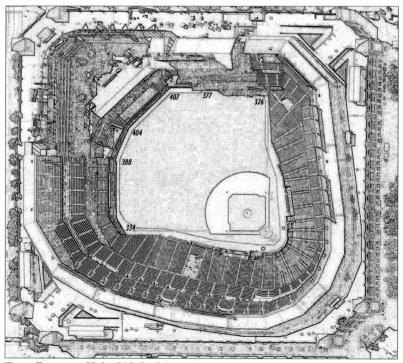

Texas Rangers, Globe Life Park in Arlington, Arlington, Texas

Globe Life have averaged 202 home runs a year, although that number has been down significantly in the last few years.

As long as you're deep in the heart of Texas, keep a-goin' and head southeast about four hours down I-45. Before long, you'll find Minute Maid Park, located smack-dab in the downtown area. It's where the Houston Astros have played their home games since the park opened in 2000.

The short distance from the Galveston Bay and the Gulf of Mexico, coupled with a southerly location, often makes for hot and humid conditions for ball games. Thirty-five years in the covered Astrodome led to a retractable roof at Minute Maid Park, giving the club an option to play indoors or out.

The prominent energy company Enron paid $100 million for a thirty-year deal to name the ballpark Enron Field. But only one year in, scandal and bankruptcy gripped Enron, and the Astros wanted nothing more to do with the arrangement, paying off Enron to go its separate way in 2002. A few months later, Coca-Cola subsidiary Minute Maid ponied up $100 million for their own thirty-year naming rights pact, and the facility became Minute Maid Park.

HOK Sports designed the 42,060-seat stadium, using the landmark Houston Union Station as a major feature of the structure. The station was built in 1911 and considered a fine representation of how the railroad contributed to the city's growth. The building is home to the Astros team store, restaurants, meeting rooms, the ball club's executive offices, and private seating for a truly unique view of the game.

Keeping with the railroad theme is a full-sized replica of a nineteenth-century steam locomotive and coal tender (loaded with oversized oranges rather than coal—Minute Maid, remember?), running along eight hundred feet of track atop

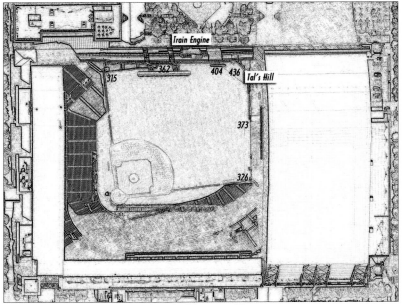

Houston Astros, Minute Maid Park, Houston, Texas

the left field wall. When one of the Astros cranks a homer or the team posts a win, the engine runs its route in celebration.

The park embraces the retro-classic style with irregular field dimensions, along with a very unique center field feature. Echoing the famed sloped left field terrace in Cincinnati's old Crosley Field, the center field area of Minute Maid Park slopes uphill a sharp thirty degrees. Ending with a dizzying distance of 436 feet, the center field—called Tal's Hill, after former Astros exec Tal Smith—also features a flagpole (yes, it's in play). Many fans and most outfielders don't have much love for the hill or the pole.

Short foul poles of only 315 and 326 feet would lead one to think Minute Maid Park would be a hitter's "Juice Box" paradise (that nickname belongs to the locals, not me). Truth be told, the park plays relatively neutral, with a home run park factor average for the last fourteen years only 7 percent above the norm.

Two hours east by plane, or eight hundred miles as the crow flies (much longer as the house flies), is beautiful Tampa Bay and Tropicana Field. It's the only home the Rays (formerly Devil Rays) have known since entering the MLB in 1998.

Built in 1990, the fixed-dome stadium's original intention was to lure the White Sox away from Chicago when a replacement for the aging Comiskey Park was slow to materialize. Chicago and the state of Illinois eventually agreed to a new stadium, and the twin cities of Tampa and St. Petersburg found themselves in search of a tenant.

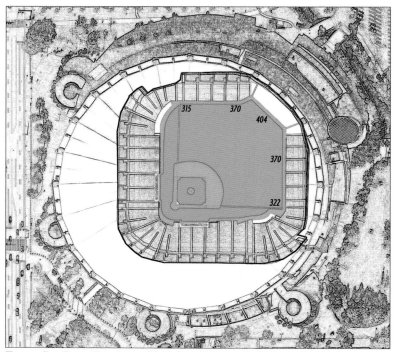

Tampa Bay Rays, Tropicana Field (Roof cutaway), St. Petersburg, Florida

After stints with arena football and hockey, the stadium—first called the Florida Suncoast Dome, then the Thunderdome—welcomed the Tampa Bay Devil Rays in 1998. Orange juice producer Tropicana had initiated a thirty-year naming arrangement in 1996, paying $1.5 million a year for the park to be known as Tropicana Field.

Design was shared by architects with HOK Sports, Lescher and Mahoney Sports, and Criswell, Blizzard & Blouin, with the 1990 construction costing $138 million. When the baseball club was awarded to Tampa Bay, another $70 million was spent to freshen and update the park for major league baseball, with seating for more than 45,000 fans (current capacity is 31,042).

The roof is made from Teflon-coated fiberglass—six acres of it—supported by a maze of struts and 180 miles of cables. Strong enough to stand up to winds of 115 miles per hour, the roof is 225 feet above second base and lights up as bright orange following a Rays win.

Four rings of catwalks—labeled A though D—hang above the playing field. Balls that strike A or B are considered to be in play; those that hit C or D in fair territory are home runs. The playing surface is Astroturf, although the infield base paths are all dirt—the only MLB park with that feature.

The outfield dimensions are a treat down the lines, with left and right field foul poles at 315 and 322 feet, respectively. But each power alley extends to 370 feet, and straightaway center field is 404 feet. As such, Tropicana Field boasts a reputation as a pitcher's park, with its average park factor for home runs over 8 percent less than regular.

Take a four-hour trip across the marshy land of Florida to the city of Miami. Just north of the ethnic area called Little Havana is a sparkling jewel of a ballpark, the newest in major league baseball. Opened in 2012, Marlins Park is the home of the National League Miami team, for which the park is named.

Since their entry to the majors in 1993, the Florida Marlins first played their home games in Sun Life Stadium, sharing tenancy with the NFL Miami Dolphins. Without any kind of enclosure, football was a comfortable fall game at the stadium, but baseball in the summer was a tropical nightmare. The average summer temperature in Miami nears ninety degrees, and the average relative humidity is close to 75 percent. Great weather for going to the beach, but lousy for an afternoon ball game.

Team owner Jeffery Loria was certain of what he didn't want in his new stadium—no retro, no nostalgia, no nod to the past. Architects at Populous got the message and came up with a contemporary design, rich with the influences of the city and its various cultures. Built for a cost of $634 million, Marlins Park was located on the site of the old Orange Bowl.

A three-panel, steel retractable roof—weighing eight thousand tons—keeps fans cool and comfortable in Marlins games, day or night. More importantly, the park reflects a major commitment to a green ecological impact. The stadium incorporates design features that consider reduced energy use, water efficiency, and recycling wherever possible.

The fan experience includes an art display throughout the park, featuring baseball-themed works by greats like Miro and Lichtenstein. There's also an

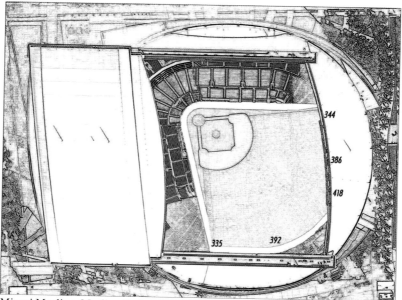

Miami Marlins, Marlins Park, Miami, Florida

original brightly colored piece by Red Grooms, aptly titled *Home Run Sculpture*. Located just beyond the left-center field fence, the seventy-foot kinetic artwork rises up whenever a Marlin hits a homer—much like the Home Run Apple at Citi Field in New York.

Marlins Park holds 36,742 people, making it one of the smallest and most intimate of major league stadiums. Yet the playing field dimensions are generous—344 and 335 down the foul lines, with power alleys a healthy 386 and 392 feet away, and center field at 418 feet at its deepest point.

Being such a new stadium, Marlins Park offers little data with regard to how it will fare with hitters and pitchers—but early returns are not encouraging for the thumpers in the game. The home run park factor for the stadium is a crippling 29 percent below the average for its first three seasons. Yet it doesn't seem to affect big bopper Giancarlo Stanton, who—in that same period—has hit 55 of his 98 home runs at home.

Better plan on driving ten hours north in order to reach Atlanta (it took Sherman a lot longer) and Turner Field, where the Atlanta Braves make their home—but not for long. The club's lease at Turner Field is up after the 2016 season, and they will move to a new open-air park called SunTrust Field, about eight miles northwest of Atlanta, in Cobb County, Georgia.

Since 1997, the Braves have played at Turner Field, which began its existence a year earlier as the Centennial Olympic Stadium. Home of the 1996 Summer Olympic Games, the stadium was reconfigured as a baseball-only facility after the Games' conclusion. The facility was named for owner and media mogul Ted Turner.

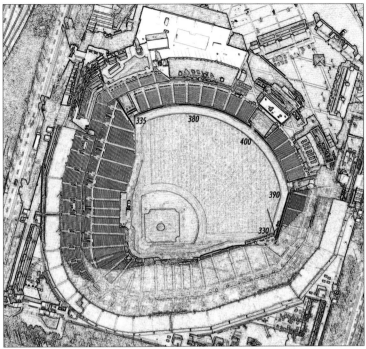

Atlanta Braves, Turner Field, Atlanta, Georgia

The Atlanta Stadium Design Team (ASDT) included architects Heery International, who also tackled the task of rebuilding the 85,000-seat stadium into a baseball facility for 49,586 fans. The cost was $235 million, which included its conversion into Turner Field.

The stadium is located a mere fifteen hundred feet south of the old Atlanta-Fulton County Stadium, where the Braves played since 1965. The old park's entire footprint is highlighted as part of a current parking lot.

Among the many sights at Turner Field are two unique items that stand high atop the left field grandstands. One is a forty-foot-tall cow, wearing a Braves helmet and holding an ever-changing (and misspelled) sign, urging fans to eat more chicken—courtesy of Chick-Fil-A, headquartered in Atlanta. The other is a forty-nine-foot bottle of Coca-Cola, representing another Atlanta-based company.

The old Atlanta-Fulton County Stadium was often called "The Launching Pad," as it was well known for the many home runs hit there. As for Turner Field, it basically plays as a neutral facility. Since 2001, its home run park factor has averaged just 7 percent below the norm. How SunTrust Park will play is anyone's guess.

Back East, Where It All Started

It's about ten hours north from Atlanta by car, across the Appalachian Mountains, to reach the Steel City of Pittsburgh. The town is home to one of baseball's oldest franchises, the Pirates, and their stadium—PNC Park.

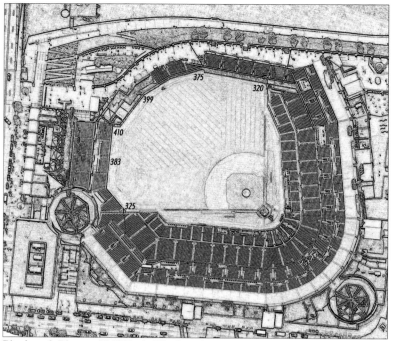

Pittsburgh Pirates, PNC Park, Pittsburgh, Pennsylvania

Located on the northern banks of the Allegheny River, across from the downtown Pittsburgh area, PNC Park is at the point where the Allegheny meets the Monongahela River, and they become the Ohio River. The Pirates spent thirty years in Three Rivers Stadium, less than a quarter-mile west from where PNC was built and opened in 2001.

Designed by HOK Sport, PNC Park is one of the neoclassical concepts (essentially, "new retro") seeking to incorporate fan-favorite features with modern conveniences. Special effort was made to include architectural highlights from Forbes Field, where the Pirates played between 1909 and 1970.

Built for $262 million, the park has only two decks, which keeps 38,362 fans lower and closer to the action on the field. PNC Bank paid $30 million in 1998 for twenty years of naming rights through 2020. The club honors Pirate greats Honus Wagner, Roberto Clemente, Willie Stargell, and Bill Mazeroski with statues of them located around the park. Also, the right field wall is twenty-one feet high in honor of the number worn by Clemente.

Like many of the retro parks, PNC has irregular outfield dimensions, with a short hike of 325 feet down the left field line that immediately expands to 383 feet and to 410 feet in far left-center field. Straightaway center is 399 feet; right field power alley is 375 feet and ends with a right field foul line of 320 feet.

The Allegheny sits just beyond the right field wall at a distance of 443 feet, making a waterlogged homer a distinct possibility. Up to the end of the 2014 season, two baseballs have left the park for a bath in the river.

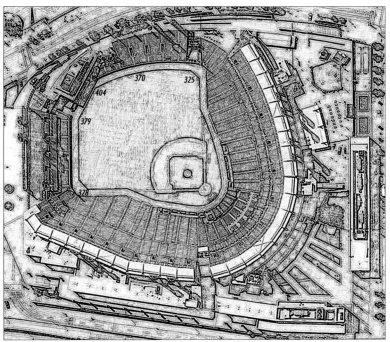

Cincinnati Reds, Great American Ball Park, Cincinnati, Ohio

Still, pitchers should like PNC Park, as home run ratings since its opening have averaged 18 percent below the norm, and only 1.7 homers leave the yard on an average per game. Andrew McCutchen has stroked less than half of his homers at PNC during his career, while he hits for a higher average and more doubles at home.

Less than a three-hour drive west from Pittsburgh brings one to the Queen City, Cincinnati, and the Reds baseball team, the oldest in professional baseball. Since 2003, the Reds have played their home games at the Great American Ballpark, named not with a patriotic touch, but a $75 million check from the Great American Financial Resources Company. They purchased thirty years' worth of naming rights that run through 2033.

The ballpark was built directly east from Riverfront Stadium/Cinergy Field, where the Reds and NFL Bengals played since 1970, with part of the new park's footprint overlapping the old. The Great American Ballpark is baseball-only, seating 42,271 fans in an open-air arrangement. The park is just south of the central downtown area and seated on the banks of the Ohio River, across from Covington, Kentucky.

Like many parks, the Great American Ballpark was designed by HOK Sport, using more than ten thousand tons of steel. Built for a cost of $280 million, the park is a far cry from the former doughnut-shaped, cookie-cutter Riverfront Stadium.

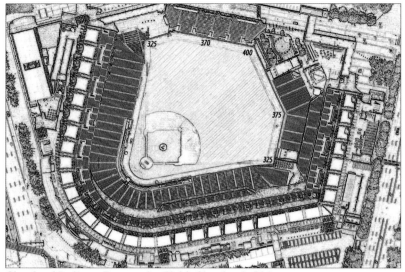

Cleveland Indians, Progressive Field, Cleveland, Ohio

Yet tradition is served with Crosley Terrace, a grass and concrete area located at the main entrance of the park, sloped at the same angle as the original terrace at Crosley Field. It includes full-sized bronze statues of Reds greats, like pitcher Joe Nuxhall on the mound, with catcher Ernie Lombardi behind the plate and Frank Robinson at bat. Slugger Ted Kluszewski stands in the on-deck circle, waiting his turn.

The outfield dimensions at the Great American Ballpark are asymmetrical but average, ranging from 328 feet down the left field line, 379 in the left field power alley, reaching 404 feet in center, back to 370 feet in right-center and 325 feet at the right field foul line.

Dimensions and other factors at the Great American Ballpark can put pitchers into a cold sweat, as the field is clearly a paradise for hitters. Since opening in 2003, home runs have left the park at a rate 27 percent more frequently than the normal stadium. Every game at the Great American Ballpark sees an average of 2.6 round-trippers.

It's only 250 miles across the state of Ohio, heading northeast toward Lake Erie and Cleveland, where the Indians have played ball in Progressive Field (first Jacobs Field) since 1994. Often called a "boutique ballpark," the Cleveland facility was the second of the then-innovative "retro classic" stadiums built, following the lead of Baltimore's Camden Yards.

The Cleveland ball club, having played in the cavernous Municipal Stadium— known as "the mistake by the lake"—since 1947, wanted a park that would anchor a revitalized downtown area known as the Gateway District. Architects HOK designed an open-air stadium for Cuyahoga County, built for $175 million. Club owner Richard Jacobs paid $10 million for the naming rights through 2006. Officially, it was Jacobs Field, but fans just called it "The Jake."

When the contract for naming rights expired in 2006, the Indians brought in a consultant to locate a party interested in seeing their name plastered all over the park. Progressive Insurance, based in a suburb near Cleveland, bought in for sixteen years at $58 million.

The park opened in time for the 1994 season, and by the end of 1995, the Indians found themselves in the World Series for the first time in over forty years. The Jake became a very popular place to watch baseball, as home games and all 43,368 seats were sold out solid between June 12, 1995, and April 4, 2001—455 consecutive dates.

Unique to the park are the light standards with a natural resemblance to toothbrushes (no word if the American Dental Association tried for the floss concessions), as well as sections in the stadium with angled seating, allowing a more comfortable viewing experience for fans.

The wall in left and left-center is an intimidating nineteen feet high—not as big as the Green Monster in Boston, but big enough to earn the moniker of "the Little Green Monster." The outfield dimensions are asymmetrical, plus turn at odd angles to keep fielders on their toes. The left field line is 325 feet—as is the right field line—then moves out to 370 feet in the power alley; the deepest part of center is 400 feet and comes back to 375 feet in the right field alley.

The Prog (not as sweet as The Jake, but that's what they call it these days) plays pretty neutral as far as pitchers and hitters are concerned. Since 2001, the home run factor has been just about 100, which is dead even. In that same period of time, each game has seen about 1.8 home runs leave the park.

It's only ninety miles from Cleveland to the Motor City of Detroit, assuming one can swim straight across Lake Erie (don't forget your passport, as directly south of Detroit is Windsor, Ontario, Canada). With a cooler head, hop on I-80 west to I-75 north and the trip will take less than three hours. In the heart of the downtown area is Comerica Park, home to the Detroit Tigers.

Opened for the 2000 season, the park stands a bit more than a mile east of where the Tigers played for nearly ninety years. Known over the decades as Navin Field, Briggs Stadium, and Tiger Stadium, the old property—devoid of any structure but still featuring a full-sized diamond and outfield—is used for pickup baseball and softball games today.

Design for Comerica Park was split between HOK Sport and locally based SHG Inc., using the grounds originally occupied by the Detroit College of Law. The stadium is adjacent to the enclosed Ford Field, home of the NFL Lions. The two sports venues share a common assemblage of outbuildings, featuring retail space, restaurants, and offices (including the Tigers' management). Comerica Bank paid $66 million for a thirty-year contract for the naming rights.

The park seeks to provide entertainment for everyone, including a food court with a merry-go-round (fans ride tigers instead of horses, of course), a Ferris wheel, and a huge colored-water fountain display in center field. The stadium's capacity is 41,681 and cost $300 million to build, with the main video screen scoreboard a massive 180 feet across.

The dirt area surrounding the batter's box is shaped like a giant home plate, and, as a nod to old-time ballparks, the area between there and the pitcher's

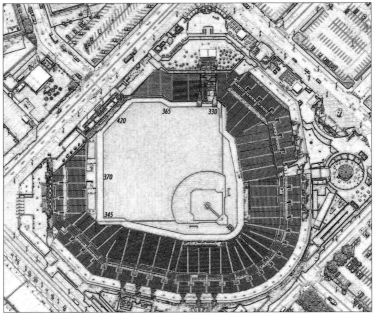

Detroit Tigers, Comerica Park, Detroit, Michigan

mound features a strip of dirt (just like Chase Field in Arizona). The generous foul area along the lines has allowed Comerica Park to record 20 percent more foul outs than the average park since 2010.

In general, the dimensions of Comerica Park quickly gained a bad reputation, leading some fans to suggest that multiple center fielders were needed to properly patrol the grass. Indeed, center field is 420 feet from home plate, and the left field wall, originally 395 feet away, was brought in to a more reasonable 370 feet in 2003.

For many players, the mindset at the park was not necessarily a "homer haven," but a "triples treat." In its first four years of existence, Comerica ranked first in triples allowed three times. Since 2010, the park has ranked no lower than fourth. Still, home runs are only 6 percent less likely at the Tigers' home park than the average stadium.

It's only about four hours east from Detroit to reach Toronto and Rogers Centre, just off the shores of Lake Erie. You can't miss the park, since it sits in the shadow of the eighteen-hundred-plus-foot-tall concrete broadcast mast next to it, known as the CN Tower.

The stadium was originally called the Skydome when it was opened in 1989 (the moniker being the winning entry in a "name the stadium" contest sponsored by the *Toronto Sun* newspaper). The Blue Jays played their first twelve seasons in Exhibition Stadium, located about a mile and a half west of the Rogers Centre. The current stadium splits time between hosting Blue Jays ball games for 49,282 fans and acting as home field for the Toronto Argonauts of the Canadian Football League.

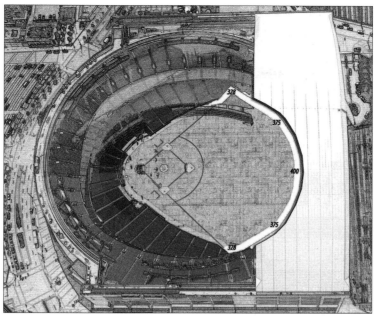

Toronto Blue Jays, Rogers Centre (Roof cutaway), Toronto, Ontario, Canada

The Skydome was designed by famed Canadian architect Rod Robbie and built for more than $470 million American. It was the first major league baseball stadium with a retractable roof—deemed a necessity in the Great White North (one must remember that the Blue Jays' very first game in 1977 started with a layer of fresh snow on the Exhibition Stadium field).

The roof was a marvel for its time (patented), weighing eleven thousand tons and built in four unique sections. Two enormous full portions roll straight back over a permanent arch, while a separate curved slice rolls around the roof's perimeter to stow away under the rest. The entire process takes about twenty minutes.

By 1998, the stadium itself had become a financial failure and went into bankruptcy. Sportsco International LP bought the park for $85 million and restored solvency to the operation. In 2004, Rogers Communications purchased the Skydome for the bargain price of $25 million, which then assumed the Rogers Centre name.

Being a multipurpose arena, the seating at the 100 Level is mounted on tracks and can be wheeled into various configurations. Attached to the Centre is a 348-room hotel, with 70 rooms facing the playing field—bringing unfortunate circumstances for more than a few baseball fans. Many couples (and a few singles) have been caught in the midst of lovemaking, recalling and revising the old Blue Jays park name—Exhibition Stadium had become Exhibitionist Stadium.

As for legitimate action on the field, Rogers Centre shares the distinction with Tropicana Field of having artificial turf. The Center also has a symmetrical outfield, with distances of 328 feet down the foul lines, 375 feet to the power alleys, and 400 feet to center.

Rogers Centre seems to favor hitters over pitchers, as the home run rating for the park since 2001 is 15 percent above the average major league arena. Visitors can count on an average of 2.34 long balls going out during a game, based on the same fourteen-year period.

Northeast

The wise baseball traveler will leave the car behind and hop a plane at Toronto Pearson International Airport, taking a nifty hour-and-a-half flight to Washington, D.C. For those who insist on staying terra-bound, the trip is about five hundred miles and should take about nine hours. Either way, once in the nation's capital, be sure to find Nationals Park, the home of the National League Washington Nationals (clearly, the word National is operative here).

With the move of the Montreal Expos to Washington, D.C., after the 2004 season, it was apparent that RFK Stadium would not be a proper long-term facility for the ball club. An industrial and residential area in southeast Washington, on the shore of the Anacostia River, was selected for the site of the new park. Naming rights were offered for sale, but no decent price was bid, so Nationals park it was.

Designed by HOK Sport (Kansas City) and Devrouax & Purnell Architects-Planners and built for nearly $700 million in time for the 2008 season, Nationals Park holds 41,506 fans in an open-air surrounding. Unlike other recently opened facilities, Nationals Park does not make a nod to the traditional and retro stadiums like Camden Yards and AT&T Park. Rather, the Washington stadium embraces the

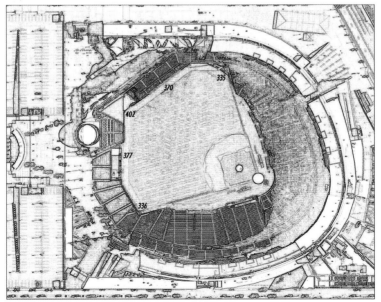

Washington Nationals, Nationals Park, Washington, DC

modern design, like Great American Ballpark and PETCO Park do. The exterior—especially behind home plate and along the third base line—features plenty of concrete, large slabs of glass, and steel.

Inside the park, fans will find a great baseball experience, combined with a solid commitment to a safe environment and renewable resources. Efforts in water and energy conservation, along with a reliance on recycled materials for construction, make Nationals Park a real twenty-first-century facility.

A forty-five-hundred-square-foot HD video screen and scoreboard in right-center field keeps everyone informed, while the odd angles and unique outfield features keep the fielders busy. The left field line is 336 feet, moving sharply to a power alley of 377 feet. A short jog in left-center field resolves to a center field depth of 402 feet, and then a long straight wall along right-center and right field—reaching 370 feet—ends in a right field line of 335 feet.

If club owners were aiming for a neutral ballpark, they got pretty close. In its first seven years of existence, the park factor for home runs is only 6 to 7 percent below the norm, with 1.79 homers hit on a per game average.

It's only forty miles up I-95 to Baltimore and the home of the Orioles (there's also MARC train service, bus, a healthy bike ride, or, as a last resort, one's thumb). Set in the southwest portion of the downtown area, the ballpark was a trendsetter when opened in 1992.

Officially, it's known as Oriole Park at Camden Yards, but everyone calls it Camden Yards (in a nod to its historic link as Camden Yard, once part of the Baltimore and Ohio railroad facility). Located in the center of what used to be an industrial park directly adjacent to the B&O warehouse and staging

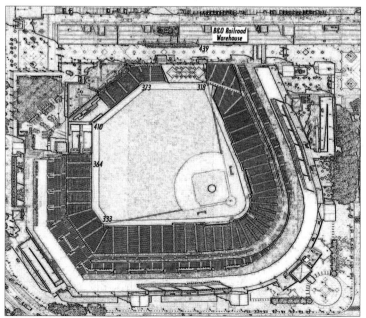

Baltimore Orioles, Oriole Park at Camden Yards, Baltimore, Maryland

yards, the park was the first of the neoclassical baseball stadiums built after the concrete donut, cookie-cutter monstrosities of the 1970s.

Camden Yards was designed by HOK Sport, seeking to embrace the architecture of the area, rather than combat it. As such, the enormous B&O warehouse—more than a thousand feet long and only fifty feet wide (ideal for storing spaghetti and pool cues)—was considered an integral part of the design. Built in 1899, the dark brick façade became a familiar sight just sixty feet beyond the right field stands. It now has Oriole team offices, and the roof features light standards to illuminate the park.

A home run off the warehouse wall is not impossible, as it is 439 feet from home plate. Even so, no one—through the 2014 season—has hit the warehouse on the fly during a major league game. Ken Griffey Jr. did accomplish the feat, but that was during the 1993 All-Star Home Run Derby. In that same time period, 79 home runs have reached Eutaw Street, the promenade that separates the park and warehouse.

With Baltimore being the birthplace of Babe Ruth, it's not surprising to find evidence of Ruth's roots at Camden Yards. The Bambino's folks owned several saloons in the area, including Ruth's Café (clever name) on Conway Street, which occupied the area that is now center field. In fact, during construction of the ballpark in the early 1990s, artifacts from the bar, such as bottles and bricks, were found and carefully preserved.

Built for a cost of $110 million, Camden Yards seats 45,900 fans and incorporates a natural grass surface. The asymmetrical outfield measures 333 feet down the left field line, is 364 feet to left-center, stretches to 410 feet in center, is 373 feet in right-center, and is 318 feet down the right field line.

For the most part, pitchers aren't the happiest of campers at Camden Yards. Hitters seem to enjoy the confines, hitting home runs at a rate of 14 percent higher than the average park. The long ball flies out at a rate of 2.37 per game.

Get back onto I-95 N and head up a hundred miles or so to reach the City of Brotherly Love—Philadelphia. The seat and site of many important events in American history, it's also the home of the National League Phillies and, more specifically, Citizens Bank Park.

After spending twenty-three seasons in the concrete bowl known as Veterans Stadium, the team built another "tip o' the cap" vintage-tinged retro park in time for the 2004 season, directly east of the old stadium. The park is in South Philadelphia, not far from the Delaware River, with the state of New Jersey on the other shore.

Designed by HOK Sport and the local firm of Ewing Cole Cherry Brott, the park relied on seating arrangements from previous Philly parks like the Baker Bowl and Connie Mack Stadium. Seating 43,500 fans, Citizens Bank Park cost more than $450 million to build, with a twenty-five-year $57.5 million naming rights agreement for Citizens Bank.

Bronze statues of Philly greats Mike Schmidt, Steve Carlton, Richie Ashburn, and Robin Roberts are located around the stadium, and a large food and entertainment area called Ashburn Alley—in honor of the aforementioned Philadelphia outfielder and broadcaster—runs the entire length behind the outfield wall. Peripheral buildings house team offices and retail space.

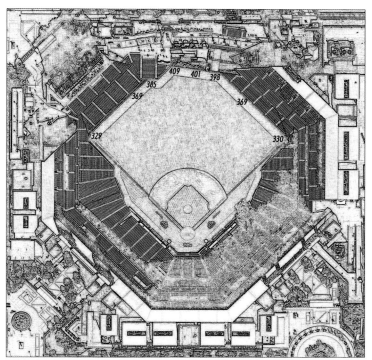

Philadelphia Phillies, Citizens Bank Park, Philadelphia, Pennsylvania

Inside the park, a seventy-four-hundred-square-foot HD video screen looms over the left field stands. In the farthest part of the right-center field stands is an eighteen-hundred-square-foot neon-lighted Liberty Bell that illuminates and rings when a Philly hits a homer or the team wins a game.

As one might expect from a retro-styled stadium, the outfield dimensions are asymmetrical—in fact, they can be downright confounding. The left field line is 329 feet, immediately cuts to 334 feet, runs into left-center at 374 feet, then all hell breaks loose. Appropriately, the locals call it "the Break," and it's caused more than one outfielder to reconsider his career choice. The wall angles back into the play field at that spot to 387 feet, then bends back to 409 feet at its furthest point. What's more, the wall height varies from nineteen feet to just under thirteen feet.

With sanity restored, straightaway center is 401 feet, angles to 398 feet, and then reaches 368 feet in right-center. The whole layout finishes with a right field foul line of 330 feet.

In general, hitters are more satisfied than pitchers at Citizens Bank Park, as the home run park factor has amounted to 18 percent above the average park since they opened in 2004. Just like Camden Yards, home runs fly out at a rate of 2.37 per game.

About ninety minutes to the northeast will bring one to the Big Apple—New York City. More accurately, the borough of Queens is the site of Citi Field, the home park for the New York Mets. Opened in time for the 2009 season, it seats 41,800 fans in an open-air, baseball-only fashion.

Built just past the center field fence of the former home of Shea Stadium at a cost of $600 million, Citi Field was designed by Populous. With thoughts of moving the fans closer to the action, the stadium was originally part of the unsuccessful proposal to bring the Olympics to New York in 2012. Naming rights were purchased by Citigroup, paying $400 million for a twenty-year agreement.

The club was well aware of its New York roots, relying on the memories of Ebbets Field to influence the appearance of the exterior façade, along with the main entrance. They also looked to the long-gone Polo Grounds as an inspiration for dark green seating, leaving the colorful rainbow assortment from Shea behind.

Still, the new park kept the popular Home Run Apple feature, placing a brand new, shiny red apple just beyond the center field fence. Four times as big as the original fruit at Shea, it rises from its confines when a Mets player puts one over the fence. Not to worry about the Shea apple, which now sits outside the main entrance of Citi Field, after spending several years of exile in the bullpen.

The original design of the playfield was, to say the least, cavernous, with right-center field measuring a distant 415 feet from home plate. In time for the 2015 season, the fences were brought in a bit, at distances anywhere from three to fifteen feet.

With those changes, the left field line is 335 feet, moves to 358 and 385 in far left-center, and reaches 408 feet to the Home Run Apple in center. Right-center

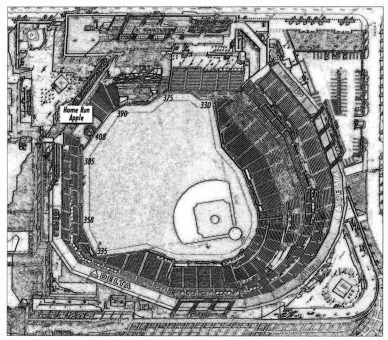

New York Mets, Citi Field, New York, New York

varies from 380 feet to 370 feet and finishes with a right field foul line of 330 feet.

Those changes will be good news for hitters (and equally bad news for pitchers), since the home run park factor has been 6 percent below the norm since the park opened. An average of only 1.6 home runs per game has been hit in the park in that same time frame. It's not known if the fence changes will tip the scale toward the sluggers' advantage at Citi Field.

It's less than ten miles from Citi Field to Yankee Stadium in the New York borough of the Bronx, across the East River by way of the RFK Bridge, but depending on the traffic, the trip may be a long one.

The Yankees have called the area "home" for almost one hundred years, but their stadium—officially called Yankee Stadium II, but Yankee Stadium is just fine—opened in 2009, the same year as their crosstown rivals. The city of New York likes to do everything big, and the new stadium was no different, costing in excess of $1.5 billion to complete (yup, billion—with a "b"). Fortunately, plans to put a retractable roof on the park were dropped, saving $200 million (did anyone notice?)

It's no surprise that Populous designed the park, drawing heavily on the old stadium for influence. Great sheets of limestone cover the exterior and inside, the decorative and familiar picket-fence-like frieze that hangs from the upper deck immediately identifies the stadium as Yankee territory. Monument Park, the collection of plaques and retired numbers of Yankee greats, was originally

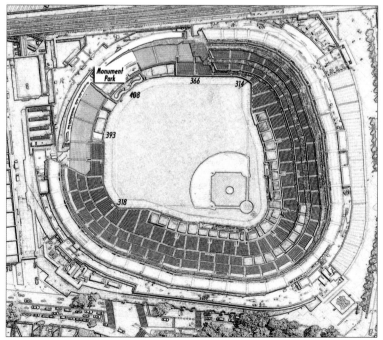

New York Yankees, Yankee Stadium, New York, New York

beyond the left field fence in the old park. The new stadium places the shrine directly behind center field.

The Great Hall runs along the right field side of the park, between the external façade and the actual stadium itself. The thirty-one-thousand-square-foot space is large enough to handle 3,300 people for various nonbaseball events, while enormous banners of Yankee greats remind visitors where they are. NYY Steak and the Hard Rock Café are also part of the right field features.

With seating for 51,800 fans, Yankee Stadium has a high-def video screen that offers nearly six thousand square feet of viewing area. The foul area in the infield is smaller than the old park, putting the fans closer to the action. There's more than two dozen fixed concession stands and over a hundred more on wheels, so grabbing a bite to eat is easy.

On the field, the dimensions are the same as the old park, but certain features in right field are unique to the new stadium. Left field is a cozy 318 feet, expanding out to 399 feet in left-center field, stretching to 408 feet in center, coming around to 385 in right center, and finishing at the familiar 314 feet in right.

Protective helmets might be needed for more than just the batters at Yankee Stadium—anyone in the outfield bleachers runs the risk of getting hit on the noggin by the numerous home runs that have flown out in the park's first six years. The park factor for long balls has averaged a monstrous 28 percent above the norm, while the average homers per game have numbered 2.58.

Move on up the road with a four-hour trip to Boston. West of the downtown area and just off I-90 is the legendary Fenway Park, home of the Red Sox. The stadium is the oldest in the major leagues, having been opened in 1912.

The year before, club owner John Taylor did not renew his lease at Huntington Avenue Grounds, and he picked the Fens neighborhood as the site for his new ballpark. Local architect James McLaughlin headed the design team, with the Charles Logue Building Company handling construction. Fenway Park was ready for the next season.

Like Wrigley Field in Chicago, the Boston ballpark was built within the confines of the main streets surrounding it—Brookline, Lansdowne, Ipswich, and Jersey (now Yawkey). As such, left field was quite close, even for the days before the dominance of the home run, so a twenty-five-foot wall was built. Along with a small scoreboard, the wall was covered with ads.

A substantial amount of bleacher seats were placed in front of the wall, on a sloped terrace known as Duffy's Cliff (named for Red Sox outfielder Duffy Lewis, who was very adept at maneuvering around the incline). In early 1934, a huge fire destroyed much of the park during a major renovation.

As a result, the terrace was flattened and the wall built to a height of thirty-seven feet, with a net placed at the top to protect the Lansdowne businesses from dive-bombing baseballs. In 1947, it was rebuilt from wood to concrete and tin; fitted with a large, hand-operated scoreboard (as it still is today); then painted green for the first time. The iconic Green Monster was officially born.

Sharp-eyed fans may note some black markings inside the white vertical lines that are part of the American League scoreboard on the wall. The marks are Morse

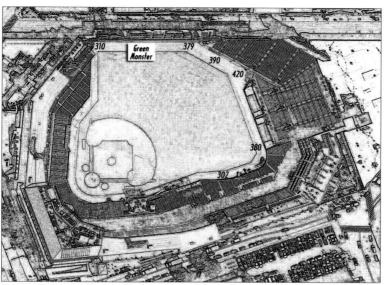

Boston Red Sox, Fenway Park, Boston, Massachusetts

code, signaling TAY and JRY—the initials of previous owners Tom A. Yawkey and his wife Jean R. Yawkey.

High in the right field stands, a single seat is painted red amid the other green ones. In June 1946, Ted Williams blasted a 502-foot homer—the longest ever hit at Fenway—that struck the fan sitting in the seat. Hitting him in the head, the ball broke his straw hat and the paint job commemorates the date and event.

Keeping a historic park like Fenway in working shape (as well as financially sound and safe for the fans) is challenging. Over the years, it has seen several major renovations that have added a bigger press box, padding to the walls, expanded seating (including on top of the Green Monster in 2003), more concessions, and new video boards.

On the field, the asymmetrical dimensions reflect the citybound park's perimeter. As noted, left field is 310 feet (long marked erroneously as 315), expanding to 378 at the far end of the Green Monster, then reaching a perilous nook of 420 feet is deep center. The right field fence angles to 380 feet at its deepest part, then quickly curves to a right field foul line of just 302 feet.

The foul area in the infield is small, resulting in 22 percent fewer foul outs than average since 2010. Overall, hitters tend to like Fenway Park, although skillful left fielders can turn hard hit balls into loud singles if they can play the wall properly. Still, homers have been about 9 percent less likely at Fenway than the norm since 2001. In that same period, an average of just about 2 homers per game have been hit at the park.

8

Past Grounds of Glory

Stadiums Long Gone

D espite the best-laid plans (or blueprints) of mice and men, baseball stadiums cannot be expected to last forever. For longtime stalwart teams like those in New York, Boston, Chicago, Cincinnati, and other pioneer entries to the game, those early playing fields are (for the most part) long gone.

As the game has changed over the last one hundred-plus years, so have the needs of the ballparks that host them. And it's not just the fact that stone, brick, steel, and concrete cannot (and will not) last eternally, but also the seating, lighting, and other amenities that enhance the fan's experience.

Still, Boston's Fenway Park and Chicago's Wrigley Field have each passed the century mark of existence—of course, not without hundreds of millions of dollars of renovations (for safety, as well as aesthetic and practical purposes). After those two, LA's Dodger Stadium is a seeming youngster at fifty-plus years old. Two other California stadiums—in Anaheim and Oakland—are nearing the half-century mark. All other fields range from fortyish years old to just a few.

A full accounting of the historic and former major league ballparks could be exhaustive (for you as well as me), so those great and long-gone stadiums will be remembered in abbreviated form. For the sake of organization, they will be presented in the order in which the team's franchise entered the majors.

Also, note that in some cases, there may be gaps in the listings. For example, St. Louis had four different facilities called Sportsman's Park at one point or another. But only three were used for general major league play, so they all may not be represented in these listings.

NATIONAL LEAGUE

Atlanta Braves: 1966–Present

Previously . . .

Milwaukee Braves	National League	1953–1965
Boston Bees	National League	1936–1940
Boston Braves	National League	1912–1935, 1941–1952
Boston Rustlers	National League	1911
Boston Doves	National League	1907–1910

Boston Beaneaters	National League	1883–1906
Boston Red Caps	National League	1876–1882
Boston Braves	National Association	1871–1875

Previous Stadiums

Atlanta-Fulton County Stadium (aka Atlanta Stadium 1966–1975)
Years: 1965–1996
Dimensions: L—330, LC—385, C—402, RC—385, R—330
Capacity: 52,800
Architect: Heery International
Today: Now parking lot for Turner Field, old playing field highlighted on asphalt.

Milwaukee County Stadium: 1953–1965
Dimensions: L—320, LC—377, C—402, RC—377, R—315
Capacity: 53,100
Architect: Skidmore, Owings, & Merrill
Today: Site is now Miller Park. Chicago White Sox played twenty home games at the park in 1968 and 1969.

Braves Field: 1915–1952
Dimensions: L—337, LC—355, C—390, RC—355, R—320
Capacity: 44,500
Architect: Osborn Engineering
Today: Right field stands are now part of Nickerson Field, a soccer and lacrosse facility, at Boston University

South End Grounds III: 1894–1914
Dimensions: L—275, LC—394, C—394, RC—400, R—235
Capacity: 11,000

South End Grounds II: 1888–1894 (Destroyed by Great Roxbury Fire in 1894).
Dimensions: L—250, LC—445, C—500, RC—440, R—255
Capacity: 6,800

South End Grounds I: 1871–1887 (Torn down in 1887).
Capacity: 3,000
Today: All three parks stood on the same land, at Walpole St. and Columbus Ave. The site now is the parking lot of the Columbus Parking Garage.

Chicago Cubs: 1903–Present

Previously . . .

Chicago Orphans	National League	1898–1902
Chicago Colts	National League	1890–1897
Chicago White Stockings	National League	1876–1889
Chicago White Stockings	National Association	1874–1875

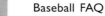

Previous Stadiums

West Side Grounds: 1894–1915
Dimensions: L—340, LC—441, C—442, RC—365, R—316
Capacity: 16,000
Today: Currently site of University of Illinois College of Medicine and UIC Medical Center.

South Side Park: 1891–1893
Today: Currently site of Dan Ryan Expressway and overflow parking for US Cellular Field.

West Side Park: 1885–1892
Dimensions: L—216, R—216
Capacity: 10,300
Today: Currently the site of the Andrew Jackson Language Academy.

Lakefront Park: 1878–1884
Dimensions: L—180, LC—280, C—300, RC—252, R—196
Capacity: 10,000
Today: Currently the site of the Millennium Memorial; a part of Millennium Park.

23rd Street Grounds (aka State Street Grounds): 1874–1877
Capacity: 11,000
Today: Currently the site of the National Teacher's Academy.

Cincinnati Reds: 1890–1953, 1960–Present

Previously . . .

Cincinnati Redlegs	National League	1954–1959
Cincinnati Red Stockings	American Association	1882–1889
Cincinnati Red Stockings	National League	1876–1880

Previous Stadiums

Riverfront Stadium (aka Cinergy Field 1996–2002) 1971–2002
Dimensions: L—330, LC—375, C—404, RC—375, R—330
Capacity: 52,300
Architect: Heery International
Today: Site occupied by commercial buildings, including restaurants, condos and apartments, and parking space.

Crosley Field (aka Redland Field 1912–1933): 1912–1970
Dimensions: L—328, RC—380, C—380, RC—387, R—366
Capacity: 33,000
Architect: Hake and Hake
Fact: Site of MLB's first night game, May 24, 1935.

Palace of the Fans (aka League Park III), 1902–1911
Dimensions: L—360, LC—418, C—400, RC—375, R—450
Capacity: 12,000
Architect: John G. Thurtle
Fact: Design based on Chicago's 1893 Columbian Exposition.

League Park II: 1894–1901
Dimensions: L—253, LC—384, C—414, RC—426, R—340
Fact: Fire destroyed League Park II, with the grand Palace of the Fans erected on its location.

League Park I: 1884–1893
Capacity: 6,000

Bank Street Grounds: 1880–1883
Capacity: 2,000
Today: Site is parking lot for Cincinnati's Metro transit system.

Avenue Grounds: 1876–1879
Capacity: 7,500
Today: Site currently occupied by railroad staging yards.

Pittsburgh Pirates: 1891–Present

Previously . . .

Pittsburgh Alleghenys	National League	1887–1890
Pittsburgh Alleghenys	American Association	1882–1886

Previous Stadiums

Three Rivers Stadium: 1970–2000
Dimensions: L—335, LC—375, C—400, RC—375, R—335
Capacity: 47,900
Architect: Deeter Ritchy Sipple Associates
Fact: One of the many multisport, "concrete donut" stadiums built in the seventies.

Forbes Field: 1910–1970
Dimensions: L—335, LC—355, C—457, RC—375, R—300
Capacity: 35,000
Architect: Charles Levitt Jr.

Forbes Field, Pittsburgh, PA, 1913.

Today: Site now occupied by Posvar and Mervis Halls, part of University of Pittsburgh campus.

Exposition Park III: 1891–1909
Dimensions: L—400, LC—461, C—515, RC—439, R—380
Capacity: 16,000
Today: Became site for Three Rivers Stadium and now, Heinz Field.

Recreation Park: 1884–1890
Capacity: 17,000
Today: Site now occupied by industrial and office buildings.

Exposition Park II: 1883 (Quickly built to replace destroyed park).

Exposition Park I: 1882–1883 (Destroyed by fire and flood in 1883).

St. Louis Cardinals: 1892–Present

Previously . . .

St. Louis Browns   American Association   1882–1891

Previous Stadiums

Busch Stadium II (aka Busch Memorial Stadium 1967–1983): 1967–2005
Dimensions: L—330, LC—375, C—404, RC—375, R—330
Capacity: 53,100
Architect: Sverdrup, Parcel, and Associates

Sportsman's Park IV (aka Busch Stadium 1954–1966): 1920–1966
Dimensions: L—351, LC—379, C—420, RC—354, R—310
Capacity: 30,500
Architect: Osborn Engineering
Fact: Shared tenancy with St. Louis Browns until 1953, built on same site as Sportsman's
  Park I.

Robison Field: 1893–1920
Dimensions: L—410, LC—458, C—441, RC—360, R—312
Capacity: 21,000
Architect: Beinke and Wees
Today: Damaged by fires in 1898 and 1901. Now the location of Beaumont High School.

Sportsman's Park II: 1882–1982
Dimensions: L—350, LC—400, C—460, RC—330, R—285
Capacity: 12,000
Today: Site currently occupied by Hoover Boys & Girls Club building, with football field
  and tennis courts.

Philadelphia Phillies: 1887–Present

Previously . . .

Philadelphia Quakers   National League   1883–1886

Previous Stadiums

Veterans Stadium: 1971–2003
Dimensions: L—330, LC—371, C—408, RC—371, R—330
Capacity: 61,800
Architect: Hugh Stubbins and Associates
Today: Site is now parking lot west of Citizens Bank Park.

Shibe Park (aka Connie Mack Stadium 1953–1970): 1938–1970
Dimensions: L—334, LC—358, C—447, RC—355, R—329
Capacity: 33,600
Architect: William Steele and Sons
Today: Shared with the Philadelphia Athletics between 1938 and 1954, site is now the
    Deliverance Evangelistic Church.

Baker Bowl (aka Huntingdon Grounds 1895–1913): 1895–1938
Dimensions: L—342, C—408, R—279
Capacity: 18,000
Architect: Heery, Heery, and Finch
Today: Built on Huntingdon Grounds property, area is now an industrial building, a car
    wash, parking lots, and a gas station.

Shibe Park, Philadelphia, PA, 1909.

Huntingdon Grounds: 1887–1894 (Burned down in 1894 fire—temporary facility built for remainder of the season).
Dimensions: L—500, C—410, R—310
Capacity: 15,000

Recreation Park: 1883–1886
Dimensions: L—300, C—410, R—247
Capacity: 2,000
Today: Used for baseball as far back as 1860, the site is now residential and small businesses.

San Francisco Giants: 1958–Present

Previously . . .

New York Giants	National League	1886–1957
New York Gothams	National League	1883–1885

Previous Stadiums

Candlestick Park (aka 3Com Park 1995–1999): 1960–1999
Dimensions: L—335, LC—365, C—410, RC—375, R—330
Capacity: 57,500
Architect: John Bolles; Chin and Hensolt
Fact: Pleasant day games became cold, windy, and raw games at night.

Seals Stadium: 1958–1959
Dimensions: L—365, LC—375, C—410, RC—360, R—335

Polo Grounds, Manhattan, New York, 1911.

Capacity: 22,900
Fact: Home to SF Seals of Pacific Coast League until NY Giants moved west.

Polo Grounds: 1911–1957
Dimensions: L—279, LC—447, C—483, RC—440, R—258
Capacity: 56,000
Architect: Harry B. Herts
Fact: Giants began playing here in June 1911. Shared with New York Yankees between 1913 and 1922.

New Polo Grounds II: 1891–1911
Dimensions: L—277, C—433, R—258
Capacity: 30,000
Fact: Burned down in start of 1911 season, one month of games played at Hilltop Park.

New Polo Grounds I: 1889–1890
Capacity: 14,300
Fact: Became parking lot for Polo Grounds when opened in 1911.

St. George Cricket Grounds: 1889 (Used for two months while New Polo Grounds were built).
Today: Located on Staten Island, now the site of Richmond County Bank Ballpark.

Polo Grounds I—Southeast Diamond: 1883–1888
Capacity: 12,000
Today: Park was closed when NYC built 111th St. through the park. Area now is directly north of Central Park, at 110th St. and 5th Ave.—near Duke Ellington Circle.

Los Angeles Dodgers: 1958–Present

Previously . . .

Brooklyn Dodgers	National League	1911–1912, 1932–1957
Brooklyn Robins	National League	1914–1931
Brooklyn Superbas	National League	1899–1910, 1913
Brooklyn Bridegrooms	National League	1890, 1896–1898
Brooklyn Bridegrooms	American Association	1888–1889
Brooklyn Grays	American Association	1885–1887
Brooklyn Atlantics	American Association	1884

Previous Stadiums

LA Memorial Coliseum: 1958–1961
Dimensions: L—251, LC—320, C—420, RC—380, R—300
Capacity: 94,600
Architect: John & Donald Parkinson
Fact: The short left field distance was somewhat neutralized by a forty-two-foot-high screen fence.

Ebbets Field, Brooklyn, New York, 1920.

Ebbets Field: 1913–1957
Dimensions: L—348, LC—351, C—384, RC—344, R—297
Capacity: 32,000
Architect: Clarence Randall Van Buskirk
Today: Now largely the Ebbets Field Housing Development, a group of high-rise
   residences.

Washington Park III: 1898–1912
Dimensions: L—335, LC—500, C—445, RC—300, R—215
Capacity: 18,800
Today: Now a shopping center and parking lot in the Gowanus section of Brooklyn.

Washington Park III, Brooklyn, New York, 1908.

Eastern Park: 1891–1897
Capacity: 12,000
Today: Site is now a junkyard, assorted businesses, and bordered on the east by the Metropolitan Transportation Authority elevated line.

Washington Park II: 1889–1890
Capacity: 8,000
Today: Site is now the JJ Byrne Playground in Brooklyn.

Washington Park I: 1884–1889 (Burned down in 1889).

New York Mets: 1952–Present

Previous Stadiums

Shea Stadium: 1964–2008
Dimensions: L—341, LC—371, C—410, RC—371, R—341
Capacity: 55,300
Architect: Praeger-Kavanagh-Waterbury
Fact: Shared with NY Yankees in 1974 and 1975 while Yankee Stadium underwent a major renovation.
Today: Site is now parking lot directly west of Citi Field.

Polo Grounds: 1962–1963
Dimensions: L—279, LC—447, C—483, RC—440, R—258
Capacity: 56,000
Architect: Harry B. Herts
Fact: Sitting empty for four years after the Dodgers went west, the Mets played in the Polo Grounds until Shea Stadium was ready for use.

Milwaukee Brewers: 1998–Present

Previously . . .

Milwaukee Brewers	American League	1970–1997
Seattle Pilots	American League	1969

Previous Stadiums

Milwaukee County Stadium: 1970–2000
Dimensions: L—320, LC—377, C—402, RC—377, R—315
Capacity: 53,100
Architect: Skidmore, Owings, & Merrill

Sick's Stadium: 1969
Dimensions: L—305, LC—345, C—405, RC—345, R—320
Capacity: 28,500
Today: Site is now retail home improvement store and parking lot.

Washington Nationals: 2005–Present

Previously . . .

Montreal Expos   National League   1969–2004

Previous Stadiums
RFK Stadium: 2005–2007
Dimensions: L—335, LC—380, C—410, RC—380, R—335
Capacity: 46,300
Architect: George L. Dahl, Osborn Engineering
Today: Only current tenant is DC United, MLS soccer team.

Hiram Bithorn Stadium: 2003–2004
Dimensions: L—325, LC—375, C—404, RC—375, R—325
Capacity: 19,000
Fact: Located in San Juan, Puerto Rico, the Expos played twenty-two home games each
in 2003 and 2004.

Olympic Stadium: 1977–2004
Dimensions: L—325, LC—375, C—404, RC—375, R—325
Capacity: 46,500
Architect: Roger Tallibert
Fact: Following the 1976 Summer Olympic Games, the roofed stadium was adapted for
baseball.

Jarry Park: 1969–1976
Dimensions: L—340, LC—368, C—420, RC—368, R—340
Capacity: 28,400
Architect: HOK Sport
Fact: Upgraded from a 3,000-seat park for amateur baseball, the park had a swimming
pool just beyond the right field fence. It was a perfect landing spot for home runs
hit by lefties.

San Diego Padres: 1969–Present

Previous Stadiums

*Qualcomm Stadium (aka Jack Murphy Stadium 1981–1996, San Diego Stadium
1969–1980): 1969–2003*
Dimensions: L—327, LC—370, C—405, RC—368, R—330
Capacity: 67,500
Architect: Frank L. Hope and Associates
Fact: Jack Murphy was a sportswriter who pressed for a major league baseball team in
San Diego.

Colorado Rockies: Nat Lge, 1993–Present

Previous Stadiums

Mile High Stadium: 1993–1994
Dimensions: L—335, LC—366, C—423, RC—400, R—370
Capacity: 76,000
Architect: Stanley E. Morse
Today: Site is now occupied by Sports Authority Stadium, home of NFL Denver Broncos.

Miami Marlins: 2012–Present

Previously . . .
Florida Marlins   National League   1993–2011

Previous Stadiums

Sun Life Stadium (aka Pro Player Stadium 1997–2004, Joe Robbie Stadium 1993–1996): 1993–2011
Dimensions: L—330, LC—360, C—394, RC—373, R—345
Capacity: 47,600
Architect: HOK Sport
Fact: Shared with NFL Miami Dolphins team

Arizona Diamondbacks: 1998–Present

Chase Field (aka Bank One Ballpark 1998–2005): 1998–Present

AMERICAN LEAGUE

Baltimore Orioles: 1954–Present

Previously . . .
St. Louis Browns   American League   1902–1953
Milwaukee Brewers   American League   1901

Previous Stadiums

Memorial Stadium: 1954–1991
Dimensions: L—309, LC—376, C—405, RC—376, R—309
Capacity: 53,300
Architect: L. P. Kooken Company
Fact: In 1954, center field was a spacious 445 feet, allowing for NFL Colts to play as well in the fall.
Today: Site is now two-thirds replica of the field as part of a YMCA park.

Sportsman's Park IV: 1909–1953
Dimensions: L—351, LC—379, C—420, RC—354, R—310
Capacity: 30,500
Architect: Osborn Engineering
Fact: Shared tenancy with St. Louis Cardinals until 1953, when the Browns moved to Baltimore.

Sportsman's Park III: 1902–1908 (Same site as other Sportsman's parks).
Dimensions: L—342, LC—350, C—390, RC—400, R—300
Capacity: 18,000

Lloyd Street Grounds: 1901
Dimensions: L—295, C—380, R—295
Today: Site is now older residential neighborhood on Milwaukee's Northwest side.

Boston Red Sox: 1907–Present

Previously . . .

Boston Americans   American League   1901–1906

Previous Stadiums

Huntington Avenue Grounds:1901–1911
Dimensions: L—350, C—635, R—320
Capacity: 11,500
Today: Site is now the campus of Northeastern University.

Fenway Park, Boston, MA, 1912.

Chicago White Sox: 1901–Present

Previous Stadiums

Comiskey Park: 1910–1990
Dimensions: L—352, LC—382, C—415, RC—382, R—352
Capacity: 51,000
Architect: Zachary Taylor Davis
Today: Site is now parking lot north of US Cellular Field. Home plate and foul lines are marked on asphalt.

White Sox Park, Chicago, IL, 1908.

South Side Park III (aka White Sox Park 1904–1910) 1901–1910
Dimensions: L—330, LC—397, C—410, RC—360, R—325
Capacity: 15,000
Today: Site is housing development directly south of US Cellular Field.

Cleveland Indians: 1915–Present

Previously . . .

Cleveland Naps	American League	1903–1914
Cleveland Bronchos	American League	1902
Cleveland Blues	American League	1901

Previous Stadiums

Municipal Stadium (aka Lake Front Stadium 1930s) 1932–1933, 1947–1993
Dimensions: L—320, LC—380, C—410, RC—380, R—320
Capacity: 74,000
Architect: Walker and Weeks
Fact: Indians played at Municipal Stadium on special occasions between 1934 and 1946 before making it their full-time home.
Today: Site is now FirstEnergy Stadium, home to NFL Browns.

League Park IV (aka Somers Park 1910–1915, Dunn Park 1916–1927): 1910–1932, 1934–1946
Dimensions: L—375, LC—408, C—420, RC—319, R—290

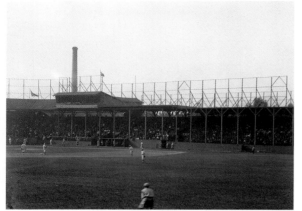
League Park III, Cleveland, OH, 1905.

Capacity: 22,500
Architect: Osborn Engineering
Fact: Short right field fence was backed by a forty-four-foot fence.
Today: Rebuilt as a city baseball field for youth and high school games in 2014, with original ticket booth and grandstand wall retained.

League Park III 1901–1909
Dimensions: L—353, LC—362, C—409, RC—390, R—290
Capacity: 11,200
Fact: Site dates back into early 1880s as grounds for baseball.

Detroit Tigers: 1901–Present

Previous Stadiums

Tiger Stadium (aka Navin Field 1912–1937, Briggs Stadium 1938–1960) 1912–1999
Dimensions: L—340, LC—365, C—425, RC—370, R—325
Capacity: 52,000
Architect: Osborn Engineering
Today: Park structure has been demolished, but diamond and playing field remain for pickup ball games.

Bennett Park, Detroit, MI, 1909.

Bennett Park: 1901–1911
Dimensions: L—295, LC—420, C—480, RC—412, R—440
Capacity: 14,000
Fact: Park razed after 1911 season, with Navin Field built on the site.

Minnesota Twins: 1961–Present

Previously . . .

Washington Senators   American League   1901–1960

Previous Stadiums

Hubert H. Humphrey Metrodome: 1982–2009
Dimensions: L—343, LC—385, C—408, RC—367, R—327
Capacity: 46,500
Architect: Skidmore, Owings, & Merrill
Fact: Shared with NFL Vikings. Domed stadium featured soft fabric roof, kept up by internal air pressure of stadium.

Metropolitan Stadium: 1961–1981
Dimensions: L—344, LC—365, C—402, RC—365, R—330
Capacity: 45,900
Architect: Thorshov and Cerny
Fact: Senators became the Minneapolis Twins in 1961, actually moving to Bloomington, MN. Shared with NFL Vikings.
Today: Site is now Mall of America.

Griffith Stadium: 1911–1960
Dimensions: L—388, LC—391, C—421, RC—373, R—320
Capacity: 28,600
Architect: Osborn Engineering
Fact: Unusual notch in center field fence allowed for five houses outside the field—and unpredictable bounces inside the field.
Today: Site is now Howard University Hospital and Howard University College of Medicine.

American League Park II: 1904–1910 (Stadium destroyed by fire in March 1911)
Dimensions: L—356, LC—410, C—442, RC—449, R—328
Fact: Site used for Griffith Stadium.

Fire at American League Park II, Washington, D.C., 1911.

American League Park I: 1901–1903
Dimensions: L—290, LC—338, C—424, RC—378, R—338
Today: Site is now residential area in east part of Washington, D.C.

Oakland Athletics: 1968–Present

Previously . . .

Kansas City Athletics	American League	1955–1967
Philadelphia Athletics	American League	1901–1954

Previous Stadiums

Municipal Stadium: 1955–1967
Dimensions: L—330, LC—375, C—421, RC—382, R—353
Capacity: 35,500
Architect: Osborn Engineering
Fact: Famous for owner Charlie Finley's zoo beyond right field, stadium was razed in 1976.
Today: Current site has single-family homes, with a historical marker at 22nd St. and Brooklyn Ave.

Shibe Park (aka Connie Mack Stadium 1953–1954): 1909–1954
Dimensions: L—334, LC—358, C—447, RC—355, R—329
Capacity: 33,600
Architect: William Steele and Sons

Columbia Park II: 1901–1908
Dimensions: L—340, LC—392, C—396, RC—323, R—280
Capacity: 13,600
Today: Site is now residential area in central part of Philadelphia.

New York Yankees: 1913–Present

Previously . . .

New York Highlanders	American League	1903–1912

Previous Stadiums

Yankee Stadium II: 1976–2008
Dimensions: L—318, LC—385, C—408, RC—375, R—314
Capacity: 57,500
Architect: Praeger-Kavanagh-Waterbury
Fact: Two renovations cost $160 million, created Monument Park in out-of-play area in left-center.

Shea Stadium: 1974–1975
Dimensions: L—341, LC—371,
C—410, RC—371, R—341
Capacity: 55,300
Architect: Praeger-Kavanagh-
Waterbury

Yankee Stadium I: 1923–1973
Dimensions: L—301, LC—440,
C—450, RC—380, R—296
Capacity: 67,000
Architect: Osborn Engineering
Fact: Monuments in left-center
were in play until renovation
in 1974.

Hilltop Park, Bronx, New York, 1908.

Polo Grounds: 1913–1922
Dimensions: L—279, LC—447, C—483, RC—440, R—258
Capacity: 56,000
Architect: Harry B. Herts
Fact: Unlike other parks with short foul lines, the Polo Grounds had no high wall or
screen to confound pulling home run hitters.

Hilltop Park: 1903–1912
Dimensions: L—365, LC—378, C—412, RC—412, R—365
Capacity: 17,000
Today: Site is now part of the Columbia-Presbyterian Medical Center.

Los Angeles Angels: 1961–1965, 2005–Present

Previously . . .

Anaheim Angels   American League   1997–2004
California Angels   American League   1966–1996

Previous Stadiums

Dodger Stadium (Chavez Ravine for Angels games): 1962–1965

Dimensions: L—330, LC—375, C—395, RC—375, R—330

Capacity: 56,000

Architect: Praeger-Kavanagh-Waterbury

Fact: In an effort to separate their team from the Dodgers, the Angels referred to
their park as Chavez Ravine.

Wrigley Field (in Los Angeles): 1961
Dimensions: L—340, LC—345, C—412, RC—345, R—339
Capacity: 20,400

Fact: Only a few miles southeast of Hollywood, the stadium was used for many film and TV productions, including Home Run Derby in the early 1960s. Built in 1921 by Cubs owner Wrigley for minor league team.

Today: Site is now Gilbert Lindsay Rec Park.

Texas Rangers: 1972–Present

Previously . . .

Washington Senators   American League   1961–1971

Previous Stadiums

Arlington Stadium: 1972–1993
Dimensions: L—330, LC—380, C—400, RC—380, R—330
Capacity: 43,500
Architect: HKS Inc.
Fact: Built in 1965 as a minor league park called Turnpike Stadium.
Today: Site is now parking lot northwest of Globe Life Stadium.

RFK Stadium (aka DC Stadium 1962–1968): 1962–1971
Dimensions: L—335, LC—380, C—410, RC—380, R—335
Capacity: 46,300
Architect: George L Dahl, Osborn Engineering

Griffith Stadium: 1961
Dimensions: L—388, LC—391, C—421, RC—373, R—320
Capacity: 28,600
Architect: Osborn Engineering

Houston Astros: 2013–Present

Previously . . .

Houston Astros   National League   1965–2012
Houston Colt 45's   National League   1962–1964

Previous Stadiums

Astrodome: 1965–1999
Dimensions: L—340, LC—390, C—405, RC—390, R—340
Capacity: 54,800
Architect: Herman Lloyd & W. B. Morgan & Wilson, Morris, Crain, & Anderson
Fact: Shared with NFL Oilers between 1968 and 1997.

Colt Stadium: 1962–1964
Dimensions: L—360, LC—395, C—420, RC—395, R—360
Capacity: 33,000
Today: Site is now parking lot northwest of Astrodome. Park was dismantled and rebuilt in Gomez Palacio, Mexico.

Kansas City Royals: 1969–Present

Previous Stadium

Municipal Stadium: 1969–1972
Dimensions: L—330, LC—375, C—421, RC—382, R—353
Capacity: 35,500
Architect: Osborn Engineering

Seattle Mariners: 1977–Present

Previous Stadiums

Kingdome: 1977–1999
Dimensions: L—331, LC—355, C—405, RC—340, R—312
Capacity: 60,000
Architect: Naramore, Bain, Brady and Johanson
Today: Site is now CenturyLink Stadium, home for NFL Seahawks.

Toronto Blue Jays: 1977–Present

Previous Stadiums

Exhibition Stadium: 1977–1989
Dimensions: L—330, LC—375, C—400, RC—375, R—330
Capacity: 43,700
Architect: Marini and Morris
Fact: Infield and outfield were Astroturf, and, to accommodate a football field, there was no seating—only grass—beyond the right field fence.
Today: Site is now portion of south parking lot and part of BMO Field.

Tampa Bay Rays: 2008–Present

Previously . . .
Tampa Bay Devil Rays   American League   1998–2007

9

Buy Me Some . . .

The Total Experience—Food, Fungoes, and Fun

For many fans (such as yours truly), the experience at the ballpark is all about the game on the field. At the most, a couple of hot dogs and beers are all I really require for the span of the contest—perhaps I'm a purist or just easily pleased.

However, others who attend the game need more than that (and that's OK, as long as they don't drip the orange cheese from their nacho platter down my back). As such, major league ballparks have gone to great lengths to enhance the experience for those who pass through their turn styles.

There's just about every kind of food—gourmet and not-so-gourmet, fan-player interaction, high-class (and high-priced) skyboxes and luxury suites, as well as amusement rides and other activities, for those who can't tell Mike Trout from a rainbow trout.

Who Wants One, How Many?

It's a standard cry from the purveyors of tubular meat surrounded by bread at the ballpark, and hot dogs are only the beginning for those starving fans who

Harry Stevens, 1911.

want to eat. And, historically speaking, hot dogs and beer were the first food items sold at ball games back in the 1870s and 1880s (most likely, beer, then hot dogs).

It's believed that the hot dog was first sold at a St. Louis Browns game in 1893, but the facts are somewhat vague. Others claim the inspiration first struck Harry Stevens some eight years later, when he sold German sausages stuffed into long buns at the Polo Grounds in 1901.

By 1908, a Chicago-based snack of peanuts, molasses, and popcorn known as Cracker Jacks was being sold in wax bags at ballparks. In 1914 and 1915, the company created a series of trading cards. Known as the E-145-1 and E-145-2 sets, they totaled 320 and featured Cracker Jack Ball Players like Christy Mathewson, Ty Cobb, and Napoleon Lajoie.

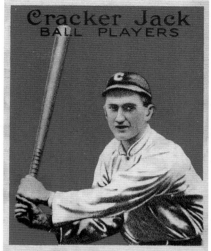

JOE JACKSON, CLEVELAND - AMERICANS

1914 Cracker Jack card, Joe Jackson.

The food was popular enough to be immortalized in the Norworth and Von Tilzer song "Take Me Out to the Ball Game." They included peanuts as a separate lyric offering, and, combined with hot dogs, these three foods all made perfect sense—they were (and still are) salty, prompting consumers to crave (and purchase) beer and soda. (Always remember, baseball is a sport and it's a business.)

During the times of Babe Ruth and Lou Gehrig, refrigeration was still sorely lacking for sodas, beer, and ice cream. While bottles of soda and beer could be kept on ice, it was likely that the average ballpark beverage was not cold like those found in the hands of today's fans.

In the 1940s and 1950s, concession stands, as well as mobile and convenient vendors, offered a number of items for consumption at a game. For example, in 1951, a ballpark menu offered a red hot for a mere twenty cents, a burger for twenty-five cents, peanuts or Cracker Jacks for a dime, and a beer for thirty-five cents.

Cigars and cigarettes were standard (and still deadly, but nobody knew it then), costing fifteen cents for a cheroot and twenty-five cents for a pack of smokes. And if your bum needed a chum, seat cushions could be rented for ten cents.

In another instance, Shibe Park in Philadelphia offered hungry fans a wider variety of food and drink, with sodas for fifteen cents, a fish cake sandwich for twenty cents, a BBQ pork sandwich for twenty-five cents, and a ham and cheese sandwich for a costly fifty cents. Oh, and a pack of chewing gum was five cents.

Wrigley Field in Chicago had its own specialties. During the 1950s through the 1970s, spicy, hardwood-smoked Oscar Mayer Smokie Links, as well as pizza (eventually tacked onto third baseman and prominent Italian American Ron Santo), were popular items at the concession stands around the park.

In Los Angeles, one could find the Dodger Dog, introduced in 1962. The mighty foot-long wiener (actually only ten inches, but we know everyone likes to exaggerate) became a popular staple at the stadium (choosing between grilled or boiled). So popular, in fact, Dodger Stadium became known as the top purveyor of red hots—in 2005, they sold more than 1.7 million wienies (one could retire with the mustard contract there).

Not every food promotion in baseball was a rousing success—witness the "Ten-Cent Beer Night." While it probably sounded like a good idea when first brought up around the Cleveland Indians marketing offices in 1974, it was a nightmarish fiasco when it became reality on June 4.

New York hot dog stand near ball park, 1906.

Actually, the Indians had a nickel-beer night in 1971 that was very calm and successful. Unfortunately, the repeat promotion did not provide repeat results. By the late innings, the field was strewn with exploding cherry bombs, streaking fans, flashing females, and all three bases were stolen (and not by the players). Visiting outfielder Jeff Burroughs had his hat swiped, and the umps were attacked.

Umpire crew leaves the field after 10-Cent Beer Nite in Cleveland, 1974.

Needless to say, the Indians forfeited the game to the Texas Rangers that night.

Today, diversity and demographics rule the ballpark kitchens, with foods for just about everyone. If—in your wildest gustatory dreams—you can imagine it, you can probably find it at the stadium (but beware—you might not always like what you find).

At a Rockies game, one can partake of Rocky Mountain oysters—yes, yes, bull testes—along with a large assortment of beer (frankly, there isn't a large enough assortment of beer in the world to convince me to taste that menu item).

A visit to Milwaukee's Miller Park will bring out the beast—actually, The Beast. It's a foot-long (bragging again?) bratwurst sausage, split lengthwise and stuffed with a grilled hot dog. Then the duo is wrapped in bacon, topped with sauerkraut and grilled onions, and shoved into a pretzel bun. Calorie count? Just a shade over 1,100. And at thirteen bucks, it's a bargain—as long as you take a week to eat it.

What's yer beef? At Yankee Stadium, it's the USDA Prime Steak sandwich, served by Lobel's. The upscale steakhouse has been serving the best in beef for more than 150 years, and, at fifteen dollars for slices of prime steak on a cheesy bun, they'll likely be around for another 150.

The Seattle Mariners have a unique offering called Ichiroll (perhaps someone should let them know that the Nippon outfield star for whom the sushi is named left the team several years ago). The tuna and cucumber roll indulges the ongoing fascination with Asian foods and trendy sushi.

1950s Concession stand: movie comic and baseball fan Joe E. Brown offers a snack to his friends.

For a taste of Southern hospitality, nothing beats The Hammer from the Atlanta Braves—appropriately named for Hammerin' Hank Aaron. It's breakfast, lunch, dinner—and a midnight snack—all in one. Surround a Southern-fried chicken breast filet with two crispy waffles, add fried onion straws, apple-smoked bacon, pepper jack cheese, and maple mayo. (Cots for a nap are optional.)

Philadelphia is famous in epicurean lore for its Philly cheese steak sandwich. At Citizens Bank Park, the item is kicked up a notch (foodies, you get it) with the Schmitter. Named for Hall of Famer Mike Schmidt, the sandwich combines top-quality sliced steak with cheese, then adds grilled salami, fried onions, tomatoes, and the not-so-secret sauce (basically, thousand island dressing). Pile it all on a big Kaiser roll, and then the park piles you on a cart and rolls you away.

Deep in the heartburn of Texas is Minute Maid Park, where the Houston Astros have—natch—the BBQ-stuffed baked potato. They start with a large spud, split it open, and then stuff it with BBQ pulled pork, shredded cheese, green onions, jalapeño peppers, butter, and sour cream. Yum.

At PETCO Park in San Diego, one can watch the Padres and partake of the Rubio Fish Taco—resulting in believing one has died and gone to Heaven (or at least, Rubio's Mexican Grill). Simple but satisfying, the fish is beer-battered and assembled on a tortilla with shredded cabbage, salsa, and a white sauce of mayo and yogurt.

Burp. (Pardon me.)

Dodger Dog bobblehead.

Of course, all this fine food and drink comes at a cost. Maybe the hot dog and beer of years ago were (literally) a nickel-and-dime operation, but today's concessions can lead to an expensive investment.

Not counting the previously mentioned gourmet sandwiches that can cost upwards of fifteen bucks and more, the costliest hot dog can be found at Citi Field. Figure on paying $6.25 for a red hot while watching the Mets. On the other hand, way up in the right field stands at the Great American Ball Park in Cincinnati, you can find a hot dog, soda, and peanuts for one dollar each (yes, really!)

The cost of a frosty beer ranges from eight dollars at a Miami Marlins game (one small, please), to half that price for a similar size in Cleveland or Phoenix. Maybe you can't tell the players without a program, but count on shelling out five dollars for one at eleven different MLB stadiums across the country (luckily, they are free at eleven more).

Overall, where can you see a cheap major league game, or where will you break the bank watching America's pastime? The Fan Cost Index (FCI) takes the following items into account for a family of four: Four average tickets to a game, two small brews (for Mom and Dad, sorry kids), four sodas, four red hots, parking for one vehicle, two programs, and two adult-sized team caps.

Based on those components, the major league baseball average in 2014 was $212.46. On the high side, the experience at Boston's Fenway Park would set you back $350.78 (after, certainly, stopping off at the bank for a loan). Of course, you could compare that to the average cost of ONE ticket to a 2014 Rolling Stones concert—$642.00 (no beer, no hot dog, no cap, just to sit down—or stand, once the 72-year-old Jagger started to strut his stuff), and the trip to see the Red Sox suddenly doesn't sound so costly.

On the other side of the coin, according to the 2014 FCI, a family of four can sit in air-conditioned comfort and watch the Arizona Diamondbacks for just $126.89. That's about a third of the Red Sox figure, and both teams have won the World Series at least once in the last fifteen years or so.

Early to Bat, Early to Write

Here's where I get to sound like the cranky middle-aged man that I've become. In the old days (aka the sixties and seventies), one collected baseball cards because they were cool looking, and when held against your rotating bicycle spokes with a clothespin, they made a real neat sound. In those days (he said, frowning in a grumpy manner), there were only three card manufacturers—Topps, Fleer, and DonRuss.

Then the wheels came off the wagon, and baseball cards became an investment option. Everyone with a printing press had their own line of baseball trading cards, and the market was glutted with product. The result was a bull market that became unbearable—card sets by the thousands diluted the hobby, and, except for the vintage cards (not to mention the tobacco and candy cards from the late 1800s and early 1900s), values plummeted.

More directly, in those days, a baseball card (or perhaps a ball) was something to hand your favorite player when the rare chance meeting occurred and politely request a signature. The autograph was obtained much like two ships passing in the night—nothing more.

Today, it's much the same, except one is a dingy (the fan) and one is a battleship (the player). Yet you can't blame them. I have personally witnessed a young fan (or bold entrepreneur, more accurately) holding an entire box of twenty-four baseballs, waiting for a ballplayer and expecting him to sign them all. Writer's cramp notwithstanding, I also watched as said player said "One ball—not all."

Did the young fan have twenty-three friends and fans waiting for a souvenir? Doubtful. Did he or she have an eBay account? Most assuredly. Collectability of artifacts of all kinds has risen to an all-time high—but so has the desire to sell them online or at a sports show. Is it wrong to want to make a buck? Of course not, but when that drive to make money muddies the waters for the true fan (especially the kid)—who only wants that one signature because the player is someone to be admired—then something is out of whack.

All that palaver is preface to some thoughts about attending a game at the ballpark, including showing up in time to watch batting practice and (just maybe) collect an autograph or two. While there's no magic trick to unveiling endless signatures, some strategies are more effective than others.

Batting practice (something I find enjoyable in its own beauty) usually starts about two or two and a half hours before game time. In other words, figure on getting to the park around 4:30 in the afternoon for a 7:00 p.m. first pitch. But also be aware that some ballparks limit access to your seat before game time (or even open the gates), while some teams require special tickets or have special days for open batting practice, so it's best to check the club's website or make a phone call. Also, the home team almost always has BP first (sometimes even before the public is allowed to enter the park, which seems to make no sense). So figure you might be limited to watching the visiting team's batting practice.

In general, players seem to be less disagreeable in signing for kids than for teens or adults. However, patience, politeness, and perseverance usually pay off, regardless of age. Standing at the rail near the infield, or by the dugout, or near the team bus, or the players' parking lot, just might get you a signature. (Do not . . . REPEAT . . . do not forget to say "Please" and "Thank you.") Some teams will even regularly assign one or two players per week to sign at a designated location, inside or outside the stadium. But here's the catch of all catches.

Kid or adult, we like to admire players for what they do, be it hitting home runs, throwing a blazing fastball, or making a diving catch. As such, they perform feats of talent and skill that we (essentially) can't perform—at least not very well and/or consistently. This makes them seem like superheroes or (at least) superhuman to us.

And, they aren't. In spite of their millions of dollars in salaries, ballplayers have wives, sweethearts, kids, good days, bad days, slumps, ingrown toenails (an ugly picture, but they still hurt like the dickens), upset stomachs, slipped discs, worries about their future—just like the rest of the world. And as much as they should be happy to do so, signing a baseball may not always be their top priority. And let's not forget—Mark David Chapman is remembered as asking John Lennon for an autograph.

Some players are more open and available to sign—again, especially for kids. Outfielder Chris Young is known to spend quality time with kids seeking a signature. Former players (and Hall of Famers) like Roberto Clemente, Frank Thomas, and Cal Ripken Jr. were known to stand for long, long periods of time to sign for fans.

Years ago, pitcher Mike Marshall refused to sign, but with an interesting rationale. Marshall believed his skills were not that stunning and kids should be seeking autographs from their teachers or parents. And there's always the (somewhat logical) excuse of: If I sign for one person, I have to sign for everybody.

But would you like a few tips? Ask to have the signed item personalized ("To Herschel, All the Best, Ty."). The personalization tends to indicate the card or ball is destined for your desk or wall at home, not an online auction. And use a blue ink—not black ink—roller ball–style pen. Why? Blue is harder to copy than black, further indicating your sincerity to the signer. Oh, don't ask, "Would you sign one more item?" The players figure that's a sure signal that the items in your hand today will be on eBay tomorrow.

Superstar starting pitcher Curt Schilling (he of the bloody sock—talk about red socks!) reminds fans that the ballplayers are working stiffs and may have somewhere to be. They may not be able to stop while walking from a workout to the dugout—there could be a team meeting, a scheduled one-on-one get-together with the skipper, or even a desperate call of nature.

Schilling also encourages fans to let the kids up front have the first crack at getting a signature. The postseason pitching star for the Phillies, D'Backs, and Red Sox also reinforces the fact that signing for one person means signing for everyone waiting, and, many times, that's just not possible. As such, and to his regret, Schilling has found himself often not stopping at all.

The pitcher also echoes the sentiments of almost every ballplayer who really doesn't want his personal time—with family and/or friends, especially in a restaurant—to be interrupted by autograph seekers. God forbid someone asks while the player is standing, pants unzipped, at a public urinal (and it has happened).

So you better forget about a handshake, as well.

Up Where We Belong

In most cases, when we arrive at the ballpark, we find our ticket location; fold open the wooden, metal, or plastic seat; plop down; and wait for the game to begin. But for the fortunate few—those with skyboxes or luxury suites—the routine is a bit different.

Many stadiums have private entrances, or even elevators, to whisk those with skybox seats to luxurious and roomy suites. Padded theater-style seats, in front of broad sliding glass windows and amid air-conditioned surroundings, give the keister a comfortable landing spot from which to watch the game (in case anyone cares).

Historically, the concept goes back to the 1880s, when the "box seat," purchased for a premium price, kept the haves isolated from the have-nots. Much could be said for the socioeconomic class and status separation that comes from luxury box seating, but this book is not necessarily the place for that kind of observation.

Suffice it to say, where one sits doesn't affect the outcome of the game (don't even bother to argue that Steve Bartman had anything to do with the Cubs' collapse in 2003). But where one sits can affect an individual's impression of how the game is played. Don't believe it? Take someone who has never seen the game of baseball (shame on them) and imagine: What kind of initial reaction and opinion would they have if they viewed it from a bleacher seat, compared to sitting in a luxury box? 'Nuff said.

At the least, the luxury box must be considered as a necessary evil for the survival of the game. Why? Because, since the 1970s, the nearly fifteen hundred skyboxes in major league baseball have largely been purchased by corporations and businesses. Those corporate purchases have accounted for anywhere from 5 to 20 percent of a club's total revenue. Without those valuable millions of dollars of income, owners would be unable to pay the multimillion-dollar contracts for top players. (The logic or sanity of that entire situation is fodder for a book of its own.)

Seeking allowable deductions for business entertainment, these firms have been somewhat limited by legislation in the last thirty years, since they can only deduct these skybox prices as face value amounts equaling any nonluxury premium seat. For example, if a skybox seat costs them $1,000 and a prime ticket

A box seat for $2.40? Sure—1946 All-Star Game at Fenway Park.

right behind home plate costs $250, then "X Company" can only deduct $250 for business entertainment.

There's no doubt, the skybox experience is wholly different from the standard ball game encounter. The value of "better or worse" is up to the individual. Along with catered food; premium liquor and broad varieties of wine; large, flat-screen TVs; private restroom facilities; and personal concierges, luxury suites can seat anywhere from fifteen to thirty people.

Other facilities, basically amounting to exclusive, private restaurants (usually called "clubs,"), offer in-seat service, large and gourmet buffet tables, white table-cloths, valet parking, and other high-priced, upscale amenities.

Amid all of it, one might just catch a glimpse of a ball game, too.

Can Anyone Here Play This Game?

Basic Skills of Baseball

Pitch the Ball, Hit the Ball, Field the Ball, Throw the Ball (No, Not All at Once . . .)

From the outset, at no time does this book profess to be the be-all and end-all in explaining the details and nuances of what makes a baseball player so great and so unique. If I could do that, I would be managing world champion teams year after year, following a stellar career of winning the MVP award year after year.

However, this book may be able to scratch the surface of the biomechanical activities required to play the game of baseball with some level of skill. In other words—for the reader—I might point you toward the water, but you'll have to do the drinking.

It's also important to bear in mind that these are general suggestions. There are as many pitching deliveries and hitting styles as there are ballplayers. However, there are also certain consistent factors that must be incorporated into any of those activities to be successful. Ignore them, and you will be left standing alone in a stadium, trying to sell peanuts from a tray.

Hey, Dude—What's UAP?

Before delving into the bucolic world of baseball basics, a few moments should be spent on what's known as the UAP. No, that doesn't refer to an "unemployed adult person" (although Lord knows there's enough of those out there). The UAP is the universal athletic position. With it, the participant is balanced and ready to move.

It doesn't matter—you can be playing baseball, football, basketball, hockey, wrestling, tennis—if there is no

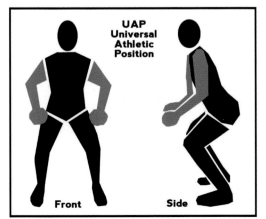

UAP (Universal Athletic Position).

universal athletic position, you're not going anywhere, athletically speaking. It's all about balance.

With slight variations, the feet are about shoulder-width apart; the knees are bent slightly; the hips are back and low; the back is straight; the torso leans forward; the hands are held out front, two feet apart and at about belly level; the head is even; and the eyes are looking forward. Voilà—les UAP.

Just imagine the other sports.

- In football, the linemen approach each other in that position, and the defensive secondary is often found in that stance at the snap of the ball (what happens after that is completely up to them).
- In basketball, the basic movement of dribbling the ball is performed in that position, and, again, the defenders take a similar position as the offense approaches.
- In hockey, imagine the players' positions as they prepare to face off.
- In wrestling (freestyle or Greco-Roman, not the head-banging, body-slamming, ticket-selling entertainment event), the grapplers assume the position as the referee prepares to say, "Ready . . . wrestle!"
- In tennis, one player prepares to serve, while the other stands at the ready, exactly in the position as described for the athletes in the other events mentioned.

Since the focus of this book is baseball, the emphasis will be placed on the UAP for hitting and fielding. But both positions are very much alike. The hitter steps into the batter's box, raises his or her hands, and there they are—UAP. The fielder gets into his or her ready position, and although a bit lower overall, it's still the UAP.

The Basics of Pitching—We Need a Pitcher, Not a Belly Itcher

Without beating a dead horsehide, balance and fundamentals are equally important to any one of the ten active ballplayers on the field at any one time (remembering there are nine fielders and one hitter in the batter's box). But the pitcher has the ball and, make no mistake, nothing will happen until the ball is thrown.

In no particular order, the pitcher has these things to consider before that can happen: stance, type of pitch to be thrown, delivery, any runners on base, and the mental state of the person holding the ball. Without being exhaustive, let's take a look at each. (We will first assume this is the start of the game.)

The pitcher stands with both feet on the rubber, not together but not too wide apart. His or her stance is erect but relaxed, with the ball held in the glove at the center of the chest. The knees should not be locked, but comfortable. It might also be a good idea to take a nice big, deep breath and exhale.

Having looked in for the catcher's signals, the pitcher now knows what kind of pitch he or she will be throwing. Consider the possibilities:

- Fastball (two-seam, four-seam, or cutter)
- Curve

- Changeup (three-finger choked, circle change, or—God forbid—Eephus)
- Slider
- Split-finger
- Knuckleball
- Illegal varieties (scuffed, doctored, spitball, foreign substances)

No pitcher can hope to throw all those pitches effectively (and the catcher does not have ten fingers for signaling, anyway). As such, mastering two, three, or perhaps four at most should make a good pitcher even better.

The fastball is what gets you to the Show. Coaches know if their player can throw 95 miles an hour with accuracy, they can teach the other pitches. In most cases, it's purely a gift—either you throw heat or you don't. Of course, good mechanics can maximize that gift, or perhaps add two miles per hour to one's fastball, but miracles are rare.

Yes, there are many variations in fastball velocity. Cincinnati closer Aroldis Chapman often exceeds 100 miles an hour with his fastball. No one can see it, but it sure sounds fast. Pitching great Greg Maddux barely reached 89 mph with his so-called heater. Despite the lack of velocity, Maddux combined pinpoint location, vexing movement, and an encyclopedic knowledge of hitters to baffle batters and earn entry as one of the 2014 Induction Class to Baseball's Hall of Fame.

A two-seam fastball means the index and middle fingers (when not being used to poke out the eyes of the opposing first base coach, who just happens to look like Larry from the Three Stooges) grip the baseball, aligned with the narrow portion of the seams. The thumb is directly underneath the ball, either bent or straight. Thrown with an overhand or three-quarters motion, the two-seamer may run in on (move toward) a right-handed hitter—especially if the grip is just a bit tight.

The four-seam fastball is different in several ways. A loosened grip places the first two fingers across the loop of the stitches, with the thumb (once more) directly underneath the ball. The key to a good four-seam fastball is a light grip and as little contact with the ball as possible (since contact equals friction and friction equals slowing things down and slowing things down equals massive home runs from the other team and massive home runs from the other team equals considering another line of work). The pitch may appear to rise, but that's merely an optical illusion—the ball cannot defy the laws of gravity, unless it studied law, which is very unlikely.

A cut or cutter fastball simply moves the grip of a four-seam fastball off-center of the seams, giving the pitch some side spin. Hopefully, it cuts in toward a left-handed hitter (for a righty pitcher), and in toward a right-handed hitter for a lefty.

The curveball—a vexing pitch that is often called an optical illusion, although physics says it's real. Without turning this into Science 101, the spin of the curveball creates an area of high pressure on top, with low pressure underneath (so expect intermittent light rain near second base tomorrow). The uneven pressure causes the ball to move downward or break in the direction of the spin. (The opposite of how an airplane flies—high pressure underneath the wing is greater than the low pressure on top and, off it goes—into the wild blue yonder.)

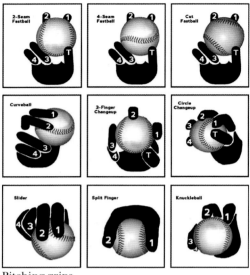

Pitching grips.

For many, many years, it was believed that allowing Little Leaguers and young teens to throw a curveball would damage their elbows and lead to an unpleasant visit to the surgeon. However, the latest studies (including one of more than thirteen hundred pitchers—more than four hundred of them were Little Leaguers) showed there was no association between curveballs and arm pain or injuries.

Yet common sense still must prevail in keeping kids under fourteen or so away from the curveball. Even with pitching limits in youth and younger leagues, throwing the fastball and some sort of changeup (coming right up) should keep pitchers' arms sound into their adulthood.

Consider the next paragraph as rated PG-13—parental guidance is suggested for children thirteen and under. Several grips can be used to throw the curveball, but for brevity's sake, consider the overhand curve. The index and middle fingers are kept together, with the middle applying pressure to the top of the right seam in the loop. The thumb completes the grip on the opposite side in the same location.

Many idioms are attached to the motion required to throw the curve, including break your wrist (not literally, of course), pulling down the window shade, and others. Perhaps the most accurate is turn the doorknob. The middle finger goes down, the thumb rotates up, and—hopefully—the batter is retired.

The key to the curveball is rotation. The more spin that can be placed on the ball, the more it will curve. Some curveballs measure a break of more than fourteen inches, most of that coming toward the end of its sixty-foot, six-inch journey. Like a musician trying to get to Orchestra Hall, the curveball takes practice, practice, practice.

The changeup, often relegated to second-class status in the past, has become a very popular pitch in the last decade or two. Meaning change of pace or change of speed, the key to throwing the change involves duping the batter into thinking a fastball is on its way. So, while the arm motion of a good changeup looks just like the arm motion of the fastball, the speed is greatly reduced.

How is that done? As mentioned previously, friction slows things down (my local post office must have a lot of friction down there). A three-finger grip places the index, middle, and ring finger across the top seam, with the thumb and little finger touching underneath. Try to increase the contact by forcing the ball into your palm.

A circle change starts with making the okay sign with your thumb and index finger. Place that along the side of the ball and spread the other three fingers evenly across the top of the ball. Upon throwing it, try to show the OK sign to the catcher (in other words, turn your wrist out slightly).

In both cases, everything else in the delivery should be just like the fastball (otherwise there's no deception). If the pitcher has worked hard and the stars are aligned just right, the difference in velocity between the fastball and the changeup should be 5 to 10 percent. A hurler with a 90-mile-an-hour fastball can expect a well-thrown changeup of somewhere around 81 to 85 miles an hour.

The Eephus pitch? Well, that's something more of legend than likelihood these days. In a world of fastballs that fly by the batter, often at speeds more than 95 miles an hour, imagine the following: a pitch that soars as much as twenty-five feet in the air, barely reaching a speed of 50 miles an hour. Sitting on a fastball, a batter might swing two or three times at an Eephus before it settled gently into the catcher's mitt.

Pirate pitcher Rip Sewell first threw the Eephus in a 1942 spring training game. It struck out a batter in a regulation game, resulting in accusations that it was an illegal pitch (denied). One disgruntled hitter spit tobacco juice at the ball as it floated by (now there's a real illegal substance). Another grabbed the ball in midair, before it ever reached the catcher, and angrily threw it back to Sewell.

Other notable pitchers to occasionally throw the Eephus include Dave LaRoche, Steve Hamilton, Bill Lee, and fireballer Randy Johnson. Most likely, the name of Eephus comes from Sewell's teammate, outfielder Maurice Robays. When Pirates manager Frankie Frisch asked what kind of pitch Sewell had thrown, Robays used a Hebrew word for zero—efes. A zero is nothing, and that's what Sewell threw.

The grip for the Eephus is very much like the three-fingered changeup, with, obviously, a much higher release point. Getting it over the plate could be a control problem, so the Eephus is best left as an amusing story to be told in the bar after the company softball game.

The slider is a greasy little hamburger, but it's also a very effective pitch. Like the curveball, bad mechanics might lead to arm soreness and injury, so leave it to the big guys. It's a speedy pitch, but not as fast as the fastball. It's a breaking pitch, but not as big and pronounced as the curveball. The movement is often side to side, with additional downward action.

While several grips can be effective, try this. With the index and middle fingers together, straddle the right-hand seam of the loop. The thumb should sit inside the seam under and opposite the top seam (from the perspective of the back of the ball, if the top seam is two o'clock, the thumb is at seven o'clock).

Increase the pressure on the thumb-side of the index finger (the grip is the key to a good slider, not wrist break or any other factor). Think fastball through the delivery toward the plate, only pulling on the ball with the grip at the last moment. The off-center spin should provide a late-breaking pitch (and often breaking windows, so stay out of the backyard).

Once the darling of relief pitchers, the split-finger has lost some of its shine, but none of its effectiveness. The splitter is seldom thrown for strikes, since it rarely stays in the zone for very long. The idea is to deke the hitter into thinking fastball, only to have the bottom drop out of the pitch at the last moment.

The grip can be uncomfortable and more suited to those with big hands, since the grip requires splitting the index and middle fingers to the outside of the left and right seams of the loop. (Some major league pitchers practice by forcing a twelve-inch softball between their fingers in the off-season. Beats selling used cars, like they used to do before the big-buck contracts hit the scene.) Throw the splitter like a fastball, using a stiff wrist and firm grip. Watch a hitter making $6 million a year look silly as he swings at something that's not there.

The knuckleball throws out everything discussed so far (except, of course, the ball itself). Forget about spin, forget about velocity, forget about location. Like many spouses and spoiled kids, the knuckleball has a mind of its own. But it's also very tough to learn and, like Kate in *The Taming of the Shrew*, a bitch to control.

Knuckleball may actually be a misnomer, with fingernail-ball being more accurate. The grip (if you could call it that) uses the fingernails of the first two or three fingers digging into the ball. The thumb and little finger wait at the sides, in case they're needed (they won't be). The ball is not even thrown; it is pushed toward the catcher, with all three fingers releasing it at the same time.

It can be difficult to catch a knuckler—because of the long time it takes to get there and the total inability to know where it's going. Baseball announcer and former big league catcher Bob Uecker shared his secret in handling the knuckle-ball—he just waited until it stopped rolling and then picked it up.

Some pitchers might be a bit insecure, so they occasionally resort to throwing pitches considered to be illegal. Basic physics tells them that a perfectly round and smooth ball tends to move smoothly—both going in and going out often, over the outfield wall. However, if the ball's cover or its stitching can be somehow altered, then the ball might move erratically and improve the chances of striking out the hitter.

Catchers have been known to use one of their metal spikes to cut the ball; pitchers have hidden thumbtacks in their gloves and nail files in their pockets. Substances like spit, Vaseline, tobacco juice, and others have been used (once legal, but outlawed in 1920 when—as noted in another chapter—Cleveland Indian shortstop Ray Chapman was struck in the temple with a spitball thrown by Yankee Carl Mays. He collapsed with a fractured skull and died the next morning).

Just recently, a Yankee pitcher (not Mays, as he died more than forty years ago) was suspended for ten days following the discovery of a large glop of pine tar on his neck. He claimed it was just dirt and it may have been, if dirt is gooey, sticky, and comes from a conifer tree. Needless to say, the game does not tolerate foreign substances on the ball—once it's found.

With the proper pitch selected for throwing, the next thing is to deliver it—like a hot and tasty pizza. For the sake of young kids learning the game, it might be time to introduce a mnemonic to arrange the basic mechanics of the delivery—STEP.

• S for step (yes, it's that simple). With both feet on the rubber, take one step back with the glove-side foot. How big of a step? Maybe a foot, tops. All you're trying to do is put your body into motion in a balanced way.

- T for turn. The throwing-side foot turns out on the rubber a full ninety degrees, Think of turning the foot from pointing at home plate to pointing at third base (for right-handed pitchers, first base for lefties).
- E for elevate. The glove-side leg elevates and the knee bends in a natural motion. Imagine a puppeteer pulling a string attached to the thigh bone. The front foot strides toward the plate, with the shoulders square and the head kept high.
- P for pitch. During the Turn and Elevate points, the throwing hand extends back (as if showing the ball to the center fielder, although he or she has probably seen a baseball before), while turning the wrist back (now the sky gets a look at the ball . . . Geez, everyone's getting an eyeball on this little white thing). At the same time, the front hand swings forward—the pitcher may look as though he or she might fly, rather than the ball. Once more, it's all for balance.

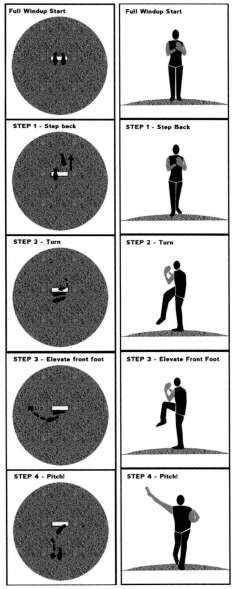

During the stride, the pitching arm comes forward (keeping it extended and the hand back) in an overhand, three-quarters, or sidearm fashion (leave the submarine delivery to the Navy). The release point (obviously, the point where the ball is released . . . duh!) is a matter of repetition, learning where the best moment is to let fly.

A quick explanation of the arm motion. The angle at which the arm comes through the pitch is called the arm slot, and it's important to keep it natural to avoid stress on the anatomy. Assuming the rest of the mechanics are sound, the best way of ensuring a proper arm slot is to keep the eyes level. If the pitcher looks like he or she has his or her head tilted, as if trying to peek around a corner, then his or her arm slot is wrong.

The follow-through is important, as the pitcher must bear in mind he is no longer a pitcher, but has magically become a fielder (the big leagues, it seems, tends to forget this). In other words, the front foot lands, the back foot follows, and the pitcher assumes a modified UAP with hands out, ready to field the ball.

Pitching, STEP Technique.

And here's an important note of safety. At any level of competition, that ball can come back in less than one second, and if the pitcher isn't ready to react, he can be seriously injured. In just the last few years, major league pitchers like the A's Brandon McCarthy, Toronto's J. A. Happ, and Cincinnati's Aroldis Chapman all suffered serious head and face injuries when the batted ball came speeding back at them. Debate continues for pitchers to wear protective helmets like batters do. Let's face it, baseball isn't a fashion show—"Those who pitch, and protect their head—come back to pitch again, he said." (So, I'm no Dr. Seuss—so what?)

With no base runners, the pitcher can deliver the ball from a full windup. But with runners on, he or she must be aware of them—and make sure they know that he or she knows, that they know . . . well, you know. To keep the runners in check, the pitcher needs to deliver the ball from what's known as the stretch.

For a righty, the pitcher faces third base (first base for a lefty), straddling the rubber. A commitment to deliver the ball is made by placing the freehand-side foot against the front of the rubber. The hands come together, the pitcher checks the position of the runner or runners, makes a full stop in his or her motion (if not, that's a balk, which is addressed elsewhere), and the pitcher delivers the ball.

Strategically, it's hard to establish a template for effective pitch location. However, if the pitcher has no worries (as in: doesn't give a rat's patoot) about giving up copious amounts of base hits and home runs, then they should keep tossing it right over the middle of the plate, waist high. In other words, variety is the spice of life for the hurler. Up and in, switched with low and away, and working the inside and outside parts of the plate, are the most general of strategies that can be recommended (not knowing who's batting, at what level the game's being played, and the control accuracy of the pitcher).

Another major point for pitchers is getting the first pitch over the plate for a strike. The advantage—more mental than strategic—of having that ump holler "Steee-rrike one!" on the initial delivery cannot be overemphasized. The hitter does not want to appear overanxious (believing what his or her dear old Mom said once about good things coming to those who wait), so the chances are very good that a good solid strike will be allowed to pass. And, at that point, the hitter is already in the hole, count-wise. The wise pitcher, oh Grasshopper, now has an immediate edge on the opponent.

If the pitcher thinks the runner at first base is getting too cocky, he or she can throw over to the first baseman. Once more, a balk must be avoided (yes, yes—addressed elsewhere), and the pitcher must not forget his primary job, which is to deliver the ball to an impatient catcher.

And that brings us to the most important part of the game—the mental part. Fans sometimes believe that, since a sport is a physical activity, the brain has minimal involvement. Nothing could be further from the truth. Focus and concentration are vital to success on the field. Studying and knowing your opponent are also paramount to success. As previously mentioned, Greg Maddux reached Cooperstown, largely due to his commitment to researching and familiarizing himself with who his hitting adversaries would be on his day to pitch.

They may or may not be gifted with great intelligence, but ballplayers must be disciplined enough to direct their intensity to the task at hand, be it pitching, hitting, fielding, or running the bases. Add in the fact that great physicality has to be included—often, without thinking about it—and playing a kid's game becomes a tall task—for young and old alike.

The Basics of Hitting—Keep the Chubby End Up

At the risk of angering fans of other sports, it is often said that the single most difficult activity in sports is hitting a baseball properly. To dredge up an old argument, and paraphrasing Hall of Fame hitting great Ted Williams: What other sport allows a player to be considered exceptional when he succeeds only three out of ten chances?

Picture a football quarterback who throws 12-for-40 during a game—it's doubtful he won that one. In basketball, how could any player show his face on the court by completing 3 out of 10 free throw attempts? How effective is the hockey player who passes the puck twenty times in a game, with only six of those passes reaching the teammate and not the opponent?

Ah, but in baseball, a major league player who reaches 200 hits in 665 at bats will have an average of .300 for the season—not too shabby. It certainly isn't easy getting to that point, with these factors utmost in importance for the batter: bat, grip, stance, recognizing the pitch, making the decision, the swing, bunting, and the mental state of the person holding the bat (last one sound familiar?).

Speaking softly and carrying a big stick might have been alright for Rough Rider Teddy Roosevelt, but it's smarter to use the right-sized stick, not necessarily a big one. True, the mighty Babe Ruth admitted to often using a thirty-six-inch bat that weighed anywhere from forty to a baseball-busting fifty-four ounces. But remember, there's only been one Babe Ruth. Imagine swinging a bat that weighs nearly as much as a half-gallon of milk—if bat control is a key, then you're out of control with that much bat.

The major league uses wooden bats only, made from hardwoods like ash, birch, or maple. The recent infestation of the ash borer beetle has jeopardized the future of ash trees, the preferred wood for many hitters, and major wooden bat manufacturers are considering alternatives.

At the collegiate level and below, all the way to Little League, the debate continues about the use of metal bats. Certainly, they're more durable and longer-lasting (read: economical), but the speed at which the ball comes off the metal bat (being hollow, scientists call it "the trampoline effect") is much higher than wood and, therefore, much more dangerous for the pitcher and infielders.

Governing organizations have started to put limits on how aluminum and synthetic bats are designed and made, seeking to reduce the speed at which the ball leaves the bat. One factor is called "the drop," a difference between the bat length (in inches) and weight (in ounces). For example, a bat that is thirty-two inches in length and weighs twenty-nine ounces has a drop of minus-three (which is the maximum allowed by many high school and college leagues. Any lighter and the bat could be swung faster, imparting greater speed to the ball. Most youth leagues accept drops of minus-nine to minus-thirteen).

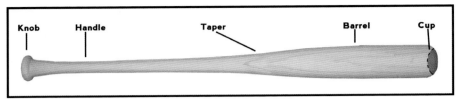

(More) Anatomy of a bat.

Another bat safety factor that looks at the trampoline effect is BBCOR—Batted Ball Coefficient of Restitution (Sheeesh! We just want to hit the ball, not design a rocket ship). Suffice it to say, it's a ratio, and BBCOR bats should be marked as equal to or less than point-five-zero. (Other details and regulations about bats can be found in the chapter on rules, so let's stick with how it relates to the batter standing in the box.)

The basic anatomy of the bat is (moving up from the part closest to the batter's hands): the knob, the handle, the taper, the barrel, and the end cap or cup (depending on how the bat is constructed). Of course, they all have a purpose. The knob? Imagine swinging the bat without a knob—it would fly right out of the hitter's hands, strike the lady in Section 104, Row 2, Seat 6 right in the head, causing the hot dog in her mouth to go flying, hitting the bald guy in front of her . . . well, this may take a while, so just accept the fact that the knob is a very necessary part of the bat.

The handle allows for a proper grip—for a right-hander, the left hand is on the bottom, with the right hand on top. That may sound rudimentary, but the great Henry Aaron arrived in the big leagues using a cross-handed grip. Trust me, the only thing Hank would have wound up hammering would have been the mashed fender of a '57 Chevy if his grip had not been fixed.

In a perfect world, the first knuckles (closest to the meaty part of both hands) should line up. In a more realistic world, the hitter must make sure the bat is not gripped too tight or too deeply in the palms. A stiff grip leads to a stiff swing—not a good thing.

Most—but not all—power hitters like to hold the bat down at the end of the handle, some even hook their little finger over the knob. It may improve their home run swing, but they may also strike out a lot more. Choking up—moving the hands up the handle, toward the taper, improves bat control, but reduces the leverage. The batting average may go up, but the power may go down.

The taper allows the natural transition, in diameter, from the handle to the barrel, where all the action happens. After all, that's where the "sweet spot" is located. If the bat is thirty-inches in length, roughly the top ten inches make up the barrel. But the sweet spot—the part that imparts the maximum amount of energy to the ball—starts about two inches from the end and extends for about five and a half inches on that barrel (with metal bats, the sweet spot can continue for another inch or two).

Like a late-night snack, handle thickness is a personal choice. A very thin handle seems to increase the whip-like action of the swing (and allows small-handed batters to feel like the Hulk). It also increases the likelihood of breakage in wooden bats. Thicker handles are better suited to longer-fingered hitters.

The stance starts with the UAP, with the bat held over the back shoulder. But before that even, stepping into the batter's box allows for a very simple action that puts the batter's balance in exactly the right position. For a righty, step into the box, take the bat in the right hand, bend forward at the waist, and touch the end of the bat to the far side of the plate. (Lefties—you know how to flip this.)

When the batter straightens the back into a UAP, the body weight should be perfectly distributed between both feet and settled over the balls of the feet (not on the toes, and not on the heels). Bringing the bat back into the launch position (hands near the right ear and over the right shoulder) will force the weight slightly onto the back foot, which is where it needs to be before taking a whack at the ball.

Another consideration in the stance is how the feet are positioned. Does the front foot lead the back foot? (as if a righty is taking a small step forward with the left foot). That's called a closed stance, and it's the preference of many hitters. If the feet are even with each other, it's a square stance. (No, I didn't say square dance. . . .) It's the most commonly seen of the three. If the back foot is ahead of the front foot (like a righty has taken one baby step with the right foot), that's an open stance, a favorite of some hitters, too.

The benefits of the three stances? The closed stance gives a slight advantage to hitting the ball to the opposite field and reaching an outside pitch. It also forces the front hip in, which is where it needs to be before starting the swing. But it also makes getting around on an inside pitch more difficult. Conversely, the open stance gives the batter a better chance to pull the ball down the line, but is trouble if the pitcher can stay on the outside part of the plate. Needless to say, a square stance gives the best of both worlds. (And a square dance gives the best in country music.)

Practice makes perfect, and the best medicine for a weak hitter is swing, swing, swing. There are several ways to get your cuts in: many arcades and fun parks have batting cages, where machines toss baseballs or softballs at various speeds for practice. As long as the dollars (and the blisters on your hands) hold out, you're OK.

A batting tee is not just for beginning kids, but hitters of all ages can benefit from getting a good tee (many have a ball tethered to the front of the plate, keeping the retrieval time to a minimum). Also, some devices attach to a fence post or other vertical pipe,

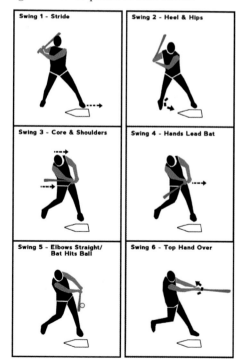

Batting swing.

which allows a ball mounted on an arm to be struck, the spring back to a ready position.

Two people can trade off in the process known as "soft toss." The batter usually faces a chain-link fence (or interior of a backstop enclosure), while a partner kneels a good four or five feet to the front and side of him or her. With a good supply of baseballs, the partner tosses one at a time into the air, with the downward arc crossing the strike zone (a batting helmet and safety glasses might be a good idea as well).

So let's get cutting. For now, assume the pitcher has thrown something we want to hit. What do we do? Imagine for the moment (or longer) the body is a machine. Basically, that machine needs to go into motion, from the bottom up. Perhaps we can bullet-point the process:

- The front foot strides directly toward the pitcher—maybe four to eight inches (depending on the size of the batter), with the toes pointing slightly out upon landing (softly, if possible). This leg is now locked.
- The back heel lifts, as the back foot turns on its ball and toes (think of squashing a bug), while the front hip pops out (not literally, we don't need no doctor here. Let's say, "Opens up from the closed or loaded position.").
- The core turns at the waist, with the shoulders starting to open up.
- The hands begin to lead the bat through the hitting zone—the bottom hand is the power hand, the top hand is the guiding hand. The wrists, however, are still cocked and the elbows haven't opened up yet.
- As the bat nears contact with the ball, the elbows are now straight and the wrists allow the top hand to start rolling over the bottom hand. This places the bat into contact with the ball.
- The top hand completes turning over the other and comes off the bat, as the arms complete the swing.
- Don't look at your great hit—Run, Forrest, Run!

Note the one anatomical item that wasn't mentioned in the sequence (No! Not that . . .) Ideally, the head has remained slightly down and stationary. This allows the eyes to watch the flight of the ball without jittering and losing focus. Hopefully, the chin has gone from touching the front shoulder to touching the back shoulder.

Perhaps, due to the hitter's foot speed or orders from the bench, the batter needs to bunt rather than swing away. Many believe the skill of bunting is lost, as the image of Rod Carew or Ty Cobb laying one down for a hit seems long ago. (Wait. It was.) The bunt, used to get on base or to sacrifice a base runner into scoring position, takes some practice, but it should be worth it.

One of my favorite memories was watching Dave Kingman—a prolific home-run-or-strike-out player from years ago (his nickname was "King Kong," if that tells you anything), successfully lay down a bunt from the cleanup position in Wrigley Field. Even power hitters should know how to bunt.

Like the full swing, a bullet-point description might be best:

- From a normal stance in the box, pivot your body toward the pitcher as the ball is released.

- While the bottom hand remains in its regular position, the top hand slides about halfway up the bat. The top hand should lightly hold the back of the barrel (the hand started with five fingers, you should go home with five fingers).
- The barrel of the bat should be parallel with the ground or slightly higher than the handle.
- As the ball enters the hitting zone, its top half should strike the bottom half of the barrel—the ball should go down, not up in the air. (Don't punch at the ball; think about trying to catch the ball with the bat, deadening the ball into the ground in front of the plate.)
- Depending on the intention of the bunt, it's best to direct the ball toward the first or third base lines. It's usually not advisable to bunt directly back toward the pitcher.

Bunt swing.

With a fairly bunted ball, run to first (of course), but don't forget—a foul bunt on two strikes is an out.

A very important part of this whole athletic dance is the ability for the hitter to recognize what kind of pitch is coming and its location. At the major league level, the batter has less than one-half second to see the pitch, correctly identify the type and location, and decide whether to swing or not. Clues to those factors can be obtained by picking the ball up as quickly as possible (no, the pitcher didn't drop it . . .) as it comes out of the hurler's hand (which is why part of their job is to try and hide the ball as long as possible).

Other indications of the type of pitch on its way could be picking up the rotation of the laces on the ball (but don't look too long), the angle of the pitcher's delivery and motion of the pitching arm, or just ask the catcher (a strategically placed twenty-dollar bill in the hitter's back pocket could help, but I doubt it).

Part of recognizing the pitch includes successfully adjusting to what the batter sees. Much of successful hitting seems to come from guessing or predicting what pitch is coming next (which I personally think is an iffy strategy at best, but then, that might be one of the reasons even the booming batter makes an out seven out of ten times).

Hall of Fame hitter par excellence Rod Carew (he of the 3,000-plus hits and the .328 lifetime average) once shared with me the following advice: Do not guess. Always look fastball and adjust to whatever else is thrown. (Many thanks, Rod.)

It begs the old story of the phenom hitter—let's call him Ken—who makes his way up the minor league ladder, sending letters home to his mom as he progresses (for today's technology, maybe he Tweets his messages instead. Myself, I don't Tweet, but I do moo, occasionally).

In Single-A ball, Ken writes, "Mom, I'm on my way, my batting average is .400." Moving up to Double-A, he writes, "Mom, I can't wait—I'm hitting .360." Arriving in Triple-A, Ken writes, "Any day now, Mom—My average is .320." The big day comes, as Ken makes it to the Show. After a week, he writes, "Mom, send me a ticket to come home—they throw curveballs up here."

Before bat selection, before the stance, before the swing; before any of the other factors must come the mental state of the hitter. Just like the pitcher, the hitter must study who the opponent is and what he throws. More, confidence and aggression are very important (more confidence, less aggression, or a strikeout is likely). Imagine what a good hit feels like. See yourself swinging properly, connecting fully, and going all out to first base. It's not mumbo-jumbo—picturization is a proven method to reaching success.

The previous batter's trouble with the curve (also a movie about the game) possibly indicates a difficulty in making quick adjustments, over-guessing, or an unsettled mindset. In any case, hitting is clearly an art, and, to borrow from the art world, "I know it when I see it."

The Basics of Fielding—It's That Round White Thing with the Red Stitches

For years, many prospective ballplayers failed to make it to the Show because they became known for "all-hit, no-field." For the last forty years or so, the implementation of the designated hitter in the American League has somewhat lessened that concern. No matter, the complete ballplayer needs to field the ball as well as hit it.

Although it's rare, a light-hitting, fielding master can make his way to the Hall of Fame. Padres and Cardinals shortstop Ozzie Smith—the "Wizard of Oz"—entered Cooperstown with an unimpressive .262 batting average. What got Smith into the Hall was thirteen consecutive Gold Gloves at the most demanding of defensive positions (and, perhaps, his unique daily entrance onto the diamond by completing a highly acrobatic backflip).

In order to properly field a batted ball . . . Hold the phone! This just in! The basic fielding position starts with the UAP. And here's an update: All fielders need to watch the ball right into their glove (film at eleven).

And here's a bulletin: Since there are more right-handers in the world than left-handers (with a ratio of 9 to 1), third base, shortstop, and left field are more likely to see base hits come their way than the other defensive positions. But that's not necessarily a constant, as pitch location, bat speed, and other factors require that all defensive players be prepared to react on *every* pitch.

As one might expect, there are separate approaches to handling the infield and handling the outfield. For the sake of simplicity, the two areas will be addressed in general, with details specific for each position following.

Roaming Charges (Playing the Outfield)

The ideal outfielder should be gazelle-like—fleet of foot, possessing a sharp eye and lightning-fast reflexes, and a strong throwing arm (discussed later). Even so, there have been some notable gorillas who patrolled the area past the diamond with decent skills—namely, Babe Ruth, Frank Howard, Greg Luzinski, Adam Dunn, among others. Still, one also has to keep the large and muscular Jose Canseco in mind—especially when he bounced a fly ball off his noggin in 1993 while misplaying right field with the Texas Rangers. The result was having the ball bound over the outfield fence for a game-winning home run for Carlos Martinez and the Cleveland Indians. (Yes, yes—that's using the old head.)

As a child, playing the outfield on a Little League team was akin to being banished to Siberia. The kids tended to think they're weren't needed (or not as important as the infielders, who got all the plays). Of course, it was nowhere near being true, but convincing them of that was (and still is) a tough sale.

With a nonexistent attention span, it's difficult to expect the young outfielder to remain focused and ready to receive a ball coming his or her way—assuming the nascent batters would ever make contact. And invariably, when they did—the ball would sail over the outfielder's head, or burn worms as it zoomed past them on the ground. Needless to say, the first and foremost skill required for being an outfielder is concentration—every pitch, every inning.

Young players often err in two main areas: not positioning themselves properly to catch the ball and letting the location of the fly ball play them.

Line drives and balls in the air seem to intimidate the kids, leading them to treat the flying object as deadly (convincing them it isn't is often tough, but they have to trust their coaches and their own abilities). They must get in line with the ball, letting the glove catch it—and watching it right into their mitt. Standing with their glove stuck straight out to the side, eyes wide shut, usually results in letting the ball fly right past it—and them.

The location of a fly ball can be very baffling to the young outfielder (also, for some major leaguers—where do you think those blooper reels come from?). Unfortunately, there is no shortcut to judging the trajectory of fly balls—that skill comes from practice, along with more practice. A coach should always hit fungoes to their outfielders, during practice and before every game. Running to catch the fly ball, the fielder should try to keep his eyes on the ball, which might require turning his head over one shoulder (or the other—not both) to track the ball's flight. Back pedaling is the "kiss of death"—no one can run backwards as quick or as adroitly as they can normally.

Young outfielders can be a funny lot. Sometimes, the ball lands between two of them, and both regard it as something the neighborhood dog left behind on its daily constitutional. The fielders simply refuse to pick the ball up. Then once they do, they hold on to the ball like it's the Holy Grail—all the while, the base runners are racking up runs like there's a bonus for double-digits.

Young outfielders must do two things: Know where to throw the ball when they get it—and then actually throw it, quickly. How? They should play the various scenarios through their head—BEFORE the ball is hit. (Oh, and make sure the ball is thrown to the base ahead of the runners, not just to the base closest to the outfielder. If the ball is thrown behind the runner, that's how cheap runs get scored.) When in doubt, throw the ball to a middle infielder.

Some other points to note: At any age, the positioning of the fielders is largely dependent on who is at the plate. Once more, paying attention is paramount—the fielder must quickly move to a reasonable distance, whether the batter is a "Punch 'n' Judy" lightweight or a bopping behemoth. Both can be trouble if the fielder is too close or too deep and doesn't adjust. But don't forget, coming in to make a catch is easier than going back on a fly ball (plus it makes throwing to the infield easier, as well).

With that comes the need for clear communication between the three (four, in softball) outfielders. In most cases, a loud and firm repetition of "Mine! Mine! Mine!" (just like digging for gold) should establish who will make the catch. Or the outfielder can yell, "You! You! You!" clearly establishing that he doesn't have the catch. Remember, this is no time to argue—someone needs to take command and catch that little white pill.

One-handed catches are NOT recommended, as it's way too easy for the ball to pop out of the (sometimes new and stiff) glove. And the fielder shouldn't snap at the arriving fly ball with his glove, like a dog's jaws nipping at a tasty treat—that can also backfire into a ball popping out of the mitt. Let the sphere settle into the webbing, then cover it with the other hand, like it might escape (which it just might).

For that matter, the outfielder should stay behind the ball a bit, rather than directly under it. You may ask yourself, "Why?" If the fielder is directly under the ball, the glove may block the view of it at some point as it descends, making the catch somewhat of a guess. Being a bit behind it allows a clear view as it lands in the glove, as well as providing an opportunity to make a crow-hop and quick throw to the infield.

Physically, the outfielder should make the most of his first step toward a fly ball, as it can mean the difference between a fly out or an extra-base hit. As once personally demonstrated by a former and fine defensive major league outfielder, a square or even stance actually puts the outfielder at a disadvantage. Rather, the ballplayer should stand with either the right or left foot slightly ahead of the other, making the valuable first step a full one instead of a stutter step to achieve a full gallop—forward or back.

The same tutor presented a simple process for fielding a ball hit over the head toward a fence or wall. Calling it "ball-wall-ball," the title referred to the order in which an outfielder should track the flight of the sphere to avoid becoming tangled up in his own feet. Moving back, the player should pick up the location of the ball, find the fence or wall, then resume watching the ball (and, hopefully, catching it). Anything more involved can lead to confusion (and a lower fielding percentage).

Suggestions for Corner Outfielders

Pay attention to whether the hitter is right- or left-handed, because the ball hit to left and right fielders does not usually stay on a straight line. For the left fielder, a righty's fly ball will tend to bend toward your foul line, moving across from your left to right. For a right fielder, the left-handed hit moves in an opposite manner, right to left.

The corner outfielders should also defer to the center fielder if he or she calls them off the ball. The outfield does not need (and can't properly function) with three generals.

The right fielder usually (not always) has a stronger throwing arm than the left fielder. This is because the throw to third base is further than from left field, and, going from first or second to third, the base runner is moving away from the right fielder.

If the ball is hit to the center fielder, that doesn't mean the corners are specta-tors. They need to back up the fielder, running to support any miscue or provide verbal directions. Even the weak side fielder (the one furthest from the play) should move to help, if necessary.

Suggestions for the Center Fielder

As previously stated, this position is the general in the outfield. He or she might be the better athlete (but not necessarily), and might have the strongest arm. By most measures, the center fielder should be the fastest of the three (think Rickey Henderson), as he usually has the most ground to cover, from the left field gap to the right field gap. In Little League, consider the best outfielder and put him in, coach—he's ready to play, center field.

The center fielder should play a bit closer in than the corners, although keep your distance with runners on base. This way, some of the balls that might drop in can be caught instead.

Should the catcher make a bad throw in an attempt to nab a runner stealing second base, guess who has to back that play up? Yup—the center fielder.

To put a cap on the whole outfield thing, kids may think outfield is a go-nowhere position. If that's the case, then just remind them where Mike Trout, or Bryce Harper, or Andrew McCutchen, or Carlos Gonzales, or Ryan Braun play.

Come a Little Closer, Dear (Playing the Infield)

Infielders can come in all shapes and sizes, with some consideration given to their specific location on the diamond. In a perfect world, the player at first should be tall; the middle infielders should be slight, agile, and quick; and the fielder at third base should be bulky enough to stop line drives and sizzling grounders.

However, in the real world, the major leagues have deviated sometimes. For example, Ron Coomer, Gregg Jefferies, and John Kruk—all under six feet tall—played much of their career at first base. Leading second sackers like Jeff Kent, Robinson Cano, and Jackie Robinson were over two hundred pounds. At shortstop, Troy Tulowitzski, Cal Ripken Jr., and Derek Jeter were all over six-foot-three-inches tall and more than two hundred pounds. Top-rated, old-timey Hall of Fame third basemen like Jimmy Collins, Freddy Lindstrom, and Judy Johnson barely weighed 175.

More important than the athlete's size is the glove. If the infielder can "flash the leather" and make the plays, who cares how big, how small, how light, or how heavy he or she is? As long as they can cover their territory, just sit back and let 'em play. While it's not written in stone, there are some general glove sizes recommended by position (an issue more important for high school, college, or pro ball, rather than the younger leagues). Shortstop and second base positions need quick access to the ball, so they use the smallest of mitts—somewhere around eleven to eleven and a half inches. Third base can be slightly larger at around eleven and a half to twelve inches (first base will be discussed later).

Wait! What's all this measuring stuff? Baseball gloves are categorized by size, measuring from the base of the heel (with a flexible tape, like the ones used for sewing), up across the pocket, to the very top of the web (don't measure in a straight line or you'll get everything out of whack).

Regardless of infield position, there are talents that are universally required and skills that need to be developed. All four positions should rely on the ol' UAP to get started, and they should have quick feet to move around their areas. With more ground to cover, the middle infielders (second base and shortstop, as if you couldn't guess) need a bit more speed and agility than the corners of third and first.

The "ready" position is based on the UAP, with one very crucial adjustment, once more with emphasis on the younger players and establishing fundamentals. The hands should be kept loose and face the batter, prepared to receive a hot grounder. It might look like they're ready with their hands on the knees, but there's wasted time and motion when the ball is actually hit their way.

Fielding a ground ball should be a simple enough task, but the young infielder has a few things to bear in mind. First, above all else—their mindset must be "get one out." Double plays, triple plays, fancy throws from midair—they're all great, but the result has to be at least one out. If necessary, play it safe and take that easy out—outs are golden.

Also, the hands need to stay down. To emphasize how important that is, let me repeat: The hands need to stay down. Young players, especially, like to play "olé" as the ball comes bouncing toward them, keeping their mitt about eight inches above the ground. At the last moment, they shove the glove down with a guillotine motion in an attempt to snare the ball—almost always too late to stop it from skittering under their hands for an error.

Infielders should bear in mind that the bouncing ball "comes up" (save for the rare hit that just rolls along the ground), so their gloves should be down and come up in sync with the ball. Once in the glove, the fielder should pull the ball and their hands in toward the midsection, firming up the grip and preparing to make the throw to the appropriate base.

The wise infielder will move toward the ball, rather than wait patiently for its arrival, like a flight from LAX. There are several reasons: Moving toward the ball reduces the distance (and number of hops), thus reducing the chances for muffing the reception. Moving toward the ball gets it to the fielder sooner, increasing the amount of time they have to throw out the runner. Moving toward the ball naturally makes the infielder more aggressive, which is what every ballplayer should be.

But he or she needs to stay low when moving, as if running to catch a mouse that has escaped his hole in search of cheese. (Wow—what a picture that paints, huh?) Traveling sideways can be done in a "step/feet-together/step/feet-together" (sort of skipping sideways) shuffling manner. Or if the ball is within arm's length, one crow-hop to the left (for the ball moving to that side on a right-handed fielder) or a crossover step to the right (for balls to the right of a right-hander) should put the ball in range to be caught.

That last movement requires one of the most beautiful sights (and personally satisfying feelings) for an infielder—the backhanded play. But be sure to extend the glove arm fully to receive the ball, because less than that can create a blind spot for the fielder. That's a sure formula for an error (and an ulcer for the coach or manager).

Once the ball is gloved, the infielder needs—very quickly—to right himself and throw. That involves setting his feet and taking the position to make the out (yes, the throwing portion of this program will follow immediately).

Suggestions for First Base

While not a clear requisite, the infielder at first base should be left-handed. Why? With the glove (a specialized first base mitt, if you want) on the right hand, and the fielder on the right side of the infield, balls in play are easier and closer to reach.

Also, with the first base fielder anchoring his or her left foot to the bag, the reach of the right arm keeps the fielder facing the infield with full extension. With a right-handed first base fielder, he will anchor his right foot and extend his left arm, maximizing the reach, but facing them away from the infield (on the right side of the infield, a left-handed fielder is also in a more natural position to make throws to second or third).

Regardless of the right- or left-handedness of the first base fielder, they should not set up too early to take the throw from their fellow infielders. Doing so—such as bending low or making a full stretch too soon—establishes them for a throw that hasn't yet been made. How do they know just where that toss is going to go? The first baseman must be prepared for any location, so stand ready, and, with the throw on its way, adjust to the placement of the arriving sphere. (Eyes open, please—watch the ball into the mitt.)

First base often finds the slowest (read: bulkiest) of the team's players, but this doesn't absolve them of the need for quickness and agility. With no runners on base, the fielder should be three to four strides off the base and back about eight to ten strides for a right-handed hitter at the plate (the fielder's individual quickness should determine his actual setup location). A lefty batter should force the fielder a stride or two closer toward the first base foul line.

As soon as the ball is put into play—and the first baseman knows the ball is not coming directly to him—he should move quickly to the base, find it with his anchor foot, and be ready to catch the ball. To make the most of a close play, the first baseman should be well stretched out and loose, prepared to extend his legs into a scissors-like position (in order to get as close to the ball in the fastest way possible).

And for corn's sake, don't anchor your foot on top of the base. That's a sure blueprint for: A—tripping the base runner and, B—inviting a painful ankleful of spikes and/or broken bones. In fact, many younger leagues (softball, too) have a "double" first base arrangement. The fielder's base is white and where it normally is found, in fair territory. But attached to it is another base (often orange) that extends into foul territory, This gives both the runner and fielder a safe place to put their respective feet, with little chance for injury.

What if the throw is in the dirt? With a lot of practice, the first base fielder learns to read hops and bounces, adjusting his or her mitt accordingly. Sometimes—also with practice—an upsweeping motion with the glove may facilitate a "nice dig."

Often, a left-handed batter will pull the ball directly to the first baseman. If he can reach the base in a timely fashion, he should do so (duh). But if the hit pulls the first baseman in the direction of second base, then it's the pitcher's responsibility to run off the mound, head toward a point about two-thirds the way up the first base line, and run toward first base. At the same time, the first baseman should feed the ball to the pitcher, leading him as he nears the base (tossing directly to the pitcher will slow him up and possibly result in an unwanted runner on first—and an unwanted error for the first baseman).

With a runner on first base, the fielder usually has to hold them close to reduce the chances of them stealing second base. Lefty or righty, the fielder should anchor their right foot to the side of the bag that faces home. Once more, the left-handed fielder is in a more natural position to receive a pickoff throw from the pitcher for a sweep tag on the runner. The right-hander will have to cross his or her body to apply the tag.

Suggestions for Second Base

With the bases empty, the second baseman should take a position relatively deep on the infield, but, once more, the individual's skills will determine exactly where he locates himself. The ball hit directly at the second baseman should be received and thrown to first.

With a runner on first, the situation changes quite a bit. The double play is now in order, and to make that a reality, several steps should be taken.

- The second base fielder should move in closer toward the infield, allowing faster access to the ball and/or the base.
- Consider whether the batter at the plate is a righty or lefty. If right-handed, then the second baseman will likely be covering second and taking the ball from the shortstop (assuming he gets it in the first place). If left-handed, it's possible the second baseman will field the ball, pivoting on the right foot and tossing it to the shortstop as he covers the base.
- Clear communication will help—the second baseman and shortstop should signal their intentions to each other (for example, holding up their glove to cover their faces from the opposing team's prying eyes, then one closes his mouth to indicate taking the throw, or keeps it open to signify the other

should receive the throw). Similar activity is used when covering second base on a steal from first, too.

Taking the throw from another infielder usually starts with the second baseman moving to the base, but don't get too comfortable. With a base runner bearing down on them, the smart second baseman needs to get the ball for the force out, pivot on the throw to first with the left foot, and then get the heck out of the way of a sliding juggernaut. The best move includes jumping up and out of the way or gliding across the base when taking the throw. With a steal of second, the fielder should straddle the bag, make the tag, and skedaddle in a motion similar to the previously mentioned evasive maneuvers.

Suggestions for Shortstop

If the center fielder is the general of the outfield, then the shortstop is the general of the infield. Shortstops need to take charge and, for younger players, they're often the best overall athlete on the team. They need to have the greatest range of all the infielders, with an arm strength equal or greater than the third base fielder.

The shortstop's position is very important, as he has to consider fielding the ball and making an accurate throw to first, while taking the speed of the batter into account. If the hitter can burn the base paths, then the shortstop needs to take a few steps in, improving his or her chances of throwing out the runner.

With a fast runner going to first, the shortstop often does not have the time to set his or her feet for the toss, so must use his or her agility and strong arm to throw, either on the run, or turning in midair (making a backhanded grab deep in the infield) and throwing while airborne.

Much of handling the area of second base—for either double plays or steals—is a mirror of what was outlined previously for the second baseman. Coverage and communication are both the same, but from the opposite angle.

For the double play or force, a ball hit right at the shortstop calls for a shovel (underhanded) toss to the second baseman for the out. On a ball hit to his or her left, the momentum often carries the shortstop across the bag, with a throw directly to first for the second out. A ball hit to the right is often a backhanded grab, so the shortstop needs to think quickly before throwing to second or just tossing straight to first. The key is to make sure at least one out is recorded—the double play is a bonus.

On foul pop-ups to the third base side, the shortstop normally has a better route than the third baseman to make the catch. While the third base fielder is forced to go straight behind his or her position, the shortstop can circle around to make an easier catch (the same is true for the second baseman on the first base side).

Suggestions for Third Base

As this position usually requires the longest throw to make the out at first (deferring to the shortstop when he or she makes that long throw from the hole), there isn't much time to think. The third baseman needs to react quickly and make accurate throws. At the very least, someone broad and bulky at third can knock the ball down, keep it in the infield, and save an extra base hit.

Because of the distance of third to first, the player at third needs to set up closer than the other infielders (also requiring quick reflexes and quicker throws). With no one on base, the third baseman should position himself three or four stride off the base, standing even or just a bit behind the invisible line between second and third.

A batter may take a full hack at a pitch, with result behaving just like a bunted ball (called "the swinging bunt"). Other than the pitcher, only the third baseman should consider making a throw to first after fielding the ball. That slow roller needs to be charged, taken with one or two hands (depending on the speed of the ball and the runner), and thrown with a side or underhanded motion to first.

If the ball is taken with one hand, be sure to mash the ball into ground as it's grabbed (the ants may not like it, but the coach will be thrilled). This naturally firms up the fielder's grip on the ball, since there's no opportunity to pull it in toward the body like a normal ground ball. Even with great natural ability, the third base fielder needs to practice this play more than others.

To start a double play, the third base fielder must wait for the second baseman to move toward the bag, but time the toss to reach the fielder as he reaches the base. As such, the third baseman is throwing to a spot in the air, much like a football QB trying to time the toss to a wide receiver. The fielder needs to throw to where the second baseman will be, not where they are. Guess what? Right—more practice to get this one down.

Making the Bunt Play (Not to Be Confused with Making the Bundt Cake)

As mentioned in the section on hitting, the bunt may be laid down, for a legit hit or as a sacrifice to advance the base runner or runners. Depending on the location of the ball, infielders have a job to do in getting the out (the catcher's job in fielding the bunt will be addressed shortly).

For balls bunted down the first base line, the first baseman comes down to field the ball, while the second baseman hurries to cover first base and the shortstop moves quickly to second base. Outfielders need to be ready to back up any errant throws.

For balls bunted down the third base line, the third baseman comes down to field the ball, although the pitcher might also be in position to grab the ball. In either case, whoever gets the ball, the other should move to cover third base—making sure to talk to each other to clarify who does what.

If the ball is bunted back toward the pitcher with a runner on first, he must make a snap judgment as to whether the lead runner can be forced at second base. Most important is getting at least one out, so when in doubt, go to first base for the sure out. If they have to wait for the shortstop to near second before throwing, it's most likely there will be no outs and runners on first and second. So get that sure out!

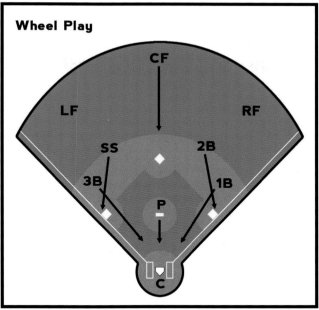

The Wheel play.

Of special importance is what is called the "Wheel play," a literal ballet of ballplayers in search of an out. Let's assume there are runners at second (or first and second), and the offense is certain to make a sacrifice bunt in order to get that runner to third base.

- As the hitter squares around to bunt, the first and third basemen rush the plate.
- When the pitcher delivers the ball, the shortstop quickly moves to third base, while the second base fielder covers first.
- The pitcher may also rush the plate after the pitch.
- The center fielder runs in to cover any possible play at second base.
- There are really only two options: The throw will (hopefully) get the runner tagged out at third (when the force is not in play), or at first base (with the center fielder coming in from such a long distance, an out at second base is not likely).

As with all fielding plays, the bunt and Wheel plays are something that require special drills and practice.

Wearing The Tools of Ignorance (Catching Behind the Plate)

Alright—at ease! Staying with the military theme, if the center fielder and short-stop are generals of the outfield and infield, then the catcher is the commander in chief. He has the entire field of play in front of him, and, even before the pitcher pitches, the catcher flashes the signs for what pitch to throw. Wearing mask, pads, and shin guards, what were often called "the tools of ignorance" surely was a misnomer. (Right! And don't call me "Shirley.")

That insulting phrase, incidentally, dating back to the 1920s, was coined by a Washington Senators catcher and lawyer (talk about winning arguments with the umpire . . .) named Herold "Muddy" Ruel. His main claim to fame in those days was catching the great Walter Johnson.

There are several types of masks for catchers, each with their pros and cons. The traditional face mask with straps used to be worn over the back-turned ball cap of the catcher. But one too many conks on the skull (present company included as an eight-year-old) led to reversing an earless batting helmet as protection for the back of the head, as well as the face. The mask itself often has a dangling throat protector (a requisite for many youth leagues).

In 1996, a Toronto Blue Jays catcher named Charlie O'Brien watched a hockey game and lightning struck him (not unlike the foul balls that had pummeled his mask earlier that day). O'Brien worked with Van Velden Masks of Ontario, Canada, to design the All-Star MVP—a one-piece, hockey-style catcher's mask that provided complete protection of the noggin, as well as improved vision.

It became a big hit with major league receivers. It's estimated that 30 percent of today's big-time catchers use the hockey-style mask. Still, some catchers find it awkward to remove quickly when needed and have stayed with the standard mask and protective skullcap combo.

Along with a sturdy chest protector and shin guards, the catcher must not venture into the fray without wearing "the cup." Even with a protective metal athletic supporter, the player behind the plate is vulnerable to what is known in the majors as "the nutshot." Usually the result of a foul tip (although also attributable to the catcher simply missing the pitch), the ball strikes the metal cup. Appropriately, the sound that follows is called a "bell ringer" (Quasimodo never had such worries at old ND). The impact often leaves the catcher incapacitated for three minutes or more, with a pain that moves all the way up into the stomach.

Obviously, the prototype catcher needs to have plenty of stamina and should be made of sturdy stuff. What's more, he must have knees made of steel, since the strain of constantly squatting behind the plate can put some serious pain into those joints. Unfortunately, after years of hard work, many former pro catchers actually do end up with knees made of steel, or some other metal alloy.

About twenty-five years ago, a doctor in Maine developed the Knee Saver, a pad originally intended to spare the knees of coal miners who spent most of their days squatting in dark caves (not sure if they were wearing chest protectors down there—doubt it). Soon, many youth leagues, and some major league catchers, were singing the praises of Knee Savers.

Worn behind the knees, attached to shin guard straps, Knee Savers may—or may not—save the knees of catchers, as there seems to be almost no valid data on their effectiveness, at any age. No matter, they are the personal choice of many and can improve the catcher's comfort, as long as they are hooked to the lowest strap of the guard. Any higher and the Knee Savers put undue pressure on the backs of the knees, becoming Knee-Unsavers.

The complete catcher is a "take-charge" kind of player, hustling all the time, positioning outfielders, and keeping the pitcher focused and on track, while keeping a sharp eye on base runners who might have larceny in their hearts. He or she must have quick feet and a cannon for a throwing arm.

It goes without saying that the position is physically demanding. In the major leagues, catchers can lose five to eight pounds of sweat in a single summer game under the blazing sun. Often, their weight can drop twenty or more pounds across a season from the labor of catching (this isn't necessarily the kind of weight loss that is healthy, since much of it can be fluids and muscle mass).

The basic catching position requires the player to squat with balance, but not just on the balls of the feet—the heels should stay down for a flat-footed stance. With no base runners to worry about, the catcher can concentrate on giving the pitcher a good target, flash the signals, and get that nasty hitter back to the bench where he belongs.

That starts with staying low in the crouch position. Some ex-pro catchers, like Manny Sanguillen and Benito Santiago, actually sat on one heel, with the other leg out straight behind the hitter. This gave their pitchers an extremely low target but, of course, could not be used with runners on base.

The catcher's mitt should provide a good location for the pitcher (although they're not aiming, per se). If the pitch should be inside, then the catcher should set the mitt on the inside part of the plate. Outside? Vice versa—the mitt is held toward the outside portion of the plate. Up or down in the zone, although down is best.

The mitt should not be held at arm's length, unless the catcher wants to catch hell from his or her manager, with the constant threat of catcher's interference with the bat. Held even with the knees, the glove should be open and ready to receive the pitch. And with the mitt in the proper location, the catcher's body should shift with it—but not until the last moment. An early adjustment with the body will tip the batter off as to the location of the approaching pitch, and then it's "Goodbye, Mr. Baseball. . . ." As the pitch arrives, the body should be directly behind the glove, wherever the location.

As the ball settles into the catcher's mitt (frustrating the batter who expected another type of pitch), the throwing hand should be kept back and behind the right ankle. This protects it from any injuries from foul balls. In the old days, before one-handed catching, receivers' bare hands and fingers were split, broken, dislocated, and, as one veteran noted, looked like "a sack of walnuts."

The cooperative catcher will help his or her battery mate by displaying the art known as "framing" (sorry, the art is on the field, not in a gallery). Framing involves receiving the ball at the corner or edge of the strike zone and quickly but gently pulling it into the invisible rectangle the umpire considers to be a strike. Many a ball outside the strike zone has been deemed valid, thanks to the capable catcher who knows how to properly frame a pitch.

Before that pitch, the catcher shows a sign or series of signs to his or her battery mate, indicating what kind of pitch to throw (often, this info is first relayed from the manager or bench coach to the catcher). With no base runners, one sign is plenty. If there are runners on, then the catcher should use a series of signs, with the second or third being the actual desired pitch. The catcher may also choose to use an "indicator," which is a signal that the next sign is the actual pitch to be thrown.

For example, one finger is for a fastball, two fingers for a curveball, and three fingers, wiggled, for a changeup. The right hand sits deep between the legs during the crouch, hiding the signs from prying eyes, and flashes the desired finger or fingers (try to avoid flashing that one special finger that can empty the benches in a second). The glove hand sits outside and below the left knee, blocking the view of that nosy third base coach.

With runners on base, especially someone on second base (with a clear view to the catcher's signs), the catcher might use four signs in succession. If a fastball is desired, the receiver may flash—two, four, one, two. Four would be the indicator, telling the pitcher that whatever comes next (one) will be the pitch. The sequence can rotate, so that base runners don't wise up to the possible indicator. To increase visibility, at night or for nearsighted pitchers, the catcher may wrap each finger with white tape.

Assuming runners are on base, the catcher stays ready to pop up quickly and throw to the appropriate bag to gun down prospective stealers. Footwork is the key for catching the would-be thieves. Still in the crouch, the ball is received with the left foot slightly ahead of the right. At this point, a lot has to happen simultaneously:

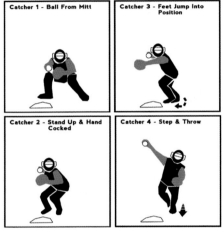

Catcher's throw to second base.

- The ball is taken from the mitt.
- The catcher springs up from the crouch, and the throwing hand cocks back near the right ear.
- The feet actually jump forward into a throwing-ready position, with the left foot in front of the body and the right foot back (both pointing to the first base dugout), ready to step with the throw.
- The catcher steps with the right foot and lets fly!
- The umpire yells, "Yer out!" (Hopefully.)

The pitcher may occasionally throw a ball low, into the dirt in front of the plate (especially breaking pitches). The good catcher must quickly adjust his or her hands and position, or the ball will skip under them to the backstop, while the base runners trot at their own desire. To block balls in the dirt, the catcher must rotate the glove to an underhanded position to protect what's known in hockey as "the five hole": the space between the ground and the legs. They hunch their shoulders to deflect the bouncing ball straight down off the chest protector, keeping it in front of the catcher.

One of the most important plays for the catcher is fielding the ball out in front of the plate. Whether the result of a bunt or a topped swing, the catcher does well to move quickly to grab the ball and make an accurate throw to first. Young catchers often hurry their throws and don't give themselves the proper position to get the out.

For these balls that dribble fair—especially ones that land only a few feet in front of the dish—the catcher must quickly move out from the point of fielding the ball. If he does not give himself a good and clear angle for the throw, it may very well end up hitting the base runner in the back as he nears first base. The catcher should remove his mask and get rid of it fast—making sure it's tossed far from the area of action, scoop the ball with both hands, move to establish a clear angle, and throw to first base.

Pop-ups behind the plate are another challenge for the catcher. He or she must keep in mind the fact that the popped up ball tends to curl back toward the field, so find the ball and be ready to backpedal. Once more, the mask is removed, but the catcher should wait until actually ready to catch the pop-up before tossing it away. An early throw of the mask can wind up creating a dangerous obstacle for the catcher to trip over.

The Basics of Throwing—It's Tougher Than You Think

"It's as simple as throwing a ball."

Perhaps that's as poorly chosen a phrase as there is. Think it's easy to throw a baseball? Just watch any number of YouTube videos of celebrities who have embarrassed themselves with the simple act of "throwing a ball" during their turns at tossing out the ceremonial first pitch of a major league game. (Among the sorry unfortunates have been US President Barack Obama and rap star 50 Cent, although his toss wasn't even worth two cents.)

Now, ramp that idea up, knowing that ballplayers at all levels have to throw quickly and accurately—as short a distance as five or ten feet, all the way to more than three hundred feet from the outfield. No wonder people go into politics or music—throwing the ball is an acquired skill that can be learned, but it requires a lot of diligence and hard work.

As a youth coach, I was constantly amazed at how poorly taught my kids were (not by me, hopefully, but by those before me). Their poor throwing mechanics often resulted in weak throws that were off the mark. Were they bad ballplayers? No—they just never had the proper instruction, that's all.

Another wayward phrase, often aimed as a taunt toward young players, is: "You throw like a girl!" The inaccuracy of that statement points in several directions (some of the best players I've ever had the privilege to coach were female), but let's rephrase that into a truer accusation: "You throw like someone who doesn't know how to throw!" (Gender plays no role in the circumstance.) Young or old, male or female, human or alien, proper mechanics can be taught that should result in a properly thrown baseball.

On Your Mark? Get Set? Throw!

Make no mistake, a proper grip is very important, but for young players, it's often limited because of their smaller hands. Still, it's never too early to get a grip on getting a grip. The goal is to firm up the ball's grasp into a four-seam grip as quickly as possible (as described in the pitching section, this places two fingers across the seams).

So, here goes: With ball in hand, point the glove shoulder and elbow (for right-handed throwers, that's the left shoulder and elbow) at the target, with the body perpendicular and the throwing elbow back on the same plane. The hands should be together at the chest. The left foot (again, for righties) should be pointed at the target and together with the right foot as well.

In one smooth motion, point the glove at the target and extend the throwing hand straight back, with the ball facing the ground (this full extension is often missed, with the result being a "short-armed" throw). Step with the left foot, then bring the ball past the right ear, with the elbow bent and the arm in an ell-shape.

Turn the shoulders to make a full arc from the starting position, with the throwing shoulder ending up pointed toward the target. The wrist should bend naturally as the ball is about to be released (this is another problem area, with kids throwing stiff-armed and stiff-wristed, which is not correct). Release the ball with fingers on top and follow through, with the right leg coming forward and the throwing hand and arm crossing the body.

For infielders and outfielders alike, it's best to come over the top with their throws as much as possible. The results will be the straightest of all throws. Various drills for accuracy can be employed, including throwing into a garbage can (insert your own joke here) for outfielders or into a pail placed at first base for infielders.

When infielders glove the ball, they need to firm up their grip and make a strong and accurate throw to the other infielders. For example, they should avoid throwing underhand or sidearm, lest the ball move in less than a straight line to the first baseman. Fielding a hot grounder and firing to first is no time to discover the shortstop also has a great, late-breaking slider.

In the outfield, the player should properly position himself to make a strong and accurate throw once he has caught the ball. Using two hands for the catch (along with providing more stability) keeps the distance during transfer from glove to throwing hand to a minimum.

Staying slightly behind the ball, he should catch it with his nonthrowing side (left for

Fielder's throw.

righties, you betcha) slightly pointed toward the infield. This allows for the throwing arm to be quickly cocked and the body back, ready to throw.

A crow-hop is handy for fielding both fly and ground balls to the outfield. Having received the ball, the fielder takes a short and quick jump, left foot to right foot. This provides momentum and the angle to make a good throw on a base runner.

It's Not Only Film Directors That Yell "Cut!"—Hitting the Cutoff

And now, the bane of all coaches and managers, amateur and pro—throwing to the cutoff man. Many field generals start with full heads of hair, only to end up as bald as their granddaddy's scalp after numerous failures by their outfielders to execute the concept properly. Just like the aforementioned "Wheel play," it's a coordinated dance that, when done right, is a beautiful thing to behold.

Kids and major leaguers alike have to believe in basic physics when throwing a ball at any large distance. Once thrown, the ball does not magically pick up speed—quite the opposite; it begins to slow down. In an attempt to nab a runner heading for the plate from first or second, the outfielder envisions a heroic cannon-shot of a long-distance in-the-air throw, arriving so early and accurately that the catcher has time to not only have a cup of tea, but to brew it as well. However, reality and science have other plans—it's gonna be awhile.

I recall proving to my adolescent ball team that a properly executed cutoff throw was able to reach the plate (or third, when needed) sooner than a single toss from the outfield. I had one of my solid fielders catch a fungo at a good distance in right field. As soon as he caught the ball and started his throw to the plate, the other kids counted "One thousand one, one thousand two," etc.

Using the same outfielder at the same distance, and an added second baseman in short right, we repeated the experiment. This time, the throw was aimed lower, with the infielder as the target. The infielder stood sideways, with his throwing shoulder pointed toward the throw. As soon as he received the throw (two-handed), he spun and threw a nice strike to the plate. Counting the same cadence, the rest of the team found themselves a couple of thousand short of their first count.

They must understand that there are two basic reasons for the cutoff: either to nab a runner trying to score or to prevent the hitter from turning a single into a double or more. Hits to right or center require the first base fielder to occupy an area between first and the pitcher's mound. Communication from the catcher should position that fielder in a direct path between the throwing outfielder and the impending play at the plate (yelling "Left—Left—Hold!" or some similar simple directive).

If the play at the plate looks good, then the first baseman lets the throw come through to the catcher. But if the receiver yells "Cut! Cut!" the first base fielder has to make the cutoff and throw to second or third base, in an effort to catch the hitter who thinks he owns the infield (thereby letting the obvious run score, but preventing another runner from reaching scoring position).

Thus, the outfielder is cautioned to keep his or her throws suborbital. A sharp, straight toss, chest to head high, will do the job in a much better fashion (and faster time) than a moon shot arc that may result in nothing more than a short-lived souvenir for someone in the stands behind the infield (and one or more runs for the opposing team). And just in case that throw gets past third base, the pitcher needs to hurry his or her patoot into foul territory by the third base coaching box. It's a good place to be in stopping errant throws from the outfield.

The Other Half of the Equation—Catching the Throw

There's nary a dry eye in the house when Roy Kinsella asks his father, "Hey Dad— You wanna have a catch?" in 1989's *Field of Dreams* (detailed elsewhere in this book). There's also beauty in the simplicity of feeling the ball settle into the webbing of the glove. But like much of the other skills outlined in this chapter, it takes practice to perfect the catch.

Without beating a dead horsehide, it's important that fielders move to the ball, rather than sticking their arms out to their sides and hoping to snag it as it moves past them (yes, that was mentioned before, but, trust me, it deserves repeating).

At all levels of the game (and many family picnics, to boot), playing catch is a great way to hone the crucial and fundamental skill. Assume the UAP, give a good target at chest height, keep your eye on the ball, and toss away.

Here's a general rule of thumb (or perhaps waist): Any throw above the waist should be caught overhand (the palm of the glove facing the toss, with the fingers pointing up), while any throw below the waist should be received underhand (the glove's palm facing the sky, with the fingers pointed away from the body). Think of it this way—above the waist, pretend you're a police officer who's holding up his hand to stop a car in traffic. Below the waist, you're lowering your hand for your Collie to sniff.

Even as a middle-aged infielder playing twelve-inch softball, I found a great challenge in warming up with my teammates by seeing how many times I could hit their mitts without their need to move them. (My best, as I recall, was twice. Wait, I think that was how many hits I had that season.). Seriously, having a catch is fun and useful, but turning the activity into a challenging game is more fun and more useful.

However, there's nothing more frustrating than trying to catch the incoming sphere with a brand new, just-out-of-the-plastic-bag glove. It's always stiffer than my knees in the morning and never closes, like the convenience stores in the neighborhood. A properly broken-in glove can literally be the difference between a win and a loss for your team.

Many mitt makers claim their products are "pre broken-in," but they're seldom if ever in an immediate usable condition. It's the owner's responsibility to break in the glove, and, if done correctly and taken care of, they can last for decades.

It seems that for every player, at every level, there's a unique way to break in their glove, some more effective than others. I had one friend who soaked his new mitt in motor oil (10W-30, but it didn't matter. It was not very successful, and he always smelled like a Buick.). I had another pal who got the mitt into a closed position and ran over it, back and forth, with the family car (more useful, but he was always late for dates).

Personally, I had the best success with the following procedure:

- Slather the inside of the glove with a foam-type shaving cream (I never tried the gel, but that might work, too).
- Rub or massage it in until the bubbles are absorbed into the leather.
- Place a ball in the pocket, wrap the entire package tight with a shoestring, and stick it somewhere until the spring.

The last action is a very common method to break in a glove, but I found the additional steps to be more effective. Some major leaguers have taken to sticking their mitts (leather, not flesh) into their microwave for less than a minute. Time is of the essence, as any longer will ruin the glove. Maybe major leaguers get their equipment for free, but the rest of us shell out anywhere from $25 to $250-plus for a good glove. Mitt conditioning should be a "no nuke" practice.

In the end, the best (and most beneficial) way for the user is to play catch . . . play catch . . . play catch.

White Ball, Black Players

Baseball's Negro Leagues

Keeping Your Head . . . in the Game

Despite the fact that the Emancipation Proclamation, along with the Thirteenth, Fourteenth, and Fifteenth Amendments to the US Constitution, ensured freedom and equality to blacks in America, those provisions were largely confined to the paper on which they were printed. Like many other sides of nineteenth-century culture, baseball maintained a "whites-only" attitude.

At the time, most of American society was surrounded by multiple instances of the "separate but equal" doctrine. It was a tenet that allowed that African Americans be provided with their own public facilities (such as restrooms, waiting rooms, transportation, etc.), keeping them segregated from whites—as long as the facilities were equivalent (they seldom, if ever, were). Black baseball was no different.

As pointed out in the chapter on early baseball, much of the game in the beginning was largely a social event, based on local teams assembled from local residents. As such, just as blacks and whites maintained their own urban areas and neighborhoods, so baseball was naturally played within its own cultural districts.

Historically speaking, the first noted game between two black teams occurred in New York, before the start of the Civil War. On November 15, 1859 (must have been a cold one), the Weeksville Unknowns (from the borough of Brooklyn) faced off against the Henson Club of Jamaica (a section of Queens, not the tropical Caribbean island). Despite the football-like final score of 54 to 43, this was indeed baseball, and the Henson team was the victor.

In 1867, an all-black baseball club called the Philadelphia Pythians—recognized as a top-echelon team and led by Octavius Catto—sought membership with the

Pythians' Octavius Catto.

Scoresheet from 1867 game between Philadelphia Pythians and Washington Mutuals.

National Association of Base Ball Players, the major amateur organization of more than four hundred teams. The Pythians were unceremoniously refused admittance, as the NABBP questioned the quality of their character (perhaps begging the comment of the great wit Groucho Marx, who once observed that he would never want to be part of a club that would have him as a member). The die was cast for black baseball players, although some slipped across the segregation border in the coming decades.

A man named John "Bud" Fowler is noted as the first black to play professionally, starting in 1874 and moving from team to team, mostly as a second baseman. But more attention is paid to Moses Fleetwood Walker, catcher and leadoff hitter for the Oberlin College team in 1878. His baseball skills were so good, Walker found himself recruited by the University of Michigan (and to where he subsequently transferred).

He was playing professionally by 1882, eventually joining the Toledo Blue Stockings of the American Association. Walker was regarded as a fine catcher (in the days when the only protective equipment was a mask and a slightly padded glove) and excellent hitter.

Make no mistake, the handful of black players who played on professional teams met with prejudice and hatred in many ways. Teammates went out of their way to get their own black players charged with errors. Along the base paths, black infielders were forced to wear wooden shin guards to avoid getting spiked by runners. At the plate (decades before protective helmets or RoboCop-like elbow guards), black players might as well have had a bull's-eye painted on their

John "Bud" Fowler, 1880s.

Moses Fleetwood Walker, 1880s.

ribcage or the side of their skull, as pitchers constantly came inside—far, far inside.

An unfortunate incident in 1883 set the table for a later event that would signal nearly sixty-four years of an unwritten agreement, keeping some of the game's greatest players from reaching their full and fair potential. On August 10, the Toledo team showed up to play the Chicago White Stockings, a major league team in the National League, for an exhibition game.

The Chicago team was led by player-manager Cap Anson, a run-producing first baseman—and outspoken racial bigot. Even though Walker was not scheduled to play, since he had an injured hand, Anson loudly averred that his team would not take the field against an opponent with a black player on the roster. (Newspaper accounts from the day included quotes, but here's no need to cite them here. Suffice it to say, Anson used the most common insulting appellation for an African American.)

Calling Anson's bluff, Walker was then announced as part of the lineup and Anson backed off, agreeing to play this time, "but won't play never no more with the (black man) in." (Nice grammar, Cap.)

Almost four years later, those same Chicago White Stockings (with the same Cap Anson) had another exhibition game, this time with the Newark Little Giants. The Giants happened to have a black catcher (the same Moses Walker), along with a fine black pitcher named George Stovey. This time around, Anson stood firmly in his bias until the White Stockings took the field, with Walker and Stovey finally sitting out the game on July 14, 1887.

That was basically it—the major league owners quietly agreed (though it was never written into the rules) that blacks would not be signed to contracts to play baseball. The decision would stand until April 1947, when Jackie Robinson and Branch Rickey wrote a new page in the history books.

That's OK, We Can Play Just as Well on Our Own . . .

As early as 1882, complete teams of black players were playing baseball for pay. But in the summer of 1885, an all-black team drawn from the wait staff of a Long Island, New York, resort called the Argyle Hotel became entertainment for guests at the inn. First called the Athletics, then the Cuban Giants, they moved south when the summer ended, playing

ADRIAN C. ANSON.
ALLEN & GINTER'S
RICHMOND. Cigarettes. VIRGINIA

Cigarette card with Cap Anson, 1887 Chicago White Stockings.

1885 Cuban Giants.

ball in Florida on a salaried basis. They remained together until 1899, winning championships at many levels.

A group of six teams of all-black players banded together in May 1887. As an initial attempt to create a league of black teams, the National Colored Base Ball League was less than successful. It lasted a mere two weeks, as poor attendance forced the league to fold.

Bud Fowler—previously noted as the first professional black player—assembled the Page Fence Giants in 1895 (not surprisingly, sponsored by a Michigan wire fence company). The team traveled in style, having their own private railroad coach with which they moved from town to town (conveniently, the combination sleeper/dining car sidestepped the issue of segregated lodging and eateries).

Going up against the Cuban Giants in 1896 for a fifteen-game series, the Fence Giants won ten of those games and established themselves at the time as the best team in black baseball. If there were any doubts, they were quickly kiboshed the next year when the Fence Giants won an amazing eighty-two games in a row, finishing the 1897 season with a record of 125 wins and just 12 losses.

But the Fence Giants fell as quickly as they rose, coming apart in 1898 and much of the team moving to the Chicago Columbia Giants for 1899.

Heading into the Twentieth Century—Separate but Equal

In 1896, the US Supreme Court ruled that the practice of "separate but equal" was acceptable racial treatment, as stated in the landmark *Plessy v. Ferguson* decision. That still didn't stop the efforts of one club owner from trying to slip a top black player into the majors.

Rube Foster, 1910.

John McGraw, co-owner and manager of the Baltimore Orioles in the new and upstart American League in 1901, found a Cherokee Indian named Tokohama at a Hot Springs, Arkansas, resort. He could hit like thunder; he could field with the grace of a gazelle; he could run like the wind. He could also lie like a rug—Tokohama was actually Charlie Grant, a great black second baseman who, with the help of McGraw, created the fake Native American alter ego. The ruse was quickly discovered, and Grant never made it to the Orioles.

The Cuban Giants came under new ownership and were renamed the Cuban X Giants. Like many black teams, a defined lack of structure lead to much barnstorming and—at best—regional organization that included teams like the Cuban X Giants, along with the powerhouse club, the Philadelphia Giants, and the Brooklyn Royal Giants (lotsa Giants teams—it must have been confusing).

Around that time, a man named Andrew "Rube" Foster emerged, leaving a major mark on the development of black baseball. Often called "The Father of Negro Baseball," Foster pitched for the X Giants starting in 1903, and his reputation quickly spread among all of baseball—including the major leagues. Seen in exhibition and barnstorming games, Foster earned the highest of praise from the likes of the Cubs' Frank Chance and the Pirates' Honus Wagner.

Assuming the role of player-manager in 1910, Foster assembled his own team of black superstars. Called the Chicago American Giants (there it is again), the team featured stars like shortstop John Henry "Pop" Lloyd, infielder Grant "Home Run" Johnson, and outfielder Pete Hill.

Foster understood the need for structure and, in 1920, formed the Negro National League (NNL). It consisted of eight Midwestern teams—his Chicago American Giants, the Kansas City Monarchs, Chicago Giants, Indianapolis ABCs, Cuban Stars, Dayton Marcos, Detroit Stars, and St. Louis Giants.

Not only did Foster run his own team, he also was the first president and treasurer of the league. Sadly, Foster became ill and was hospitalized in 1926. He died in 1930, and without his leadership, the NNL broke up in 1931 (although they reorganized a few years later and lasted into the late 1940s).

Getting It Together

While Negro leagues popped up in various geographic locations on a regional basis, the Great Depression kept a lid on large-scale development of organized black baseball in America. Once more, barnstorming was quite prominent among black teams.

But in 1937, the Negro American League (NAL) was formed, with the Chicago American Giants, Kansas City Monarchs, Detroit Stars, and St. Louis Stars from the old NNL, plus the Memphis Red Sox, Birmingham Black Barons, Cincinnati Tigers, and Indianapolis Athletics.

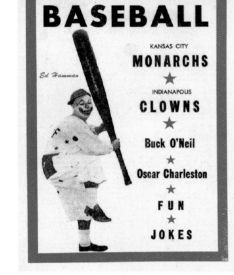

Other teams came and went throughout the 1940s and 1950s, but the NAL finally provided a structure that equaled the NNL. By the late 1930s, the NNL had teams like the Baltimore Elite Giants, Homestead Grays (based out of Pittsburgh, then Washington, D.C.), Philadelphia Stars, New York Cubans, Newark Eagles, and the New York Black Yankees, among others.

Dominant teams soon emerged from both leagues—the Grays in the NNL and the KC Monarchs in the NAL—with a well-attended East-West All-Star game every year. In 1942, a World Series was initiated in the Negro Leagues, with the Grays appearing in

Program from 1954 Indianapolis Clowns vs. KC Monarchs.

five and the Monarchs in four. The Series ran between that year and 1948.

Even though the players had contracts with Negro League teams, they often broke ranks to go where the money was. Many of the top stars spent off-seasons (or even some summers) playing in Mexico, Cuba, or the Dominican Republic. More often than not, they returned to their league teams in due time, with little or no consequences.

The story of the long-deserved integration of baseball by black players, with Jackie Robinson the first of many in 1947, is outlined elsewhere in this book. When that occurred, the segregated Negro Leagues would not last much longer.

The NNL would play its last season in 1948. By 1952, more than 150 black players had moved from the Negro Leagues to the majors, either onto major league rosters or in the minors. Even so, the Negro American League moved forward, resorting to gimmicks and self-deprecation in some cases.

The Indianapolis Clowns became baseball's version of the Harlem Globetrotters—heavy on entertainment and light on sport. With decreasing finances, the NAL had only four teams remaining by 1960 and they closed in 1962, with the Clowns remaining as a barnstorming attraction until 1988.

Greats from the Negro Leagues

It should be noted that, due to the lack of consistent media coverage and record keeping, many stats for Negro League players are incomplete.

Oscar Charleston, 1920s.

Oscar Charleston

A longtime Negro League player, major league coach, and scout named Buck O'Neil once said Oscar Charleston was "Ty Cobb, Babe Ruth, and Tris Speaker, rolled into one." High praise indeed for a black player who started in 1915 as an eighteen-year-old and played until 1941, retiring at age forty-four.

At six feet tall and two hundred pounds, Charleston was a left-handed power hitter who could also speed around the base paths. Never shy or reserved, his temper got him arrested for assaulting an ump in his very first year. He peaked in the 1920s, hitting over .400 several times and becoming a player-manager for the Pittsburgh Crawfords in the 1930s and the Philadelphia Stars in the 1940s.

An outfielder and first baseman, Charleston was inducted to Cooperstown in 1976.

Cool Papa Bell

Pure and simple, James Bell was the fastest man in the game. A story often told by teammate Satchel Paige claimed that, when on the road with the Pittsburgh Crawfords, he saw Bell turn off the light and get into bed before the room was dark (a nice tale, but no one is faster than the speed of light—not even The Flash).

Nearly six feet tall and only 150 pounds, the switch-hitting Bell was a pitcher and outfielder. Starting with the St. Louis Stars in 1922, he played until 1946, including four seasons in Santo Domingo (now the Dominican Republic) and Mexico.

A member of the Pittsburgh Crawfords, the Homestead Grays, and the Kansas City Monarchs, Bell was selected for the Hall of Fame in 1974.

Cool Papa Bell, 1922.

Judy Johnson

Considered to be one of the top third baseman to play in the Negro Leagues, William Julius "Judy" Johnson was quiet and shy. Judy let his bat and glove do all the talking that was needed.

Slightly built at five eleven and 150 pounds, Johnson started as a nineteen-year-old in 1918, playing until 1936. His best days were as a player-manager with the Homestead Grays in the early 1930s and five seasons with the Pittsburgh Crawfords in the mid-1930s.

Nearly twenty years after retiring from the game, Johnson became a coach and scout for teams like the Athletics and the Dodgers. He eventually became the first full-time black coach in the majors, joining the Phillies in 1954. Johnson was elected to the Hall of Fame in 1975.

Buck Leonard

He was called "the black Lou Gehrig," but Buck Leonard needed no nickname to prove his skills. The lefty was a sure-handed first baseman, as well as a feared hitter at the plate. Playing for semipro teams until he was twenty-six, Leonard got a late start in the Negro Leagues, playing his entire career with the Homestead Grays.

Burly at five ten and 190 pounds, Buck Leonard was known as a steady influence and complete gentleman in the game. Like many players from the Negro Leagues, Leonard spend many of his winter seasons playing in Latin American and South American Leagues.

Yet when offered the chance to play in the majors in 1952, Leonard declined—at age forty-five, he felt his opportunity had already passed and now he was too old. He was among the first blacks elected to Cooperstown, being inducted in 1972.

Judy Johnson, mid-1930s Pittsburgh Crawfords.

Buck Leonard, early 1940s Homestead Grays.

Josh Gibson, early 1940s Homestead Grays.

Satchel Paige, early 1950s St Louis Browns.

Josh Gibson

If Leonard was "the black Lou Gehrig," then Josh Gibson surely was "the black Babe Ruth." Many who played with Gibson said, simply, he was the best to play the game—ever. Yet timing and bias kept him from actually proving that.

Ruthian in stature, at six foot one and 220 pounds, right-handed Gibson was a strong-armed catcher with prodigious power. He was said to have once hit a 580-foot home run at Yankee Stadium, and some record books credit Gibson with 84 homers in a single season.

Gibson joined the Homestead Grays in 1930, spent four seasons with the Pittsburgh Crawfords in the mid-1930s, then returned to the Grays for the rest of his career that ended in 1946. Likable and easygoing, his abuse of alcohol and other substances contributed to an early death at age thirty-five. Like Leonard, his longtime Grays teammate, Josh Gibson entered the Hall of Fame in 1972.

Satchel Paige

Being among the all-time greats is one thing; being a colorful character is something entirely different. And, it is agreed, Satchel Paige was both. Playing eighteen seasons in the Negro Leagues—for seven different teams, mostly with the Kansas City Monarchs—Paige established a reputation that led to five seasons in the MLB between 1948 and 1953.

Tall and lanky at six three and 180 pounds, Satchel was loud and a showman, but able to back up any boast. Indeed, he did occasionally pull his outfielders from play and then strike out the opposing side. Paige was an effective relief pitcher for the Cleveland Indians and St. Louis Browns after the color line was crossed in 1947.

His autobiography was titled *Maybe I'll Pitch Forever*, and he seemed destined to make that come true in 1965. At age fifty-nine, Paige pitched three innings for the KC Athletics—he gave up one hit, struck out one, and allowed no runs.

Appropriately, Paige was the third black player, after Jackie Robinson and Roy Campanella, elected to the Hall of Fame. He entered Cooperstown in 1971.

Stories from the Dugout

An Offer He Couldn't Refuse

To say the early African American ballplayers had a tough time, both on and off the field, in the major leagues is an enormous understatement. Cubs shortstop Ernie Banks, always smiling, always beaming, always ready to "Play two!" had his own share of difficulties as a black ballplayer.

Cub teammate, and fellow Hall of Famer, third baseman Ron Santo once related the story of a particular opposing pitcher who constantly drilled Banks with the ball across several seasons in the early sixties. While it might have been due to Banks' back-to-back MVP trophies in 1958 and 1959, it's more likely it was due to the color of Banks' skin.

Tired of being the target of this certain pitcher's prejudice, Banks called his own pitching teammates together and offered fifty dollars cash to any one of them who would plunk the offending hurler when he came up to the plate.

Santo, a young ballplayer making barely five grand a year (decades before the multiyear, multimillion-dollar contracts kicked in), and ever the protective Italian, told Banks, "Heck, Ernie—give *me* the fifty bucks and I'll just slug the guy."

Chicago Cubs' Ron Santo and Ernie Banks at the batting cage, early 1960s.

Effa Body Meet a Body . . .

The game has always had its share of colorful characters, and the Negro Leagues were no exception. Many of the club owners came from worlds of bootleg liquor, nightclubs, and illegal gambling. Perhaps the most unique of owners was—surprise! A woman named Effa Manley.

The daughter of a black mother and white father, Effa was raised in a black family and, despite her light complexion, was a bold member of the black community in Newark, New Jersey. Effa loved baseball and, with her husband, Abe Manley (who also loved the game), became co-owner of the Brooklyn Eagles of the NNL in 1934 (moving to Newark after the 1935 season).

Effa's confidence and outgoing demeanor were perfect for handling player negotiations and public relations for the Newark Eagles. Unfortunately, Effa also

Newark Eagles owner Effa Manley.

engaged in private relations with some of the players, including Terrie McDuffie, a top pitcher with the team. Effa was known to order field manager George Giles on when to start the hurler, to show off the stud to her friends. (Husband Abe got even by trading McDuffie to the Black Yankees.)

Effa Manley was also active in social issues and civil rights, using her power and visibility to champion those causes. And, even though she knew it would hurt the Negro Leagues, Effa worked diligently for racial integration in the game. Her contribution to baseball was rewarded in 2006 when she became the first woman to be elected to the Hall of Fame.

Minor League Baseball

The Best Seat on the Bus

Life in the Sticks

No other professional sport has the structure and depth of progressive development that baseball does (although, football somewhat does it under the guise of the "college game," and hockey has just started its own minor leagues). Even though the total makeup of minor league baseball can be mind-numbingly complex and confusing, suffice it to say it somewhat resembles a ladder. The rungs lead from the ground level of the major league draft, up to the very top—the major leagues (or "the Show," as it is known).

The reality of making it all the way up that ladder is this: It is one backbreaking, spirit-breaking, dream-breaking climb. The math tells the story.

At any one point, there are only 750 players in the game of major league baseball. Unless another team is added (not likely for a while), that number will not change. As one might imagine, the competition for one of those spots is enormously fierce. So that comprises one side of the number game.

On the other side, the estimate is one out of every two hundred high school players is drafted by a major league team, making that about .5 to 1 percent. At the same time, about eleven high schoolers out of those two hundred—5.5 percent—go on to play NCAA college ball. Of every two hundred college players, about twenty-one—10.5 percent—are drafted or sign as free agents with a major league team to play minor league ball.

While the number of players drafted can vary from year to year, estimates are that only one of every thirty-three minor league players ever plays at least one day of major league ball—about 3 percent. Viewed another way, only 1 in 6,600 high school baseball players makes it to "the Show." That's about the same odds that a crafty thief has in guessing your ATM PIN in the first shot.

Still want to be a big leaguer? Keep in mind: The chance of making the big league is always zero—if one never tries at all. So it's no wonder these players give it all they've got.

On a team of one, you're always going to be the best player. As you go up the ladder, the value of your talent is diluted by your teammates. Maybe you were All-Conference on your team, but guess what? So were all your teammates. Never forget, in the minors, your teammates are also your competition.

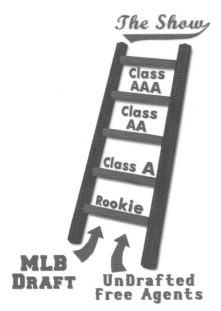

The Show

Class AAA

Class AA

Class A

Rookie

MLB DRAFT   UnDrafted Free Agents

Climbing the ladder to the major leagues.

Minor leaguers at the top—AAA level—are Minutemen. At a moment's notice, they must be ready to drop everything and get to wherever the big league team is. And that could be for a day, a week, or (rarely) the rest of the season. One of the mantras in AAA is "a player is one injury away from the big leagues." For the most part, their trip up will be as long as a snowball's life in June.

A Draft No One Wants to Dodge

The best ballplayers have played on travel teams, high school, college, etc., and just might have caught the eye of a scout who represents a major league club. Each team can have dozens of scouts—many are former players themselves—who literally scour the world for the best talent (especially since the emergence of the Asian players, along with Latin and other global sources).

The scout looks at five talents—or "tools"—hitting, hitting with power, fielding, arm strength, and foot speed. Each tool can be rated on a scale from twenty to eighty. Fifty is considered the MLB average, twenty is the low end, and eighty is the top of the chart. To be impressive to a scout, one needs to demonstrate excellence in more than one tool—otherwise, the player is considered "one-dimensional," and not very bankable.

Many times, a player's talent is regarded as being "plus" or "plus-plus." That means one or more of the tools is rated as above average or at sixty (plus) or above average by a wide margin or at seventy (plus-plus). For pitchers, the fastball is key (the other pitches, it is said, can be taught). The average of fifty is 88 to 89 miles per hour. A "plus" is 90–92 mph, and "plus-plus" is 93–97 mph.

With a huge network of front-office personnel at the big league level, scouting reports are tallied for the First-Year Player Draft, held every June. Eligible players are from the ranks of high school, upper-year (junior or senior) college, or junior college rosters. Up to fifty rounds of players can be drafted (perhaps as many as fifteen hundred players every year). Those eligible but not drafted can sign as a free agent with any club.

Welcome to the Club, Kid

For the most part, a ballplayer comes to the team that drafted him with good physical conditioning. After all, he's been playing the game for as many as fifteen or more years at this point. But now it's his mental conditioning that needs work.

The player now belongs to the Yanks, or the Blue Jays, or the Cubs. The player must be schooled in the Yankees Way, or the Blue Jays Way or the Cubs Way.

That sounds not unlike the communist indoctrination programs of decades ago, but it's nowhere near as intimidating. Simply, it's a campaign to get all new players to think, act, and do things in accordance with the philosophy of winning that that particular team believes in. (Come to think of it, it does sound like the brain is put through the wash, rinse, and tumble-dry cycles.)

Anyone who has been involved with an organization of some size (a team, a business, a school) knows that whoever runs that group needs to have everyone—at all levels—pointed in the same direction, sharing a common vision or philosophy. It's no different for a professional baseball team, so newly acquired players in the minors are quickly informed of "the Way."

Properly oriented, the young player can look forward to long bus trips between small towns; smaller and dingier hotels on the road; ballparks of varied quality, cleanliness, and age; living with a host family in the team's hometown; and trying to eat healthy and sufficiently on twenty-five dollars a day in meal money (greasy burgers and sodas are usually what's on the menu).

As a player (hopefully) moves up the ladder, the perks become a bit more plentiful. But the first rung has to be mastered before moving on. The minor league baseball system is basically (from bottom to top): Rookie ball, Class A (actually low-A and high-A advanced), Class AA, and Class AAA. There is also a Short-Season Class A, where teams play about 75 games in a season, as opposed to the normal 140-game schedule for the minors.

Salaries for those leagues range from a minimum of $850 a month to a maximum of $1,100 (for the initial contract season), up to a base of $2,150 a month in the higher classes. Bonuses, if they are offered, can be thousands of dollars and up. (There are, however, clubhouse fees and tips that can eat into a player's meager earnings.)

If a player shows promise but seems slow to respond to minor league ball, or needs to work on one particular aspect of his game, there's also the Instructional Leagues, the Arizona Fall League, and Winter Ball. All provide drills, individual coaching and teaching, and games for sharpening a player's abilities and maximizing the club's investment (yes, yes . . . never forget, baseball is a business).

For many young players, the minor leagues are all about change. For one, there is a major adjustment in changing from aluminum bats to wooden bats. What used to be long home runs soon become warning track fly outs, and the player must adapt. Also, a player who has always been a shortstop or catcher—both possessing rifle arms—may find himself suddenly being groomed as a pitcher, based on the needs and determination of the parent club.

Helmets and uniforms are provided by the club, as well as just about anything with the team's logo—travel bags, jackets and windbreakers, water bottles, etc. Bats and gloves, being a very personal choice, are usually the property of the player. Many of those items have the individual's name engraved on them.

But consider just how fragile the minors can be. After T-ball, Little League, travel teams, high school, college (for some), the draft—easily more than a dozen years of hard work in having fun. It can all come crashing down without warning (although common sense is handy at any level).

Take the story of a bunch of young players, sitting in the bullpen of their Class A ballpark. Some kids venture over, seeking autographs from these potential big leaguers. One pitcher—never thinking about the consequences—signs not his name, but several inappropriate anatomical words. Big laughs all around—until two days later, when the rowdy group is summoned into the skipper's office. Obviously, someone registered a complaint.

Suddenly, there is a brand new vacancy in the bullpen. No questions, no second thoughts, no appeals process—budding pro pitcher to cell phone salesman, with one stroke of the pen. A lot of hard work has been wasted (as well as money invested by the drafting team), all because of a brief lapse in judgment.

It's real life, down on the farm.

The Yo-Yo World

Today, it is rare (emphasis: RARE) for a ballplayer to go directly from high school or college to a major league baseball team. In the good old days, players with great natural talent could possibly make that kind of move. Consider names like Mel Ott, Al Kaline, Sandy Koufax, Ernie Banks, Bob Feller, Catfish Hunter, and Dave Winfield. They all joined the bigs without a day of minor league ball. You might notice one other similarity with those names—all are in the Hall of Fame.

Yes, there are similar superstars today. But even top players like Stephen Strasburg, Bryce Harper, and Mike Trout all played in the minors, A through AAA, albeit for relatively short periods of time before hooking up with their major league teams. Being young prospects, it's important that they move up in a controlled, orderly fashion. After all, someone has to show then "the Way."

Cubs' phenom Mark Prior, 2002.

But there is also another type of minor league ballplayer. No longer young, no longer a prospect, this player has been to the mountaintop, only to come tumbling down. For whatever reason, he wishes (or feels driven) to make the climb again. Bear in mind, we're not talking about the major leaguer who returns to the minors for a short period of time as part of a rehab assignment from an injury.

No, this player made it to the majors and then—for reasons of marginal talent, serious injury, self-abuse, insufficient attitude, lack of hard work, a squeeze in the numbers of players at his position, or perhaps unknown cause—was unable to perform or impress at the level required to stay in the majors. He might leave the game entirely, then sign on later as a free agent; or the team might send him down, with the hopes of resurrecting his career as a productive player.

While many stories stand out, consider the one that belongs to pitcher Mark Prior. He was an award-winning hurler for the USC Trojans when taken by the Chicago Cubs as the second overall selection in the 2001 MLB Draft. With only nine games in Classes AA and AAA, the pitcher joined the major league club in mid-2002. He started nineteen games that year for the Cubs, going 6 and 6, with a 3.32 ERA. He supposedly had perfect pitching mechanics and gold running through his arm.

In 2003, Prior practically owned the National League. At the age of twenty-two, he was an All-Star, finished third in Cy Young Award voting, and went 18 and 6, with a 2.43 ERA. Prior had 245 Ks in 211.1 innings. Needless to say, it was a heckuva year, despite missing four games on the disabled list with a shoulder injury, sustained in a collision with Braves base runner Marcus Giles.

He was on the mound in the eighth inning of Game Six in the NLCS, with a 3–0 lead against the Marlins, when a foul ball went uncaught (by neither left fielder Moises Alou nor unfairly scapegoated fan Steve Bartman—it's OK, Steve), leading to a continued inning. Shortstop Alex Gonzales booted an easy double play ball, and the wheels fell off for the Cubs, leaving them only a few outs short of the World Series.

In the next three years, Prior began to break down physically. He had a problem with his Achilles' tendon, inflammation to his pitching elbow, and several surgeries on his right shoulder. Some point to the workload Prior carried in 2003—Cub manager Dusty Baker let his young pitcher throw more than 120 pitches in ten games; in four of those games, he threw more than 130 pitches.

Prior never pitched in a major league game after the 2006 season. The Cubs released him a year later, and, in a series of disappointing attempts to keep his pitching career alive, Prior signed with (and was released by) the Padres, the Rangers, the Yankees, the Red Sox, and the Reds between 2008 and 2013. In that period, he played for six minor league teams between Rookie and Triple-A levels, pitching a total of just sixty innings as a reliever in that period of time. After several years of million-dollar salaries, it was back to riding buses for Prior.

No longer a heralded phenom in his early twenties, Prior officially retired in 2014. At age thirty-three and full of scars, he realized that he needed to move on. Like many former major leaguers, he moved on by joining the front office of the game, becoming a special assistant for the Padres. Succeeding in the majors and then playing in the minor leagues, Prior's story in one of many who tried to come back and, in that time, matured and learned from his mistakes.

But What Are My Options?

Other players travel somewhat irregularly between their major and minor league teams, continuing that idea of a yo-yo life. How does it work? Simply put, major league teams maintain two different types of rosters: a twenty-five-man roster (called the active roster) and a forty-man roster (called the expanded roster).

The twenty-five-man active roster is comprised of major league pitchers and position players that suit up for the day's game. The forty-man expanded roster is restricted to all of a team's players who are signed to major league contracts. Obviously, fifteen of these players must play in the minors, but can be called up to the parent club at any point (usually to fill the spot of an injured player).

A player on the expanded roster has three years of options, in which he can be moved from his minor league team to the major team (and back) as many times as needed. But this roller-coaster ride is not endless. After the third year, the player is "out of options" (a phrase we've all heard and perhaps scratched our head over at times).

At this point, the team has to place the player on waivers before they can send him down—one or more of the other twenty-nine teams can claim the player within three days. If they don't, the player "clears waivers" and continues down to the minor league team. But if one or more teams do claim him, the waiver can be canceled or the team with the worst record (if more than one claims him) gets the player.

The parent club can also "outright" a player to the minors. This move takes the player off the forty-man roster—a pretty serious action. But a player with five years of major league service has to give his okay before he can be outrighted. If he doesn't want to go to the minors, the player is released and becomes a free agent.

Commensurately, a club can "purchase" a minor league player, which adds him to the forty-man roster (assuming there is a vacancy). At that point, his minor league contract becomes a major league deal, with all the associated major league perks (and moolah).

Finally, a player can be "designated for assignment," which means it's pretty much the end of the line with that club. With that move, he's off the forty-man roster, and the team has ten days to trade the player to another team, release him, or outright him. (Yes, there will be a quiz on all this tomorrow).

And then there's the question of starting the arbitration clock on a sure-fire future major leaguer. Since this is not a textbook on sports law, we'll try to keep this simple.

After three seasons of major league service, a player without a contract becomes eligible for salary arbitration. That means the club can offer a certain amount of money for the upcoming year. The player (or, more accurately, his agent) can accept that deal or come back with a request for a higher amount.

At that point, an impartial judge (or "arbitrator") looks at the two figures and decides on the lower or higher figure. No appeals, no questions asked—the team wins or the player wins (and with millions of dollars at stake, does the player really lose in either case? Only in comparison to fair market value).

If, then, the team delays calling up a minor league player for the first time (usually about two months' time, which "starts" the arbitration clock), they can keep control of that player for another year before he is eligible for arbitration.

In essence, it's good business for the team—economically. But it's bad business—competitively, if the player can make a difference for the team in winning.

The Leagues and Teams

Whaddya Mean, You Played Class D Ball?

As we know it, minor league baseball was born in late 1901 with fourteen leagues and ninety-six teams, following the first full year in which the American League played. By the end of the decade, there were thirty-five minor leagues and nearly 250 teams. But the upstart Federal League raided the minors, and, along with the impact of World War I, only nine leagues were in existence by 1918.

In 1919, years before he added Jackie Robinson to the Dodgers' team to break the color barrier, Branch Rickey was president of the St. Louis Cardinals. He devised a system of minor league teams at varying levels, all owned by the Cards. The following year, the main minor league organization—

Branch Rickey in 1913, just a few years before starting baseball's farm system.

the National Association—agreed to let major league teams buy minor league teams. (However, few major league teams today actually own their minor league teams—most hold affiliation agreements with them.)

In 1949, the number had grown to fifty-nine leagues and nearly 450 teams, with almost 40 million fans attending minor league baseball across the entire country. Around that same time—in 1946—the structure of the minor leagues was changed, with the addition of AAA ball to the existing levels of AA (previously the highest level). The Class A1 level was renamed AA, and then there were lower levels of Class A through Class D.

With major league expansion in 1962, another major reorganization for the minor leagues was needed in 1963. The progressive alphabet classes were dropped, and the present-day rankings of AAA, AA, A (low-A, A-advanced, and short-season A), and Rookie were established. As one might expect, these changes also lead to a great deal of reassignments of teams and leagues within the new structure.

The addition of two new teams to the majors in 1998 brought about another round of changes and reorganization to minor league baseball between that year and 2001. Teams were added, leagues were realigned, and, overall, the level and quality of minor league ball was evened out.

The Minor Leagues, As They Are Today

It should be noted that while a town may have its own minor league team year after year, the affiliation with a major league team can change often, sometimes in an abrupt manner. In fact, the relationships are only as firm as the contracted time frame. Just like the ballplayers themselves, minor league organizations often

1948 Dallas Rebels scorebook.

become "free agents" and negotiate the best deal they can with a major league franchise.

So the 2013 Nowhere Widgets, Class A team for the Toronto Blue Jays in Nowhere, Iowa, can become the 2014 Nowhere LazerCats, Class AA team for the Milwaukee Brewers, if the contract comes up for renewal or negotiation.

And, like some of those aforementioned players, a minor league team can go unsigned. Which means the busy ballpark in Nowhere, Iowa, of 2014—home of the LazerCats—can become the empty and unused ballpark—home of no one—in 2015.

Currently, the highest level of minor league ball—Triple-A—has three leagues. The International League has fourteen teams that are located along the East Coast and as far west as Ohio and Indiana.

The Pacific Coast League has sixteen teams, and in spite of the name, they are established from the West Coast, through the Southwest and the Rockies, all the way to Tennessee and Louisiana. The Mexican League has sixteen teams across the eastern and southern portions of Mexico.

Double-A baseball has three leagues as well. The Eastern League has twelve teams, from Maine and New England into Pennsylvania and Ohio. The Southern League has ten teams, spread across the Deep South. The Texas League has eight teams, and, even though Texas is a big state, the teams are actually there, as well as Arkansas, Missouri, and Oklahoma.

High-A ball also has three leagues. The California League has ten teams across the state. The Carolina League has eight teams, from Maryland and Delaware, through Virginia, into the Carolinas. The Florida State League has twelve teams all over the Sunshine State.

The Low-A leagues are the Midwest League with sixteen teams and the South Atlantic League with fourteen teams. There's also two Short-Season A leagues: The New York-Penn League has fourteen teams. and the Northwest League has eight teams.

Ten teams make up the Appalachian League, and eight teams comprise the Pioneer League in the upper Rockies (even two teams in Montana!). Both leagues are the components of the Rookie-Advanced League. The Rookie League has four subsections: the Arizona League has fourteen teams; the Dominican Summer

League has thirty-four teams (a clear indication of how important the major leagues consider the Dominican Republic); the Gulf Coast League, with all fifteen teams in Florida; and the Venezuelan Summer League, with nine teams.

The Arizona Fall League, started in 1992, has six teams for the further development of top minor league players. They play a thirty-two-game schedule between October and November.

There are also dozens and dozens of independent leagues and teams, not affiliated with the MLB.

Enjoying the Game as a Fan

Personally speaking, I enjoy the minor league experience just as much as a major league game. In many cases, more—the parking is easier, and I can usually get the best seat in the house (close enough to the umpire to let him know if he missed one) for under twelve bucks. The beer is just as cold, the hot dogs have just as much nitrates as their big league brothers, and the concrete is just as sticky under your shoes.

But here's the other reason to enjoy a minor league game—being able to watch the player on his marvelous journey. In the majors, the players are the very best, and, in a simple sense, they've made it to the top of the mountain. Yes, they must work hard every day to stay at the top, but—hopefully—they have reached the level to which they aspired. Their story isn't over, but a big chapter of it is.

But for the minor leaguers, the story is still being written. Either they haven't reached the peak yet (and may never reach it, who knows?), or they have been there and are trying to make a successful and satisfying return. In other words, they're hungry . . . they're tired of riding the bus and want to ride a chartered plane flight

A minor league at bat: the Akron Aeros, 2013.

Akron Aeros, Canal Park, Akron, OH, 2013.

to their next game. In my view, as a fan, they're playing for higher stakes and, therefore, are playing harder.

Sure, there are errors, and there are lapses in memory and judgment, but those can happen anywhere. Yes, the big marquee names are missing (unless you're fortunate to catch on a rehab assignment), but they still throw hard, they still strike the ball with authority (and, often, a long way), and still make some great defensive plays.

Yet the owners and front-office folks of a minor league team know what they have and what they need to do in order to get people into their park. With the variance of quality and stability, they know there must be more than just the game on the field. As a result, minor league teams can offer some of the most innovative (and downright bizarre) promotions for fans to enjoy.

Many have the standard "little kids race the mascot around the bases" and "spin your head around a bat many times and run like a drunken fool toward the field intern" promotions, but some teams are more creative than others.

While they haven't yet resorted to "Hard Liquor and Handgun Night," here are just a few examples of fan fun done on the farm:

After one night of giving away toilet plungers, an upper New York team followed up the next year with a toilet seat giveaway. The first 3,000 fans received oval commode covers that (conveniently) doubled as seat cushions.

An Ohio team hosted County Fair Night, complete with cow-milking contests, steer-lassoing (real heifers were safe, as interns took the place of cattle being roped), horse races— (on kiddies' stick horses), and hay-baling. Instead of the usual public address announcer, a fast-talking auctioneer took his place.

A Texas team showed its generosity by giving away a car one night, albeit a used car. (Oil and gas were probably extra.)

Many teams have sponsored speed-dating nights, with the intention of getting folks together and—just maybe—building families with future fans, as well.

There was "Awful Night" in a Pennsylvania league, where the giveaway was a "spork" (part spoon, part fork), the fans were encouraged to wear awful clothes (which they usually do, anyway), and the PA announcer did an awful job in reading the players' names.

A Minnesota team gave fans the chance to bid in an online auction, with the prize being an actual at bat during one of the team's games. One fellow paid more than $5,500 to take his cuts in the eighth inning—where he popped out to the catcher.

Then there was "Nobody Night," where fans were locked out of the game until the fifth inning. When they were finally let into the park, it resulted in an official paid attendance of zero.

Yes, you just can't beat fun at the old ballpark—either down here or up there.

Baseball at the Movies

Playing at Playing Ball

Lights . . . Camera . . . Play Ball!

The love affair between Hollywood and the game of baseball has been long, torrid, and very public. Even pioneer inventor Thomas Edison made the game a subject of his early filming efforts, shooting less than a minute of a Newark team playing an unidentified opponent in 1896.

Called *The Ball Game*, it was the precursor to Edison's silent version of Ernest Thayer's "Casey at the Bat" poem filmed in 1899. Titled *Casey at the Bat or the Fate of a "Rotten" Umpire*, it was a dramatization of the verse, shot on the inventor's New Jersey lawn. It would be the first of at least seven versions of the story, including two feature-length films in 1916 and 1927, and five short films.

The growing popularity of cinema ran parallel to the growth of baseball in the early 1900s. Shorts like 1909's *His Last Game* and 1912's *The Ball Player and the Bandit*—both just twelve minutes each—combined baseball with the Wild West. Before long, it wasn't unusual to see many baseball stars appearing on the big screen, acting as . . . well, acting as ballplayers.

One-sheet poster, *Casey at the Bat*, 1927.

Pitchers Chief Bender and Jack Coombs showed up in a 1911 comedy short, *The Baseball Bug*, while Frank "Home Run" Baker starred in a 1914 short, curiously titled *Home Run Baker's Double*. Pitching great Christy Mathewson appeared in *Love and Baseball* and *Matty's Decision*, in 1914 and 1915, respectively.

Ty Cobb got in the act, starring in *Somewhere in Georgia* in 1916. Based on a not-so-original story by sportswriter Grantland Rice, the film features Cobb as a ball-playing bank clerk (years later he probably owned the bank). Discovered by a scout for the Detroit Tigers, the bank clerk leaves his sweetheart—the banker's daughter—behind to play ball and steal bases, while a sneaky coworker tries to steal his girl. When Cobb is kidnapped by thugs hired by the competing cashier, the Georgia Peach beats the bejesus out of them, then arrives at the big game in time to win it, and his girl. Cobb made a cozy $25,000 for the two-week project.

Somewhere in Georgia, starring Ty Cobb, 1916.

It wouldn't be long before the Bambino himself—Babe Ruth—brought his broad face and big personality to the screen. With only one season under his (then-slim) belt with the Yankees, Ruth starred in a seventy-one-minute 1920 feature called *Headin' Home*. Once more, the story was not complex. A simple country boy named Babe (what a stretch . . .) doesn't play baseball very well, until he blasts a long homer one day against the local team. Branded as a traitor to his town, he moves to New York and becomes a Yankee. With a return to his hometown, Babe is now a hero.

Ruth's cinematic career continued as his success with the real Yankees grew. He starred in two comedy features in 1927 and 1928, *Babe Comes Home* and *Speedy*. The Babe also showed up in half a dozen shorts in the 1930s, making his final film appearance as himself in 1942's *Pride of the Yankees*.

Early feature films focusing on the game included *The Pinch Hitter* in 1917, *The Busher* in 1919, and *Slide, Kelly, Slide* in 1927. The Great Stoneface, Buster Keaton, went out for baseball in 1927's *College* and performed a masterful baseball pantomime in 1928's *The Cameraman*. A real fan of the game, he was known to assemble pickup ball games with the film crew whenever there was a break in the shooting.

In the early 1930s, comic Joe E. Brown—he with the loving-cup ears and saucer-sized mouth—a former semipro ballplayer who passed on an offer to play with the Yankees, made three baseball films: *Fireman, Save My Child* in 1932, *Elmer the Great* in 1933, and *Alibi Ike* in 1935. In all three films, Brown was a simple man with a passion for baseball. As an interesting afteract, Brown's son eventually

One-sheet poster, *Babe Comes Home*, 1927.

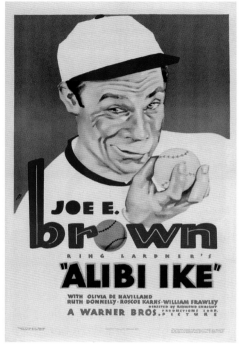

One-sheet poster, *Alibi Ike*, 1935.

became the general manager with the Pittsburgh Pirates.

Ever since then, dozens and dozens of films with a baseball theme have captured the attention (and, more often than not, the admission price) of millions of moviegoers. Some of the cinema stands out more than others, just like the ballplayers portrayed on the screen.

For many fans of the game, certain scenes and certain quotes remain, long after the projector has been shut down and the stale popcorn is tossed in the bin. For me, two particular moments stand out, both from films to be addressed in just a few paragraphs.

A key exchange in *A League of Their Own*, between manager Jimmy Dugan and star player Dottie Hinson, reaches far beyond the game of baseball. The catcher has decided to quit because, as she puts it, "It just got too hard." Jimmy replies with a corny but still very true observation: "It's supposed to be hard! If it wasn't hard, everyone would do it. The hard . . . is what makes it great." Trite? Yes. Sappy? Yes. But a challenge to always reach higher? Yes.

In *The Natural*, slugger Roy Hobbs—confined to a hospital bed with his childhood sweetheart Iris Gaines at his side—reminisces about his life. Very simply, he pauses and quietly says, "God, I love baseball." Truer words were never spoken, even if they're just on film.

The following films are a cross section of some of the celluloid offerings across the last eighty years—some well known, some obscure.

42

(2013—American/**Warner Bros**—128 Min/Color)
Director: Brian Helgeland
Original Music: Mark Isham
Film Editing: Peter McNulty, Kevin Stitt
Production Design: Richard Hoover
Cast: Chadwick Boseman (**Jackie Robinson**)
Harrison Ford (**Branch Rickey**)
Nicole Beharie (**Rachel Robinson**)
Christopher Meloni (**Leo Durocher**)
Lucas Black (**Pee Wee Reese**)
Andre Holland (**Wendell Smith**)

Alan Tudyk (**Ben Chapman**)
Max Gail (**Burt Shotton**)
Jesse Luken (**Eddie Stanky**)

With the war over in 1945, America returned to peacetime activities. Despite fighting gallantly in the conflict, African Americans were still not allowed to play major league baseball. As such, some of the game's best players were confined to playing in the Negro Leagues. But that would soon change.

Branch Rickey, top exec of the Brooklyn Dodgers, plans to add a black player to his major league roster. Jackie Robinson, a star player on the Kansas City Monarchs, is selected to be the first black player in the game. But it won't be an easy task.

Sportswriter Wendell Smith will chronicle Robinson's entry to the majors, while Jackie's wife Rachel joins them. His first stop is the minor league Montreal Royals. With a solid season behind him, Jackie joins the big league club—managed by Leo Durocher—in 1947. A group of Dodgers players refuse to play with Robinson, but players like shortstop Pee Wee Reese support him—and Durocher loudly puts a quick end to the mutiny.

But the Dodgers manager is suspended for the year, as he openly dates married actress Laraine Day so, reluctantly, Burt Shotton will skipper the team. In a game at Ebbets Field against the Philadelphia Phillies, manager Ben Chapman unleashes a terrible racist tirade against Robinson at the plate. Jackie flies out, without acknowledging the abuse. Next at bat, the words continue and Robinson pops out, glaring at the Phillies manager. Jackie keeps his cool as he heads down the Dodger runway, finally exploding in a rage of anger and tears when he's alone.

Chapman's assault returns in Jackie's third at bat, which puts Dodger second baseman Eddie Stanky over the edge. He charges Chapman, offering to shut the manager's mouth if he doesn't do it himself. Robinson then singles, steals second, advances to third (on a bad throw), then scores on a single.

When the Dodgers arrive in Philadelphia for a road game, they are not warmly welcomed. Chapman is forced to apologize for his vile actions by taking a picture with Robinson on the field. Other teams routinely brush back the Dodgers player, often hitting him with inside pitches. In Cincinnati, Reese once more shows his support for Jackie by embracing him on the infield as the crowds scream at Robinson.

The Dodgers win the 1947 NL pennant, guided by the play of Robinson and his teammates, as well as the foresight of Branch Rickey.

Afterwords

Director Brian Helgeland first made an impact on Hollywood by writing the screenplay for 1997's great film-noir thriller *L.A. Confidential*. So great, in fact, the young man won an Oscar for it. Despite the fact he wasn't much of a baseball fan, Helgeland soon met with Rachel Robinson, the widow of the Dodger great. They agreed that the seminal year of 1947 would be the focus of the proposed biopic, and Helgeland was in as director.

Advance one-sheet poster, 42, 2013.

After bringing in Chadwick Boseman, a young actor with ten years of TV roles—and more inclined to play basketball than baseball—to play the iconic Jackie, Helgeland was very hesitant to cast a big-name movie star in the important part of Dodgers' GM Branch Rickey. No question, he did not want someone like Harrison Ford.

But Ford, determined to leave Han Solo, Jack Ryan, and Indiana Jones behind him, convinced Helgeland that he was right for the character role of Rickey. Makeup effects artist Bill Corso—a longtime associate of Ford's—added a wig, prosthetic nose and jowls, age stipple—as well as Rickey's trademark bushy eyebrows to complete the transformation.

Former MLB relief pitcher C. J. Nitkowski played Phillies pitcher Dutch Leonard. Nitkowski admitted that he never thought much about the impact of Robinson's struggle as a black ballplayer—until he spent several years playing ball in Asia. As a white player—and a minority—the pitcher said he received less than fair treatment for the first time in his career. He didn't like it at all, and that experience—plus his role in 42—allowed Nitkowski to finally appreciate Robinson's contribution to the game.

Along with finding performers who looked like ballplayers, filmmakers were hard-pressed to find a ballpark that could look like the hallowed Brooklyn-based Ebbets Field, which had been torn down in 1960. After looking at stadia of all sorts, location manager Eric Hooge arranged for Engle Stadium—owned by the University of Tennessee at Chattanooga—to be transformed into Ebbets, as well as other stadiums like Crosley in Cincinnati, Sportsman's in St. Louis, and Shibe in Philadelphia.

With a construction budget of more than half-a-million dollars, dugouts were demolished and buildings were razed to create a clean slate, then more than eleven hundred feet of plywood walls, covered in green material for digital image replacement later, were erected along the perimeter of the field. A three-story scoreboard, complete with an eight-foot-tall clock, was built in right-center.

Shooting at the park took about three months. As part of the deal, Engle Stadium, originally built in 1930, had to be restored (with improvements) to what it was before filming began. That process took two and a half months, with everyone pleased with the final results—on film and on the field.

Made on a budget of $40 million, *42* was released to commemorate the sixty-fifth anniversary of Jackie Robinson's historic entry to the major leagues. The film grossed more than $95 million in America. As might be expected, the story didn't draw much interest in foreign markets, with only $2.5 million taken in—mostly in Japan.

61*

(2001—American/**HBO**—129 Min/Color)
Director: Billy Crystal
Original Music: Marc Shaiman
Film Editing: Michael Jablow
Production Design: Rusty Smith
Cast: Barry Pepper (**Roger Maris**)
Thomas Jane (**Mickey Mantle**)
Anthony Michael Hall (**Whitey Ford**)
Richard Masur (**Milt Kahn**)
Bruce Mcgill (**Ralph Houk**)
Chris Bauer (**Bob Cerv**)

With the 1998 record-setting home run efforts of Mark McGwire as the backdrop, the summer of 1961 is recalled. Mickey Mantle and Roger Maris, teammates and good friends on the New York Yankees, battle to break the single-season home run record of Babe Ruth. Mantle is clearly the fan favorite, while Maris is considered an outsider.

Mickey's drinking and carousing seem to be taking their toll, and Maris convinces him to move into his quiet apartment that he shares with teammate Bob Cerv. While the M&M Boys head toward Ruth's record, Commissioner Ford Frick states that unless the record is broken within the same 154-game period that Ruth had, the broken record will be considered as a separate entry.

Mantle suffers a disabling injury and has to stay on the sidelines as a stressed Maris hits 61 home runs, albeit in the full 162-game season. In 1991, six years after Maris' death, Commissioner Fay Vincent rules that a season is a season and Maris' record stands.

Afterwords

Comedian, actor, popular Oscar host, and all-around baseball fan Billy Crystal grew up in New York City, loving the Yankees and Mickey Mantle. Crystal would eventually forge a close friendship with "The Mick" in the early 1980s. In fact, Mantle once told Crystal that, if they ever made a biopic of his life, the slugger wanted Crystal to direct it—and he did.

Aside from Crystal's obvious passion for the $16 million project, the film is great because of the dead-on portrayals (and physical looks) of Mantle and Maris by Thomas Jane and Barry Pepper, respectively. Still, neither was any kind of ballplayer coming into the film and had to be tutored by switch-hitting former pro Reggie Smith, who ran a baseball school in Southern California.

Along with finding look-alikes for Mantle and Maris, Crystal needed to find a facility that looked like Yankee Stadium in 1961. With the real thing renovated in 1974 (and shooting in August), a substitute would be required. Tigers Stadium, closed in 1999 when Comerica Park opened, had a close resemblance, and once production designer Rusty Smith dressed the park (and Centropolis FX masters digitally enhanced the view), Yankee Stadium in 1961 appeared.

Other cinema tricks involved Anthony Michael Hall, who played left-handed pitcher Whitey Ford. With Hall being a right-hander, the decades-old trick of dressing the player with backwards script and numbers on the uniform, shooting the scene normally, then reversing the footage in postproduction, resulted in Hall looking like he was throwing left-handed (a similar process was used with Gary Cooper in *Pride of the Yankees* nearly seventy years before).

Originally, *61** was planned to be a theatrical release, but recent baseball films like 1992's *The Babe* and 1994's *Cobb*—box office duds—made that route a bad idea. Cable's HBO embraced the project, with the resulting film winning Emmys for casting and sound editing amid a dozen nominations—including one for Crystal as best director.

A League of Their Own

(1992—American/**Columbia**—128 Min/Color)
Director: Penny Marshall
Original Music: Hans Zimmer
Film Editing: Adam Bernardi, George Bowers
Production Design: Bill Groom
Cast: Tom Hanks (**Jimmy Dugan**)
Geena Davis (**Dottie Hinson**)
Lori Petty (**Kit Keller**)
Madonna (**Mae Mordabito**)
Rosie O'donnell (**Doris Murphy**)
Jon Lovitz (**Ernie Capadino**)
Megan Cavanagh (**Marla Hooch**)
Garry Marshall (**Walter Harvey**)
Jon Lovitz (**Ernie Capadino**)
Bill Pullman (**Bob Hinson**)

Dottie Hinson, a former star of the All American Girls Professional Baseball League, travels to Cooperstown in 1992, where the Hall is opening an exhibit about the AAGBPL.

Flashing back to 1943, catcher Dottie and her kid sister, Kit—a pitcher–are scouted by the gruff Ernie Capadino to join a girls' baseball league in the Midwest during World War II. The two soon join others to form the Rockford Peaches, managed by ex-major leaguer Jimmie Dugan. An outright drunk, Dugan

The Rockford Peaches team, *A League of Their Own*, 1992.

reluctantly accepts the assignment from candy bar magnate Walter Harvey, giving his female players no respect for their skills.

The girls are fine players, but Dottie really excels and adds flash when the league is close to going under. The AAGBPL is soon a success, with Kit suddenly traded to a rival team. When Dottie's husband Bob comes back from the war with an injury, she suddenly quits to return home with him, a move that Jimmy thinks she will regret.

The Peaches reach the World Series against the Racine Belles, Kit's new team. Proving Dugan right, Dottie returns to play the final game. A collision at home plate allows Kit to score the winning run against her sister, who is unable to hold on to the ball.

Back in the present, Dottie and Kit share a tearful reunion at the Hall, along with many of their old teammates.

Afterwords

As with many films based on fact, regardless of the subject, *A League of Their Own* took certain liberties with the truth in an effort to make the movie more entertaining. Yet much of what appeared on the screen happened in the twelve-year history of the AAGPBL. The skimpy uniforms; the lessons in poise and manners; and, particularly, the seriousness with which the women played the game of baseball, all were spot-on.

The big challenge for director Penny Marshall was finding actresses who could play ball. In fact, before she would read with the auditioning performers, they had to first pass muster with Rod Dedeaux, longtime baseball coach at USC. A couple of Marshall's personal picks ended up having to pass on the lead role of Dottie Hinson, opening the door for Geena Davis.

Demi Moore was slotted to star, but wound up pregnant with then-husband Bruce Willis' child, daughter Scout. Debra Winger was then cast, but quickly backed out when Madonna hired on to play a significant part. Davis, admittedly not a ballplayer, worked hard to gain the skills needed to make Dottie believable.

Peaches' manager, Jimmy Dugan, was patterned after slugger Jimmie Foxx, and, while Marshall wanted an older actor to play the part, Tom Hanks—not yet a back-to-back Oscar winner—pressed hard for it. Once cast, he gained thirty pounds, with help from Dairy Queen, to reinforce the look of a self-abusive ex-ballplayer. While some of the performers showed pretty good natural baseball skills—particularly Lori Petty, Rosie O'Donnell, and Tracy Reiner—others, like Madonna and Megan Cavanagh, trained hard to portray baseballers with believable skills.

A League of Their Own was a solid summer hit at the box office, grossing $107 million on a budget of $40 million. It also spawned a short-lived (six episode) TV spinoff on CBS, with Reiner and Cavanagh reprising their roles.

Babe Ruth

(1991—American/**NBC-TV**—**99 Min/Color**)
Director: Mark Tinker
Original Music: Steve Dorff
Film Editing: Stanford C. Allen
Production Design: Donald Lee Harris
Cast: Stephen Lang (**George Herman "Babe" Ruth**)
Donald Moffat (**Jacob Ruppert**)
Bruce Weitz (**Miller Huggins**)
Lisa Zane (**Claire Hodgson Ruth**)
Pete Rose (**Ty Cobb**)

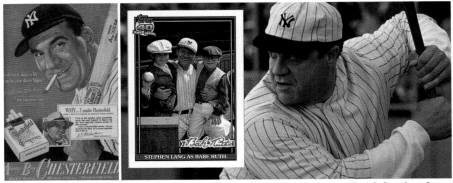

Cigarette ad with William Bendix as Babe Ruth, 1948; 1991 Topps card with Stephen Lang as Ruth; John Goodman as *The Babe*, 1992.

The Babe

(1992—American/**Universal**—115 Min/Color)
Director: Arthur Hiller
Original Music: Elmer Bernstein
Film Editing: Robert C. Jones
Production Design: James D. Vance
Cast: John Goodman (**George Herman "Babe" Ruth**)
Kelly Mcgillis (**Claire Hodgson Ruth**)
Trini Alvarado (**Helen Woodford Ruth**)
Bruce Boxleitner (**Jumpin' Joe Dugan**)

The Babe Ruth Story

(1948—American/**Allied Artists**—106 Min/Color)
Director: Roy Del Ruth
Original Music: Edward Ward
Film Editing: Richard Heermance
Art Direction: F. Paul Sylos
Cast: William Bendix (**George Herman "Babe" Ruth**)
Claire Trevor (**Claire Hodgson Ruth**)
Charles Bickford (**Brother Matthias**)

Based on the 1949 Bob Considine/Babe Ruth book.

The greatest baseball player of all time starts out as a troublemaking kid, eats hot dogs, drinks, fools around with women—marries two of them—and hits a lot of home runs.

Afterwords

As much as I would like to embrace these films as celebrations of the greatest ballplayer ever, I always promised my mom I would never lie. As such, all three films about the mighty Babe Ruth—separated by more than forty years—failed to do his very colorful life story any justice. They might be like the person who, in an effort to do everything he or she can to please the family, ends up stumbling around, tripping over and breaking everything in sight.

In essence, they all suffer from twisted time frames of events, omission or aberration of known facts, and poor prosthetic noses. One's time is better spent reading *Babe: The Legend Comes to Life*, the great bio on the Babe written by Robert Creamer.

John Goodman is better in the role than William Bendix (who, at age forty-one, had the thankless job of playing Babe as a teen as well as an adult. No one is that good an actor). Goodman admitted that, although he worked hard on the baseball skills (he's a righty, whereas the Babe, of course, was a lefty), he expected everything to fall into place—and they didn't. Goodman wishes he could have gotten a "do over" for *The Babe*.

Bendix—a fine character actor who could play comedy as well as drama—was once a batboy for the Yankees and personally watched Ruth slam many of his home runs. *The Babe Ruth Story* was in production as the Bambino neared his last days, dying of cancer. Even so, he worked with Bendix when he could, giving him tips on his batting style and other baseball-related details. Still, the actor believed *The Babe Ruth Story* was the "worst picture" he ever made—not an easy task to count, considering he appeared in nearly one hundred film and TV projects in his career.

Goodman was originally pitched the NBC-TV role but turned it down, so Stephen Lang took it on. The successes of *The Natural, Field of Dreams*, and *Major League* made baseball a hot theme for the media, so TV and film both clamored to get their own take on Ruth out in the early 1990s. The best thing about the TV film is seeing Pete Rose trying to play Ty Cobb in a fictitious encounter with the Babe.

The Babe, released against blockbusters like *Basic Instinct* and *White Men Can't Jump*, stumbled out of the box office. Made on a budget of $12 million, it grossed only $17 million in US theaters.

Bad News Bears

(1976—American/**Paramount**—102 Min/Color)
Director: Michael Ritchie
Original Music: Jerry Fielding
Film Editing: Richard A. Harris
Art Direction: Polly Platt
Cast: Walter Matthau (**Coach Morris Buttermaker**)
Tatum O'neal (**Amanda Whurlitzer**)
Vic Morrow (**Roy Turner**)
Joyce Van Patten (**Cleveland**)
Jackie Earl Haley (**Kelly Leak**)

(2005—American/**Paramount**—113 Min/Color)
Director: Richard Linklater
Original Music: Ed Shearmur
Film Editing: Sandra Adair
Art Direction: Bruce Curtis
Cast: Billy Bob Thornton (**Morris Buttermaker**)
Greg Kinnear (**Roy Bullock**)
Marcia Gay Harden (**Liz Whitewood**)
Sammi Kane Kraft (**Amanda Whurlitzer**)
Jeffery Davies (**Kelly Leak**)

Morris Buttermaker is an ex-minor leaguer, as well as a beer-swilling, cigar-smoking grouch, who is paid to reluctantly coach the Bears—a Little League team of just about the most inept players in Southern California. One of the opposing coaches is Roy Turner, a hard-nosed, win-at-all-costs father, who consistently takes his Yankees to the finals. After the first practice, it's clear that Buttermaker and his team have their work cut out for them.

The opening day game between the Bears and Yankees is a one-sided rout, with Buttermaker mercifully forfeiting after a half-inning score of 26–0. Despite suggestions of breaking up the Bears, Buttermaker adds hard-throwing, no-nonsense Amanda Whurlizer to pitch, along with tough-guy athlete and Harley-riding Kelly Leak to play outfield.

Soon, the Bears are winning games and playing like a real baseball team. As a result, the Bears face off against the Yankees for the championship. Unfortunately, Buttermaker catches himself acting as cutthroat and aggressively mean as Turner—and he doesn't like the feeling.

Turner embarrasses his son, Joey the Yankees pitcher, by slapping him. Joey gets back at his dad by fielding a grounder, then holding onto it as the Bears base runner circles the infield for an inside-the-park homer run—then he quits the Yankees.

Buttermaker fields some of his second-stringers in the game's last inning, giving everyone the chance to play. The Yankees take a 7–3 lead, and the Bears make an exciting comeback before losing by a run. Buttermaker's team is excited and celebrate, as there's always the next year.

Afterwords

Mainstream America was hardly prepared for the kind of baseball seen in 1976's *Bad News Bears*. With a coach that drank constantly and kids who cursed like sailors, it wasn't the usual neighborhood Little League. Or perhaps it was, as director Michael Ritchie was cynical enough to focus on the need that parents often have to win—vicariously—through their children's sporting events. (Although, after years and years of coaching youth baseball, I know if I had talked and acted like Buttermaker or Turner, I wouldn't have been allowed to coach a rock on how to play dead.)

Lobby card, *Bad News Bears*, 1976.

Ritchie was at home directing sports films, with entries like 1969's *Downhill Racer* (skiing), 1977's *Semi-Tough* (pro football), 1986's *Wildcats* (high school football), and 1994's *The Scout* (baseball, covered elsewhere in this chapter). The director had cast young Tatum O'Neal as the Bears' star pitcher, following her Oscar-winning performance in 1973's *Paper Moon*. Aged ten when she won the award, it made O'Neal the youngest ever Academy Award recipient.

Yet Ritchie knew O'Neal alone would not have the drawing power to make the film viable, so he approached another Oscar winner—the gruff and grumpy Walter Matthau. The actor first refused the role, balking at working with kids' characters who cursed. Ritchie convinced Matthau that it was just how kids talked, and once he meet the likable young cast, he joined *Bad News Bears*.

Other standouts were Vic Morrow and Joyce Van Patten, along with child actor Jackie Earl Haley, who would continue his acting career into adulthood. Most of the other kids veered away from Hollywood as they grew up.

Tatum O'Neal worked for three months learning how to pitch, although many of her pitching scenes involved a boy wearing a wig and creative camera angles. She later recalled that Matthau was a very unique person. Several years after *Bad News Bears*, the actress was in a car accident that put her in the hospital. She was stunned when Matthau entered her room one day, saying he just wanted to "see that (she) was all right."

The 1976 film grossed more than $32 million, a fine return for its $9 million budget. Two sequels followed (original plans called for five!): *The Bad News Bears in Breaking Training* in 1977, and *The Bad News Bears Go to Japan* in 1978, neither of which had the impact or inspiration of the first film. CBS-TV produced two seasons of *The Bad News Bears*, with Jack Warden as Coach Buttermaker, in 1979 and 1980.

In 2005, a remake of the film was released, with Billy Bob Thornton in the Buttermaker role and directed by Richard Linklater. The character of Roy Turner was renamed Roy Bullock. But time had seemed to change how kids' behavior was accepted in the nearly thirty years between the two films. What had been shocking in 1976 became mundane in 2005.

Curiously, the 2005 version grossed almost the exact same $32 million that the 1976 version did. Of course, the latter had a budget of $35 million, and the average ticket cost was three times the amount of 1976. Those factors made the 2005 version of *Bad News Bears* a flop and, once more, proved that nothing is better than the original.

Bang the Drum Slowly

(1973—American/Paramount—96 Min/Color)
Director: John Hancock
Original Music: Stephen Lawrence
Film Editing: Richard Marks
Production Design: Robert Gundlach
Cast: Robert De Niro (**Bruce Pearson**)
Michael Moriarty (**Henry "Author" Wiggen**)
Vincent Gardenia (**Dutch Schnell**)

Phil Foster (**Joe Jaros**)
Tom Ligon (**Piney Woods**)

Based on the 1956 Mark Harris Novel.

Catcher Bruce Pearson is a simple, even ignorant, journeyman catcher for the NY Mammoths. His friend is bright and self-centered ace pitcher Henry Wiggen, whose nickname is Author (he once wrote a book). Pearson, diagnosed with a fatal case of Hodgkin's disease, keeps Wiggen as his confidant—the only person to know about the illness.

At spring training, Bruce is in jeopardy of being released in favor of the eccentric rookie, Piney Woods. Henry signs his new contract, with the stipulation that he and Pearson are a matched set: One can't go anywhere without the other. Manager Dutch Schnell reluctantly accepts the deal.

Some of the players have teased and insulted Pearson, ragging him. Henry quietly tells them that Bruce is dying, hoping they will lay off taunting him. When Dutch brings in a detective to investigate what Wiggen and Pearson were doing at a hospital, Henry deftly lies and says Bruce was being treated for syphilis.

Before long, everyone on the team knows about Pearson's condition, and Piney Woods is brought back from the minors, despite Bruce's decent showing on the field. Those who used to rag on the catcher—even Dutch—regret how they acted. The Mammoths start pulling together as a team.

A rained-out game leaves the team stuck in the clubhouse, and Piney, not knowing about Bruce, sings the sad lyrics to "Cowboy's Lament—Streets of Laredo." The story of a cowboy dying too young brings a silent pall over the team.

Heading into the last weeks of the season, the Mammoths are winning. In spite of Pearson's rapidly declining health, he continues behind the plate, and his teammates work together to cover his ebbing play. They make the World Series, but Bruce is now too sick and goes home.

In the fall, Pearson passes away, and Henry is the only member of the Mammoths organization to attend the funeral. Wiggen resolves that from now on, after knowing Bruce Pearson, he rags nobody.

Afterwords

Long before Travis Bickle or Jake LaMotta or even Paul Vitti, Robert De Niro played a simple-minded catcher named Bruce Pearson in *Bang the Drum Slowly*. It was his first

B&W Still, *Bang the Drum Slowly*, 1973.

big role, as *Mean Streets*—the beginning of a beautiful friendship with director Martin Scorsese—was released several months later. Even at the start, De Niro indulged his personal philosophy of becoming immersed in the role he was to play.

Not quite thirty years old, De Niro played Pearson without much personal baseball experience from which to draw (a requisite of Method Acting). Still, he spent hours in full catching gear, taking fastball after fastball, before the cameras began to roll. De Niro watched a lot of ball games, as well as spent time with the Cincinnati Reds in spring training and worked with future Hall of Fame catcher Johnny Bench.

As might be expected, the immersion worked. Michael Moriarty, playing ace pitcher Henry Wiggen, once said he didn't know De Niro, but he did know Bruce Pearson. As for Moriarty's pitching prowess, director John Hancock worked him two hours a day for three weeks. The workouts left the actor with an arm so sore he couldn't even comb his hair. But his pitching on screen was just fine.

This was not the first time Mark Harris' novel had been brought to the screen. Shortly after the book's release in 1956, the TV anthology series *The U.S. Steel Hour* presented a live production, starring Paul Newman as Wiggen and Albert Salmi as Pearson.

Director Hancock shot the film on a slim budget of $850,000, using New York's Shea and Yankee stadia as backdrops for the fictional NY Mammoths team. The film did alright at the box office, as Hollywood had noticed the success of the made-for-TV film *Brian's Song*, released in 1971. The story focused on Chicago Bears running back Brian Piccolo, who died of cancer at the age of twenty-six.

Baseball Bugs

(1946—American/**Warner Bros**—7 Min/Color)
Director: Friz Freleng
Original Music: Carl Stalling
Cast: Bugs Bunny (**Mel Blanc**)
Additional Voices (**Tedd Pierce, Bea Benaderet**)

Bugs Bunny, an angry fan at a baseball game, ends up taking on the entire team by himself—and wins.

Afterwords

Warner Brothers Studio clearly hit a homer with this Looney Toon, covering just about every aspect of baseball in only seven minutes. With the war just ended, the sport would be back at full strength in a few months from the cartoon's release in February 1946.

Bugs is a carrot-in-a-bun-munching fan, watching as the Gas-House Gorillas—obviously based on the scruffy and unshaven St. Louis Cardinals, who were known as the Gashouse Gang when they won the 1934 World Series—clobber the Tea Totallers, a team of aged and frail players who look like they just stepped out of

Elysian Field. When Bugs loudly claims that he could beat the Gorillas single-handed, the villainous team takes him up on his boast.

Based on the scoreboard, the Gas-House Gorillas are the visiting team. But when Bugs enters at the top of the fifth inning, he is now the visitor and the Gorillas are the home team (setting up the eventual "one-run-down" scenario for the bottom of the ninth).

The stadium is referred to as the Polo Grounds, but the frieze at the top of the grandstands looks very Yankee Stadium-like. A close look at the batter's box reveals that home plate is drawn backwards, with its point aiming back at the pitcher—by the ninth inning, it's just a white square.

One particular scene has lasted in my mind over time, since I've played in my share of one-sided slaughters (invariably on the losing side). Early in *Baseball Bugs*, a hapless Tea Totaller pitches, while a conga line of Gorillas forms completely around the diamond. As the ball is delivered, every player crushes it for a base hit and moves forward one place for the process to endlessly repeat and repeat. For years, I could only laugh at the memory of this image, as it seemed to be replaying in front of me as my own team was being shellacked.

In the bottom of the ninth, Bugs has taken a one-run lead. A Gorilla cranks a ball way out of the park and Bugs gives chase, grabbing a crosstown bus. Arriving at the "Umpire" State Building, the rabbit elevators to the roof, climbs a flagpole, and tosses his glove to catch the ball as it sails by. An umpire has climbed the side of the building (a monkey's uncle to King Kong, no doubt) and calls the Gorilla hitter for the final out. Bugs has won the game.

MLB Rule 7.05 awards three bases if a player touches a fair ball with a thrown glove, hat, or other detached part of the uniform. If, in the umpire's judgment, the ball would have gone over the fence in fair territory, he may rule the batted and interfered-with ball to be a home run and not a called out.

But this was just a cartoon.

Batty Baseball

(1944—American/**Metro-Goldwyn-Mayer**—6 Min/Color)
Director: Tex Avery
Original Music: Scott Bradley
Cast: Ball Players (**Jack Mather**)

A series of baseball-themed jokes—visual and verbal—presented while a game between two rivals goes on.

Afterwords

Predating the Warner Brothers' *Baseball Bugs* by nearly two years, this six-minute cartoon is full of the visual gags that made Tex Avery famous. One of the first oddities is the fact that the well-known roaring Leo the Lion opening to all MGM pictures does not open this cartoon. Only when one of the ballplayers notices it hasn't shown up—about forty seconds in—does the feline make its appearance.

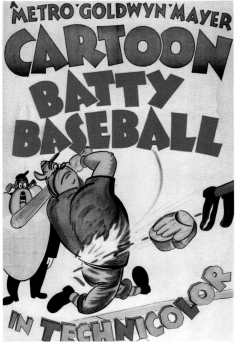

One-sheet poster, *Batty Baseball*, 1944.

The imaginary "fourth wall" that often separates the audience from a movie screen is almost immediately torn down in *Batty Baseball*. The scene opens in a dripping-in-corny fashion at the ballpark known as W. C. Field, after which the audience is informed that the writer of that joke is no longer around the MGM lot.

Many of the gags are related to the war, which was still under full rage at the time of the cartoon's release. At one point the infield is empty, with 1-A draft rating signs noting the reason for the missing players. Fortunately, the pitcher is still on the mound, since he wears a 4-F on his back.

Like many of the MGM animated shorts of the day that were obviously aimed at the adult audiences in movie theaters, *Batty Baseball* is full of violence, death, and sex—just how we like our cartoons (and they thought Ren and Stimpy were a rough pair!).

A base runner is out at the plate—literally—as the catcher cracks his head with a bat. Using a bombsight on his shoe, the pitcher squarely takes aim at the batter's head. Once conked with the ball, the batter obliges by quietly laying his hat and bat down and then lies down on a stretcher to be taken away.

A rowdy fan yells the familiar phrase of "Kill the umpire." A gunshot follows, and the crowds stand and remove their hats in respect for the recently departed arbiter. The pitcher tosses a tantalizing curve—complete with the outline of a shapely woman—that elicits a chorus of wolf whistles from the men in the stands. A pitcher is warmed up in the dugout—by the numerous kisses from two attractive women.

Countless official rules of the game are broken, including the pitcher throwing three baseballs at once, a bowling ball, a heavy iron ball, and using a slingshot at one point. An enormous batter steps into the box—shades of Frank Howard, Adam Dunn, or Frank Thomas! Appropriately, he wears the number of B-19, also the designation of America's largest bomber in the war.

A running gag includes a catcher who constantly encroaches on the batter's territory to catch the pitch, while his fast-paced patter encourages his battery mate to keep up the good work. Only his crouch saves him from decapitation by the hitter's vicious swing—until the last one. The catcher ascends skyward, with wings and a halo (even though the Angels wouldn't join the majors for nearly twenty more years).

The Bingo Long Traveling All-Stars & Motor Kings

(1973—American/**Universal**—110 Min/Color)
Director: John Badham
Original Music: William Goldstein
Film Editing: David Rawlins
Production Design: Lawrence G. Paull
Cast: Billy Dee Williams (**Bingo Long**)
James Earl Jones (**Leon Carter**)
Richard Pryor (**Charlie Snow**)
Ted Ross (**Sallison Porter**)
Stan Shaw (**Esquire Joe**)
Dewayne Jessie (**Rainbow**)

Based on the 1973 Novel By William Brasher.

In 1939, funeral home owner Sallison Porter is also the owner of the St. Louis Ebony Aces in the Negro League. Tight-fisted and cold, his mistreatment of the players leads flamboyant Bingo Long—his star pitcher—to quit and start up his own barnstorming team, featuring all-star black players from around the league, like slugging catcher Leon Carter and outfielder Charlie Snow.

Bingo's team enters towns with a lot of flash and flair, parading down the streets in full uniform. The convoy always draws the attention of the locals, and the ballparks are always filled. Their play on the field is slick and almost always leads to one-sided wins for the Motor Kings. Along the way, Bingo signs up Esquire Joe Callaway, a young kid with great talent for the game, to play center field.

Porter and other club owners are not happy with losing their players and seeing them successful as the Motor Kings, so they resort to strong-armed tactics to intimidate the black game promoters. The problem is quickly solved by taking on amateur teams of white players.

But a new problem comes from the white fans, who quickly show their contempt for the black team. The Motor Kings swing the crowds into their corner by clowning around on the field—while still winning the games.

Porter gets rough with Bingo's team—sending goons to steal money from Rainbow, the Motor Kings' treasurer, and attacking Charlie Snow with a razor, injuring him badly. Angry and dejected, Leon quits the Motor Kings. Bingo replaces him with a little person.

Bingo receives an offer from Porter—one game against the league's all-stars. If the Motor Kings win, they can join the league. If they lose, everyone goes back to their old teams. Bingo convinces Leon to rejoin the team, but Porter has him kidnapped as the game begins.

Carter escapes in one of Porter's coffins, as the league all-stars take the lead in the game. Leon arrives at the field in Porter's hearse, just in time to stroke a game-winning three-run homer. Esquire Joe receives an offer to play in the major leagues, while a recovered Charlie Snow has a new scheme to join the big leagues—with his head shaved into a Mohawk, he'll claim to be a Native American.

One-sheet poster, *Bingo Long Traveling All-Stars & Motor Kings*, 1973.

Afterwords

Motown Records founder Berry Gordy purchased the film rights to *Bingo Long* from author Bill Brasher. Together with producer Rob Cohen, they sought to bring the great traditions and entertainment of the Negro League baseball to film audiences of the 1970s. The focus was aimed at replicating teams like the Indianapolis Clowns, who combined baseball with vaudeville for an experience that differed from more serious teams like the Kansas City Monarchs.

John Badham was a TV director whose first chance to direct a feature film was *Bingo Long*. Although born in England, Badham was raised in Birmingham, Alabama—home to the Birmingham Black Barons of the Negro League. The young Badham had firsthand knowledge of how black players played the game before the color barrier was broken in 1947. Steven Spielberg was originally slotted to direct, but his chores in finishing up *Jaws* left him unavailable.

Top black performers were brought onto the project, seeking to appeal to crossover audiences of all types. Billy Dee Williams, well known from TV's *Brian's Song*, as well as big-screen films like *Lady Sings the Blues* and *Mahogany*, played the titled pitcher whose character was largely based on Satchel Paige.

James Earl Jones, an established Tony Award–winning theater performer, played catcher Leon Carter, based on the power-hitting Josh Gibson. While he had starred—on stage and on screen—as boxer Jack Jefferson in *The Great White Hope*, Jones admitted he was no athlete and had to work hard to look like he knew how to hit a baseball, with or without power.

Richard Pryor, a huge comedic talent with stand-up, television, and writing experience (he was part of the team that penned Mel Brooks' *Blazing Saddles* in 1974), portrayed outfielder Charlie Snow. His on-screen character sought to break into the majors by pretending to be, first a Cuban named Carlos Nevada, then a Native American named Chief Takahoma. Played for laughs, the ploy was not far from reality for many black players in the day, who tried many ways to break into the majors.

Included in the cast was DeWayne Jessie as Rainbow. The actor would gain much greater fame a few years later as R&B singer Otis Day in John Landis' *Animal House*. Also, Leon Wagner appeared as Motor Kings first baseman Fat Joe. Wagner had a twelve-year career in the MLB with five teams, including a great season in 1962 with the Angels, where he hit 37 homers and drove in 107 runs.

Bingo Long was made on a $3 million budget—not a bad amount of money for 1976 films, considering *Rocky* was made for just $1 million, while *King Kong* cost $23 million.

Bull Durham

(1988—American/Orion—108 Min/Color)
Director: Ron Shelton
Original Music: Michael Convertino
Film Editing: Robert Leighton, Adam Weiss
Production Design: Armin Ganz
Cast: Kevin Costner (**Crash Davis**)
Susan Sarandon (**Annie Savoy**)
Tim Robbins (**Ebby Calvin "Nuke" La Loosh**)
Trey Wilson (**Jim "Skip" Riggins**)
Robert Wuhl (**Larry Hockett**)

Durham, North Carolina, is home to the Class A minor league Durham Bulls. Annie Savoy is a smart and sexy local—a baseball fanatic and loyal supporter of the Bulls. Every year, she takes a rookie under her wing and helps him reach the next level.

Manager Skip Riggins and pitching coach Larry Hockett watch as hurler Ebby LaLoosh hits 95 mph on the radar gun, as well as the Bulls' mascot in the head. Veteran minor league catcher Crash Davis is only twenty home runs away from the all-time minor league record and joins the Bulls for one reason—to mentor pitching phenom (and total head case) LaLoosh as he develops into a major leaguer.

After a rocky start, Davis and LaLoosh become battery mates, although LaLoosh second-guesses his seasoned catcher and thinks he knows everything. While Crash passes on Annie's romantic advances, LaLoosh becomes Annie's paramour, and she nicknames him Nuke.

Davis gains immediate credibility with Nuke and his teammates when he admits he spent three weeks in the major leagues, "the twenty-one greatest days in my life." But the team—and Nuke—are in a big slump.

With the help of Annie and Crash, LaLoosh starts to pitch well and the Bulls start to win. With Nuke winning, he's superstitious and won't sleep with Annie until he loses—a notion that doesn't sit well with her. In the midst of a tough game, a mound meeting turns into a discussion about a cursed first baseman's glove and wedding presents, with coach Hockett quickly concluding that "candlesticks make a nice gift" and the team should get a double play.

Nuke is promoted to the major leagues, so it seems that Annie and Crash have done their jobs. But that means Davis is no longer needed by the Bulls and is released. He finds comfort with Annie.

Catching on with another team, Davis breaks the minor league homer record, while Nuke spouts clichés to major league reporters just like Crash taught him. One evening, Crash returns to Annie's house to stay, retiring from the game of baseball.

One-sheet poster, *Bull Durham*, 1988.

Afterwords

Writer and director (first-time) Ron Shelton had been an infielder in the Orioles minor leagues for five years before he realized he would never make it to "the Show." He turned his attention to art and film, with *Bull Durham* coming close behind his football-based *Best of Times* in 1986.

Shelton had a tough time convincing Orion Pictures to take Tim Robbins as the wild-armed Nuke LaLoosh. They wanted Anthony Michael Hall, a young actor fresh from his stint on NBC-TV's *Saturday Night Live*. The studio finally agreed after Shelton threatened to quit the project. Incidentally, the premise of LaLoosh making the direct jump from Class A ball to the majors would be highly improbable in the real world.

Costner, a former high school baseball player, made *Bull Durham* the first of several baseball-themed movies on his résumé (along with 1989's *Field of Dreams* and 1999's *For Love of the Game*). The actor was not a lightweight at the plate, demonstrating good switch-hitting skills (lefty in his first at bat and righty in the batting cage with Annie) and cranking 2 homers during the shooting of the film. He also took great pleasure in gunning down base-running actors going for second.

Not that Costner was the film's first choice, either. Other actors considered for Crash Davis (a name from real life, although the inspiration hit only 2 home runs in his three-year minor league career, rather than the movie's 247 round-trippers) were Harrison Ford, Kurt Russell (a former minor league infielder himself after a child acting career with Disney), and Mel Gibson. Likewise, Kim Basinger and Ellen Barkin were considered for Annie Savoy before Susan Sarandon got the part.

The actress relished the role, as Shelton wrote the character of baseball groupie Savoy as the antithesis of the one-dimensional "dumb sexy girl" that so often appeared in films of the day. The role also introduced Sarandon to Robbins, with whom she ended up spending more than twenty years.

As pitching coach Larry Hockett, Robert Wuhl ad libbed the mound meeting suggestion of candlesticks making a good wedding present, then uttering the standard baseball axiom, "Let's get two!" Friends of the actor were getting married soon, and a week before the film started shooting, Wuhl asked his wife about an appropriate gift. He just used the highlights from the conversation in the scene—which the studio twice asked to be cut from the final version.

Shelton took a $7 million budget and turned it into a $50 million hit at the box office. *Bull Durham* also earned Shelton an Oscar nomination for best original screenplay. A sequel was discussed for many years, although the writer admits that the cast is now too old to revisit the characters.

Cobb

(1994—American/**Warner Bros**—128 Min/Color)
Director: Ron Shelton
Original Music: Elliot Goldenthal
Film Editing: Kimberly Ray, Paul Seydor
Production Design: Armin Ganz, Scott Ritenour
Cast: Tommy Lee Jones (**Ty Cobb**)
Robert Wuhl (**Al Stump**)
Lolita Davidovich (**Ramona**)

Based on the 1962 Al Stump article "Ty Cobb's Wild Ten Month Fight to Live" and 1994 biography Cobb: The Life and Times of *the Meanest Man in Baseball.*

In 1960, well-known sportswriter Al Stump takes on his toughest assignment— writing the biography of now-seventy-three year-old Ty Cobb, with the ex-ballplayer's personal input and assistance. Unfortunately, the pair differ on exactly what type of story to tell. Stump wants to tell all, while Cobb insists on showing only the positive side of his career and life.

Eventually, after a hair-raising car trip over snow-packed roads into Reno, Stump decides to secretly write the real story, while appeasing his subject with a false manuscript in the works. Seriously ill, Cobb shows himself to be mean, abusive, alcoholic, paranoid, and racist. At one point, he physically assaults a cigarette girl who showed an interest in Stump.

The duo travel across the country to attend a testimonial for Cobb at the Hall of Fame. Once there, many of Cobb's famous contemporaries are in attendance, but hate him so much that they refuse to allow him into their private parties. Cobb discovers Stump's private book notes. Enraged and betrayed, he winds up in a hospital and angrily tells Stump to print whatever he wants.

Cobb soon dies, and Stump finally decides to publish the false story that shows the man in a positive light. The writer admits his weakness by burying the truth about Ty Cobb.

Tommy Lee Jones as *Cobb*, 1994.

Afterwords

Hollywood is often referred to as "the land of make believe." *Cobb*, the 1994 movie about the Georgia Peach, seems to embrace much of that concept. A lot of the problem occurs after the fact, with many questions surrounding the veracity of what sportswriter Al Stump actually did see and experience in his efforts to commit the real story of Ty Cobb to paper back in the early 1960s.

Since the movie was based on Stump's magazine articles and books about the Detroit Tiger, any questions about the writing must have, unfortunately, transferred to the film. Yet the film did succeed in showing the complex and less-than-likable Cobb, mostly from his postplaying years. Consider it this way—as a truthful biography, *Cobb* fell short. But as an intriguing speculative story about one of baseball's best players, *Cobb* scored.

Writer and director Ron Shelton—as previously noted in the *Bull Durham* section—scored successes with sports films like that entry and 1992's *White Men Can't Jump.* Yet the mere thought of Shelton making a biopic about a man as disliked as Cobb sent Twentieth Century Fox—the original studio attached to the project—heading for the exits. Warner Brothers took on the film, then—at the last minute—abandoned it to flounder in its Christmastime release.

Tommy Lee Jones, a former offensive guard on the Harvard football team, took on the difficult job of portraying Cobb. Jones would play the outfielder in a few abbreviated baseball scenes, but mostly in makeup—by master artist Ve Neill—as a seventy-something-year-old man in the last year of his life. The actor quickly picked up the unique, split-handed, lefty batting stance of Cobb, but did his homework a bit too hard on the base paths. While practicing sliding at his Texas ranch, Jones broke his ankle, delaying the start of production.

During spring training of the 1994 season, Red Sox flamethrower Roger Clemens was brought down to Rickwood Field—the oldest existing baseball stadium in America—in Birmingham, Alabama. Shelton wanted "the Rocket" to portray an opposing pitcher to face off against Jones' Cobb.

Some media reports said that Clemens was portraying Big Ed Walsh, but that's unlikely. Clemens wore a Philadelphia A's uniform in the film, and Walsh never played for that team. It's more likely that he was taking the role of Jack Coombs or Chief Bender, both outstanding hurlers for the 1910 A's, who won 102 games that year. They also beat the Cubs in five games to win the World Series.

Despite Shelton's previous successes with his other sports films, *Cobb* was a dud at the box office. Critics were split on the movie, with many acknowledging the difficult but proper handling of Cobb's life story. Still, the movie grossed only $1 million in theaters across the country.

Damn Yankees!

(1958—American/**Warner Bros**—111 Min/Color)
Director: George Abbott, Stanley Donen
Original Music and Lyrics: Richard Adler, Jerry Ross
Film Editing: Frank Bracht

Production Design: Jean Eckart, William Eckart
Cast: Tab Hunter (**Joe Hardy**)
Gwen Verdon (**Lola**)
Ray Walston (**Mr. Applegate**)
Russ Brown (**Benny Van Buren**)
Robert Shafer (**Joe Boyd**)

Based on the 1954 Douglass Wallop novel *The Year the Yankees Lost the Pennant.*

Middle-aged Joe Boyd is a long-suffering Washington Senators fan, cursing the dreaded New York Yankees as he watches a game on TV. Oh, if the Senators had just one legitimate home run hitter . . .

A dapper man named Mr. Applegate appears out of nowhere, agreeing to grant Boyd's wish—he can sell his soul to the Devil to be that one power hitter on the Washington team. But Joe negotiates an escape clause, which Applegate reluctantly accepts. Boyd is suddenly transformed into young and virile Joe Hardy.

Senators manager Benny Van Buren reminds his sad team that talent isn't everything—winning players must have heart, as well. Acting as an agent, Applegate presents Joe Hardy to the Senators for a tryout. His display of power and skillful fielding gains Joe a major league contract with the Washington team.

Rookie Joe Hardy makes an immediate impact on the Senators, but he quickly becomes homesick for his wife, Meg. As Hardy, he convinces the lonesome woman to rent him a room—back in his own house. Applegate doesn't like the idea and brings in his assistant, sultry red-haired vamp Lola, to seduce Joe and get him to forget Meg.

Lola's wiles seem lost on Joe, as he remains committed and loyal to Meg. Applegate is not happy with the result and spreads gossip about Meg and Joe Hardy in the neighborhood. Joe is hesitant to leave, but knows it's the right thing to do.

With only one game left in the season, the Senators are poised to overtake the Yankees for the pennant. Fans celebrate—perhaps prematurely—by hosting a gala tribute to Joe.

Applegate, fearing Joe will opt out of their deal, tips a reporter with a lie

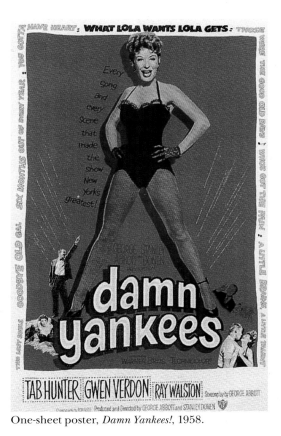

One-sheet poster, *Damn Yankees!*, 1958.

that Joe is actually a crooked ballplayer on the lam for throwing a game some years back. The mudslinging story hits the papers, prompting a hearing with baseball's commissioner and doubts about Joe's true identity. He's found innocent, but the time for the escape clause lapses, and Joe seems doomed forever in service to Applegate.

Falling in love with Joe, Lola drugs Applegate with sleeping pills, but he wakes in time to make it to the ballpark for the ninth inning in the last game. He's angry with Lola for what she did and turns her into an old witch. The Senators lead the Yanks, 1—0.

Mickey Mantle launches a deep fly to the outfield. Applegate transforms Joe back into Joe Boyd in mid-stride while he's tracking the fly ball, and Joe awkwardly stumbles to the ground. Miraculously, he still makes the catch, and the Senators are victorious and win the pennant, while Joe slips out through an outfield door and disappears.

Aching and bruised, Joe Boyd returns to Meg. Applegate shows up, with a final offer to turn Boyd back into Hardy and go on to the World Series. But the love between Joe and Meg is strong, and the villain gives up, vanishing as quickly as he first arrived.

Afterwords

Damn Yankees! originally gained fame as a Broadway musical, running for more than one thousand performances in New York City, starting in May 1955. With dance numbers first choreographed by well-known Bob Fosse, *Damn Yankees!* continues to be produced today, everywhere from middle school to community and off-Broadway theater stages around the world.

A number of performers from the Broadway show appeared in the feature film, including Gwen Verdon as Lola and Ray Walston as Mr. Applegate. However, the folks at Warner Brothers would have preferred dancer Cyd Charisse and suave Cary Grant for the respective film roles. Tab Hunter, a legitimate Hollywood hunk of the day, took the role of slugging savior Joe Hardy.

It's no secret that the basic premise of *Damn Yankees!* was based on the German legend of Faust, a story that dates back more than five hundred years. The tale tells of a magician who sold his soul to the devil, in exchange for youth and all things good.

When *Damn Yankees!* was released in England, its title there was *What Lola Wants*—for several good reasons. First, while the New York Yankees were commonly known in the USA, the Bronx Bombers—and baseball in general—were quite foreign to the Brits. More, it was feared the title might mislead filmgoers into thinking they were about to see a rousing movie about the American Civil War.

Once more, reliable Wrigley Field—in Los Angeles—served as the ball field for shooting, dressed up to resemble Griffith Stadium in Washington, D.C. A second-unit crew also shot three games between the Yankees and Senators at the actual park to use throughout the film.

Warner Brothers paid $750,000 for the film rights to *Damn Yankees!*, along with agreeing to split the profits fifty-fifty with the stage musical producers. While

South Pacific and *Auntie Mame*—both musicals—were the top two grossing films in 1958, *Damn Yankees!* was not as successful, as it didn't even place in the Top Ten for the year.

Eight Men Out

(1988—American/**Orion**—119 Min/Color)
Director: John Sayles
Original Music: Mason Daring
Film Editing: John Tintori
Production Design: Nora Chavooshian
Cast: John Cusack (**George "Buck" Weaver**)
Clifton James (**Charles Comiskey**)
Michael Lerner (**Arnold Rothstein**)
Christopher Lloyd (**"Sleepy" Bill Burns**)
John Mahoney (**Kid Gleason**)
Charlie Sheen (**"Happy" Felsch**)
David Strathairn (**Eddie Cicotte**)
D. B. Sweeney (**"Shoeless" Joe Jackson**)
Michael Rooker (**"Chick" Gandil**)
Don Harvey (**"Swede" Risberg**)
James Read (**"Lefty" Williams**)
Perry Lang (**Fred Mcmullin**)
Gordon Clapp (**Ray Schalk**)

Based on the 1963 Eliot Asinof book *Eight Men Out: The Black Sox and the 1919 World Series.*

The City of Chicago in 1919 is buzzing, and the White Sox are the talk of the town, as sportswriters Ring Lardner and Hughie Fullerton keep everyone informed. Yet club owner Charles Comiskey is unappreciative of his players, and they resent his stingy nature.

Some small-time gamblers offer payoffs to eight of the Sox players to throw the upcoming World Series against the Cincinnati Reds. Many folks believe this Sox club is the best to ever play the game, so bets against them would pay big money if they lost.

The crooks have very little money of their own, so they approach professional gambler Arnold Rothstein to back their scheme. Initially, he turns the deal down but soon is tied up in the plot to throw the Series.

The games begin, with Sox skipper Kid Gleason ignoring rumors that his team will tank the Series. By the third game, it's obvious that something is amiss. But the money promised to the Sox players comes up short, and despite their last-ditch efforts, the Sox lose the Series.

In the off-season, Lardner and Fullerton stoke the fires of doubt, with enough impact to prompt an investigation. Club owners, looking to stem the endless cheating, select Judge Kenesaw Mountain Landis as the first Commissioner of Baseball.

Eight Men Out, 1988 (Back) James Read, Michael Rooker, David Straithairn (Middle) Charlie Sheen, Don Harvey, Perry Lang (Front) John Cusack, D. B. Sweeney.

The investigation results in indictments of eight Sox players, but they are acquitted of the charges. Still, Landis rules with an iron fist and bans them forever. Some years later, Shoeless Joe Jackson plays in an outlaw league, while Buck Weaver quietly maintains his innocence.

Afterwords

The basic story of the 1919 Black Sox scandal is covered elsewhere in this book, while author Eliot Asinof went all the way in telling the tale of arrogance and greed. Way back in 1960, the writer interviewed as many of those involved as he could find. In fact, White Sox catcher Ray Schalk—never implicated in the scandal—had become the head baseball coach at Purdue. He warmly welcomed Asinof into his office, then promptly threw him out when asked about the Black Sox.

Writer and director John Sayles was fascinated by the story and wrote a screenplay based on it in 1977. Nearly ten years later, he convinced Orion Pictures—a new player in Hollywood—to pony up a slim $6 million budget to bring *Eight Men Out* to the screen.

One thing Sayles insisted on was finding actors who knew the game of baseball and could play it. As a result, he cast David Strathairn—known to have a good curve, as well as a convincing knuckleball—as Eddie Cicotte. Shooting in Indianapolis, the actor noted the walls of Bush Stadium were covered in ivy—poison ivy.

Newcomer D. B. Sweeney, cast in the pivotal role of Shoeless Joe Jackson, spent seven weeks with the Kenosha Twins—Class A affiliate for the Minnesota

Twins—to research the feeling of playing pro ball in a no-frills atmosphere. A natural right-handed hitter, Sweeney had to actually turn around and learn to bat lefty, since there was no money in the budget to optically flip the film. He took great pride in being able to get a solid hit whenever needed for the cameras.

Charlie Sheen had a baseball scholarship offer from University of Kansas, but never graduated from Santa Monica High. Sweeney convinced him to consider the project, and, relishing the ability to play ball near his beloved Cincinnati Reds, Sheen signed on to play Happy Felsch. Other actors, like Chicagoans John Cusack and Michael Rooker, joined the cast as Buck Weaver and Chick Gandil, respectively.

Sayles brought in former major league outfielder Ken Berry—a defensive star with the White Sox, Angels, Brewers, and Indians—to be a technical advisor and teach everyone the finer points of the game. For example, chewing tobacco quickly became apricots for most of the players trying to emulate the smokeless tradition. One accidental swallow of chaw was enough to turn the actors off to the practice. Berry noted that Sweeney, Sheen, and Cusack were particularly adept at the game.

Casting himself as sportswriter Ring Lardner, Sayles also tapped the great author and broadcaster Studs Terkel to play fellow scribe Hugh Fullerton. The cast was rounded out by solid character performers like John Mahoney, Clifton James, Christopher Lloyd, and Michael Lerner, among others.

In spite of crafting an excellent drama about baseball, Sayles' project did not make its budget back at the box office. Released around the Labor Day holiday, *Eight Men Out* grossed only $5.7 million in America.

Fear Strikes Out

(1957—American/**Paramount**—100 Min/Color)
Director: Robert Mulligan
Original Music: Elmer Bernstein
Film Editing: Aaron Stell
Art Direction: Hilyard Brown, Hal Pereira
Cast: Anthony Perkins (**Jimmy Piersall**)
Karl Malden (**John Piersall**)
Norma Moore (**Mary Piersall**)
Adam Williams (**Doctor Brown**)

Based on the 1955 Al Hirshberg biography *Fear Strikes Out: The Jim Piersall Story*.

Young Jim Piersall dreams of playing professional baseball. John, his dad, also fires up that dream in the boy—perhaps too much. Jim's high school team wins the state championship, but rather than celebrating the victory, his dad points out his low points. And when Jim breaks his ankle ice skating, John nearly has a heart attack.

The young man is good enough to catch the eye of the Boston Red Sox, starting out as an outfielder on a minor league team in Scranton, Pennsylvania. He meets Mary Stevens one day at the park, and a romance quickly blooms. They get married and move in with Jim's parents.

After several seasons in the minors, the Red Sox call Jim up—but they want to make him a shortstop. He balks at the idea of changing from the outfield and returns home. The anxiety is too great, and Jimmy tries to hide in the bleachers of his high school ball field, where John convinces him to give it a shot.

But Jimmy's intensity and desire to succeed lead to tense relations among the team, as well as a brawl with one of his teammates, which gets Piersall suspended for two weeks. When Jim returns, he's back playing the outfield.

At the plate, Jimmy finally snaps. He climbs the backstop fence in a rage as his teammates pull him down. Jimmy is admitted to the hospital with a mental breakdown, under the care of Dr. Brown. Treatments of all kinds, including electroshock, provide no relief, and Jim becomes withdrawn.

With the doctor's help, Jim begins to improve, and John wants his son to come home. But Dr. Brown is firm—Jimmy needs help and must stay under his care. When John tries to sneak his son out of the hospital, Jimmy refuses and finally admits it was his father's constant prodding and urging that made him crack. He just could never please his dad.

After many weeks, Jimmy sees his dad once more and shares his hopes that he can play for Boston once more. Opening day comes, and Jimmy starts in the outfield for the Red Sox.

Afterwords

More than twenty years ago, I had the rare opportunity to spend several days with one of baseball's most skilled outfielders—and the subject of *Fear Strikes Out*—Jimmy Piersall. I asked him, point-blank, what he thought of the film.

"That scene of me climbing the fence? That's a bunch of malarkey! I never did anything like that," he insisted. "The folks in Hollywood gave me a good amount of money, so they had some right to dress the story up, I guess." The ex-major leaguer didn't appreciate the film's inaccurate take that his mental problems were due to an overbearing and high-pressure dad.

Piersall also had a very strong opinion of actor Anthony Perkins as an athlete, who played the troubled ballplayer in the film. However, decorum and respect for those who have passed on prevent me from elaborating on the real outfielder's pointed and somewhat disappointed observation of Perkins' portrayal.

Part of Perkins' unconvincing baseball skills were based on a simple problem: Piersall was a right-hander and the actor was left-handed. Curiously, the film producers brought in former major leaguer (and fellow left-hander) Tommy Holmes to teach Perkins a righty approach (despite Holmes' left-handedness), but the results were less than successful—as the film demonstrates.

The 1957 movie was not the first time Piersall's story was told. His 1952 mental breakdown with the Red Sox was revealed in a 1955 book by the ballplayer and writer Al Hirshberg. Later that year, Tab Hunter (pre-*Damn Yankees!*) played Piersall in a TV version of the story, presented as part of the CBS anthology series *Climax!*

The big-screen version of *Fear Strikes Out* was made in 1957, a period for Hollywood that saw much emphasis on bug-eyed-monsters and other such sci-fi fodder for the drive-in scene. Marketing a baseball film to nonbaseball fans was a challenge. Consider that most of the movie posters for *Fear Strikes Out* illustrated nothing that had to do with baseball. Rather, they heralded the love story with, "Here's the whole heart-story of today's mixed-up kids," and the volatile and exciting notion of "He's dynamite—Ready to explode!"

In spite of Piersall's negative feelings about much of the film, he still came to appreciate his own predicament. He once reasoned that, in his words, "Probably the best thing that ever happened to me was going nuts. Whoever heard of Jimmy Piersall until that happened?"

Still, the outfielder played for seventeen seasons with the Angels, Indians, Senators, and Mets, as well as the Red Sox. He was a two-time All-Star and Gold Glove winner, posting several solid seasons with averages of .322, .314, and .293.

Field of Dreams

(1989—American/Universal—107 Min/Color)
Director: Phil Alden Robinson
Original Music: James Horner
Film Editing: Ian Crafford
Production Design: Dennis Gassner
Cast: Kevin Costner (**Ray Kinsella**)
Amy Madigan (**Annie Kinsella**)
Gaby Hoffman (**Karin Kinsella**)
Ray Liotta ("**Shoeless**" **Joe Jackson**)
Timothy Busfield (**Mark**)
James Earl Jones (**Terence Mann**)
Burt Lancaster (**Dr. Archibald "Moonlight" Graham**)
Frank Whaley (**Archie Graham**)
Dwier Brown (**John Kinsella**)

Based on the 1982 W. P. Kinsella novel *Shoeless Joe.*

Ray Kinsella lives in rural Iowa, a young farmer with his wife Annie and daughter Karin. Ray's deceased father, John, loved the game of baseball and Shoeless Joe Jackson. In a cornfield, Ray hears a strange voice that urges, "If you build it, he will come."

The image of a baseball diamond fills Ray's head, and, in spite of his skeptical wife, he plows under some of the corn and builds a ball field. Neighboring farmers heckle Ray, and as time passes, nothing happens. His brother-in-law, Mark, urges Ray to dump the field before he goes broke.

One night, Karin sees a man in the field. Ray discovers it's Joe Jackson, who somehow has returned to play ball in his field. Soon, the other 1919 White Sox join Jackson on the field—to hit, to field, to play ball.

The local PTA advocates banning the books of sixties writer Terence Mann, tagging them as smut. Ray feels a connection and is moved to find the reclusive Pulitzer Prize–winning author. In Boston, Ray convinces a dubious Mann—who just wants to be left alone—to attend a Red Sox game at Fenway Park.

At the game, Kinsella and Mann discover they must find a man named Archibald "Moonlight" Graham, an old-time ballplayer, in Minnesota. But Graham—who played only one game in the majors before becoming a doctor—died in 1972. Unexpectedly, Ray finds himself back in 1972, where he meets Graham.

The elderly doctor confides that he regrets not getting an at bat in the majors, but Ray has a place where that can happen. Graham refuses the offer, and Ray heads back to Iowa with Mann. On the way, they pick up a young hitchhiker—a budding ballplayer named Archie Graham.

Back home, the field is filled with long-gone ballplayers, and Archie joins them in the game, where he drives in a run with a sacrifice fly. Mark, not seeing the game or players, has bought the note on Ray's farm and threatens foreclosure.

Young Karin assures her father that people will come to the park and pay to watch the games.

Mann reinforces the idea, reminding him that, "the one constant through all the years . . . has been baseball."

When Ray argues with Mark, Karin falls from the bleachers and is knocked unconscious. Archie steps from the field, becoming the wise and experienced Dr. Graham, and revives her. But he cannot go back to the game—or his younger self—and that's fine with Moonlight. Suddenly, Mark sees the players and frantically urges his brother-in-law not to sell the farm. Mann joins Jackson and the others as they disappear into the cornfield.

Suddenly, it's clear why the park is there, as Ray's father appears in catcher's gear—Ray will have a chance to have a catch with his father after all. And, with the park's lights on, long lines of people arrive to see the games.

Afterwords

Canadian-born novelist W. P. Kinsella published *Shoeless Joe* in 1982, based on his twenty-page short story. The tale caught the eye and imagination of film writer and director Phil Alden Robinson. When Paramount and Twentieth Century-Fox studios passed on making the film, Universal picked it up.

Unlike then-recent successful baseball films, like *The Natural* and *Bull Durham*, the story in *Field of Dreams* went much further than just activities on the diamond, including the search for secluded writer Terence Mann. In Kinsella's book, the writer was real-world recluse J. D. Salinger, but Universal feared legal issues in using the writer's real name in a fictional film.

Robinson called on USC baseball coach Rod Dedeaux to work with the actors on their baseball skills (a task he would also undertake in *A League of Their Own*). Even though he had just finished *Bull Durham*, baseball-savvy Kevin Costner was cast in the lead role.

Ray Liotta signed on, although he has admitted that he really didn't get the story when he first read the script. But the chance to work with actors like James Earl Jones and Burt Lancaster was something he just couldn't pass up.

The voice that spoke to Ray Kinsella, while credited as "Himself," has been said to belong to actor Ed Harris. The novel's author was told this fact, and it probably has a good chance of being true, as Harris was (and is) the husband of Amy Madigan, who played Annie Kinsella in the film.

After considering everywhere from New Mexico to Ontario, the location of the Kinsella farm was—logically—set in Iowa (where the story took place). The tiny town of Dyersville—just west of Dubuque and the Mississippi River—was overrun with cast and crew. A house and property, including a cornfield, was secured from the Don Lansing family, and a ball field was built in just three days' time.

The summer of 1988 in Iowa was hot and dry, to which I can personally attest. Entering a small antiques and collectibles shop in Dubuque one day back then, I found the shelves almost empty. The owner grumbled, "Yeah—They're shooting some film called *Shoeless Joe* down the road and they (the production crew) came in here and cleaned me out." At the time, I had no idea of the film that was coming.

The disagreeable weather led to major issues for the production. For one, the cornfield from which the players were to step was only knee-high, rather than up past their shoulders. Water was pumped in to encourage rapid growth. The grass was dry and brown as well, so the production team had to paint it a lively green before every day's shoot.

The site was maintained after filming completed, becoming a mecca of sorts for families to come and "have a catch" for free. The Lansings sold the 193-acre property to a group hoping to turn the site into a major tourist attraction (which it already had become, anyway). However, zoning questions have delayed its progress.

Field of Dreams was shot on a budget of $15 million and returned a healthy $60 million in box office receipts (as the folks at Paramount and Fox repeatedly kicked themselves). More, the film received three Oscar nominations, including for Best Picture.

The Funny or Die.com website produced a hilarious mock trailer in 2011 for *Field of Dreams 2: Lockout*. The three-minute film features Taylor Lautner and a bunch of pro footballers, with football basically replacing baseball as the theme. Ray Liotta shows up as NFL commissioner Roger Goodell, along with another pleasant surprise at the end.

Long Gone

(1987—American/**HBO**—110 Min/Color)
Director: Martin Davidson
Original Music: Phillip Namanworth, Kenny Vance
Film Editing: Gib Jaffe
Production Design: Glenn Ganis
Cast: William Petersen (**Cecil "Stud" Cantrell**)
Virginia Madsen (**Dixie Lee Boxx**)
Dermot Mulroney (**Jamie Don Weeks**)
Larry Riley (**Joe Louis Brown**)
Henry Gibson (**Hale Buchman**)
Teller (**Hale Buchman Jr**).

William Petersen and Virginia Madsen in *Long Gone*, 1987.

Based on the 1979 Novel By Paul Hemphill. In 1957, Stud Cantrell has the sorry role of pitcher/manager for the last-place Tampico Stogies, a sorrier minor league team in the Gulf Coast League. Local beauty pageant winner Dixie Lee Boxx hooks up with the cigar-smoking, hard-drinking Cantrell while the team takes a long and uncomfortable road trip by bus.

Jamie Weeks is a churchgoing, soda-drinking rookie second baseman sent to the Stogies. The kid has the looks of a fine ballplayer, but cheapskate owners—Hale Buchman and his son, Hale Jr.—are hesitant to pay Weeks any more than what he's worth.

Cantrell was once a top switch-hitting prospect with the Cardinals, going head-to-head with Stan Musial for a starting position. But Stud was wounded in World War II, ending his chances at a big league career.

Also joining the Stogies is Joe Louis Brown, a powerful and cocky black catcher. But below the Mason-Dixon line, fans (and the Klan) wouldn't take to a player of his color, so Stud decides to say he's a Venezuelan named Jose.

With the new talent, the Stogies start winning ball games and are poised to win the pennant. The owners of rival Dothan Cardinals offer Stud the job of managing their team next season, with the chance to move up to the majors—if he agrees to throw the race for this season and lets the Cards win the pennant. He reluctantly agrees.

Disappointed, Dixie leaves Cantrell. More, the Buchmans' mortgage is held by the Cardinals owners, and if the Stogies win, they'll lose their team. Weeks finds out and angrily confronts the man he idolized.

The final game sees Cantrell and Brown nowhere to be found, so Weeks takes command of the team. Cantrell meets Brown in an empty bar, realizing the owners got to him, too. But, recognizing their foolish decisions, they hurry to the park to get into the game.

The Stogies are down a run in the bottom of the ninth. With two outs, Dothan tries to intentionally walk Brown, but he reaches out and homers to tie the game. Weeks triples, and the next two batters are intentionally walked to load the bases, for a force anywhere.

With Cantrell at bat, the Cards put in a relief pitcher who has totally dominated Stud in his career. But Cantrell angers the hurler, and he hits Stud in the head with a pitch. But the hit batsman goes to first, and the Stogies win the pennant. Proud of Cantrell, Dixie agrees to marry him.

Afterwords

Even though *Long Gone* seemed to be part *Major League*, part *Bull Durham*, and part *Alibi Ike*, it actually first aired on the HBO cable network in May 1987, more than a year before the release of *Bull Durham* and almost two years before *Major League*. Many have lauded the film, although it remains hard to find today—having never been released on DVD.

The film was in good hands, directed by Martin Davidson, who had helmed cult favorites like 1974's *Lords of Flatbush* and 1983's *Eddie and the Cruisers*. William Petersen, still more than a decade away from his role as Gil Grissom in TV's

CSI, took the role of Cecil "Stud" Cantrell. Virginia Madsen, cast as Cantrell's girlfriend, Dixie Lee Boxx, was in the beginning years of a successful and diverse career in TV and movies.

The same can be said for Dermot Mulroney, playing infielder Jamie Weeks. All three actors shared a common connection with the city of Chicago. Petersen and Madsen grew up in the North Shore area (Madsen's older brother is actor Michael), and Mulroney graduated from Northwestern University.

The film—occasionally found on VHS—is worthwhile to seek out. If not for the compelling story and baseball scenes, then only for seeing Teller—the silent half of the magic act of Penn and Teller—taking the role of Hale Buchman Jr. (Yes, he actually speaks in *Long Gone*.)

Like the novel, HBO's *Long Gone* was set in the late 1950s. Shot on an eight-week schedule, the film has Tampa's William Field dressed up to play the home of the Tampico Stogies. Petersen, Madsen, and Mulroney all admitted the experience during production was among the best they'd ever had.

Major League

(1989—American/**Paramount**—107 Min/**Color**)
Director: David S. Ward
Original Music: James Newton Howard
Film Editing: Dennis M. Hill
Production Design: Jeffery Howard
Cast: Tom Berenger (**Jake Taylor**)
Charlie Sheen (**Ricky Vaughn**)
Corbin Bernsen (**Roger Dorn**)
Margaret Whitton (**Rachel Phelps**)
James Gammon (**Lou Brown**)
Rene Russo (**Lynn Wells**)
Wesley Snipes (**Willie Mays Hayes**)
Dennis Haysbert (**Pedro Cerrano**)
Bob Uecker (**Harry Doyle**)

The city of Cleveland has not seen a pennant from their Indians for many years. Unlikeable owner Rachel Phelps has a scheme to move the team to Miami: Put players on the field who are so inept that no one will want to watch.

Spring training arrives, and so do players like aging catcher Jake Taylor, ex-con and wild-armed pitcher Ricky Vaughn, voodoo-loving slugger Pedro Cerrano, snobbish third baseman Roger Dorn, and would-be speedster Willie Mays Hayes. Manager Lou Brown hopes Taylor can be a leader. He also has to play peacemaker, as Dorn and Vaughn take an immediate dislike to each other.

The season starts, and Jake is unsuccessful in rekindling his romance with his old flame, Lynn. Hard-drinking radio announcer Harry Doyle is challenged to keep listeners engaged with the faltering team. Phelps makes conditions worse by forcing the team to fly in a broken-down prop plane (then switching to a broken-down bus) and not fixing the whirlpool or water pipes in the clubhouse.

With three-quarters of the season over, the Indians are playing even ball. Brown shares Rachel's wicked scheme with the team, and Jake angrily urges them to win it all. The Indians go on a tear, ending in a first place tie with the Yankees, in spite of Phelps' attempts to derail them.

In a one-game playoff, the Indians and Yanks are tied 2–2 in the top of the ninth. Vaughn—now nicknamed Wild Thing—is brought in to face Clu Haywood, who has hit very well against Ricky all season. Reaching back for something extra, he throws a 101 mph fastball to set the slugger down for the third out.

The Indians come up in the bottom of the ninth. Hayes legs out an infield chopper, then steals second. Taylor, gimpy knees and all, lays down a bunt as Willie heads for third. With the play going to first, Hayes heads straight for the plate. Jake is safe at first, Willie is safe at home, and the Indians win the pennant. More, Jake and Lynn pick up their romance where it left off years ago.

Afterwords

If *Bull Durham* went for high-brow baseball humor, then *Major League* aimed at a target lower down in the strike zone. However, it never reached the "funny-as-heck-but-in-the-gutter" fun of the baseball scenes in *The Naked Gun*, like baseball

wives spitting in unison. *Bull Durham* opted for story, while *Major League* chose laughs.

The 1989 film was written and directed by David S. Ward, an Oscar winner in 1974 for penning *The Sting*. The popularity of then-recent baseball films like *The Natural*, *Bull Durham*, and *Eight Men Out* led Ward to pitch (yes, that was intentional) his five-year-old script about a hapless Cleveland Indians ball club—with the working title of *Dead Last*—to relative newcomer production companies Morgan Creek and Mirage. A long-suffering Indians fan in real life, Ward figured the only way to see his team win the World Series would be to make a movie of it.

Similar to the process that worked for director Penny Marshall with *A League of Their Own*, Ward insisted on first checking the auditioning performer for his baseball skills before doing an actual script reading. Charlie Sheen, fresh from his role in *Eight Men Out*, has since

2014 Topps card set of 1989's *Major League*, Tom Berenger, Corbin Bernsen, Chelcie Ross, and Charlie Sheen.

admitted that he boosted his fastball into the mid-eighties by using steroids during the shooting of *Major League*.

Dennis Haysbert, playing a voodoo-practicing power hitter, was just about as prolific as he was supposed to be. Although he hadn't played ball since adolescence, whenever he was scripted to go yard as Cerrano, Haysbert really cranked the home runs. But, despite an athletic background that included advanced belts in martial arts, Wesley Snipes was never shown throwing a baseball—he just wasn't very good at it.

Shot in the midst of a blistering summer, the film supposedly took place in Cleveland's Municipal Stadium. In actuality, Milwaukee County Stadium played the part, which made the role of boozing announcer Harry Doyle easy enough to cast. Bob Uecker, former major league catcher and—conveniently—the radio announcer for Brewers games right there in Milwaukee, ad libbed most of Doyle's hilarious comments.

Also well known in Milwaukee was Pete Vuckovich, who played Yankee slugger Clu Haywood. He had an eleven-year career in the majors as a pitcher, including winning the Cy Young Award in 1982 with the Brewers.

One oddity for the sharp-eyed (and eared) filmgoer: While the end credits refer to Rene Russo's character as "Lynn Wells," Jake makes a call during the movie, asking for "Lynn Westland"—who isn't at the Cuyahoga Body Shop (the fake phone number she gave Taylor).

Budgeted at $11 million, *Major League* grossed more than $50 million at US box offices. The film's success resulted in *Major League II*, directed once more by Ward and released in 1994. This time, Baltimore's Camden Yards filled in for the Cleveland park, and almost all of the stars from the first film reprised their roles. The result was a modest success, with a gross of $30 million on a budget of $25 million.

The same cannot be said for *Major League: Back to the Minors*. Released (many suggest "got loose from the bullpen" is a better phrase) in 1998, only Bernsen and Haysbert returned to the team. Filmgoers noticed, as the film only grossed a bit more than $3 million and was quickly banished to DVD and cable hell.

David Ward has revealed that he does have a script for *Major League 3* (actually, *ML 4*, but he refuses to acknowledge the *Back to the Minors* debacle, of which he had no part). More encouraging is the fact that almost all of the principal actors—including Wesley Snipes and favorite Bob Uecker—have expressed great interest in taking part in the new film, where they would play manager and coaches for the Indians team. Production and release dates remain to be seen.

Million Dollar Arm

(2014—American/**Disney**—124 Min/Color)
Director: Craig Gillespie
Original Music: A. R. Rahman
Film Editing: Tatiana S. Riegel
Production Design: Barry Robison
Cast: Jon Hamm (JB)

Pitobash Tripathy (**Amit Rohan**)
Suraj Sharma (**Rinku Singh**)
Madhur Mittal (**Dinesh Patel**)
Alan Arkin (**Ray Poitevint**)
Bill Paxton (**Tom House**)
Tzi Ma (**Mr. Chang**)

Based on the 2014 book by J. B. Bernstein.

JB Bernstein is a sports agent, hard-pressed to sign any new talent—football, baseball, or otherwise. With all his big clients retired or signing with other agencies, JB needs a new source of talent.

While watching *Britain's Got Talent* one night, a thought strikes JB—India has millions of cricket players. Perhaps some of their bowlers could become baseball pitchers—all captured for a reality TV show called *Million Dollar Arm*. JB convinces Mr. Chang to financially underwrite the venture, as long as it's within one year's time. Pitching coach Tom House balks at the idea, but JB gets him to help out.

JB arrives in India, stunned at the cultural and lifestyle differences from America. Word of the upcoming show spreads quickly in the media, and a young local named Amit who loves baseball talks his way onto the project as an interpreter. Retired scout Ray Poitevint joins JB to help select the potential contestants. But, with the fundamental differences between bowling and pitching mechanics, the early results are not promising at all.

Eventually, twenty candidates emerge, and the show begins. Two young men, Rinku and Dinesh—oddly, neither like the game of cricket—win the contest and the chance to pitch in America.

Half-sheet poster, *Million Dollar Arm*, 2014.

The pair arrive in the US, just as stunned and amazed as JB was in India. After setting off a fire alarm at their hotel, Rinku, Dinesh, and Amit are forced to move in with JB. They start working with coach House at the USC campus.

But JB's work to get more clients leaves Rinku and Dinesh feeling abandoned, and House sees them struggling as a result. Plus, they are homesick. JB loses patience with them, having lost control of his life because of them.

It's clear that JB must be more involved with the pair, and he begins to focus more on them. In turn, the young pitchers begin to improve in their baseball skills. But Mr. Chang insists that the pair try out within the year that was agreed upon.

With worldwide media and two dozen MLB scouts watching, Rinku and Dinesh freeze up. Their pitching is mediocre at best, and they are not signed by anyone. Yet Chang is satisfied that JB delivered on their agreement and will finance his business for another three years.

The boys are disappointed, believing they failed. Sacrificing Chang's support, JB realizes that he is the one who failed and Rinku and Dinesh deserve another tryout. No one is interested, but thanks to Ray, the Pittsburgh Pirates will take a look.

JB stresses that baseball should be fun—not all business—and the tryout begins, with Ray, House, and Chang watching, along with the Pittsburgh scout. This time, their pitching is outstanding, and the Pirates offer contracts to them both.

Afterwords

It is often said that "truth is stranger than fiction," and the case of *Million Dollar Arm* is a somewhat strange—and true—story. A sports agent, his stable gone dry, seeks athletic talent from India and the game of cricket—by way of a reality TV show. With records of under .500 for every season since 1992, it's no surprise the Pittsburgh Pirates would be willing to take a shot at the two pitchers who won the *Million Dollar Arm* TV show.

J. B. Bernstein started the Access Group of Miami sports agency in 1993, where he represented sports figures like Barry Bonds, Barry Sanders, and Emmitt Smith. When the economy took a turn for the worse in 2008, Bernstein needed to rethink who he could represent. He wound up in India, where cricket bowler Rinku Singh and javelin thrower Dinesh Patel won an *American Idol*-type of TV competition, with baseball pitchers instead of singers.

The story was snapped up by Columbia Pictures, but, as often happens in Hollywood, the proposal wound up in turnaround—also known as development hell—where a project becomes something no one wants to make any more. Fortunately, Disney Studios picked it up and cast Jon Hamm, popular as ad man Don Draper in AMC's *Mad Men*, in the lead as Bernstein.

The cast was rounded out with Suraj Sharma, from 2012's *Life of Pi*, as Singh; Madhur Mittal, from 2008's *Slumdog Millionaire*, as Patel; and Oscar winner Alan Arkin as an aged baseball scout. Bill Paxton appeared as pitching coach and former Braves, Red Sox, and Mariners lefty Tom House.

Million Dollar Arm ends with lefty Singh and righty Patel signing with the Pirates, but their real story continued from there. Both made their first professional appearances by pitching back-to-back innings in a rookie Gulf Coast League game in July 2009.

Rinku Singh continued pitching for Pirates' minor league teams, reaching A ball in 2012. He also pitched in the Australian Baseball League All-Star Game, but injuries—including Tommy John surgery—kept him out of the game in 2013 and 2014.

Dinesh Patel was less successful, as he pitched for two seasons in the Gulf Coast League before being released and returning to India. He finished his schooling—which he had quit to pitch—and spent time coaching a new group of prospective pitchers for a new TV season of *Million Dollar Arm*. Patel has also gone back to working on his javelin throwing.

Disney's film opened in May 2014, amid the popular Memorial Day release frenzy that included *The Amazing Spider-Man 2*, *Godzilla*, and *X-Men: Days of Future Past*. Shot on a $25 million budget, *Million Dollar Arm* grossed more than $36 million, with another $2 million overseas.

Moneyball

(2011—American/**Columbia**—133 Min/Color)
Director: Bennett Miller
Original Music: James Horner
Film Editing: Ian Crafford
Production Design: Dennis Gassner
Cast: Brad Pitt (**Billy Beane**)
Jonah Hill (**Peter Brand**)
Philip Seymour Hoffman (**Art Howe**)
Robin Wright (**Sharon**)
Chris Pratt (**Scott Hatteberg**)
Stephen Bishop (**David Justice**)
Nick Porrazzo (**Jeremy Giambi**)
Arliss Howard (**John Henry**)

Based on the 2003 Michael Lewis book *Moneyball: The Art of Winning an Unfair Game*.

Oakland A's GM Billy Beane sits in a dark and empty stadium while, across the country, his team loses the 2001 ALCS to the New York Yankees. With a payroll budget of less than $40 million, Beane can hardly compete with teams like the Yanks and their bulging payroll of three times as much.

Upcoming free agency will strip the A's of valuable talent, and Beane needs to assemble a competitive lineup for the 2002 season, despite the club's limited financial resources. Sitting in a conference room full of A's agents, Billy realizes they are old-time solutions to modern-day issues. As a former ballplayer, he knows the game from all sides, but meetings with other ball clubs are fruitless in getting new players.

In an Indians meeting, Beane notices a young fellow named Peter Brand, a numbers savant who uses computers to analyze players' performance. This new way of evaluating talent fits Billy's needs, so he hires Brand to join the A's. Peter quickly puts his computer to work and develops a list for Beane—misread and undervalued by other teams, these affordable players could lead the A's to a championship.

But the A's manager, Art Howe, feels slighted by having just a one-year contract, and the old-time scouts have little faith in Beane, or Brand and his spreadsheets. Billy's plan (according to Brand's figures) to replace first baseman Jason Giambi's OBP with three new players—Jeremy Giambi, David Justice, and Scott Hatteberg,—is met with skeptical looks and negative comments.

Opening day of 2002 comes, and the A's roster has everyone scratching their heads. Manager Howe doesn't buy into Billy's scheme and plays rookie Carlos Pena at first base instead of Hatteberg. When the A's

Advance one-sheet poster, *Moneyball*, 2011.

stumble out of the blocks and continue to lose, Beane is vilified for going against proven scouting procedures and embracing Bill James' Sabermetrics methods.

Billy finally gets Hatteberg in at first base by trading Pena, as well as Giambi—another set of moves that don't sit well with Howe. Beane urges Justice to be a leader for the team. Slowly, the A's begin to buy into Billy's plan, and the results show as they move up in the standings. At one point, they streak to first place by winning an amazing twenty consecutive games and finish the season with 103 wins and 59 losses.

In the AL Division Series, the A's two wins are tied with the Twins, but Oakland loses the deciding fifth game. In the off-season, Boston Red Sox owner John Henry makes a pitch for Beane to become his GM, having just hired Bill James as a special analyst. But Billy passes, choosing to stay with the A's. Two years later, using Beane's new baseball model, the Red Sox win their first World Series since 1918.

Afterwords

Michael Lewis' book about Billy Beane and the Oakland A's spent fifteen weeks on the bestseller list when it came out in the summer of 2003. Columbia Pictures bought the film rights in 2004, with George Clooney suggested for the role of Beane. Many folks thought *Moneyball*'s story of baseball's "new math" let the genie out of the bottle, as the other twenty-nine teams now had the A's formula for low-cost success.

By 2008, Brad Pitt was slated to play the A's GM, with the surprise casting of former funny guy Jonah Hill as stats expert Peter Brand. Brand was a character created for the film when Paul DePodesta—the Harvard economics grad who put much of the Sabermetric analysis in place for the A's—requested his name not be used in the film. Steven Soderbergh—Oscar winner for helming 2000's *Traffic*—was all set to direct.

But Sony Pictures suddenly got cold feet in the summer of 2009 and, not liking the script, pulled the plug as shooting was just about to begin. A year later, with a rewritten script and Bennett Miller named to direct, shooting for *Moneyball* began.

Early reports for *Moneyball* had real Athletics first baseman Scott Hatteberg, outfielder David Justice, and manager Art Howe playing themselves in the film. Cooler heads eventually prevailed, as Chris Pratt (pre-*Guardians of the Galaxy*), TV's Stephen Bishop (former minor leaguer with the Atlanta Braves), and Oscar winner Philip Seymour Hoffman in those respective parts. Real former MLB players Royce Clayton (as Miguel Tejada) and Derrin Ebert (as Mike Magante) added to the believability.

Oakland Coliseum played . . . well, played Oakland Coliseum, while the A's clubhouse was meticulously recreated on a Sony soundstage for its six weeks of shooting. Other facilities used included LA's Dodger Stadium, Boston's Fenway Park, Blair Field at Cal State-Long Beach, and Stengel Field at Glendale Community College.

As of the 2015 season, Billy Beane was still the GM for Oakland, having held the spot since 1998. As for Paul DePodesta, he became GM for the LA Dodgers in 2004, lasting only two seasons. Since then, he has been a front-office executive with the Padres and Mets.

The difficulties in getting *Moneyball* to the screen were worth it in the end. Shot on a budget of $50 million, it grossed nearly $76 million in the US, with another $25 million overseas. Even better, it earned six Academy Award nominations, including for Best Picture. Pitt was nominated for Best Performance in a Lead Role, while Hill was honored with a nod for Best Performance in a Supporting Role.

The Natural

(1984—American/Tri-Star—138 Min/Color)
Director: Barry Levinson
Original Music: Randy Newman
Film Editing: Christopher Holmes, Stu Linder
Production Design: Mel Bourne, Angelo Graham
Cast: Robert Redford (**Roy Hobbs**)
Robert Duvall (**Max Mercy**)
Glenn Close (**Iris Gaines**)
Kim Basinger (**Memo Paris**)
Wilford Brimley (**Pop Fisher**)
Barbara Hershey (**Harriet Bird**)
Robert Prosky (**Judge Banner**)
Darren Mcgavin (**Gus Sands**)

Based on the 1952 Bernard Malamud novel.

In the early 1900s, Roy Hobbs is a teenager with a great talent for baseball. A lightning bolt strikes a tree one night, and Roy fashions a special bat from the split wood. He calls it "Wonderboy." Roy leaves his home, and girlfriend Iris Gaines, for a chance to play for the Chicago Cubs.

Hobbs meets sportswriter Max Mercy and the game's greatest hitter, the Whammer, on the train to Chicago. At a water stop, Hobbs wins a bet by striking out the Whammer on just three pitches. The feat catches the eye of mysterious Harriet Bird. She lures Roy to her room, then shoots him and jumps to her death from the hotel window.

Fifteen years pass, and Pop Fisher manages the last-place New York Knights. Hobbs joins the club as a middle-aged rookie, but Pop wants nothing to do with him. An amazing display of power at batting practice changes Pop's mind, and Roy becomes the Knights' right fielder.

Replica card of Roy Hobbs, *The Natural*, 1984.

The club is owned by the miserly Judge Banner, who has a deal to take the club away from Fisher if the team doesn't win the pennant. Suddenly, the team starts to win consistently, with Roy motivating his teammates.

A romance grows between Roy and Memo, Fisher's niece—and cohort of gambler Gus Sands. The distraction puts Roy into a slump, but he breaks out in Chicago, where Iris appears to inspire her long-lost beau. They reminisce and find they still have strong feelings for each other. Iris is not married, but she has a teenage son.

The Knights and Roy get back on track, heading for the pennant. Sands might lose a bundle in bets, so he convinces Memo to slip Roy a poison that puts him in the hospital. Once there, the Judge leaves a bundle of money to ensure that Hobbs will throw the game. Doctors remove a bullet from Roy's stomach, an unpleasant memory from Harriet that has left Roy at the risk of dying if he continues to play ball.

Mercy threatens Hobbs with incriminating photos of him and Bird, but he'll have none of it. At the ballpark, Roy returns the money to the Judge and states he's ready to win. But the days in the hospital have left Roy weak, and he strikes out in his first appearances in the game, while his injured abdomen is bleeding. Iris slips Roy a note, informing him that her son is also his son.

He steps into the batter's box, and, as thunder crashes around the stadium, Hobbs blasts a game-winning home run. In epilogue, Roy enjoys playing catch with his son, while Iris happily watches.

Afterwords

Robert Redford's starring role as Roy Hobbs was his first cinematic effort since acting in 1980's *Brubaker*, as well as winning an Oscar in 1981 for best director on *Ordinary People*. The performer knew he wanted to move away from the "handsome leading man-type" roles he often played and, with a passion for baseball, brought a script by Roger Towne to director—and fellow baseball fan—Barry Levinson.

Even though it strayed a great deal from Malamud's novel (for example, the novel's finale has Hobbs striking out to end the game), Redford saw the flaws in the character and relished the chance to play Hobbs. Plus, he got to play ball on film—lots of ball.

As a teen, Redford had earned a baseball scholarship to the University of Colorado in Boulder, but eventually moved toward acting. Still, he had plenty of power left in his bat, as Levinson noted that the star—at age forty-six—hit several legitimate home runs when shooting the film at War Memorial Stadium in Buffalo, New York. While growing up, the actor had admired Ted Williams, so he had Hobbs wear the number "9" as a nod to the Splendid Splinter.

Early in the film, Hobbs faced off against a well-known slugger called The Whammer, in a wager that the young phenom could strike the major leaguer out on three pitched balls—the Whammer's character was obviously based on Babe Ruth.

Even though the part was nicely played by Joe Don Baker (who gave the slightest bit of a respectful smile to the young Hobbs in the end), thought was given to casting a real major league home run hitter. Levinson recalls meeting with Harmon Killebrew and Boog Powell, but the idea was nixed when the producers thought their notoriety might detract from the scene.

The Natural grossed nearly $48 million and garnered four Oscar nominations, including one for composer Randy Newman's stirring and memorable music score. It also opened the doors for a rash of baseball films like *Bull Durham*, the *Major League* franchise, and others in the late 1980s, proving baseball was a viable theme for successful cinema.

The Naughty Nineties

(1945—American/**Universal**—76 Min/B&W)
Director: Jean Yarbrough
Original Music: Paul Dessau, Edgar Fairchild
Film Editing: Arthur Hilton
Art Direction: John B. Goodman, Harold H. Macarthur
Cast: Bud Abbott (**Dexter Broadhurst**)
Lou Costello (**Sebastian Dinwiddle**)

Frame grab of "Who's on First?" from *The Naughty Nineties*, 1945.

Captain Sam Jackson is the captain of the River Queen showboat that sails the Mississippi River in the 1890s. When he loses the ship to some conniving crooks in a fixed poker game, Abbott and Costello—as performers Broadhurst and Dinwiddle—help to get the ship back for Captain Sam. As part of their entertainment on the showboat stage, they perform their famed "Who's on First?" routine, as well as other hilarious bits.

The "Who's on First" bit begins with Broadhurst singing "Take Me Out to the Ball Game," accompanied by the showboat orchestra, while Dinwiddle hawks peanuts and popcorn to the audience. When Broadhurst takes exception to the interruption, Dinwiddle proclaims his love for baseball and pleads with Broadhurst—dressed in a St. Louis Wolves uniform—to teach him all the players' names. The result is a seemingly never-ending confusion between their nicknames and adjectives, pronouns, and adverbs.

Afterwords

By 1945, the comedy team of Abbott and Costello were one of the biggest box office draws in Hollywood. Their success almost single-handedly brought Universal Studios from the brink of bankruptcy. Along with films, they had several popular radio shows during the 1940s.

The Naughty Nineties was the duo's thirteenth film for Universal in just five years. Felix Adler, longtime writer for the Three Stooges and their Columbia shorts, contributed additional comedy scenes to this film.

The seminal "Who's on First" routine (also known as "the Baseball Routine") often credited to Abbott and Costello actually has roots that date back to burlesque theater and the 1880s. Similar gags—using the confusion between pronouns and people and/or places—were known as The Baker Scene (located on "Watt" Street), and Who Dyed (the clothes maker is named "Who"). Other comics from the early days of vaudeville, like Phil Silvers and Milton Berle, were among the many to do a version of the gag. Bud and Lou first performed it on the *Kate Smith Hour* radio program in March 1938.

The key to the success of the bit lies solely in the timing of the give and take—the questions and responses. As someone who has endured watching countless failed attempts (usually by high school variety show performers) at presenting the routine, I've noticed that rapidity is the solution for laughs, not groans. The words are just silly, but the precise timing of Bud and Lou (plus Costello's slowly building frustration and anger) make this perhaps the single funniest bit ever committed to film.

Despite the vague origins of "Who's on First," the team was honored by having the routine copyrighted under their names in 1944, and the comic clip from *The Naughty Nineties* runs continuously today in the Baseball Hall of Fame.

Pride of the Yankees

(1942—American/RKO—128 Min/B&W)
Director: Sam Wood
Original Music: Leigh Harline
Film Editing: Daniel Mandell
Production Design: William Cameron Menzies
Cast: Gary Cooper (**Henry Louis "Lou" Gehrig**)
Teresa Wright (**Eleanor Twitchell**)
Babe Ruth (**Himself**)
Walter Brennan (**Sam Blake**)

A written prologue compares Lou Gehrig facing death with valor and fortitude, just as soldiers in battle were doing in World War II.

Young Lou Gehrig, the only son of immigrant parents, wants to play the American game of baseball. But his domineering mother has other plans; she wants Lou to go to college and become an engineer, "like Uncle Otto."

Like a good son, Lou follows his mother's wishes and attends Columbia University. But his gift for baseball is hard to ignore, and with the help of sportswriter Sam Blake, Lou signs a minor league contract to play with the New York Yankees. Papa is thrilled, but Lou's new job must be kept a secret from Mother.

Gehrig makes the big league team, and when Wally Pipp's health forces him to sit, Lou gets his chance to play first base for the Yankees. Playing alongside great players like Babe Ruth, Gehrig proves he belongs. He meets Eleanor Twitchell, and despite the jealous concerns of Lou's mother, he soon marries Ellie.

Some of the Yankee players visit a St. Louis hospital during the World Series, and when Ruth promises a home run in front of the press for Billy, a bedridden fan, Gehrig ups the ante by promising 2 homers. At the ballpark, the Babe makes good on his pledge with a long drive over the fence. Lou delivers as well, cranking 2 out of the park to win the game.

Lou and Ellie have a fine marriage, in spite of Lou's meddling mother. At stadiums across the country, he continues his streak of consecutive game appearances, earning him the moniker of "the Iron Horse."

In the midst of an outstanding major league career, Gehrig finds he's growing weak for some unknown reason. Doctors discover Lou has a fatal disease, and the slugger wants it kept quiet. Still, Ellie can sense the truth, knowing that Lou doesn't have much time.

The Yankees have a day honoring Gehrig's great career. Entering the park, Lou is greeted by Billy, the bedridden boy from years back. Lou had encouraged the boy, and now, fully recuperated, Billy wanted to thank him. At the mic, Lou tells the packed stadium that, in spite of the bad break, he's "the luckiest man on the face of the Earth." He walks into the dugout as thousands of fans cheer.

Afterwords

Director Sam Wood is remembered for making what are considered by many film fans the two best Marx Brothers comedies—1935's *A Night at the Opera* and 1937's *A Day at the Races*. The prolific director headed over eighty films in a career that lasted more than three decades. He also had a reputation as an unpleasant, right-wing bigot—but enough of the accolades.

Producer Sam Goldwyn wasn't sure he wanted to make *Pride of the Yankees* for RKO Pictures, calling it "box office poison." He knew that women comprised more than half of the moviegoing audience, and they didn't particularly care for sports films. Also, with America entering World War II, the prospect of any foreign markets embracing a baseball film was very slim. Still, Goldwyn ponied up $30,000 to Gehrig's widow, Eleanor, for the film rights.

Gary Cooper receives hitting tips from Babe Ruth, *Pride of the Yankees*, 1942.

Gehrig died in June 1941, and production was under way within just a few months. The finished film was ready for release only thirteen months later. A wide variety of actors were suggested for the lead role, including Spencer Tracy, Eddie Albert, and Cary Grant. Mrs. Gehrig thought Barbara Stanwyck or Jean Arthur would be ideal to play her own role, feeling Teresa Wright—at just twenty-three—was too young for the part. Once Eleanor saw Wright's performance, she was thrilled with the choice.

Personally, I am always thrilled to see Babe Ruth in the flick, of course, playing himself. Any reported animosity between Ruth and the real Gehrig was nonexistent in *Pride of the Yankees,* considering the tone of the entire film. The Babe had been seriously ill before shooting started, and in order to get into playing shape for the cameras, he lost nearly fifty pounds. The sudden weight loss resulted in pneumonia for the Bambino, putting him back in the hospital when shooting completed.

A long-standing story tells of actor Gary Cooper, a natural right-hander (albeit an overall poor athlete), not being able to convincingly bat left-handed in his role of Lou Gehrig. Producers had even brought in Lefty O'Doul, a former major league outfielder, to tutor Cooper, with no apparent success. To solve this, he was shot wearing a jersey with backwards lettering and running to third base after swinging right-handed, then the footage was reversed in postproduction. A Washington, D.C., newspaper writer even confirmed the story.

In 2013, a fine researcher from the Baseball Hall of Fame named Tom Shieber made like someone from *CSI* and, using a sharp eye and photographic evidence, studied the film and proved that Cooper did his own left-handed hitting (or at least swinging). Further scrutiny by Shieber (including locating comments by Gehrig himself) noted that the film was actually flipped only to accommodate several scenes of Cooper believably throwing left-handed. Kudos and a "well done" go to Mr. Shieber, while O'Doul's comment needs to be remembered—Cooper threw "like an old woman tossing a hot biscuit."

Babe Herman, an outfielder and first baseman with a twelve-year major league career, doubled for Gary Cooper in many of the long shots of the actor supposedly running the bases and playing the infield. Other Yankees, like catcher Bill Dickey, outfielder Bob Meusel, and shortstop Mark Koenig, show up as themselves throughout the picture.

There can be no question that *Pride of the Yankees* set the standard for uplifting and inspiring sports films. It also did boffo business at the box office, landing in the year's Top Ten and taking in $3 million—in a day when ticket prices were only twenty-five cents. The film earned a lot of attention from the 1943 Oscars, securing eleven nominations—including Best Picture, Best Leading Actor, and Best Leading Actress. The final tally was just one statue, for film editing (even though Wright won a Best Supporting Actress that year for *Mrs. Miniver*).

The story of Lou Gehrig was retold several times over the years, with Cooper reprising his performance on an October 1943 radio broadcast of *Pride of the Yankees* on the Lux Radio Theater. A 1978 NBC-TV movie, *A Love Affair: The Eleanor and Lou Gehrig Story,* told the tale from Mrs. Gehrig's viewpoint. It starred Edward Herrmann as the Iron Horse and Blythe Danner as Eleanor.

Safe At Home!

(1962—American/**Columbia**—**84 Min/B&W**)
Director: Walter Doniger
Original Music: Van Alexander
Film Editing: Frank P. Keller
Cast: Mickey Mantle (**Himself**)
Roger Maris (**Himself**)
William Frawley (**Bill Turner**)
Patricia Barry (**Johanna Price**)
Don Collier (**Ken Lawton**)
Bryan Russell (**Hutch Lawton**)

In Palms, Florida, ten-year-old Hutch Lawton lives on a fishing boat with Ken, his single father. The boy loves baseball, especially the Yankees—sluggers Mickey Mantle and Roger Maris are his favorites.

Hutch brags to his Little League teammates that his dad knows all the Yankees, even Mantle and Maris—which is a complete lie. When Hutch agrees to invite the Yankee stars to an upcoming banquet, he's feels pressured to run off and slip into the Yankees' spring training camp.

The boy sneaks into the Yankees' hotel room and comes face-to-face with his heroes, as well as their gruff coach, Bill Turner. Hutch spends the night alone at the ballpark, while his friend's parents back home discover he's missing.

Mantle and Maris convince Turner to let Hutch watch the Yankees' practice from the dugout, pretending he's the old man's nephew. Ken and his girlfriend Johanna show up to retrieve Hutch, as he explains his problem to Mickey and

Lobby card, *Safe at Home!*, 1962

Roger. But the M&M Boys chide the boy for lying to his teammates and won't appear at the banquet. They insist that he face his friends and tell the truth.

Back home, Hutch and his father meet the Little League team, where the boy admits his lie to them and apologizes. But instead of having to cancel the banquet, all the boys have been invited to be the guests of Mantle and Maris at the Yankees training camp.

Afterwords

The Yankees winning the World Series in 1961, along with the exciting performances of Mickey Mantle and Roger Maris, made *Safe at Home!* a no-brainer. The Yanks had also opened a sparkling new spring training facility in Fort Lauderdale, Florida, so they were anxious to show it off in the film. *Safe at Home!* was released in April 1962, just in time for the brand new baseball season.

Mantle and Maris each received $5,000 for three days of shooting. Both proved they were very well suited as ballplayers, and not so suited to appearing on the big screen. The Mick was more outgoing and seemed a bit more comfortable in front of the camera. As might be expected, Maris was about as stiff as a newly made Louisville Slugger. Naturally introverted, Maris must also have been exhausted from his season-long pursuit of Ruth's record. Other Yankees rounded out the background, including manager Ralph Houk and players Whitey Ford and Joe Pepitone.

Still, the M&M Boys weren't given much in big-name backing, as the only recognizable member in the supporting cast was William Frawley. Known as the cranky Fred Mertz from *I Love Lucy* in the 1950s, Frawley had been seen in other baseball-themed films, such as 1950's *Kill the Umpire* with William Bendix and 1948's *The Babe Ruth Story*—again, with Bendix.

The Scout

(1994—American/**Twentieth Century Fox**—101 Min/Color)
Director: Michael Ritchie
Original Music: Bill Conti
Film Editing: Pembroke J. Herring, Don Zimmerman
Production Design: Stephen Hendrickson
Cast: Albert Brooks (**Al Percolo**)
Brendan Fraser (**Steve Nebraska**)
Dianne Wiest (**Doctor H. Aaron**)
Lane Smith (**Ron Wilson**)
Michael Rapaport (**Tommy Lacy**)
George Steinbrenner (**Himself**)

Based on the 1976 Roger Angell article "Scout" in *New Yorker* magazine.

Al Percolo is a longtime scout with the Yankees, known for more strikeouts than hits in finding good baseball talent. One example is young pitcher Tommy

Director Michael Ritchie, Brendan Fraser, and Albert Brooks from *The Scout*, 1994.

Lacy, who, after signing a big contract, makes his debut by throwing up—in the clubhouse and on the mound—and then running out of the park.

As a result, Al is banished to scout deep in the Mexican Leagues, where talent and simple comforts are sparse. Surprisingly, he comes across Steve Nebraska— a pitcher so highly regarded by the locals, he's ceremonially brought to the mound on a sedan chair. The kid's fastball is so good, it can't be hit—nor can it be held on to by the catcher. Plus, he can hit. Percolo quickly signs Nebraska to a deal with the Yanks.

But Ron Wilson, the Yankee GM, hates Al and fires him, making Nebraska a free agent. Still, the Yanks sign the young pitcher to a huge contract at an open tryout. The down side is Steve is somewhat flaky and insecure, along with a large dose of immaturity. Considering Al's doubtful reputation, the kid needs a letter from a psychiatrist verifying he's OK to play ball.

Steve sees Dr. H. Aaron—a lady with a coincidental name. But she notes that Steve is troubled and will not write the letter—he needs therapy and should not play ball. Al desperately convinces Aaron to OK Nebraska, with the caveat that she treats the young man. In fact, Steve could be dangerous.

Al becomes a bit too controlling, and Steve angrily reminds him who's the Yankee and who's the scout. When the Yankees win the pennant, Steve is set to pitch the first game of the World Series, but he doubts that he's ready. The anxiety drives him to the roof of Yankee Stadium, where he stands frozen with fear.

Al and Steve find their relationship is more important than the World Series, and Nebraska realizes that losing—if that happens—isn't such a bad thing. A helicopter, belonging to Yanks owner George Steinbrenner, plucks Steve from the roof and delivers him to the mound as the crowd roars.

The kid's performance against the Cardinals is nothing less than absolute perfection, as he strikes out all twenty-seven Redbird batters. Nebraska's two home runs account for all the offense needed, as the first game is a 2–0 win for the Yankees—and Steve Nebraska.

Afterwords

A well-known and respected writer of all things baseball for the *New Yorker*, Roger Angell has also penned many books on America's pastime, including *The Summer Game* and *Late Innings*. As one of his "The Sporting Scene" articles, Angell shadowed California Angels scout Ray Scarborough and wrote about the processes of, and difficulties in, predicting the future for promising baseball prospects.

Screenwriter Andrew Bergman, who had made his mark by helping to write 1974's *Blazing Saddles* with Mel Brooks and others, was inspired by Angell's article and wrote a script based on it. Pitched to Warner Brothers, with Peter Falk attached in the scout's role, it went unproduced until nearly twenty years later.

By 1994, with the success of *A League of Their Own*, Bergman dusted off the script. After thoughts of starring Rodney Dangerfield passed, the project drew the attention of comic and writer Albert Brooks. With a healthy rewrite from Brooks and his writing partner Monica Johnson, *The Scout* was finally seeing the light of day.

Michael Ritchie came on to direct, being well accustomed to helming sports films, including 1976's *Bad News Bears*, 1977's *Semi-Tough*, and 1986's *Wildcats*. Yet he ultimately felt *The Scout* was much more about relationships than sports.

Brooks worked closely with Phil Pote, who had spent decades scouting for the A's, Dodgers, and Mariners. The actor also gained twenty pounds and wore a hat that almost every scout seemed to wear. In rewriting the script, he imagined Brendan Fraser as the young phenom Steve Nebraska. The beefy actor had made his mark in films like 1992's *Encino Man* and 1994's *Airheads*.

Despite its best efforts, the film was a complete bust at the box office, as *The Scout* grossed a mere $2.6 million. The biggest finger of blame can probably be pointed at the MLB strike in 1994, which was going into its eighth week when the film was released at the end of September, leaving everyone sour on the game.

Soul of the Game

(1996—American/**HBO**—**94 Min/Color**)
Director: Kevin Rodney Sullivan
Original Music: Lee Holdridge
Film Editing: Victor Dubois
Production Design: Chester Kaczenski
Cast: Delroy Lindo (**Satchel Paige**)
Mykelti Williamson (**Josh Gibson**)
Edward Herrmann (**Branch Rickey**)
Blair Underwood (**Jackie Robinson**)
Jerry Hardin (**Happy Chandler**)

With black ballplayers banned from playing in the major leagues, stars like flashy pitcher Satchel Paige and serious catcher Josh Gibson are forced to play in Mexico and the Dominican Republic—where they dominate their opponents. Brooklyn Dodgers executive Branch Rickey has plans to change those conditions, so he can bring black players into the game.

The Negro Leagues also appear in American ballparks, but with segregated players who play to segregated fans. Here, Paige, playing for the Kansas City Monarchs, goes face-to-face against Gibson, who plays for the Homestead Grays. Oozing confidence, Satchel calls his players off the field and Josh singles—against an empty infield. Paige figures he and Gibson are destined for the Dodgers. Meanwhile, young and speedy Jackie Robinson wants none of the nonsense—he just wants to play ball.

Rickey has some concerns about Josh's mental state, with word he's been treated for headaches and odd behavior. And Satchel has a lingering shoulder ailment that could affect his chances of making the big leagues. Happy Chandler, the game's new commissioner, personally feels black players should be allowed in the majors, but also knows the country may not yet be ready for it.

On loan to the Harrisburg team for one game, Paige and Robinson still encounter racist attitudes. They roll off Satchel with little effect, but Jackie is troubled by the injustice. And despite the skills and confidence of Paige and Gibson, Rickey believes Robinson has the character to be the first black ballplayer in the majors—the first of many.

More, Paige is forty years of age, and Gibson has an awkward public incident that confirms the rumors of his instability. In the Negro Leagues All-Star Game, Paige walks the bases full so he can face Gibson. With a swinging strike and a long foul ball, Gibson goes down swinging at a Paige fastball. Later, Josh homers off another All-Star pitcher.

At the end of the 1945 season, Robinson signs a contract to play with the Dodger organization. Paige is devastated at the news, having made a private and personal pitch with Rickey to consider himself and Gibson. Both ballplayers confront Jackie with their anger and frustration, with Josh winding up in a mental facility. Paige and Robinson convince the head of the hospital to release Gibson into their custody.

At Griffith Stadium in Washington, D.C., all-stars from the major leagues play against the best from the Negro Leagues in an exhibition game. Satchel, Jackie, and Josh make it to the park just in time, but a soaking rain cancels the game before Paige can throw his first pitch. Gibson roars in anguish at the skies, while Robinson and Paige escort him to the clubhouse.

Robinson made the majors, as did Paige, but Gibson died at age thirty-six.

Afterwords

Much like *Cobb* in 1994, *Soul of the Game*—produced for the HBO cable network in 1996—scored high in baseball storytelling and not so high in accuracy. Still, very few projects have ever attempted to tell the stories of these three outstanding black ballplayers.

Certainly, the story of Jackie Robinson, and his breaking of baseball's color barrier, has been told in 1950's *The Jackie Robinson Story*. The film starred the titled man himself because, let's be honest, in 1950 it was either Robinson or Mantan Moreland. Then there was 1990's made-for-television drama on TNT, *The Court Martial of Jackie Robinson*. With Andre Braugher as the soldier-ballplayer, the film focused on Robinson's face-to-face dealings with racism during his military service prior to joining the major leagues.

Granted, 2013's *42* is covered elsewhere in this chapter, and Louis Gossett Jr. starred as Satchel Paige in the 1981 ABC-TV movie *Don't Look Back: The Story of Leroy Satchel Paige*. But Josh Gibson has never been the subject of a biopic.

Director Kevin Rodney Sullivan, having previously directed network and cable TV projects, defended the charges of inaccuracy and copious amounts of artistic license with *Soul of the Game*. Along with screenwriter David Himmelstein, Sullivan asserted they were making "a film, not a documentary." The director's budget for *Soul of the Game* was between $6 million and $7 million.

Sullivan was inspired by the idea of placing most of the film's action in 1945, which allowed it to look at the end of Gibson's career, Paige in the midst of a long, long career, and Robinson as he was about to embark on his. Harking back to *Cobb*, much of the shooting took place in the Deep South, using Rickwood Field in Birmingham, Alabama, for many of the baseball scenes.

Delroy Lindo, playing pitcher Satchel Paige, was born in England and raised in Jamaica, where he played a lot of cricket and soccer as well—but no baseball. Amid a long and successful career in TV, on the stage, and in the movies, Lindo was very proud of his performance as Satchel Paige.

Mykelti Williamson was challenged to assume the character of slugger Josh Gibson, often called "the black Babe Ruth." Unlike the other players, no historic footage of Gibson exists, leaving Williamson to find alternative ways to physically portray the hitter. He spent time with several Negro League players who knew Gibson, quizzing them for every detail he could find about Gibson's ways and mannerisms.

In the end, *Soul of the Game* accomplished what it set out to do by shining a spotlight on greats from the Negro League that many people never had the chance to see. Fabricating relationships on the screen that didn't really exist was a necessary device used by Sullivan and Himmelstein to get their story across.

Baseball Honors and Awards

To the Victors Belong the Spoils

Bravos and Kudos

et's face it, everyone likes to be recognized for their outstanding achievements—as an employee, as a family member, as a performer, and, yes, as an athlete. However, the recent habit of handing out trophies to every kid on every youth baseball team tends to dilute the accomplishments of the winning teams, not to mention prolonging the philosophy of entitlement (but then, this isn't a book on modern culture and sociology; it's just about baseball).

No matter, competition among the thirty major league teams and 750-plus ballplayers every year is a healthy thing. By October, the best team in the game wins the World Series, and in the weeks following that, other annual honors get handed out. Much like Hollywood's Oscars, it's nice to compete, but winning is much, much nicer (and, usually, more lucrative).

Back in the mid-1800s, before the game was "pro," winning baseball clubs were usually awarded the game ball from the losing team after a tournament (as stipulated by the 1857 Knickerbocker rules). These "lemon peel balls" were usually marked with the date and score of the contest, then retired to a trophy case—prominent or not—in the winner's clubhouse. Silver or gilded balls and bats also made good subjects for early award hardware.

The National Association of Professional Base-Ball Players (NAPBBP) was the first real professional organization, established in 1871 (as noted in another chapter). They were committed to establishing a single Champion of the United States, among other items on their agenda. Members of the top annual team received ornate china vases, commemorative medals, pins, watch fobs, or pocket watches—a practice that continued into the early 1920s.

Starting in 1926, ornate and jeweled rings became a standard award for players who won the World Series (and remains so today), although rings had been occasional prizes prior to that year. They often incorporated team colors, such as green for the Athletics, crimson for the Cardinals and Reds, and blue for the Yankees.

Dauvray Cup, 1887 to 1893.

There's No "I" in Teamwork—Team Trophies

Dauvray Cup 1887–1893

As baseball grew in the mid-1880s, a stage actress named Helen Dauvray—desperate for fame and notoriety—became a strange bedfellow of the game. A fan of the New York Giants, Dauvray commissioned the making of a Grecian-style loving cup, designed and created by the Gorham Silver Company at the cost of $500, to be awarded to the championship winner of the National League and American Association matchup.

Of course, the cup would be named after her, despite Dauvray having no direct connection to the game. Unfortunately, her beloved Giants were not in the 1887 championship, as the Detroit Wolverines took the cup against the St. Louis Browns. Her Giants did take the cup in the next two years, and the Louisville Colonels received it in 1890. In the meantime, Dauvray caught the eye of Giants shortstop/second baseman Monte Ward. They had a brief and tumultuous marriage in the late 1880s.

The Dauvray Cup went to the Boston Beaneaters in 1891, 1892, and 1893. Somewhere, en route to the offices of the Boston team, the cup vanished and has been lost to the ages ever since. The same could be said for Dauvray's acting career.

Temple Cup 1894–1897

By 1893, the American Association was swallowed up by the National League, and a championship series between first- and second-place NL teams was proposed by William Temple, owner of the Pittsburgh Pirates. Having lost out to the Beaneaters the previous year, Temple had a trophy cup (of course named after himself) made for the best-of-seven series.

In the four years that the tournament existed, the Pirates finished neither first nor second and the series ceased, with the Pittsburgh team never getting a chance at the trophy. The winners between 1894 and 1897 were the Giants, the Cleveland Spiders, and the Baltimore Orioles—twice. Fortunately, this time someone kept a closer eye on the Temple Cup, and it's in safe hands at the Hall of Fame in Cooperstown.

Chronicle-Telegraph Cup 1900

In 1900, Pittsburgh would get its shot at a trophy. The *Pittsburgh Chronicle-Telegraph* newspaper offered a silver cup valued at $500 to the winner of a best-out-of-five series between the second-place Pirates and league-leading Brooklyn Superbas.

Sadly, the Pirates' defense never showed up, as they made fourteen errors in four games, resulting in ten unearned runs—and three wins—for the Suberbas. The Chronicle-Telegraph Cup went to Brooklyn and can be found at the Hall of Fame today (Brooklyn was closer to Cooperstown than Pittsburgh anyway).

World Series—The Commissioner's Trophy 1967–Present

As might be expected, when the game was properly organized in the early 1900s—two leagues and a central governing body—the winner of the World Series became a big deal, for fans and teams alike. Yet there was no official team trophy awarded until 1967.

Under the direction of retired Air Force Lieutenant General William Eckert—chosen as baseball's commissioner in 1965 after the retirement of Ford Frick—an official trophy was designated as the team award for winning the World Series every fall. The first one, conceived by Minnesota designer Lawrence Voegele, went to the Cards, who defeated the Red Sox in seven games.

Unlike hockey's Stanley Cup, which is passed from winner to winner every year, baseball's top award is individually created for each winning team. The Commissioner's Trophy was actually named as such in 1985, after nearly twenty years passed with no moniker. (Up until then, the Commissioner's Award was originally the label attached to the trophy given to the MVP of the All-Star Game.) And unlike the other three major American sports—football, basketball, and hockey—the Commissioner's Trophy does not carry the name of an individual person.

The trophy has stayed with Voegele's original concept over the years, with only minor revamping. It has a circular base measuring eleven inches in diameter, rimmed with thirty gold-plated pennants on graduated posts that rise two feet—one for each MLB team. In the center is a baseball, as well as lines of longitude and latitude that symbolize the world.

Other than the gold-plating, the trophy is sterling silver that totals thirty pounds and is currently made by the fine jeweler Tiffany and Company. The cost to produce it is estimated at $15,000, but if melted into a solid silver ingot, the trophy's value would be about half that at $7,800.

Sharp-eyed (and large-walleted) collectors have occasionally found a Commissioner's Trophy to call their own—for a price. For example, Orioles manager Earl Weaver's edition of the 1970 World Series trophy was purchased at

Replica of 1993 Commissioner's Trophy, World Series.

auction in 2011 for $12,000. Outfielder Frank Robinson's award from the same season was a veritable bargain, going for $8,000.

National League Pennant—Warren C. Giles Trophy

Started in 1886, the *Sporting News* newspaper noted, in an edition from that year, that teams were vying for a league pennant. If there's any question if the flag was symbolic or actual cloth, the paper also noted that the pennant was "a silk banner, costing about $100, and will be suitably inscribed." Prior to that, evidence shows that part of a team's entry fee in 1877 went toward a pennant, "emblematic of the (National) League championship."

Put simply, the team with the best record in the National League at the end of regular season play had won the pennant and the right to go head-to-head against the winner of the other league. At the time it was the American Association, but that concept carried through to the twentieth century and the firm establishment of the American League. The New York/San Francisco Giants have earned twenty-three NL pennants, the most in the league.

In 1969, the leagues were broken into two divisions each—East and West. Since then, League Championship Series have been played to establish the winner of the entire league (considering the 1994 addition of the Central division and Divisional Championships, et al.).

National League Championship, Warren C. Giles Trophy.

In that same 1969, a trophy was created to honor the champion of the National League. It was named for Warren C. Giles, former GM and president of the Cincinnati Reds and president of the National League since 1952. Unlike the World Series trophy, the Giles Trophy moves from winning team to winning team every year, with their name engraved on it.

It is a practice that is not without its risks. In 2003, the (then) Florida Marlins apparently celebrated their winning season with gusto, as the Giles Trophy ended up in pieces. MLB had to rebuild it before it could be passed on to the 2004 winning Cardinals (no word on who footed the repair bill).

The Giles Trophy, designed by cabinetmaker Harry Arrington Jr., is composed of hand-carved mahogany, with twelve wooden columns—one each for the NL teams that were playing in 1969 when it was introduced. The upper and lower portions are mahogany and eighteen-karat gold-plated square boxes, with a carved baseball at the very top.

American League Pennant—William Harridge Trophy

At the risk of being redundant, the winner of the American League has received a pennant in every year they played since 1903 (except, of course, in 1904 and 1994). It should not be surprising to know that the Yankees have won forty AL pennants, far more than any team in either league.

Starting in 1969, a trophy was added for winning the American League Championship, named for William Harridge, who had been league president between 1931 and 1959. It has a solid beveled base, topped with a gold baseball and large golden eagle that holds an American League pennant in its beak. In all, the Harridge Trophy is about eighteen inches tall.

There's Three "I"s in Individual—Player Awards

Perhaps it's the fragility of the athletic ego, but ballplayers crave accolades like hobos going after a ham sandwich. There seems to be a need for acknowledgment of success, and that's a good thing, since many believe success breeds success. Of course, things can get out of hand, and before you know it, there's an annual award for left-handed pinch-hitting in Tuesday night games.

American League Championship, William Harridge Trophy.

As previously noted, keeping track of a ballplayer's stats was not very complete in the early days of the game. A tip of the cap goes to Henry Chadwick, the British-born sports writer who made early attempts to codify the game in the 1800s. He gave meaning to batting averages and earned runs, laying the groundwork for publications like the *Sporting News* and other papers that told the game's story via numbers.

Boston Red Stockings' James "Deacon" White received the first semblance of an MVP award in 1875, when a rich fan gave him a silver trophy engraved to the "most valuable player." Apparently, that was a one-time occurrence.

Chalmers Award 1911–1914

In the never-ending search for publicity, Hugh Chalmers—owner of the Chalmers Motor Company—announced in 1910 that he would award a Chalmers 30 Roadster to the batting champion from the National and American Leagues. Not surprisingly, Detroit's Ty Cobb leads the Indians' Napoleon Lajoie by seven percentage points on the final day of the season.

As Cobb sat out the last game, Lajoie played in a double-header against the St. Louis Browns. But Cobb was so disliked in the game that the St. Louis manager played his third baseman very deep, allowing the opposing Lajoie to bunt many times for a total of six hits. The Indian wound up going seven-for-eight in the two games, but that still left him .000975 behind Cobb for the season.

The sleazy outcome was brought to the attention of AL president Ban Johnson, who said all averages were final and official (although the Browns' manager was

Ad for Chalmers 30 Touring Car, awarded as The Chalmers Award 1911–1914.

fired for his actions). Still, while Cobb was named champion, both he and Lajoie got cars from Chalmers.

In the next four years, one sports writer from each of the sixteen major league team cities voted for the "most valuable player" in each league. In the AL, Ty Cobb won in 1911, while Cubs outfielder Frank Shulte won in the NL. All players were eligible, as seen in 1913 when Senators pitcher Walter Johnson won the AL Chalmers Award.

By 1915, Chalmers Motors noticed their sales had not increased much (let's face it—has anyone driven a Chalmers lately?). Also, there were grumblings of cheating, along with the restriction that players could not win more than once. All told, those reasons led to the demise of the Chalmers Award after that season.

League Award 1922–1929

Knowing what we know about the contributions from early sports writers, it's fitting that they were among the first to acknowledge the accomplishments of the best ballplayer at the season's end.

That process continued in 1922, when baseball looked to newspaper writers to select a player "who is of the greatest all-around service to his club." The winner received a bronze medal, called the "League Award," and $1,000. Yet it was not without its flaws. Only one player per team could be nominated on the ballot (in the AL only), and a player could not win the award more than once.

These rules almost immediately led to conflicts and unfair conditions, namely, two guys called Ruth and Gehrig (among many others). For example, when Ruth won the League Award in 1923, he posted an outstanding line of .393/41/130. But that made him ineligible to win in 1927, when he hit .356, with a then-unheard-of 60 homers, along with 165 RBI. But not to worry—Gehrig won the award that year, with deserved numbers of .373/47/173. (Yikes!)

The National League also adopted the League Award in 1922, but baseball writers could not agree on any player worthy of winning until 1924. Pitcher Dazzy Vance of the Brooklyn Robins (yes, they were the Dodgers, but fans called them all sorts of names, as one might guess) won the League Award, posting a record of 28–6, with an ERA of 2.16 and 262 strikeouts.

By the decade's end, the US was nearing the grip of the Great Depression and couldn't have given two apple cores for who was the most valuable baseball player. Plus, amid the country's economic woes, winning ballplayers used the award as leverage for salary increases—something club owners wanted nothing to do with.

In 1929, the American League selected no one (it's not known if anyone even noticed). The National League followed suit in 1930, and the League Award became one of many smaller points in baseball history.

Most Valuable Player Award—Kenesaw Mountain Landis Memorial Baseball Award

As the dominant media presence in the game at the time, the *Sporting News* took up the selection of the most valuable players in the leagues. In the AL, they named A's outfielder Al Simmons and Senators shortstop Joe Cronin in 1929 and 1930, respectively. In the NL, the Giants' first baseman Bill Terry was selected.

The weekly paper also extended an offer to readers in 1931, allowing them to select the most valuable and most popular players in the game. Those who wrote the best and most convincing letters won prizes of ten dollars, five dollars, or subscriptions to the *Sporting News*.

Meanwhile, the Baseball Writers' Association of America (BBWAA), established in 1908, decided they would begin an annual selection of a Most Valuable Player from each league—a practice that continues today. While the definition of an "MVP" is left to the discretion of the voter, the process is clearly defined.

Two baseball writers from each of the MLB cities vote for ten names placed on a ballot, using a weighted scale for the first through tenth position (for example, a first-place vote is worth fourteen points). NL city writers vote for NL players and the AL does the same, before the postseason play begins. Winners are then announced in November, after the World Series is completed.

Pitchers and designated hitters, as well as everyday players, are eligible for selection, and a player can win more than once. For example, Barry Bonds won a record seven MVP awards (albeit with pharmaceutical assistance), and greats like Joe DiMaggio, Jimmie Foxx, Mickey Mantle, Albert Pujols, and Mike Schmidt, among others, have each won three times. Outfielder

Replica of Most Valuable Player Award.

Frank Robinson holds the distinction of being the only player to win in each league—the NL Reds in 1961 and the AL Orioles in 1966.

In 1944, following the death of commissioner Kenesaw Mountain Landis, the MVP Award was officially renamed the Kenesaw Mountain Landis Memorial Baseball Award.

The actual award is a stop sign–shaped silver plaque, mounted on a round base of sixteen inches across. On the plaque is a baseball diamond, engraved with the award's name, the winner's name and team, and a gold cameo of Landis, among other details.

Some of the older awards have made their way to the auction blocks, going for big dollars to private memorabilia collectors. For example, Roger Maris' 1960 AL MVP Award went for over $18,000 in 2007, Yogi Berra's 1955 AL MVP Award sold for more than $36,000 in 2013, and Roy Campanella's 1951 NL MVP Award landed nearly $178,000 in 2014.

Cy Young Award

In the mid-1950s, Commissioner Ford Frick noticed that, by the design of their limited appearances in a season (as opposed to everyday players), pitchers didn't seem to have the same opportunity to win very many MVP Awards.

Curiously, in the first twenty-five years of the award, eleven pitchers won the MVP out of fifty chances—second only to the twelve outfielders who won. Frick's reasoning may have been askew. No matter, the commish (himself a former baseball writer) assigned the BBWAA with the task of annually selecting the top pitcher in the game and honoring him with a separate award.

The trophy was named after Cy Young, who had passed away in 1955. He was the winningest pitcher in MLB history with 511 victories. (The other side of the coin is that Young also had the most losses in the game with 316. You wanna make an omelet, you gotta break some eggs.)

Replica of Cy Young Award.

In the first eleven seasons, only one winner was selected from both leagues— five of them went to Dodgers, three alone to Sandy Koufax. Shortly after Frick's retirement, starting in 1967, the award was given to the best in each league.

Since 1969, the BBWAA has used a weighted voting system, similar to the MVP process. The Cy Young Award ballot has five candidates from each league, and writers cannot split their votes between two entries.

Arthur "Bud" Lorden, a designer for the L. G. Balfour Company, assumed the task of creating the award (Lorden would go on to design the World Series Commissioner's Trophy some years later). The resulting plaque was fifteen inches tall, with two large silver star rays that support an arch with the name of the award on it. Between it is a hand that holds a baseball with a two-seam fastball grip, while the winner's name is engraved underneath.

Multiple winners of the Cy Young Award include seven-timer Roger Clemens (again with a quick stop at the pharmacy); five-time recipient Randy Johnson; four-timers Steve Carlton and Greg Maddux; and three-peaters Clayton Kershaw (so far), Pedro Martinez, Jim Palmer, Tom Seaver, and the aforementioned Koufax.

It should be noted that except for Kershaw, who is still very active, and Clemens, whose performance lies under the shroud of PEDs, all those named pitchers have a plaque at the Hall of Fame.

The Cy Young Award has not been reserved for just starting pitchers. Starting with the Dodgers' Mike Marshall in 1974, nine relief pitchers have won the trophy. Closers Rollie Fingers, Bruce Sutter, and Dennis Eckersley (who was also a dominant starter before going to the bullpen) also have made it to Cooperstown.

Milwaukee Braves' Warren Spahn, Hall of Famer with the most wins for a left-hander in history at 363, won the award in 1957. His plaque was put up for auction in 2013 and brought a whopping price of $110,000. Likewise, Rollie Fingers' 1981 Cy Young trophy was sold for more than $38,000 in 2013.

Rookie of the Year Award—Jackie Robinson Award

The Chicago chapter of the BBWAA began selecting their own Rookie of the Year in 1940. In the first seven years, they chose a top rookie among both leagues, but being only a Chicago media practice, it held little interest for the rest of the country.

In 1947, the national BBWAA membership was asked to vote, making the Rookie of the Year a national award. It was named the J. Louis Comiskey Memorial Award, after the Chicago White Sox owner of the 1930s and son of Charles, "the Old Roman." Memorably, Jackie Robinson, the player to break the game's color barrier, won the first RoY. Each league got its own Rookie of the Year Award in 1949, and in honor of Robinson's accomplishment, it was renamed the Jackie Robinson Award in 1987.

In the beginning, the BBWAA self-regulated their own definition of "rookie," although some requisites of at bats and innings were attached in 1957. Current criteria establish a rookie as having less than 130 at bats, fifty innings pitched, or forty-five days of activity on a major league roster.

Some folks have scratched their heads regarding the fairness of foreign players'

Replica of Jackie Robinson's Rookie of the Year Award, 1947.

eligibility as the Rookie of the Year. The prime example was Ichiro Suzuki, who burst into the majors in 2001 with the Seattle Mariners. Ichiro made his presence known by hitting .350, with 242 hits, 52 stolen bases, and 127 runs scored. His breakout season earned him the AL MVP Award, as well as AL Rookie of the Year.

At twenty-seven years of age, he was a rookie only by MLB rules. But he arrived in the US game having previously played nine seasons with the Orix Blue Waves of the Japan Pacific League. Other RoYs with Japanese League experience were pitchers Kazuhiro Sazaki in 2000 and Hideo Nomo in 1995.

A similar argument could be made for RoY winners like Robinson, Don Newcombe, and Willie Mays, among other early black players, all of whom had played for the Negro Leagues before their MLB careers.

In Ichiro's case, he already had a .353 career average, with close to 1,300 hits, playing in nearly one thousand games, and stealing almost two hundred bases. He was a three-time Nippon Pro Baseball MVP, a seven-time Pacific League batting champ, along with winning seven Mitsui Golden Glove Awards.

Of course, Suzuki's Japanese Pacific League experience only enhanced his resulting MLB career. Ichiro has been a ten-time All-Star, two-time AL batting champ, won ten Gold Gloves, as well as setting all-time records for single season hits with 262, and ten consecutive 200-hit seasons. Entering the 2015 season, he had more than 2,800 MLB hits for a .317 lifetime average. Combined with his Japanese stats, he's amassed more than 4,000 hits in pro ball—a feat only topped by Pete Rose and Ty Cobb.

The BBWAA votes on a ballot of three candidates, awarding points of five, three, and one to first, second, and third places, respectively. There have been seventeen unanimous Rookie of the Year selections since 1947, with prominent names like Frank Robinson, Willie McCovey, Carlton Fisk, Sandy Alomar, Albert Pujols, and Derek Jeter among them.

Of course, not all RoYs make a lasting impact on the game. Names like Joe Charboneau, Angel Berroa, and Pat Listach are just some of the players whose star burned very brightly early on, but burned out with the same intensity soon after.

At first, the Rookie of the Year Award was a carved wooden plaque, ten and a half by fifteen inches, with a platform that held a small gold statue of a hitter having completed his swing. When the award was renamed in 1987, the plaque was redesigned as a rectangle, with a bas-relief of a runner sliding into home plate, an umpire waving him safe, as the catcher covers the play.

Jackie Robinson's original Rookie of the Year Award wound up at auction in 2014. Some lucky collector ponied up more than $400,000 for it—equal to the MLB minimum annual salary in 2009.

Sophomore of the Year Award 1953–1962

There is a superstition in sports—particularly in baseball—that says if your first year is great, then your second year will be a failure. It's known as the "sophomore jinx," and in tandem with the Rookie of the Year Award, the Sophomore of the Year Award was created in 1953 by our friends at the BBWAA.

Obviously, its intent was to honor players in the American and National Leagues who thumbed their noses at the jinx and excelled in their second full MLB season. Demonstrating that their success was no fluke, AL players Harvey Kuenn and Herb Score, along with NL players Frank Robinson and Orlando Cepeda, won the Sophomore of the Year Award after winning Rookie of the Year.

Other notables who received the SoY were Eddie Mathews, Ernie Banks, Ron Santo, and Willie Davis in the NL, with Jimmy Piersall, Al Kaline, and Jim Gentile being among those honored in the AL. But as one might imagine, there was little interest in how someone fared in their second year of play, and the award was discontinued after the 1962 season.

Triple Crown for Hitters (Average, Home Runs, RBI)

For some folks, mentioning the "Triple Crown" conjures images of thundering hooves and ears pinned back against the wind (and we're not talking Prince Fielder here). The Triple Crown of Horse Racing happens in the spring, as three-year-old thoroughbreds compete in the Kentucky Derby, the Preakness, and the Belmont Stakes.

However, this book focuses on baseball (as if you hadn't noticed), so a Triple Crown has a whole different meaning. It's one of the more difficult accomplishments in the game, and isn't getting any easier. For hitters, leading the league in batting average, home runs, and runs batted in a season secures the Triple Crown.

The problem is, the honor is hard to track from the early days of the game, for two reasons. One, the record keeping from the late 1880s into the first decades of the 1900s can be questioned, as many of those stats have been reassembled from box scores and newspaper accounts of the period—at least, from those that are available. Second, the RBI stat was not considered official until 1920, so that body of data might not be as complete as necessary. As such, players from the Dead-Ball Era and before are sometimes not included in the Triple Crown count (including the exclusion of greats Ty Cobb and Napoleon Lajoie).

While various versions of an actual crown have been given out—unofficially—over the years, the most recent Triple Crown Award was actually given to the Detroit Tigers' Miguel Cabrera in 2012. Awarded on behalf of Major League Baseball, the honor was a golden crown with large false stones, a script "D," and an oval badge engraved with all the pertinent info. A gold baseball was affixed to the top, and the crown was adorned with a deep purple fabric. (No, it wasn't fashioned from an old Crown Royal whiskey bag.)

Cabrera's accomplishment was the first in the game, and the American League, since Boston's Carl Yastrzemski in 1967—a span of thirty-five years. The drought in the NL has been even longer, with the last Triple Crown going to the Cards' Joe "Ducky" Medwick in 1937. Up to 1967, the modern-era AL hadn't gone more than ten years or less between wins. In the NL, the gap was eight or less before 1937.

Prior to Yastrzemski, the Orioles' Frank Robinson had won the Triple Crown in just the previous year of 1966. At that point, it was realized that no official trophy existed. In stepped Jerold C. Hoffberger, president of the National Brewing Company and, conveniently, board chairman of the Baltimore team.

2012 Triple Crown awarded to Miguel Cabrera.

He commissioned Samuel Kirk and Son, prestigious silversmiths, to design a beautifully engraved sterling silver bowl to honor the winner of the Triple Crown.

However, in one of the stranger points of interest in baseball, the two silver bowls given to Robinson and Yaz—along with a sample on hand at the Hall of Fame—are the only Triple Crown Awards of that sort in existence. When Cabrera took the Crown in 2012, there was none to be had. The MLB turned to Todd Radom, a graphic designer specializing in sports, who whipped up the previously mentioned gilded coronet at the last minute.

The loss of continuity—despite the decades between winners—could be partly due to the National Brewing Company, makers of National Bohemian Beer and Colt-45 Malt Liquor, which underwent several mergers in the 1970s and lost its prominence.

The problems in achieving such a lofty goal as the Triple Crown are twofold: The increase in relief specialists in the last forty years has somewhat hampered the overall batting averages of hitters. And, for the most part, hitters tend to work toward hitting for average or hitting for power, but not both.

Imagine, though, having a season of .356, with 48 homers and 163 RBI—Jimmie Foxx did it in 1933. Even better, Lou Gehrig had a line of .363/49/165 in the following year. Rogers Hornsby—the Rajah—wore the Triple Crown twice in 1922 and 1925 with the Cardinals. He broke the .400 mark each time—.401 and .403, adding home run totals of 42 and 39, with 152 and 143 RBI, respectively.

Ted Williams won the Triple Crown two times in the 1940s. In 1942, he hit .356, with 36 home runs and 137 runs batted in. Five years later, in 1947, he hit .343, with 32 homers and 114 RBI. Mickey Mantle impressed in 1956 as a twenty-four-year-old, posting a Triple Crown line of .353/52/130.

Triple Crown for Pitchers (Wins, Ks, ERA)

While the pitching side of the game also has a Triple Crown, it's not as rare as the hitters' award. In fact, there is no official trophy or plaque to mark its achievement. Its winner must post the most wins and strikeouts in a league's season, plus having the lowest earned run average.

Fittingly, names like Cy Young, Christie Mathewson (twice), Grover Cleveland Alexander, and Walter Johnson (each three times) appear in the early records as Triple Crown winners. Other two-time winners include Lefty Grove, Lefty Gomez, and Roger Clemens.

Earlier still, the great Old Hoss Radbourn had one heckuva Triple Crown season in 1884 for the Providence Grays, with 59 wins, an ERA of 1.38, and 441 Ks. Bear in mind, though—he started seventy-three games that year and finished every one of them (there's no truth to the rumor that his shirts were custom-made, with the sleeve of his pitching arm nine inches longer than the other).

Sandy Koufax earned the honor three times in the four-year period of 1963 to 1966. Just picture having three seasons with a total of 78 wins, a composite ERA of 1.88, and over 1,000 strikeouts. Wow.

Silver Slugger/Silver Bat

One of the more current awards given, the Silver Slugger has been around since 1980. It was begun by prominent bat manufacturer Hillerich and Bradsby after a long history of giving the Silver Bat Award to batting champs from each league. That practice started in 1949, and even before that, the Silver Bat—also called the Louisville Slugger Trophy—had been given to the minor league batting leader since 1934.

Replica of Silver Slugger Award.

The Silver Bat, still received today by the AL and NL player with the highest batting average for the season, is sterling plated and weighs four and a half pounds (shades of Babe Ruth!) The trophy is thirty-four inches in length, with the winner's name and stats engraved on the barrel. The great Padres hitter Tony Gwynn totaled eight Silver Bats in his career—more than anyone else.

For the Silver Slugger, major league managers and coaches are polled to select players at each position (excluding their own team's players), including the best hitting pitcher in the NL and best DH in the AL. Voters consider a player's offensive stats, including average, OBP, and slugging percentage. As such, nine Silver Slugger Awards are given in each league after every season.

The Silver Slugger Award is also a silver-plated bat, thirty-six inches in length and mounted on a wooden platform shaped like home plate. It is backed by another wooden plank, which also features the Louisville Slugger logo, plus the name of the winner and the fellow recipients in his league.

Gold Glove

Defensive skills in the game are also worthy of an award, as the Gold Glove is given to the top fielder at each position in each league. Rawlings, maker of baseball gloves and gear since 1887, has sponsored the trophy since its first appearance in 1957.

In that year, a sales manager at the company discovered that four out of five pro players used their Rawlings products and suggested a golden glove to honor the best leather-men in the game. St. Louis' Brown Shoe Company delivered a load

1966 Gold Glove Trophy, awarded to Bob Gibson.

of gold-tanned leather to Rawlings, and nine awards were made in the first year—one for the best fielder at each position in the game. The following year expanded to the best at each position in each league.

In the first fifty years of its existence, the Gold Glove Award was a full-sized glove mounted on a walnut base with a trapezoid riser, accompanied by a gilded baseball and plaque with the player's particulars. Each award's glove reflected the position of the winner—catcher awards had catcher's mitts, first basemen awards had first basemen mitts, fielders and pitchers had fielder's gloves. By the 1970s, the glove had been centered, with a gold baseball on either side. A plaque had the player's name and image engraved on it.

In 2007, in honor of its fiftieth anniversary, Rawlings upgraded the look of the trophy. They added a black lacquered base, dark cherry wood, a prominent company logo, and a clear glass plate, etched with the player's image.

Over the years, many players have earned their status as defensive specialists by measuring their number of Gold Gloves. Some suggest that showmanship and a player's preceding reputation for defense adds to a favorable vote. No matter, top stars—like third baseman Mike Schmidt, second baseman Robert Alomar, and catcher Johnny Bench—all won ten trophies each. With a record seventeen, pitcher Greg Maddux has the most of any player.

From time to time, baseball memorabilia collectors have coughed up some impressive amounts of money to purchase an authentic Gold Glove Award. For instance, first baseman Steve Garvey's 1974 trophy was auctioned off for more than $10,200 in 2013. The previously mentioned Mike Schmidt placed his 1980 award on the block, where it fetched almost $44,000 in 2014. The 1968 award of the "Say, Hey Kid," Willie Mays, was a veritable bargain for a bit more than $17,000 in 2011.

GIBBY/This Year in Baseball Awards

Major League Baseball—the official business organization of you-know-what—realizes that, just as with any consumable product, marketing and consumer awareness of baseball are important parts in being successful. As far as the game was concerned, MLB decided back in 1977 to produce a weekly half-hour television program that would highlight the best and most unique occurrences in the game during the previous seven days.

Called *This Week in Baseball*, the program was syndicated across the country during the baseball season, and, while entertaining and informative, it served as a thirty-minute commercial for all that was good in baseball. Mel Allen, a fine and familiar baseball announcer who spent the better part of seven decades broadcasting the Yankees and other teams, voiced the TV show.

Affectionately known as the acronym *TWiB* (pronounced as it was written), the popular show ran until 1998 (remembering that specialty cable networks like ESPN had only just begun when *TWiB* started, but then took over much of the sports broadcasting by the 1990s). After a one-year hiatus, Fox Sports revived the show in 2000, using it as a lead-in for their Saturday game broadcasts. *TWiB* stayed on the air until 2011.

Tapping into the well-established brand, MLB began the This Year in Baseball Awards in 2002, using the Internet to provide online voting by fans to select six winners in a broad variety of categories—from Player of the Year to Blooper of the Year.

The honors had also morphed into the GIBBY Awards in 2010—Greatness in Baseball Yearly. By 2014, the categories had grown to twenty-four, with players and plays both being selected by fans, as well as media, MLB alumni, and front-office people.

Just some of the honors in the GIBBY list include Defensive Player of the Year, Everyday Player, Postseason MVP, plus Best Outfield Throw, Best Moment, and Best Oddity. Today's technology and accessibility to archived video almost anywhere makes voting for such a vast variety of awards possible.

Manager of the Year Award

The Baseball Writers Association of America has chosen a Manager of the Year from each league since 1983, picking up the award from the Associated Press, who began the honor in 1959. The AP continued to choose their own single Manager of the Year until 2000.

One might assume that the choices are obvious—just pick whoever took their team to the World Series. But the process, and results, are based on other criteria. The BBWAA uses a weighted voting system, giving five, three, and one point to third-, second-, and first-place selections.

As a result, winning managers may have taken their teams into second or third place. In 2006, Joe Girardi—at the time skipper of the NL Marlins—won Manager of the Year, despite the fact that his team finished in fourth place, with a sub-.500 record. Girardi kept the Marlins in the pennant race all season, earning the award—and a firing from the Florida front office. (That's OK, since Joe picked up with the Yankees—finishing first three times and claiming the World Series in 2009.)

Tony La Russa has won the award four times—once with the White Sox, twice with the A's, and once with the Cardinals. Similarly, Bobby Cox has also won four times—once with the Blue Jays and three times with the Braves.

"Sweet" Lou Piniella received the award three times—twice with the Seattle Mariners and once with the Chicago Cubs. Jim Leyland also won three times—twice with the Pirates and once with the Tigers. Dusty Baker has taken the award three times—all with the Giants.

Executive of the Year Award

Baseball, of course, is won (and lost) on the field. But more than the players who hit, pitch, run, and catch, their teams are built by the front-office personnel. General managers and their staffs keep tabs on the best up-and-comers, watch the waiver wires for available vets, and do their best to assemble a winning team.

In 1937, the *Sporting News* first recognized these efforts by creating the Executive of the Year Award. Votes from GMs and assistant GMs select the top exec from the major league clubs (excepting 1966, when Lee MacPhail was chosen from the Office of the Commissioner).

Repeat winners include George Weiss, who built a little dynasty called the Yankees. He won four times, with three years in a row—1950, 1951, and 1952—and again in 1960. Branch Rickey received the award three times—twice with the Cards and once with the Brooklyn Dodgers in 1947, when Jackie Robinson broke the color barrier.

More recently, Walt Jocketty has won three times since 2000. His first two were with the St. Louis Cardinals and most recently, in 2010, with the Cincinnati Reds.

Players Choice Award

In many cases, the most satisfying honor is being recognized by one's peers. Since 1992, the Players Choice Award allows members of the Major League Baseball Players Association (MLBPA, the players' union) to select outstanding players from their own ranks. Those chosen are honored for activities—on and off the field—and designate thousands of dollars from the Players Trust to charities of various types.

In the first two years, the Outstanding Player of the Year was selected from each league, and that was the extent of the Players Choice Awards. Since then, the categories have expanded to include Comeback Players of the Year, Outstanding Pitchers, and Outstanding Rookies—one from each league. A singular Player of the Year is also chosen, as well as the Marvin Miller Man of the Year Award.

Named for the first director of the MLBPA, the Marvin Miller Man of the Year Award is given to the player whose actions—on and off the field—are most inspiring to other to reach higher and achieve greater things. Greats like pitcher John Smoltz and first baseman/DH Jim Thome have won the honor twice.

Hank Aaron Award

To commemorate the twenty-fifth anniversary of Hank Aaron's breaking Babe Ruth's record of 714 home runs, the Hank Aaron Award was first given in 1999. A point system including hits, home runs, and RBI was used to honor the top offensive player in each league.

The next few years gave baseball's broadcasters the chance to vote for the winners. In 2003 and later, fans—along with a panel of Hall of Famers, including Aaron himself—voted to select the NL and AL winners. Despite (or perhaps because of) their methods, Alex Rodriguez won the award four times, while Barry Bonds received it three times.

The award is impressive, designed by FineAwards.com. A beveled wood base holds a polished marble home plate, with silver ribbons engraved with the name and date of the award, and a silver bat topping off the trophy. Aaron has presented the award to winners during the World Series.

Hank Aaron Award.

Roberto Clemente Award

In 1971, MLB began giving the Commissioner's Award (not to be confused with the aforementioned Commissioner's Trophy, presented to World Series winners). The Commissioner's Award was to honor the ballplayer that excelled in sportsmanship on the field, as well as community involvement off the field. Willie Mays received the first award.

Two years later, after the tragic death of Roberto Clemente—killed in a plane crash while bringing supplies to victims of a Nicaraguan earthquake—the award was renamed in honor of the great Pirate outfielder.

Each of the thirty major league clubs names a local recipient among the team, and that player becomes eligible for the national award. Including a fan vote component, the national winner is selected by an elite panel that includes former Clemente Award winners; the Commissioner; Clemente's widow, Vera; and various baseball broadcasters and analysts. Winners choose charitable organizations to receive cash donations in their name.

Up to 2013, one player in the game was chosen annually. Then in 2014, one from each league was honored with the Clemente Award—the White Sox' Paul Konerko and Phillies' Jimmy Rollins were the first recipients in that year.

Branch Rickey Award

Also offering kudos for community service, the Branch Rickey Award has been given since 1991 by the Rotary Club of Denver. Named in honor of the pioneering baseball executive, the award is given to one person, chosen from candidates named from each team. Those eligible include players, managers, coaches, front-office execs, as well as scouts, and even owners.

Winners are chosen by a committee of sports media figures, past award winners, and Rotary District Governors from Major League cities. Fans can also cast their votes via Facebook.

The award itself is a two-foot-tall bronze statue by Colorado sculptor George Lundeen. The figure, a replica of The Player sculpture that stands outside Coors Field, is a ballplayer, with a bat on his shoulder and a baseball held at his side. The trophy is presented during a banquet held in Denver after the season.

Comeback Player of the Year

In the "I'm as Confused as Heck" category is the Comeback Player of the Year honor. The previously mentioned GIBBYs and Players Choice Awards have their own award for the player who overcomes a downtick in his career, coming back to help a team once again.

Along with those two groups, the *Sporting News* has given its own Comeback Player of the Year Award, dating back to 1965. In their cases, several players have won twice—Norm Cash (both with the Tigers in 1965 and 1971), Boog Powell, Andres Galarraga, pitchers Rick Sutcliffe, Bret Saberhagen, and Chris Carpenter (twice with the Cards).

Starting in 2005, MLB began giving yet a fourth version of the Comeback Player of Year Award, based on nominations made by the staff from MLB.com. Fans then vote online for the winner—one from each league.

That's clear—isn't it?

Fireman/Reliever of the Year/Rolaids Relief Man Award

Replica of Rolaids Relief Man Award.

In 1960, the specialty known as the "relief pitcher" was just starting to make its impact. Up to then, former starting pitchers, too pooped to pitch more than five innings, and those not quite good enough to crack the rotation, were called upon to finish games.

That changed in 1959, when Pittsburgh Pirate Roy Face—never a starter—finished the season with an astounding 18–1 record, all in relief. Even though the save wouldn't become an official stat until 1969, he had ten in 1959. The reliever had arrived.

The *Sporting News* noted that no pitcher who pitched in relief had ever won the Cy Young Award. They responded by creating the Fireman of the Year Award, honoring the player in each league who had the highest total of wins and saves. The nine-by-twelve-inch plaque featured an engraved silver image of the winner.

The publication continued the award until 2010, changing its name to Reliever of the Year in 2001. Kansas City Royals' Dan Quisenberry won five trophies, while the Yankees' Mariano Rivera won a record six.

Major League Baseball instituted its own award for closers in 1976, sponsored by the Rolaids antacid tablet. Called the Rolaids Relief Man Award, it was based on a weighted point system for saves and wins (plus negative points for lost contests). Like the *Sporting News* award, Quisenberry and Rivera led the all-time competition with five trophies each.

Reflecting the way a closer "comes to the rescue of the team," the Rolaids Relief Man Award was a metal firefighter's helmet atop a wooden base. A prominent badge on its front proudly displayed the award's title, while a brass plaque on the base heralded the winner's accomplishment. The wooden base gave way to a metallic spire around the turn of the millennium.

Variations of the trophy include the 1991 version awarded to Rollie Fingers for being the first reliever to ever earn three hundred saves. The familiar helmet sat on an acrylic column with large metal numerals exclaiming "300." That trophy was sold at auction in 2010 for more than $7,000.

Other relief trophies ending up in the hands of collectors include Finger's 1980 Fireman of the Year plaque, going for nearly $2,300 in 2013. Goose Gossage's 1978 Rolaid's Relief Man Award went for more than $9,000 in 2013 as well.

When Rolaid's was acquired in a business deal, their sponsorship—and award—disappeared after 2012. But MLB resurrected the concept in 2014, creating the Mariano Rivera Reliever of the Year in the AL and the Trevor Hoffman Reliever of the Year in the NL. The two pitchers hold the top two spots in career saves and, along with a panel of other Hall of Fame closers, select the award winners.

All-Star and Postseason Awards

As might be expected, there's a myriad of honors given out during the All-Star Game and postseason tiers of playoffs. Some include the All-Star MVP Award (named for Ted Williams in 2002), League Championship MVP Awards in the NL and AL, and the World Series MVP. (Two-time winners include Sandy Koufax, Bob Gibson, and Reggie Jackson.)

Baseball's Valhalla—The Hall of Fame in Cooperstown, New York

According to Norse mythology, the god Odin created a place where great warriors could dwell after their battles were over. He called it Valhalla. (Me? I'm Italian—what do I know about Norse mythology?)

It's only fitting that the grand game of baseball have a similar spot where the greatest of all time could repose in honor when their playing days are over. That spot, as mentioned numerous times throughout this book, is the Baseball Hall of Fame, in Cooperstown, in upstate New York.

Its bucolic setting between the Catskills and Adirondacks was a glorious mislocation based on fiction. No matter; once visited, you can picture no other area for

Main entrance to Baseball's Hall of Fame, Cooperstown, New York.

its placement. While Elysian Fields in Hoboken, New Jersey, would be historically accurate, it's difficult to imagine the Hall anywhere else.

In 1909, a wealthy man named Stephen Carlton Clark, along with brother Edward, built the beautiful Otesaga Hotel on the south shore of the lake that lent its name to the lodge. The lake abutted Cooperstown, founded by William Cooper in the late 1700s. Hs son, James Fenimore, wrote novels like the *Leatherstocking* series, which included *The Deerslayer* and *Last of the Mohicans.*

The impact of the Great Depression in the 1930s was felt not only in metropolitan areas, but small towns like Cooperstown. Clark, a fan of baseball, sought to boost the local economy (including putting bodies in his hotel rooms). He asked NL President Ford Frick for permission to open a museum and Hall of Fame that honored America's pastime. Frick gave the go-ahead in March 1936.

By the time the actual museum structure was ready to open in June 1939, four elections had placed twenty-six people into the Hall (based, as it still is today, on receiving at least 75 percent of the vote). Players worthy of the first induction included relatively recent players with names like Wagner, Mathewson, Cobb, Young, Gehrig, (and a guy named Ruth), as well as historic notables like Anson, Cummings, Chadwick, and Cartwright. Fittingly, Abner Doubleday is not a member of the Hall, although the ball field just steps from it is named for him.

Since then, more than three hundred names have been elected to baseball's Hall of Fame. The hall gallery itself is cavernous and solemn, almost like a chapel. On its walls are plaques that honor players, managers, owners, executives, and umpires that made their impact on baseball. Each bronze plaque has raised text, identifying the honoree as well as their career highlights. A bas-relief image of the winner is located above the wording.

Along with the Hall's gallery itself are three floors of exhibits and artifacts, including artwork; historic items; and displays of bats, balls, and uniforms from the entire history of the game. Individual exhibits honor African Americans, Latin Americans, and women in baseball. Thousands of additional items are stored in the Hall's archives.

A separate wing houses a library, children's activities, the Giamatti Research Center, and a permanent exhibit called Scribes and Mikemen that recognizes broadcasters and writers who have made their way into the Hall of Fame (as award "recipients"—not to be confused with HOF "inductees").

Ford C. Frick Award—Broadcasters

In 1978, the Hall began honoring radio and television announcers, acknowledging their contributions to the game since the beginning days of broadcasting. Some of the game's greatest sports voices are featured, with their picture and bio on the wall of the exhibit. The award was named for former sportswriter, broadcaster, and commissioner Ford C. Frick.

First recipients of the honor were Mel Allen (previously noted as the seven-decade sportscaster) and Red Barber (announcer for the Reds, Dodgers, and Yankees for more than thirty years). A single winner was revealed in the years that followed, including broadcast greats like the Tigers' Ernie Harwell, the Cubs' Jack Brickhouse, the Cards/White Sox/Cubs' Harry Caray, the Cardinals' Jack Buck, the Brewers' Bob Uecker, and Mets/network staple Tim McCarver, among others.

J. G. Taylor Spink Award—Writers

The *Sporting News*, long the weekly paper for all things baseball, was started in 1886 by the Spink brothers. Less than twenty years later, J. G. Taylor Spink took the reins from his dad and uncle, editing *TSN* (as it's known) until his passing in 1962. In that same year, the Hall began recognizing baseball writers on an annual basis for their "meritorious service" with the J.G Taylor Spink Award.

It was only fitting that the very first recipient was none other than the man for whom the award was named. Other notable names in baseball journalism who have received the Spink Award include Ring Lardner, Grantland Rice, Damon Runyon, Red Smith, Jerome Holtzman, Wendell Smith, Peter Gammons, and Roger Angell, amid other deserving winners.

Buck O'Neil Award—Lifetime Achievement

One of the newest honors given by Baseball's Hall of Fame, the Buck O'Neil Award started in 2008. O'Neil was a veteran from the Negro Leagues, mostly playing with the Kansas City Monarchs. He also scouted for the Cubs (whom he also coached in the 1960s) and the KC Royals. In total, O'Neil spent the better part of eight decades in the game. A full-sized bronze statue of O'Neil stands in the museum, with award recipients added as they are chosen.

The O'Neil Award is selected once every three years, given to a member of the baseball community whose lifetime of service boosted the game, in terms of its impact on society, its appeal, and did so with great integrity. It made sense for the first recipient of the Buck O'Neil Award to be Buck himself, who had passed away in 2006 at the age of ninety-four. Since then, executive Roland Hemond won the honor in 2011, and player/broadcaster Joe Garagiola received it in 2014.

Beating the Best Baseball Bar Bets

Great Answers to Crazy Questions

Oh, Yeah?—You Wanna Step Outside?

Through the haze of sudsy beer and salty pretzels, a company softball team gathers in the local watering hole after a satisfying win on the diamond. The mood is cheery, increasing with each foamy pitcher of brew.

Suddenly, a fight breaks out! Is it the beefy first baseman Bruce "Tater" Carbona and the lanky left fielder, Kenny "Number 52" Hasenpheffer, bruising each other with fists like matured hams? Is it solid second-sacker Stephen "Noomby" Noodleman and slick shortstop Jimmy "Blonde Boy" Coogan, throttling each other with wrenching hands at their throats?

No, it's just the quiet catcher Johnny "The Ham" Berger and forever bench-warmer Lucius "Splinter-Butt" Micheals engaging in the lively art of conversation. Everyone watches as the pair test their baseball acumen with round after round of brain-busting questions about the game they love.

While some folks like to show off their skills on the field, others may be more adept away from the ballpark. In the world of names and numbers, records and streaks, baseball offers no end of challenging questions about its legacy.

Just as some pub regulars can bounce a quarter into a shot glass, or flip a fiber coaster tumbling into the air and deftly snatch before it hits the bar, others like to flex their mental muscles by demonstrating the depth of their knowledge about everything there is to know about America's pastime.

Number, Please?

There is nothing that can compete with the thrill of being elected to Baseball's Hall of Fame, but having your number retired might come close. It's a tradition that is sacred—no one ever wears that number from now on, so it becomes associated with that player (or manager or even owner, on occasion).

Major league baseball retired its first number—4—on July 4, 1939, when the New York Yankees honored Lou Gehrig, suddenly leaving the game and in the midst of dying from ALS—amyotrophic lateral sclerosis, a disease that would

Retired Yankee numbers in Monument Park, Yankee Stadium.

eventually be named after Gehrig himself. Only one player—Jackie Robinson—has had his number 42 retired by all thirty major league teams, who honored his memory on April 15, 1997.

Feisty and clever managers like the Yankees' Casey Stengel (37) and the Braves' Bobby Cox (6) have had their numbers retired. In a few rare instances, owners like the Angels' Gene Autry have been so honored (number 26, although there's no record of the singing cowboy ever wearing the number on the back of his chaps. But his horse, Champion, just might have had it branded on his hide).

So, of the thirty current major league teams, which two have never retired any numbers of their players? Hint: There's one in each league. (Washington Nationals and Seattle Mariners)

More Numbers, Please?

What was the attendance figure for the game between the Baltimore Orioles and Chicago White Sox on April 29, 2015? (Zero. For the first time in major league history, a scheduled game was played with no fans in attendance.)

Baltimore and the area around Camden Yards had been the site of unrest for several days, following the death of a black man in police custody. After postponement of Monday and Tuesday night games, the Orioles and Commissioner Rob Manfred agreed that a Wednesday afternoon game could be played. But in the interest of safety and law enforcement needs in other more important areas, no tickets were honored, and, except for the players, umpires, the media, and a few Orioles employees, the park was completely empty.

The situation didn't seem to faze the Baltimore club, as they won the game easily by a score of 8–2.

Take Yer Base!

Back in the 1950s, a lot of talk in the boys' locker room of the local high school centered around a young man's ability to get to first base—and they weren't talking baseball. (However, don't get your hopes up—this story is about baseball, ladies and gentlemen.) But, much like that aforementioned situation, you have to reach first base before you can score.

In most cases, that feat (in baseball) is accomplished with a skillful hit, or even a successful bunt. The rules of the game do allow for other ways to get to first base, some without ever touching the ball with the bat. In fact, there are five ways (paying no attention to errors or the fielder's choice . . . the bat is used in those situations, obviously).

Name the five ways an offensive player can reach first base without hitting the ball. (Walk/intentional walk, hit by pitch, dropped third strike, catcher interference, pinch runner.)

Making the Hit Parade

Other than pitcher, what one position has never had a player with 3,000 hits? (Catcher. Even the designated hitter is represented by Brewer/Blue Jay/Twin Paul Molitor, who amassed 3,319 hits and reached the Hall of Fame in 2004. The catcher closest to the mark was Ivan "Pudge" Rodriguez, with 2,637 knocks.)

Pitching Greatness . . . and Batting Lateness

Only one current major league team (with Washington including Montreal) has never had a no-hitter . . . .SD.

Yes, They All Played Baseball, But . . .

Here's a quickie: What do Tom Seaver, Sparky Anderson, Dallas Green, and Babe Ruth all have in common? (They all share the common first name of George).

Tom Seaver, Sparky Anderson, Dallas Green, and Babe Ruth.

More Strikes Than Balls

Back in the late 1980s, I happened to be visiting some good friends in Wausau, Wisconsin. One evening, we attended a minor league ball game featuring the Wausau Timbers (at the time, a Class A affiliate of the Seattle Mariners). As minor league parks tend to often do, they asked a trivia question, with a prize of two tix to a future Timbers game (assuming the Timbers had a future, which was questionable) as well as a large pizza from the local pie purveyor.

At the time, there was only one answer to their question—which I admit that I immediately knew and gave to my friends to submit (knowing it would be who-knows-when I would be back in Wausau).

The question, currently posed for your consideration, now has four answers.

Name the only four pitchers in major league history to each have a lifetime record with more than 3,000 strikeouts, and less than 1,000 walks.

(Fergie Jenkins, Greg Maddux, Curt Schilling, Pedro Martinez)

You Could Look It Up . . .

Another quickie: Name the winner of the 1994 World Series.

No one. And it certainly wasn't the fans of baseball, as a labor strike canceled the last month and a half of the season, all playoff games and the World Series. The strike wasn't settled until April 1995.

Who's on First?—Part 1

In the classic above-named comedy routine made famous by Abbott and Costello, only one defensive position is never named. What is it? No, what's on second; who's on first . . .

(The right fielder. When the Selchow and Righter Company made a "Who's on First" board game in the 1970s, they named the right fielder Nobody).

Who's on First?—Part 2

There have been quite a few Major Leaguers who have played all nine positions in their career—especially in the pre-1900 days, when even Hall of Famers Cap Anson, King Kelly, and Deacon White showed they could really get around.

However, only four have pulled the nine-position duty in just one game. Name them. (Shortstop Bert Campaneris, with the Kansas City A's in 1965; outfielder Cesar Tovar, with the Twins in 1968; and the Rangers' infielder Scott Sheldon and the Tigers' infielder Shane Halter, both in 2000.)

Oh, that guy . . .

Who was Sidd Finch?

He was a young pitcher in 1985, invited to the Mets spring training camp. Hidden behind an enclosed canvas, the twenty-eight-year-old right-hander astounded the coaches by throwing at a blistering radar-measured speed of 168 miles per hour. Finch had never played organized ball at any level and learned his rare talent by throwing rocks in the mountains of Tibet. The few who witnessed the practice sessions were always left speechless. But the fellow was torn between the prospect of a major league career or becoming a Buddhist monk.

Or so the story went.

Perhaps the greatest hoax in sports history, the curious case of Hayden "Sidd" Finch was published in *Sports Illustrated* magazine—on April 1, 1985. Yes, it was an April Fool's gag, written on assignment by journalist and sports writer George Plimpton. The scribe's article was rich in details, including first-person accounts from a pain-suffering practice catcher, an assigned Mets driver, Finch's landlady, even a specialist in Eastern religions. Only a few select Mets players and front-office staff were let in on the story as it was being prepared.

The quirky and reclusive character of Finch was also minutely described as a tall, string-bean fellow with a delivery like Goofy from the Disney cartoons. He had French horn skills worthy of a major philharmonic orchestra and pitched wearing one hiking boot and the other foot bare. Finch was even issued the uniform number of "21."

The *SI* article was complete with pictures—starring a Chicago-area middle school art teacher who was a friend of the staff photographer. Named Joe Berton, he was tickled at the opportunity to tweak the noses of America's sports fans. To this day, thirty years later, he still gets recognized as Finch and is asked for his autograph.

As for the magazine story, the fallout included several readers who angrily canceled their subscriptions. A couple of MLB managers asked Peter Ueberroth, the baseball commissioner, how their batters would be kept safe from such an unhittable flame-throwing hurler. The Mets and *SI* finally fessed up to the joke, and Plimpton wound up expanding the article into a 1987 novel. In the book, Finch went on to join the Mets after his newfound girlfriend encouraged him to go for it.

It's All Just a Myth-tery . . . Part I

Heard in dugouts all over is the familiar cry of, "C'mon, kid—Knock the cover of that ball!" A well-turned phrase, but can a ballplayer actually do it?

It depends on who you ask. And when.

The folks at Discovery Channel's *Mythbusters* tackled the question in a 2007 episode that dealt with baseball. With their usual methodic and thorough process of scientific research, the Mythbusters Team used a mechanical rig (for consistency) to fire standard baseballs at a wooden bat, with the intention of ripping the cover from the ball.

While Reds reliever Aroldis Chapman had yet to throw a world-record pitch of more than 105 mph in 2010, pitches of more than 100 miles per hour have been reached since the days of Indians great Bob Feller. With that in mind, the Mythbusters cranked their rig up to fire the ball at nearly twice that speed—200 mph. The ball survived, but the bat was smashed into splinters.

In true Mythbuster fashion, the speed of the ball was ramped up to a mind-numbing 437 mph. The result was a handful of twine, separated from its horsehide cover. At those numbers, the concept of a batter "knocking the cover off the ball" was deemed realistically impossible and, as such, "busted."

Fast-forward to April 14, 2014. In a game between the visiting Milwaukee Brewers and the home team Pittsburgh Pirates, Brewers backup catcher Martin Maldonado took a healthy cut at a fastball from Charlie Morton. The ball was grounded to third baseman Pedro Alvarez, who fielded something that looked like a partially peeled orange. He gathered the mass and tossed it to first like a knuckleball, with a confused shrug of his shoulders.

The quasi-ball rolled into Gaby Sanchez' mitt, although Maldonado had already crossed the bag with an infield single. The first baseman handed the oddity to first base ump Jim Reynolds, who laughed at the misshapen ball. In fact, everyone on the field—including Prates manager Clint Hurdle—had a good laugh at something they thought they'd never see.

It was the cover knocked off the ball.

It's All Just a Myth-tery . . . Part 2

Much has been made in recent years concerning the sometime (and longtime) major league practice of using a corked bat to propel a ball farther than with a legal bat. The principle is supposedly twofold: The cork is less dense than wood, so the bat is lighter and allows the hitter to swing faster. By the same token, the difference in materials results in a so-called trampoline effect, imparting positive and reciprocal energy to the impact of the ball. Supposedly.

Essentially, the end of a wooden bat is drilled out with a three-quarter- to one-inch bit, up to the "sweet spot"). Then the void is filled with bits of cork, and a wooden plug is glued into the end to camouflage the scam.

Does it work? Nah.

Once more, the Mythbusters team tackled this tale in 2007, using a rig similar to their "knock the cover off the ball" setup. An air cannon was able to consistently fire baseballs at an electrically timed swinging bat, with incoming and outgoing speeds accordingly measured.

A standard bat returned a ball traveling at 80 miles per hour at the same speed. The corked bat—which should have given the ball a higher outgoing speed—actually returned the ball at only 40 miles per hour. Not a result that's conducive to long balls and large contracts.

Corked bats, in a word—busted.

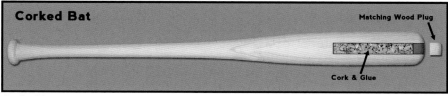

Corked bat.

Of course, if you don't believe their results, then you can consider research published in 2011 by four eminent physics scientists. The trampoline effect? Balderdash (although there's a wholly different answer when talking about an aluminum bat). Lighter bat? Nonsense. A lighter bat means less mass, which (thinking back to high school physics) means less distance.

These scientists came to the simple conclusions of: Home runs? Heavier bat. Higher batting average? Lighter bat.

What's in a Name?

With a vast community that includes thousands of players across nearly 150 years, the variety of baseball players is bound to be wide and diverse. Yet if one takes a closer look, there can be certain categories under which seemingly disparate players, some decades apart, share a common trait—their name. The next time the conversation wanes at the local watering hole, try some of these labels for a laugh.

Players with Very Colorful Names

Bud Black—Left-handed pitcher from the 1980s and 1990s and manager of the San Diego Padres.

Devon White—Solid center fielder and multiple Gold Glove winner between 1985 and 2001.

Shawn Green—Outfielder and two-time All-Star between 1993 and 2007.

Vida Blue—Dominant starting pitcher in the 1970s and 1980s—Multiple All-Star, as well as Cy Young and AL MVP Award winner.

Gates Brown—Lifetime Detroit Tiger and pinch-hitting specialist in the 1960s and 1970s.

Red Ruffing—Hall of Fame Pitcher from 1920s through the 1940s. Also effective at the plate, often used in the outfield or as a pinch hitter on his off days.

Players with Names Found in Nature

Kerry Wood—Starting pitcher in the 1990s and 2000s, including posting a 20-strike-out performance against the Astros in 1999.

Steve Stone—Starting pitcher from the 1970s, winning the AL Cy Young Award in 1980. Also a longtime broadcaster for the Chicago Cubs and White Sox.

Chip Glass (minor league)—Outfielder in the 1990s, winning the College World Series Most Outstanding Player award in 1994.

Heinie Sand—Philadelphia Phillies infielder in the 1920s.

Chris Waters—Starting pitcher for Baltimore Orioles in 2008.

Tim Raines—Base-stealing outfielder between 1979 and 2001, swiping more than 800 bases and amassing more than 2,600 hits in his career.

Curt Flood—Sure-handed outfielder in the decades of the fifties and sixties. Also known for being the first to challenge the long-standing "reserve clause" that kept players indentured to their team.

J. T. Snow—First baseman between 1992 and 2008, winning six Gold Gloves.

Players with Names One Can Bank On

Bobby Bonds—Outfielder who combined power and speed between 1968 and 1981.

Wes Stock—Pitcher and pitching coach between 1959 and 1981.

Don Money—Defensively superior third baseman who played between 1968 and 1983.

Norm Cash—Power-hitting first baseman, playing for the White Sox and Tigers between 1958 and 1974.

Ernie Banks—Hall of Fame shortstop and first baseman for Chicago Cubs in the 1950s, 1960s, and 1970s.

Brad Penny—Often-traveled starting pitcher, playing for six teams between 2000 and 2014.

Doug Nickle—National League relief pitcher between 2000 and 2002.

Curt Schilling—Dominating starting pitcher, winning more than two hundred games and striking out more than three thousand hitters between 1988 and 2007.

Bryan Pounds (minor league)—Infielder, reaching as high as Class AAA in the 2000s.

Buddy Yen (minor league)—Relief pitcher in low minors at the end of the twentieth century.

Mark Teixeira—Switch-hitting first baseman since 2003, with more than 350 homers and 1,100 RBI.

Players That Make One Hungry

Herman Franks—Former catcher and coach, as well as manager for the Giants and the Cubs in the 1960s and 1970s.

Billy Bean—Former outfielder for the Tigers, Dodgers, and Padres, who in 1999 bravely revealed he is gay.

Rob Burger (minor league)—Class AA pitcher between 1994 and 2000.

Pickles Dillhoefer—Based on the "dill" in his last name (as in dill pickles), he caught for the Cubs, Phillies, and Cards between 1917 and 1921.

Greg Bunn (minor league)—Class A pitcher between 2004 and 2008.

Chili Davis—Reliable outfielder and DH in the 1980s and 1990s.

Bob Veale—Effective pitcher for the Pirates and Red Sox between 1962 and 1974.

Bobby Wine—Light-hitting shortstop for the Phillies and Expos in the 1960s and early 1970s.

Darryl Strawberry—Power-hitting outfielder with the Mets, Dodgers, Giants, and Yankees during the 1980s and 1990s. A good player who could have been great, but his career was derailed by substance abuse.

Bob Lemon—Hall of Fame pitcher, as well as managing the Yankees and winning the 1978 World Series.

Harold Apple (minor league)—Triple-A pitcher in the early 1960s.

Pie Traynor—Hall of Fame third baseman with the Pirates in the twenties and thirties.

Candy Maldonado—Full first name is Candido; was an outfielder in the 1980s and 1990s.

Cookie Rojas—Little but mighty infielder in the 1960s and 1970s, with brief managing stints with the Angels and Marlins.

Coco Crisp—Sounding like a tasty breakfast cereal, the speedy outfielder has spent his thirteen-year career in the American League since 2002.

Peanuts Lowrey—Pinch-hitting specialist with the Cubs, Reds, Cards, and Phillies in the 1940s and 1950s.

Johnny Oates—Part-time catcher in the 1970s and 1980s, going on to manage the Rangers to three division championships.

Zack Wheat—Hall of Fame outfielder between 1909 and 1927, finishing with a .317 lifetime average.

Jim Rice—Intense and powerful outfielder with the Boston Red Sox during the 1970s and 1980s, entering the Hall of Fame in 2009.

Players with Watery Names

Mike Trout—Amazing Angels outfielder, bursting into the majors as a nineteen-year-old and winning Rookie of the Year honors in 2012.

Tim Salmon—Setting the tone for the previously mentioned Trout, Salmon was also Rookie of the Year for the Angels (albeit in 1993), playing all fourteen seasons in the outfield and DHing for the team.

Kevin Bass—Fourteen-year outfielder in both leagues, spending most of his time with the Houston Astros.

Mike Carp—First baseman/outfielder in the American League since 2009.

Catfish Hunter—Hall of Fame pitcher with the A's and Yankees, winning more than twenty games for five consecutive seasons and earning the Cy Young Award in 1974.

Jess Pike—Cup-of-coffee outfielder with the New York Giants in 1946.

Robert Fish (minor league)—Seven-season stint pitching for Angels and Braves affiliates.

Preacher Roe—National League pitcher during the 1930s, 1940s, and 1950s.

Junior Lake—Chicago Cubs outfielder during 2013 and 2014 seasons.

Mickey Rivers—Fleet leadoff man and outfielder for the Angels, Yankees, and Rangers between 1970 and 1984.

Jason Bay—Well-traveled outfielder with several solid offensive years between 2003 and 2013.

Players That Embody Body Parts (Only the Clean Ones)

Bill Hands—Journeyman pitcher during the sixties and seventies, winning twenty games for the Cubs in 1969.

Rollie Fingers—Hall of Fame relief pitcher from the 1960s through the 1980s, known for his massive handlebar mustache.

Barry Foote—Catcher often used in a backup role with the Expos, Phillies, Cubs, and Yankees in the 1970s and 1980s.

Greg Legg—Infielder with the Phillies in 1986 and 1987.

George Bone—Switch-hitter with the 1901 Milwaukee Brewers.

Ed Head—Pitcher with Brooklyn Dodgers between 1940 and 1946.

Roy Face—One of baseball's first relief specialists as a closer in the fifties and sixties, winning eighteen games while losing only one for the Pirates in 1959.

Brandon Backe—Pitcher with Tampa Bay and Houston between 2002 and 2009.

Mike Palm—Pitched three games for Boston Red Sox in 1948.

Ted Beard—Outfielder with the Pirates and White Sox in the late 1940s into the 1950s.

Harry Cheek (he should have shaved)—Briefly played for the Phillies in 1910.

An Uneven Playing Field

The Dark Days of Baseball

Say It Ain't So, Joe . . .

Into every life, a little rain must fall," and, over the years, baseball has had its share of downpours. Even though the balance of this book is meant to celebrate the game, it would not be fair or complete to ignore the part of its history that isn't so joyous. If anything, the sage observation of philosopher George Santayana from way back in 1905 applies: "Those who cannot remember the past are condemned to repeat it" (no matter how you may have originally heard this quote). Put simply: Let's hope baseball can learn from its mistakes.

A team may have made its own money deal on the side when they weren't properly paid for being successful. One of the game's top players ever is denied entrance to the Hall of Fame when he places bets on baseball. Labor issues bring baseball to a halt several times. With no immunity from exercising poor judgment, baseball's owners agree to freeze out some of the game's best players. Substance abuse, whether it was the personal indulgence of cocaine or the pursuit for improved stats via PEDs, left black marks on a game lauded as all-American as apple pie.

Yet, in spite of these bumps in the road, baseball has continued to be a great sport, great entertainment, and a great way to spend a summer evening.

1919 Black Sox

Charles Comiskey was a first baseman with a fair thirteen-year baseball career in the late 1800s. Retired from the game, he worked with Ban Johnson to assemble the American League in 1902 (as outlined elsewhere in this book). Comiskey—known as "Commy" (having nothing to do with Russian politics) or "the Old Roman" (most likely in observation of his prominent "Roman nose")—owned the new Chicago team. He called them the White Sox (after the Chicago White Stockings became the Colts and then the Orphans, before becoming the Cubs in 1902).

Comiskey's team won the World Series in 1917 and was poised to win it again in 1919. The owner had the reputation of being open and generous—he gave away free tickets to school children and soldiers, while letting the city of Chicago use the ballpark (named after Comiskey himself) for many special events.

However, the same generosity with the fans didn't always make its way down to the Sox players. A big bonus promised to them turned out to be a case of flat champagne. Other teams paid their players four dollars per diem; Comiskey's White Sox received only three bucks a day. The Chicago players paid their own laundry bills, prompting them to wear the same filthy uniforms for weeks. It would earn them the nickname of "the Black Sox" long before their 1919 scandal. Yet a review of the actual contract records from the day (kept somewhere deep in the files at Cooperstown) has shown that the 1919 White Sox were one of the highest-paid teams back then, collectively making $93,000 a year.

Also, one often-told story should be clarified. The great 1988 film *Eight Men Out* (again, covered elsewhere in this book) showed pitcher Eddie Cicotte nearing a thirty-win season in 1919, for which Comiskey had promised a $10,000 bonus. The owner then told manager Kid Gleason to keep Cicotte on the bench until the Series, thereby "keeping him fresh" (and denying the pitcher his bonus). While some have pointed out that it actually happened in 1917, recent research of box scores and other evidence from the period shows that the whole story is not true.

The players could have been divided into the "haves" and "have-nots": One group, headed up by second baseman Eddie Collins, was basically an educated lot

Eight Men Out: (*Top*) Cicotte, Felsch, Gandil, Jackson (*Bottom*) McMullin, Risberg, Weaver, Williams.

and had negotiated yearly salaries as high as $15,000. The "have-nots" were led by first baseman Chick Gandil. This bunch only made around $6,000 a year (some as little as $3,000) and clearly held hard feelings toward the "haves." Both groups' income was a result of the reserve clause that stood for many years.

Gandil had made the acquaintance of a gambler and bookmaker named Joseph "Sport" Sullivan. Several weeks before the start of the 1919 World Series between the heavily favored White Sox and the Cincinnati Reds, Gandil offered Sullivan a deal: For $80,000—in advance—the Sox first baseman would recruit enough teammates to throw the Series, allowing Sullivan to make a killing in well-placed bets.

Gambling on baseball was not a unique practice, and although crooked ball-players were seen less frequently, the idea was not unknown. Ty Cobb and Tris Speaker were involved in a gambling fix around the same time the White Sox were (although word of it didn't break until 1926). Even umpires had been approached to illegally influence the outcome of games.

And this wasn't the first time the White Sox found themselves in the midst of a scandal. In 1917, Sox players actually formed a pool to collect money, donating it to Tigers pitchers for "helping" the Sox sweep a late-season, four-game series with them. Sox management knew all about the arrangement—which allowed the Sox to reach the World Series, and win it—but said and did nothing.

As the 1919 Series approached, Gandil rounded up the following players for the fix (with varying amounts of involvement, from eager agreement to cautious skepticism). More or less in the following order:

- Right-handed pitcher Eddie Cicotte (who obviously had his reasons to get back at the miserly Old Roman)
- Shortstop Charles "Swede" Risberg
- Utility player Fred McMullin
- Left-handed pitcher Claude "Lefty" Williams
- Third baseman George "Buck" Weaver (who never agreed to the fix)
- Left fielder "Shoeless" Joe Jackson
- Center fielder Oscar "Happy" Felsch

With possibilities of gambling and fixing the game hardly a secret, it's no surprise that competition came from another group of lowlifes—ex-pitcher "Sleepy" Bill Burns and ex-fighter Billy Maharg (what—no nickname?)—who made their own offer of $100,000 to the eight Sox players.

Of course, the pair didn't have a pot to plant petunias in, so now they had to find the payoff money somewhere. Burns and Maharg hit up Arnold Rothstein, the biggest gambler in America. Rothstein declined their offer at first but before long, Rothstein, Sullivan, Burns, Maharg, and an ex-world boxing champ named Abe Attell were all involved in the deal. (Rothstein would eventually reap more than a quarter-million dollars in gambling winnings from the 1919 Series.)

The only thing missing was the actual fix money. While Cicotte received his $10,000 up front, the others were angered that their double-cross had been double-crossed. Attell and Sullivan came up with another $70,000—eventually, of which Gandil kept $35,000—but that was not the $100,000 that was discussed.

It was a nine-game series in 1919, and after five games—down four games to one—the betrayed Sox decided to go for the win. They quickly won the next two games. But Rothstein, having bet heavily on the Reds, sent a goon to threaten Lefty Williams and his family. The pitcher was scheduled to start game eight, and if the Sox won, the Williams family would lose.

Losing their fifth game (Williams surrendered four runs in the first inning), the Sox lost the Series. Sox manager Kid Gleason, who had stuck up for his players when rumbles of cheating erupted, felt betrayed.

Even though Comiskey was aware of what had happened (Jackson told him about the fix, but Commy turned a blind eye to the whole situation), he publically stated the Series had been played fairly. Despite other rampant suspicions—including those of Chicago sportswriters Hugh Fullerton and Ring Lardner—the 1920 season started with little impact from the previous year. Except for Gandil, the whole 1919 White Sox team returned.

But by September, the game suspected many teams of taking money under the table, a grand jury found enough cause to indict the eight White Sox players with "conspiracy to defraud" the public. In other words, for fixing the 1919 World Series.

The resulting trial was a farce. Signed confessions from Cicotte, Jackson, and Williams suddenly disappeared. Comiskey had promised the players that if they were found innocent, their suspensions would be canceled and they'd still be White Sox. (No surprise—that didn't happen.) Lacking hard evidence—and the missing confessions—a jury took less than three hours to acquit the defendants of all charges.

The legendary and heart-tugging story of a young boy confronting Joe Jackson on the steps of the courthouse, tearfully asking, "Say it ain't so, Joe"—just ain't so. Jackson himself, in a 1949 magazine article, denied any such incident. The apocryphal story can be traced to a front-page item in a Chicago paper—journalism in those days tended to stress sensation over accuracy.

Tired of the gambling that raged unchecked in the game, baseball club owners saw the Black Sox Scandal as the final straw. Less than two months after the eight White Sox players were found innocent of conspiracy, a stern Federal judge named Kenesaw Mountain Landis was hired as the first Commissioner of Major League Baseball. Owners felt his salary demand of $50,000 a year (less his $7,500 government pay) was more than fair—if Landis could clean the game up.

His first act was to banish the eight White Sox players—for life—even though they had been found innocent. Throwing a blanket over the bunch (and firmly demonstrating there was a new sheriff in the ballpark), Landis believed that anyone even suspected of throwing a baseball game deserved permanent expulsion.

Some of the eight tried to play ball with barnstorming teams, but their days of baseball were basically done. Ringleader Gandil became a plumber in the Napa Valley of California, until his death in 1970. Cicotte lived until 1969, working as a game warden and strawberry farmer. Risberg was a dairy farmer and ran a tavern until his death in 1975. McMullin ended up in California law enforcement, up to his passing in 1952. Williams had a landscaping business until he died in 1959.

Felsch played outlaw ball for a number of years, then ran a tavern in Milwaukee and became a crane operator. He died in 1964.

The cases of Weaver and Jackson were somewhat different than the rest. Weaver had never taken any money and hit a robust .324 in the 1919 Series. Jackson (who had tried to return the $5,000 he received) hit .375 and drove in six runs—hardly an indication of throwing games.

Buck Weaver sought reinstatement, even penning a request to Commissioner Ford Frick in 1953—thirty-three years after the Black Sox Trial—but it was denied. He barnstormed a bit, then became a house painter until his death in 1956.

There's no doubt that Joe Jackson was one of the great ballplayers, in his time and perhaps in the history of the game. In his shortened thirteen-year career, he collected 200 or more hits four times, hit more than 40 doubles four times, drove in 80 or more runs five times (while never hitting more than a dozen homers in the Dead-Ball Era), and scored 90s or more runs six times. He had top averages of .408, .395, and .392, finishing with a lifetime .356 average, as well as more than 200 stolen bases. Jackson was also a top-notch outfielder with a crackshot arm. In three consecutive years with the Indians, he had 30, 32, and 28 assists, respectively.

Joe Jackson referred to his bat as "Black Betsy," all thirty-six inches and forty-eight ounces of it. The mighty Babe Ruth claimed to have patterned his successful batting swing after Jackson's. He acquired the nickname of "Shoeless" after playing a minor league game in his stocking feet—his new spikes had left him with blisters.

The native from Pickens County in South Carolina was essentially illiterate, once stating that "it don't take school stuff to help a fella play ball." Many have pointed to his basic lifestyle and innocence as proof that he likely wasn't involved in the fix—he was too simple and pure. Like some of the others who were banned, Jackson played outlaw ball for a number of years afterward. He opened a restaurant and liquor store in South Carolina, running it until his death in 1951. Still, his banishment from the game sticks, despite the continued efforts of fans across more than ninety years since Landis' decision, denying Joe Jackson a deserved spot in Cooperstown.

A Rose by Any Other Name

Yes, he was known by another name—Charlie Hustle. Pete Rose, a bulldog of a guy who played the game of baseball like it should have been played for twenty-four seasons. He set records, took part in six World Series—winning three times—and turned something as simple as a base on balls into excitement, as he always ran to first on a walk—as if he had just slashed a sharp single to left.

One example of his hard-nosed method of playing the game was evidenced in the 1970 All-Star Game. With the game knotted at 4–4 in the bottom of the twelfth inning, Rose singled to center with two outs. Billy Grabarkewitz (as great a mouthful of a name as there's ever been) stroked another single, with Rose advancing to second. Jim Hickman singled to center, and Rose came roaring around third like the proverbial runaway freight train.

AL catcher Ray Fosse—a promising twenty-three-year-old who was playing in his first full year with the Indians—was flattened as Rose buried his shoulder into the catcher, just as the ball arrived. Rose scored the winning run in front of his hometown fans in Cincinnati.

Fosse suffered a broken and separated shoulder, but without MRI technology, it went undiagnosed until the following year. More, his career was never the same after the collision. Up to the All-Star Game, the catcher was hitting .312, with 16 homers and 45 runs batted in. In the seven years following, he compiled a .255 average, with only 41 home runs.

Some fans believe Rose, playing in a meaningless contest, should have backed off as he neared the plate—at that time, the All-Star Game had no bearing on the season's outcome (unlike today, where the winning league gets home field advantage in the World Series). Others see the play as exemplary of how the game should always be played, with Rose as a symbol of that philosophy.

Yet, at some point, Pete Rose showed a major lapse in judgment and, as a result, earned a lifetime ban from baseball, instead of a plaque in the Hall of Fame—which he also earned. He traded in his years of accomplishment for betting on baseball, and in 1989, Commissioner A. Bartlett Giamatti decided Rose should be banished for his indiscretions.

Originally joining the Cincinnati Reds in 1963 as a second baseman, Rose earned Rookie of the Year honors. In the years after, he played all three outfield positions, as well as third base and first base, for the Reds, the Phillies, and one year with the Expos, before returning to the Reds as a player-manager. He spent the better portion of 1985 and 1986 in that dual role, continuing to manage through most of the 1989 season.

The seventeen-time All-Star was a feared switch-hitter, with a crouching batting stance that begged to have a chair slipped under it. In 1978, Rose amassed a forty-four-game hit streak, tying the NL record set by Wee Willie Keeler. Furthermore, he set the all-time record for hits in 1985, breaking Ty Cobb's long-standing mark of 4,191.

Rose finished his career with 4,256 hits, along with all-time records for most games played, at bats, and singles, and a National League record for doubles with 746. He had 200 or more hits an ML record of ten times, and is the only player to ever play at least five hundred games at five different positions.

By the start of the 1989 season, talk was all over that Pete Rose liked to gamble—a lot. Appointed by the MLB, investigator John Dowd revealed that the Reds manager was betting thousands of dollars on baseball, every day in 1987. He even bet on more than fifty Reds games—although never against his team. Even though he denied the findings, Rose was banned from baseball in September of that year.

Pete Rose, 1976 Cincinnati Reds.

In the years following, Rose applied—unsuccessfully—for reinstatement with Commissioners Fay Vincent and Bud Selig. In 2004, Pete published *My Prison Without Bars*, in which he admitted to gambling on baseball, but steadfastly averring that he never bet against his own teams.

Rose has hosted radio shows since the banishment and for many of those years, signed autographs at a Cooperstown memorabilia store—just a block down from the Hall—during HOF Induction Week. When not there, he signs in a Las Vegas shop and hopes to get another chance at reinstatement.

Current Commissioner Rob Manfred has avoided any direct consideration of Rose, even though Pete submitted a new application for reinstatement just prior to the start of the 2015 season. And while he can hope, the all-time hitting king isn't betting on a positive outcome.

The Ump Doesn't Always Call the Strikes—The Labor Problems of 1981 and 1994

The game of baseball survived two world wars, three major military conflicts, dire economic conditions in America, and even an earthquake. But it was the almighty buck that put the kibosh on the Fall Classic—the first time in ninety years that there was no World Series. Across the years, labor issues have helped to change the course of how the game was played—outside the foul lines.

First appearing in the mid-1970s, free agency allowed players to play with teams they chose, and allowed club owners to assemble teams, not just by drafting young players and making trades, but also by signing established stars. But the folks in the front office weren't happy with losing their best players without receiving any compensating players of similar value (in other words, major leaguers) in return.

The Players Association, having just achieved free agency, felt such an arrangement would foul the waters. With a new collective bargaining agreement (CBA) being negotiated during the 1980 season, it looked like the divide over free agency compensation would result in a strike. At the last minute, the agreement was signed—with the free agency issue unresolved. A committee of owners and players would study the matter, and if agreement couldn't be reached by early 1981, the owners retained the right to put their own plan into place. In fairness, if that happened, then the players had the right to go on strike.

It wasn't, they did, and they did. On June 12, the players walked out, and the ballparks were empty. The rest of the month, as well as all of July, was lost. As August began, the owners finally gave ground and agreed to loosen their demands of accepting only major league players as compensation. With a new four-year CBA signed, baseball would return on August 9 with the All-Star Game. The 1981 season wound up losing about 50 games from its 162-game schedule.

At the end of regular play that year, the split-season records were combined to determine postseason matchups, leading to some hard feelings among fans and teams. In the NL East, for example, the Phillies had the most wins before the strike and the Expos had the most afterward. But with both halves combined, the Cards actually had the best overall record. Similarly, the NL West had the Dodgers and Astros with the most wins, pre and post respectively, but the Reds had the most for the entire year and went to the postseason.

The time off seemed to affect some teams in strange ways. Before the strike, the Angels had a record of 31–29, but after, they played to only a 20–30 second half. The Yankees started out with 34–22 in the first half, but fell to only 25–-26 in the games after the strike. Likewise, the Phillies had posted a 34–21 first half, but could only muster a 25–27 record when they returned. In the other direction, the Astros had a disappointing 28–29 record before the strike, but soared to 33–20 afterward.

The players also held a two-day strike in August 1985 (with lost games made up at the season's end), in reaction to the owner's demand for a cap on salary arbitration awards. The owners dropped the idea, and in return, the players agreed to delay their eligibility for arbitration from two to three years (in negotiation, the key is a willingness to concede on some points, while modifying others).

And the worst was yet to come.

When MLB Commissioner Bart Giamatti suddenly died in September 1989, his deputy, Fay Vincent, took over the helm. He quickly became unpopular with the club owners and resigned in 1992 after they overwhelmingly gave a vote of "no confidence" by a ratio of two-to-one. As a result, the owners named Bug Selig as acting Commissioner—it was no coincidence that Selig was an owner himself and one of the leaders to oust Vincent.

By 1994, the owners proposed a salary cap (basically a potential cut in pay, something the players certainly didn't want to see), as well as revenue sharing. With it, larger market teams (with larger money resources) would share their revenues with smaller market teams (and their smaller money resources). The players believed those measures were just a way for club owners to solve their ongoing money management problems—at the expense of their players.

With no agreement in sight, the ballplayers walked out on August 12. Of course, the fans lost out, the owners lost out, and the players lost out. In particular, Padres outfielder Tony Gwynn was hitting .394 when the strike was called, dashing any hopes of hitting .400. Similarly, the Giants' Matt Williams had 43 home runs when the strike started, losing forty-five games in which he had a very good chance to tie or break Roger Maris' single-season record of 61 homers.

What's more, the work stoppage canceled the World Series in October, a first since they started. You know the situation was getting bad when the president of the country (Bill Clinton at that time) tried to play umpire, asking both sides to accept a deal of binding arbitration in February 1995. The owners refused and began to make preparations for the new season with replacement teams of minor leaguers, college players, and retired major leaguers (not many from that last group, as most stood firm with their current union brothers). Managers like the Tigers' Sparky Anderson refused to work with the second-stringers.

With opening day only a few days away, the National Labor Relations Board (NLRB) asked for an injunction on behalf of the players' union. US District Court Judge Sonia Sotomayor (eventually a member of the US Supreme Court, and a longtime Yankees fan from the Bronx) ruled that the owners were guilty of federal labor law violations and ordered that the rules from the old CBA be put back into use. The 234-day strike came to an end, with play resuming at the end of April—the 1995 season would be shortened by eighteen games.

Worse, the fans were angered, as they considered both players and owners a big bunch of rich and selfish people. While the 1993 season had seen a grand increase in attendance for baseball, the 1994 and 1995 seasons showed a drop of 20 percent overall. It would be several years before the game recovered from the effects of the strike.

Revenue sharing for the teams eventually became reality by 2000, with a separate luxury tax (the "competitive balance tax," if one wants to get technical) established in 1997. It's not, as some believe, the same thing as revenue sharing. Basically, teams with high payrolls that exceed a certain limit are penalized by paying millions of dollars in the form of a tax. Unlike revenue sharing, the money collected doesn't go to other teams. It funds player benefits, as well as furthering the development of baseball as a business.

In Cahoots—Club Owner Collusion (Part I, II and III)

Going back to the mid-1980s, baseball club owners felt their hands were tied, considering free agency in general, an unsatisfactory compensation process for lost players, and no salary cap (of course, forgetting they had called all the shots for the first one hundred years of the game). Commissioner Peter Ueberroth, recently replacing long-serving Bowie Kuhn, met with the owners after the 1985 season. Like a father scolding his son, Ueberroth admonished the group for crying over lost dollars. Perhaps with a wink, he told them, "I know and you know what's wrong. You are smart businessmen. You all agree we have a problem. Go solve it."

And they did, even though they got caught for solving their problem illegally. Privately, they all agreed to avoid signing up each other's free agents, and if they did, they would stay away from long-term contracts. All this, despite the CBA having specific language prohibiting such acts of "collusion."

Suddenly, big-name free agents like Kirk Gibson, Carlton Fisk, Tommy John, and Phil Niekro were going unsigned and forced to stay with their 1985 teams. The Players Association took notice and filed a grievance in early 1986, charging the owners with an action that became known as "Collusion I." Meanwhile, the practice continued. Following the 1986 season, once again free agents like Jack Morris, Tim Raines, and Ron Guidry went untouched by new teams—Collusion II, the Sequel.

Andre Dawson, a star outfielder with the Montreal Expos, was fed up with the obvious shenanigans and signed a blank contract with the Chicago Cubs, telling GM Dallas Green he would play for whatever money the club wanted to pay. It was a steal for the team, as "The Hawk" was paid $650,000 for one year (when he was worth millions).

He responded with an amazing season in 1987, collecting 178 hits for a .287 average, 49 homers, driving in 137 runs, and scoring 90 runs. The Cubs finished last in the NL East, but Dawson won the MVP Award, as well as a Gold Glove. He played five more seasons with Chicago, being paid as much as over $3 million a year. (Dawson was elected to the Hall of Fame in 2010 after posting a .279 lifetime average, with 438 homers, 314 steals, nearly 2,800 hits, and a reputation as a feared outfielder with a cannon for an arm.)

Meanwhile, the Players Association recognized that free agent salaries actually went down for the first time since the practice began in the 1970s, dropping 16 percent. They also noticed that team revenues increased 15 percent in that same period. Smelling something fishy, they filed a second grievance in early 1987.

As the 1987 season wound down, independent arbitrator Thomas Roberts ruled that baseball owners had indeed colluded in 1985 to restrict free agent signings. Players received damages of more than $10 million from the owners in early 1988, along with seven players who were free agents in 1985 being awarded "second looks" or chances to sign with new teams. Yet club owners secretly agreed to refrain from big free agency signings for a third consecutive year—Collusion III was afoot, and still another grievance was filed.

One year later, in late 1989, another arbitrator named George Nicolau assigned damages of $38 million in Collusion II, along with another group of second-look free agents from 1986. Nicolau also reviewed the charges of Collusion III and made a final determination in late 1991. Lost wages and salaries, along with penalties, would cost club owners a total of $280 million for all three acts of collusion.

In 1989, while this was all going on, Ueberroth left the Commissioner's Office, Bart Giamatti had just one year before suddenly passing away, and Fay Vincent took command. As mentioned earlier, Vincent was no friend of the owners. He, too, admonished them, forcing them to realize they "stole two hundred-eighty-million dollars from the players . . . you got caught."

It was all a matter of trust—there was none.

I Wanna New Drug—Passing the Acid Test

When people talk about performance-enhancing drugs in baseball (which is a lot these days), they seldom consider hallucinogenics as an example of one. Yet back in 1970, Dock Ellis (yes, that's his real first name) dropped acid—LSD—before a game and came out pitching a no-hitter.

More than forty years ago, the drug culture was widespread, and for baseball, it focused on amphetamines. Stimulants—not the occasional caffeine tab, but serious drugs like speed and pep pills—were common to help players get up for their games. Maybe they'd had a tough night of partying or were feeling the drain of a long season, but they looked to "greenies" and "bennies" to get game-ready.

Dock Ellis, a promising and outspoken twenty-five-year-old starting pitcher with the Pittsburgh Pirates in 1970, relied on pep pills as much as any player. Plus, he embraced the philosophy of Timothy Leary, a pop culture psychologist and writer at the time who touted the use of psychedelic drugs with the mantra of "turn on, tune in, and drop out."

The Pirate was scheduled to pitch against the San Diego Padres in their Southern California stadium on Friday, June 12. Ellis took LSD at the airport, and when he arrived at his girlfriend's place, he admitted he was "High as a Georgia pine." But Ellis had lost track of the days and thought it was Thursday, while it was really Friday—his day to pitch.

At the park, Ellis grabbed a handful of Benzedrine and, still tripping, started the game. While he didn't recall much of what happened that day, Ellis did admit to not seeing the batters, thinking at one point that President Richard Nixon was the ump behind the plate, and the ball changed from being very small to very large. At one point, he covered first base on a play and exclaimed, "Oh, I just made a touchdown."

When it was all over, Dock had given up no hits, no runs, recorded 6 strikeouts and 8 walks, and hit one batter. He won the game with a 2–0 score. While his teammates knew he was high on something, no one suspected LSD was involved. It would be nearly fifteen years before the word of the drug-influenced no-no came out, long after Ellis' baseball career was over.

The former pitcher eventually got his act together, cleaning up and becoming a drug counselor. While known most for the psychedelic pitching performance, he was not proud of it and talked about the incident with shame and disappointment. Dock felt he had looked to drugs in an effort to mask his fear of losing and failing.

Dock Ellis, 1970 Pittsburgh Pirates.

Ellis regretted the fact that his greatest achievement on the field was a blur of broken memories for him and would always have the stigma of drug abuse attached to it. He passed away in 2008 at age sixty-three from cirrhosis of the liver.

I Don't Wanna New Drug—Cocaine in the 1980s

Baseball fans under thirty-five probably think "steroids" when someone mentions drugs in the game. But the relatively recent concern with PEDs—performance-enhancing drugs—is not baseball's first drugstore rodeo. The decade of the 1980s saw rampant recreational abuse of cocaine among players, with some prominent stars being suspended for their involvement—or worse.

Starting in the 1980s, suspicion was widespread that cocaine use in baseball was a common occurrence. In 1983, drug dealer Mark Liebl fingered more than a dozen AL players as some of his cocaine customers. Four KC Royals—Willie Aikens, Vida Blue, Jerry Martin, and Willie Wilson—pled guilty to misdemeanor drug charges and were jailed.

The issue was still a hot one in 1985, when a number of drug dealers were brought up on cocaine distributing charges in a Pittsburgh courtroom. With promises of immunity from prosecution, some of baseball's biggest stars—Keith Hernandez, Dave Parker, and Lonnie Smith among them—testified, admitting to using cocaine and buying from the defendants. Tim Raines, a top base stealer with the Montreal Expos at the time, revealed he always made sure to slide head-first—he didn't want to break the vial of cocaine he always kept in his back pocket.

The spindly vines of drug use reached into every corner of the game. Even Kevin Koch, the Pittsburgh Pirates' Parrot—the team mascot (!)—admitted to being a drug delivery boy (or bird) in the clubhouse. Hernandez suggested that as many as 250 MLB players might have been cocaine users, and Parker admitted that years of use had seriously (and negatively) affected his play on the field.

While the witnesses were legally untouchable, Commissioner Peter Ueberroth made sure they didn't escape unscathed. Ten players were suspended, although those penalties were lifted when they agreed to donate a substantial percentage of their salaries to drug programs. They, along with ten additional players, consented to take drug tests for the remainder of their careers.

Other abusers didn't get off so easy. Pirates reliever Rod Scurry had a promising career before cocaine took over his life, leading to a fatal cocaine-related heart attack in 1992. Like Scurry, NBA's Boston Celtics draft star Len Bias and NFL Cleveland Browns' Don Rogers both died from cocaine-related heart attacks. All were healthy, well-paid athletes who couldn't shake their drug abuse and became the kind of role models no one wanted to be.

I Still Don't Wanna New Drug—Steroids and PEDs in the 1990s

In sports, it's only human nature that makes an athlete want to succeed. Despite the tenet of Lincoln's Emancipation Proclamation that "all men are created equal," Honest Abe was not referring to baseball players. As such, the matchup of a shortstop hitting .206 against a pitcher of, say, Roger Clemens' skills would seem hardly fair and evenly matched.

Then wouldn't it make sense that the .206 hitter would be seeking an edge of any sort—perhaps pharmaceutical—in facing off against the Rocket? You'd think so. So why was Clemens the one (among many) connected to the use of illegal steroids and HGH—human growth hormone? With a blazing fastball in the upper nineties and a knee-buckling curve, Clemens hardly appeared to be a needy candidate for artificial enhancement.

Barry Bonds, Alex Rodriguez, and Roger Clemens all have career WAR levels that place them in the Top Twelve position players and pitchers of all-time, but the ominous shadow of PEDs brings doubt as to the true value of their accomplishments.

For example, A-Rod was clearly on the fast-track to superstardom as a young shortstop with the Seattle Mariners. In 1996, at just twenty years old, he had 215 hits for a .358 average, along with 54 doubles, 36 homers, and 123 RBI. From all accounts, it was a clean performance.

But Rodriguez admitted in 2009 that he had used PEDs from 2001 to 2003, when he signed with the Texas Rangers as a free agent. At the time, it was the largest contract in the game, a ten-year deal worth more than $250 million. Traded in 2004 to the Yankees (and later re-signing in 2007 as a free agent, for ten years at $27.5 million per year), A-Rod continued to pile up big offensive numbers and accompanying accolades.

The three-time MVP started having hip problems in 2009, where his stats began to fall off. Despite stating that since his Rangers days, he had not taken steroids, A-Rod finally admitted to drug agents and prosecutors that he did use them between 2010 and 2012.

The confession gave A-Rod immunity from prosecution, but not from the wrath of MLB, which suspended him for the entire 2014 season. In early 2015, he apologized to his team, in the hopes of regaining some semblance of his potential Hall of Fame career. Even if he never played again, his 654 homers, 2,939 hits, over 500 doubles, and more than 1,900 RBI would seem to make him a lock for Cooperstown. But his poor decisions might have derailed that course.

The shame is, considering their skills and numbers before their alleged (or admitted) substance use began, many of these players—like A-Rod—were already on Hall of Fame tracks. Placing their achievements, albeit under the cloud of suspicion, above WARs of greats like Stan Musial, Rogers Hornsby, or Greg Maddux—whose on-field reputations are without question—seems unfair and invalid.

It should be noted that Clemens was indicted for perjury in 2010, for lying to Congress about never taking PEDs. In all fairness, though, it should be understood: The pitcher was acquitted of all charges in 2012, after an initial mistrial. Still, previous testimony from former teammates implicated that Clemens had routinely used PEDs, supplied by a private trainer. The stigma of suspected illegal activity remains.

Just how do PEDs work? Without turning this into the start of a pharmaceutical degree, let's focus on steroids and HGH, human growth hormone. While there are other substances banned in baseball, these two garner the most attention.

First developed in the 1930s, anabolic steroids adds artificial testosterone (the male hormone that makes one's muscles bulge and voice sound deep) to an athlete's system. The added "juice" makes the body produce more proteins in muscle cells and increases muscle mass. Intense or prolonged use can also result in acne, impotence, violent fits of anger, along with heart and liver damage.

HGH is produced naturally in the pituitary gland. A synthetic was developed in the mid-1980s to medically help patients with growth disorders. Abused by athletes, HGH reduces body fat, while it encourages an increase in muscle mass and quick recovery from injuries. Side effects can include nerve or joint pain, increased fluids in body tissue (called edema), and increased cholesterol. In both cases, an athlete who abuses these drugs can hope to perform higher, farther, and faster—after a quick stop at the drugstore.

Not wanting to ignore the eight-hundred-pound gorilla in the room (obviously an animal with no need for steroids), baseball instituted random drug testing in 2004. Yet the concern for drug abuse continued, resulting in a 2005 Congressional hearing on the use of steroids in baseball. Seven high-profile players—Jose Canseco (who had just written a tell-all book), Jason Giambi, Mark McGwire, Rafael Palmeiro, Curt Schilling, Sammy Sosa, and Frank Thomas—were called to testify, along with baseball executives like Commissioner Bud Selig.

There were enough unanswered questions from the hearing to prompt Selig to request an official investigation, headed by former Senator and prosecutor George Mitchell. His report, unofficially but logically called *The Mitchell Report*, was released in 2007. It concluded that the abuse of steroids in the game was

Mark McGwire, 1987 Oakland A's and 1999 St Louis Cardinals.

widespread, and while baseball had been initially slow to respond, attempts to correct the problem were under way.

After years of denying the use of steroids, Cards first baseman Mark McGwire admitted, in a January 2010 television interview with Bob Costas, to using PEDs since 1989. This same Mark McGwire won the AL Rookie of the Year award in 1987 as a twenty-three year-old, standing six-foot, five-inches and listed at 215 pounds. With the use of PEDs, his weight rose to 250 pounds (as he stated in the Costas interview), so there's an example of how steroids can add as much as 35 pounds of muscle in a short period of time.

Like Bonds and Clemens, McGwire's pre-PED performance (81 homers and 217 RBI in his first two years with the Athletics) indicates he was and could have been a longtime superstar in the game. Continuing at that pace, McGwire would have clearly been Hall of Fame worthy. By his own admission, he took drugs—not to enhance his performance, but to recover from a series of recurring injuries so severe that they had him considering early retirement. In other words, the improved statistical performance was a handy side effect of getting and staying well.

The impact of PEDs in amassing HOF-level credentials is evidenced by the plights of players like first baseman Rafael Palmeiro and outfielder Sammy Sosa. In Palmeiro's case, he was a promising young first baseman for the Cubs in the late 1980s. He hit nearly .300 for his three seasons with the team, but had a yearly average of only 8 home runs and 30 RBI in that period of time. Wanting more run production in that position (and with Mark Grace coming up soon), the Cubs traded Palmeiro to the Rangers in 1989.

For the remainder of his seventeen-year career—playing twice each with the Rangers and Orioles—Palmeiro suddenly began averaging 32 homers and 100 RBI every year. Finishing with more than 3,000 hits, more than 560 home runs, over 1,800 RBI, and a career .288 average, one would think Palmeiro would be an absolute lock for the Hall of Fame.

Despite his testifying before the 2005 Congressional subcommittee that he "never used steroids—period," Palmeiro tested positive for a substance banned by baseball just a few months later and was suspended for ten games. More than that, when he became eligible for the Hall in 2011, he received only 11 percent of the votes needed for enshrinement.

The next year, he bumped up to 12.6 percent, then dropped to only 8.8 percent in 2013, and, in 2014, only 4.4 percent. Having less than 5 percent of the vote dropped him from the ballot, and now he can only return for consideration after twenty-one years of retirement and, hopefully, be one of twelve candidates selected by the Hall's Screening Committee. Suffice it to say, Palmeiro's use—intended or unintentional (as he claimed)—of PEDs has probably solidified his omission from Cooperstown.

In a story somewhat similar to McGwire's, outfielder Sammy Sosa first joined the majors with the Texas Rangers in 1989 as a wafer-thin, twenty-year-old player. At the time, Sosa was listed at somewhere around 170 pounds and standing six-foot even. He was traded to the Chicago White Sox later that year and, in two seasons, hit 25 homers and drove in just over 100 runs. He was then traded across town to the Cubs in time for the 1992 season, although he played his first full year in 1993.

By then he was well over two hundred pounds and began an amazing career of offensive production. In his thirteen years with the Cubs—while growing to 240 pounds by way, according to Sosa, of "Flintstones vitamins"—Sosa had an annual average of 42 home runs, 109 RBI, and 140 Ks, and amassed a .284 average. A single season with the Orioles and, back once more with Texas, left Sosa with 609 home runs for his career. If "500 homers" is the golden number for Cooperstown, then "600" is pure platinum.

At the time, only four other players in the history of the game had hit as many as Sosa—three were named Ruth, Aaron, and Mays, all in Cooperstown. Sammy seemed to be headed there, having testified in front of Congress—just as McGwire and Palmeiro had done—that he was clean.

Then in 2009, a *New York Times* report said that Sosa was among 104 baseball players who tested positive for PEDs in an anonymous 2003 survey, the results of which were leaked, despite their supposed confidentiality.

That revelation clearly affected Sosa's supposed slam-dunk for his induction into the Hall of Fame. On his first eligible ballot in 2013, he received only 12.5 percent of the vote. The next year, Sosa nose-dived to 6.6 percent, seemingly headed below the 5 percent threshold and falling off the ballot, just like Palmeiro.

While Palmeiro had played with little fanfare, Sosa was bigger than life during his days with the Cubs. Always hustling from the dugout to right field, Sosa energized the crowds, and, adding a theatrical hop to his frequent home run trot, he was a fan favorite.

In 1998, the country was still smarting from the damaging strike of 1994 that kept the World Series from happening, while it lingered into 1995 and shortened that season by eighteen games. The popularity of baseball was affected, and the ensuing contest in 1998 between Sosa and McGwire to break the 61-homer single-season mark of Roger Maris was just what the doctor ordered.

Both players showed an affinity and respect for each other, as they sent ball after ball out of the parks that summer. In early September, the two sluggers went face-to-face in St. Louis, with McGwire hitting his 62nd homer off Cub pitcher Steve Trachsel. After the Cardinal crossed home plate, Sosa ran in from right field to embrace him and happily acknowledge the victor.

At the time, it was an event that was tailor-made for putting a positive spin on baseball. McGwire and Sosa were heroes. Unfortunately, what we now know about those two players leaves a sour taste in the mouths of baseball fans. One can't make a proper judgment based on what one doesn't know (via rampant speculation), but one can judge based on what one does know.

We know Babe Ruth stroked 60 home runs in 1927 and, thirty-four years later, Roger Maris bested that record by one. Thirty-seven years after that, McGwire hit 70. Suddenly, in the short span of four years, the magic line of "60 home runs"—a mark achieved only twice across seventy years—was crossed another five times. Doesn't really make sense, does it?

When it's all said and done, McGwire's years of 70 and 65 home runs, Sosa's years of 66, 63, and 64 home runs, and Bonds' year of 73 home runs are at the most, downright dishonest, and the least, highly suspect. As a result, Roger Maris' 1961 record of 61 home runs appears to stand as the only legitimate single-season record.

Baseball By the Numbers

Stats and the World of Sabermetrics

Traditional Tracking

For many fans of baseball, it's all about how many, how fast, and how long . . . and that's just the hot dogs at the concession stand. For the statistically minded, baseball is a game of numbers. But as anyone with a checking account or weight problem knows, numbers can be "adjusted" favorably for one's benefit, or be just plain misleading.

Still, the basic baseball statistics are based on mathematic absolutes, after all—two-plus-two equals four (unless you know something I don't). The main group of metrics, many of them assembled by English-born sportswriter Henry Chadwick in the mid- and late-1800s, provides rudimentary measurements of a ballplayer's accomplishments.

Bear in mind, as with all statistical analysis, the absolutes apply only to the past (take note, fantasy players who are seeking a sure payoff). Using numbers from yesterday to predict tomorrow's outcome is an iffy and unproven science—just ask your local weathercaster. Yes, the forecast (baseball, not beach conditions) considers probabilities to a certain level of assured success. But there's always the margin for error (any shortstop knows that).

So keep that close to you when your favorite outfielder is hitting .403 in late May, or your beloved starter begins the season with a record of 9–0. It may look good, but the season is a long one. The probability of the hitter ending the year over .400, or the pitcher going undefeated, is very, very low.

Consider these basic statistics (and appropriate abbreviations) for players of baseball:

Hitting and Baserunning

Raw Numbers

Games Played (G), **At Bats** (AB), **Hits** (H), **Extra Base Hits** (XBH), **Runs Scored** (R or RS), **Walks** (BB), **Strikeouts** (K), **Hit By Pitch** (HBP), **Intentional Walk** (IBB), **Sacrifice Bunt** (SH), **Sacrifice Fly** (SF), **Fielder's** Choice (FC), **Grounded Into Double Play** (GIDP),

Runners In Scoring Position (RISP), **Runners Left On Base** (LOB), **Stolen Bases** (SB), **Caught Stealing** (CS)

Formulas

Plate Appearances (PA = At Bats + Bases on Balls + Hit By Pitcher + Sacrifice Hits + Sacrifice Flies). The difference between at bats and plate appearances is simple: An at bat considers only the batter's chance to strike the ball fairly, while a plate appearance takes those into consideration, as well as walks, hit-by-pitches, and sacrifices. Those circumstances remove the batter's opportunity of reaching base, either by his or her own choice, or out of his or her control.

Total Bases (TB = Number of (Singles + (2 x Doubles) + (3 x Triples) + (4 x Home Runs).) Total bases includes all hits, but assigns a graduated value to each one, equal to the (surprise!) total bases accrued with each hit. The total base count comes in handy when differentiating between a batting average and a slugging percentage.

Batting Average (BA = Hits/At Bats). The batting average is the most basic measurement of offensive ability. If the batter has 100 at bats and safely hits the ball thirty times, then his or her average is .300. A single or homer, it doesn't matter, as long as he or she reached base with a hit of some kind.

Slugging Percentage (SLG = Total Bases/At Bats). On the other hand, slugging percentage is more accurate in measuring power or extra-base offense (sometimes, a better measure of driving in runs, too). Dividing total bases into at bats, rather than the number of hits, results in a higher percentage.

Look again at that same batter who had 100 at bats and safely hit the ball 30 times for a batting average of .300. Of those 30 hits, 20 were singles, 4 were doubles, 1 was a triple, and 5 were home runs. That means 20 bases for singles (20*1), 8 bases for doubles (4*2), 3 bases for the triple (3*1), and 20 bases for the 5 homers (5*4), for 51 total bases. The resulting slugging percentage is .510.

Note that a greater gap between batting average and slugging percentage is also a quick indicator of extra-base ability. If the batter is hitting .286, and the slugging percentage is only .293, this player is obviously a singles-hitter. But if the batting average is the same at .286, but the slugging is .476, then there are more extra-base hits coming off the bat.

And yes—the slugging percentage can be over 1.0 (most likely in softball, but a player early in the year who's having a silly home run surge could also achieve it). Don't believe it? The numbers never lie. Consider 20 at bats, with 4 singles, a double, and 4 home runs. The batting average is a robust .450 (9/20), but the slugging percentage is an eye-popping 1.100 ((4+2+16)/20). Just don't look for those numbers in mid-September.

On Base Percentage (OBP = Hits + Walks + Hit-By-Pitch)/(At Bats + Walks + Hit-By-Pitch + Sac Flies + Sac Bunts). The ability to get on base means the ability to score runs. If you're not on base, you can't score—plain and simple. Ideally, a team's leadoff hitter should have a respectable OBP—around .400 is very good.

The formula, which is based on the batting average, includes all permutations of reaching first base, minus the noble art of sacrifice. It's assumed that the sacrifice fly and bunt magnanimously surrender the batter's chance to get to first, in exchange for advancing runners already on base.

Stolen Base Percentage (SB% = Stolen Bases/(Stolen Bases + Caught Stealing).) Once on base, the effective runner may try to improve his or her status, stealing a base to get into scoring position (considered at least second base). A good base stealer should be able to steal seven or eight bases out of every ten attempts.

Pitching

Raw Numbers

Games (G), **Games Started** (GS), **Innings Pitched** (IP), **Wins** (W), **Losses** (L), **No Decision** (ND), **Strikeouts** (K), **Walks** (BB), **Intentional Walks** (IBB), **Hit Batsmen** (HBP), **Games Saved** (SV), **Earned Runs** (ER), **Unearned Runs** (UR)

Formulas

Winning Percentage (Wins/(Wins + Losses).) There's not much to say about measuring a pitcher's winning percentage. If the hurler wins more than he or she loses, then the percentage is over .500, and that's what you want (at the very least).

For example, if your favorite starter has a year where he goes 13–12, then he ended up on the plus side with a .520 winning percentage (13 divided by 25). Of course, some pitchers have amazing years, like the Yankees' Whitey Ford did in 1961. With a record of 25–4, he had a jaw-dropping winning percentage of .862.

Earned Run Average (ERA = Earned Runs*9/Innings Pitched). After the win-loss record, the most cited stat for pitchers is the ERA—a formula that measures the number of earned runs that cross the plate on a pitcher's watch, based on nine innings. The good thing about the ERA is that it's an effective evaluation for starters and relief pitchers alike.

Years ago, an ERA of 3.00 or under put you on the A-list, but today, under 4.00 seems to be admirable and/or acceptable. The Dodgers' Clayton Kershaw currently holds a lifetime ERA of 2.53, a superb number. Through mid-2014, the starter had given up 367 earned runs in 1,308 innings (367*9/1308) equaling 2.525, which is rounded up to 2.53.

Recently retired closer, Yankees' Mariano Rivera, also sported a stellar 2.21 ERA in his career. His stats of 315 earned runs given up in 1,283.2 innings pitched—almost all in a relief role (315*9/1283.2)—came to 2.21. Actually, his stats aren't far from Kershaw's, but Rivera amassed them in nineteen years, while Kershaw is only at six and a half (so far).

Strikeouts per Nine Innings Pitched (K/9 = Total Strikeouts*9/Innings Pitched). Once more, this formula projects a pitcher's estimated number of strikeouts in a complete game, although that certainly is a rarity these days. As such, starters and relievers can both be evaluated equally with this stat.

Long and lanky, Randy Johnson's lifetime K/9 of 10.61 is the game's all-time best. Essentially, the figure means he struck out more than one hitter per inning, or nearly eleven in a complete game. He had 4,875 Ks in 4,135.1 innings across twenty-two years, with (4875*9/4135.1) equaling a K/9 better than greats like Nolan Ryan and Sandy Koufax.

Ace closer Trevor Hoffman posted a K/9 of 9.36 in an eighteen-year career, with 1,133 strikeouts in 1,089.1 innings (1133*9/1089.1). With the closer's role usually aimed for the ninth inning, Hoffman was averaging just about one strike out in every outing he pitched.

Fielding

Raw Numbers

Assists (A), **Put Outs** (PO), **Errors** (E), **Total Chances** (TC), **Caught Stealing** (CS), **Passed Balls** (PB), **Pick Off Attempts** (POA)

Formulas

Fielding Percentage (F% = Put Outs + Assists/Put Outs + Assists + Errors). This is one more of the old-school stats that is quite one-dimensional in assessing a fielder's skills. They make put outs (catch a fly ball, tag a runner, or force an out at a base), as well as assist others (fielding a ground ball and throwing to a base to force the out).

If the fielder is perfect throughout the year (not gonna happen very often), then his F% is 1.000. More realistically, infielders excel if they carry a fielding percentage of .970 to .980 (first base is usually higher, with high put outs and lower assists, since most ground ball outs are thrown to first). In the outfield, most players would like something in the .990s, although less than a dozen have had perfect 1.000 seasons.

But it's not easy. The Orioles' Brooks Robinson—often cited as the best of the best infielders—had a lifetime F% of .971 in twenty-three seasons. Holding down the "hot corner" at third base, he made 2,697 put outs, had 6,205 assists, and committed 263 errors ((2697+6205)/(2697+6205+263)) equaling a .971 fielding percentage.

The New Stat-sation

If the basic baseball stats that have existed since Henry Chadwick's day are simple math, then Sabermetrics are advanced algebra. The complex formulas that Sabermetricians use to evaluate players seem to dissect their skills and accomplishments at a subatomic level. Yet they are vital numbers in today's game, used by the front office for trades, acquisitions, and salary negotiations. The field manager also uses these figures to forge the most formidable lineup against the opposing team on a daily basis, or the one-on-one matchup of hitter to pitcher at a decisive point in the game.

Yes, they are valuable but, no matter how many slices you cut from a pie, it's still pie (not 3.14159 pi, but blueberry, cherry, peach . . . .mmmm, peach pie). In other words, as valuable as advanced analysis like Sabermetrics may be, they still fall short in taking the human factor into the process. A .204 hitter may not measure up well against a multiple Cy Young award winner, but the chance still holds that he could hit a homer in a crucial situation—despite where all the numbers point. And that is part of the beauty of baseball.

Baseball historian and all-around smart guy Bill James coined the word Sabermetrics in 1980, as a nod to SABR—the Society of American Baseball Research, started in 1971 at the Baseball Hall of Fame. Considered as

Henry Chadwick, Father of Baseball Stats.

"the search for objective knowledge about baseball," Sabermetrics is not, as one might assume, numbers and nerds with pocket protectors who never lifted a ball or bat in their lives. The society is comprised of more than six thousand members worldwide, all with a passion for the game. The use of statistical analysis only serves to feed that passion, as well as other aspects of SABR's varied research and activities.

What, then, does Sabermetrics actually do? It provides an accurate and balanced method with which we can compare players from different eras of the game—a process useful for determining Hall of Fame worthiness. It also takes a new (and, often, more accurate) look at player performance that traditional stats seem to miss. And while one doesn't need to be a mathematician or statistical analyst to use or understand Sabermetrics, a little background in statistics doesn't hurt.

That's not to say that the serious study of stats married with baseball is a phenomenon born in the times of bell bottoms, the Vietnam War, and "Tricky Dick" Nixon. F. C. Lane, editor for *Baseball* magazine between 1912 and 1937, made a study of 1,000 major league baseball hits and their relationship to run production sometime before 1920. He may have been the first to assign various weighted values to singles, as well as extra-base hits.

Bill James, Father of Modern Sabermetrics.

Still, for the sake of sanity (mine as well as yours), this section will stay as far away as reasonably possible from mean, median, and standard deviation sort of factors. The Sabermetric massage of data can be very intense and detailed, and, quite frankly, this book just can't delve into those depths. And don't forget, not all Sabermetrics require NASA-level formulas.

One note about Sabermetrics and their tools: Some of the more encompassing formulas include stats that have not always been kept in the game's history, nor have the rules always been equal. For example, the run-batted-in (RBI) wasn't officially tallied until 1920; at one point in 1887, walks were counted as hits (huh?); historically, sacrifice flies have not (and, at times, have) been considered as at bats.

As such, the attempt to evaluate players from the early days in a more exact manner might be foiled somewhat, since their stats are not in complete sets like more current players. Nevertheless, Sabermetrics have made a valuable contribution to the game—not so much in the way it's played, but certainly in the way it's measured.

Hitting and Baserunning

Formulas

OPS (On-Base Percentage + Slugging Percentage). This number is handy in making an overall assessment of a player's offensive history, although it does falter somewhat. The OPS stat fails to include what happens once the batter reaches the base paths, omitting base running and base stealing in the equation.

Still, the OPS has become a mainstream stat in today's game, often mentioned by radio and TV broadcasters. Current players like Albert Pujols and Miguel Cabrera (.996 and .960, respectively, lifetime) prove that an OPS of .900 and up is considered tops in the game. No surprise to know that Babe Ruth—with a lifetime OBA of .474 and slugging .690—has the highest all-time OPS of 1.164 (.474 + .690).

It should be noted that Sabermetric stats like OPS-Plus—adjusted OBA + adjusted slugging—dig deeper, including the factor of ballpark differences into a complex formula. Similarly, wOBA—weighted on-base average—acknowledges that while a double has twice the mathematic value of a single, it does not have double the offensive baseball value.

The wOBA attaches a relative value to each component of the OBA formula, producing a more accurate assessment of a player's offense. As the body of offensive data changes from year to year, so do the various coefficients used to determine the wOBA.

Total Average (TA = (TB + BB + HBP + SB)/(AB−H+ SH + SF + CS + GIDP). Basically, this is a stat of overall offensive production, making a comparison of a batter's on-base activity to outs made. A number of .900 or more gets into superstar territory, and over 1.000 is astronomical, since that means the player is getting more bases than outs. I suppose it doesn't need to be said that the Bambino holds the career record for a TA of 1.400.

But looks can be deceiving, since the TA measures bases versus outs. What looks like a useful Sabermetric stat might have a fault, since the job of the batter is to produce runs somehow, not accumulate bases. Perhaps there's a better way . . .

Runs Created (RC = (H+BB)*(TB)/(AB+BB). The basic runs–created formula achieves the desired result of considering both getting on base and, once there, advancing—either the batter himself or those already on base. Why? Elementary, Watson: to score a run.

Let's look at one season for Yankee great "number two, Derek Jee-tah." In 1999, he stroked 219 hits and walked 91 times. His total base count was 346, and he had 627 at bats. According to the RC formula, Jeter created about 150 runs for the Yankees that year. ((219+91)*346)/(627+91). Playing in 158 games, the shortstop basically created about one run every game (according to the formula). Offense like that helped the Bronx Bombers to win the World Series that year.

Other versions of the RC formula take stolen bases into account, as well as outs made and other factors. But for a simple and accurate measure of a batter's run productivity for a team, the RC (according to Bill James, its creator) comes within a 5 percent margin of error in predicting a team's run total.

Pitching

Formulas

Walks and Hits per Inning Pitched (WHIP = (Walks + Hits)/Innings Pitched). The standard ERA is good in predicting the number of runs a pitcher gives up in any given game, but WHIP looks at how many players a pitcher allows on base in any given inning.

The WHIP stat is widely used in the game today, with tallies of 1.000 or so pointing to a highly effective pitcher. One of today's top pitchers, David Price, had a great WHIP of 1.109 in 2012. He walked 61 and gave up 173 hits for the year, pitching in 211 innings (61+173)/211 = 1.109). The lifetime leader in the modern game (since 1901) is reliever Mariano Rivera, with a WHIP of only 1.000.

Fielding Independent Pitching (FIP = (13*HR+3*(BB+HBP)-(2*K)/IP + constant). Let's be honest; once the ball leaves the pitcher's hand, there's little he or she can do to influence the outcome of what happens to it. With that in mind, FIP isolates a pitcher's effectiveness, considering only those things over which he or she has control.

The FIP also places relative weights on pitching results, recognizing the large impact of the home run, the lesser impact of walks and hit-by-pitch, and even less value of the strikeout. The constant, which like the coefficients of the wOBA, changes from year to year, is based on the average MLB ERA for each year.

Once more, it's not surprising to see that Clayton Kershaw is the FIP leader for current pitchers, with a 2.77 FIP two-thirds through the 2014 season. ((1027+1311-2738)/1316.1+Constant of ERA average between 2008 and 2014). (PS—I worked it out twice to make sure it's correct, so don't spend your own time on it.)

Fielding

Formulas

Range Factor (RF = 9*(Put Outs + Assists)/Defensive Innings Played). Intended to be a stat superior to Fielding Percentage, the RF ignores defensive errors and focuses on the skill at accumulating the number of outs made by a player at any given position. The formula then extends that over a standard nine-inning game for a nine-inning average.

While only an estimate and not a solid number, the RF—as originally proposed by Bill James in 1976—counted put outs and assists, dividing them by games played. But after a while, it was realized that games played did not always equal the number of defensive innings played. So that number replaced the games played denominator, increasing the accuracy of the formula.

Still, the number can be deceiving, as a first baseman invariably would have a higher RF than a shortstop. For example, consider Hall of Famer Ozzie Smith, known as "The Wizard of Oz" for his defensive prowess. In nineteen seasons, he made 4,249 put outs, with 8,375 assists. The innings played totaled 21,785.2, giving Smith a lifetime RF of 5.22 (9*(4249+8375)/21785.2). This meant you could project that Ozzie would make a little more than five defensive outs in a nine-inning game.

But Cardinal and Mets first baseman Keith Hernandez (Smith's teammate for two seasons) was an eleven-time Gold Glove winner, showing sure hands at first. In his career, Hernandez made 17,916 put outs and 1,682 assists, playing a total of 17,317.1 innings. With those numbers, he had a lifetime RF of 10.19 (9*(17916+1682)/17317.1)—almost twice the RF of Smith.

Does that mean Hernandez was twice as good a fielder as Smith? Of course not, their respective RFs indicate the position of first base, manned by a top fielder, probably made about twice as many outs as the position of shortstop, also manned by a top fielder.

Of Course You Know—This Means WAR!

In the baseball world of " What If?", WAR has become the ultimate stat. WAR—Wins Above Replacement—is a metric applicable to both position players and pitchers, taking offensive, baserunning, defensive, and (where relevant) pitching factors into account. The result is a single number that measures a player's worth to the team, despite their position or role.

Essentially, WAR demonstrates a player's replacement value, compared to what an easily available player of the same position—through waiver, free agency, or the minors—would be worth. WAR supposes the number of wins a given player contributes to the team, above what a replacement player would add. Expressed as a positive or negative, the WAR figure for players will change every year, as the pool of replacement players also changes.

Suffice it to say, there are several variations of WAR calculators, but they all use advanced Sabermetric formulas with factors of various weights (so there won't be any deep explanations here—Hey! Printer's ink is expensive.). But one of the good things about WAR is that it ignores factors like parks and leagues, so fair comparisons across the history of the game can be made (assuming the required raw stats are available).

So who has the highest career WAR overall? Let's just say his first and middle names are George and Herman, and his name sounds sorta like a popular candy bar. As a pitcher, his WAR reached as high as 8.7 in 1916. As a position player (right field), his WAR was as high as 14.1 in 1923.

By comparison, great players like Ted Williams' WAR peaked at 10.9 in 1946, and Albert Pujols' WAR has been as high as 9.7 in 2009. In pitching WAR, Walter Johnson had a high of 14.6 in 1913, and Greg Maddux reached 9.7 in 1995. While other players may have had single seasons with exceptional WARs, it's clear that numbers of nine or more place them in the rare class of exceptional baseball performance.

Taking a Walk in the Park Factor

We can be thankful that folks like Bill James have spent much of their time developing detailed and complex formulas with which we can view the game in entirely new and unique ways (and keep us normal folks from buying too many headache remedies). One of James' innovations is the Park Factor (PF), which includes a series of indices that quantify many aspects of how a ballpark influences the teams that play in them.

Actually, the PF is not as difficult as some of its cousins. Take a team's runs scored at home and add them to the runs scored against them at home. Do the same, using the same data sets from the road. Divide the home number by the road number. Multiply by 100 and there it is—the Park Factor. A PF of 100 means the park is neutral; a PF over 100 favors the hitter, while a PF under 100 favors the pitcher.

For example, take the 2014 Baltimore Orioles' stats. They scored 341 runs at home and had 285 scored against them at home, for a home total of 626. On the road, they scored 364, and had 308 scored against them for a road total of 672. Divide 672 into 626 for .931, then multiply by 100. The Park Factor is 93.1, which means pitchers fared better than hitters in Camden Yards in 2014.

Now, let's look at the 2014 Colorado Rockies record. They scored 500 runs at home and had 444 scored against them at home, for a home total of 944. On the road, they scored 255, and had 374 scored against them for a road total of 629. Divide 629 into 944 for 1.507, then multiply by 100. The Park Factor is 150.7 for Coors Field. As a hitter, where would you like to play? (Yeah, me too.)

The Best There Ever Was

Baseball's Greatest Players

According to the Numbers

Can ballplayers who roamed the fields one hundred years or more apart be fairly compared? Just how equally can Pie Traynor and Mike Schmidt be assessed? Babe Ruth or Henry Aaron—who's tops? Walter or Randy—who is the better Johnson? (Yeah, I know, I know . . . .)

OK—Different rules, different equipment, different parks, different training and preparation—all tend to muddy the waters for establishing ballplayer parity across the ages. Plus, some excelled in their defensive skills, while others have made their mark at the plate, on the mound, or on the base paths. With those factors in mind, who is better—Lou Gehrig or Greg Maddux? Cy Young or Rickey Henderson? Honus Wagner or Albert Pujols?

Then again, what about the actual pool of talent—considering varied factors in lifestyle, technology, and the evolution of the game—in a given time period? For example, how can a player's accomplishments be measured, knowing they used medicine balls in the 1920s and hi-tech weight rooms nowadays for strength development?

Such is the dilemma in attempting to quantify the achievements of these great ballplayers in some sort of order. Thanks to organizations like SABR (Society for American Baseball Research, which is covered elsewhere in this book), some efforts have been made to develop tools that can measure greatness in the game.

However, just as it would be difficult (and unwieldy) to compare a Ferrari with a hi-tech racing bicycle, a distinction must be made between pitchers and other players. Yes, they all play ball, but their skill sets are wholly separate. Therefore, in an attempt to wrap our arms around this whole thing (and leave this meager stab at trying to sound like I know what I'm talking about), let's lay some ground rules.

Pitchers will be measured within their own group, and position players will be assessed separately. Yet, recognizing the vast differences—in rules, restrictions, existing (and accurate) statistics, and experience—we can really only look at players from 1900 or so to the present day.

More, the sum of a person's career should be considered, as opposed to one outstanding year or accomplishment. For example, I happen to hold Roger Maris and his home run achievement with very high respect—knowing the stress and condemnation that he endured in reaching it. But few realize that in that amazing 1961 season, Maris struck out less than 70 times, while walking more than 90 times. That is not a usual stat for a record-setting home run hitter.

Still, despite his record (asterisk, begone), Maris only had a few outstanding years—yes, two of them leading to earning the league's Most Valuable Player Award. As such, while Maris was a very good ballplayer, those who do make this list must show—year after year—their ability to dominate the game. Sadly, he did not.

Also, much like entry to the Hall of Fame, players must be retired (five years or whatever). Why? Today's superstars, like Clayton Kershaw or Mike Trout or Albert Pujols, are clearly talented and, possibly, headed for spot on a later version of this list. But, like a book with chapters that remain to be written (hmmm, like this one . . .), their careers are not yet complete. If we are looking at the sum of a player's career, then today's top players and their legacies remain to be seen.

While the subject is covered in its own chapter, players who have admitted to, been suspended for testing positive, or have been implicated in substantive media reports for performance-enhancing drugs cannot be considered for this list. So names that belong here, like Clemens and Bonds, will not be found.

In all fairness, there are enough deviations in circumstances—era, players, ballparks, and so on, along with other intangibles—to put these lists into order alphabetically, rather than ranked in an order, up to the best ever. After all, who can say Gehrig was better than Mantle, unless they faced the same pitchers in the same number of at bats, in the same weather conditions (if one really wants to get ridiculous about it). So let's just consider these ballplayers as elite groups of "the best of the best."

The scale for this will be largely (if not entirely) using common, time-tested stats. For pitchers, that includes total wins, earned run average, strikeouts, walks (low, not high numbers), games saved (where appropriate), and WHIP—walks and hits per inning pitched. For position players, total hits, extra-base hits (not just home runs), on-base percentage (including hits, walks, and hit-by-pitch), runs scored, stolen bases, and fielding. With these criteria, the field of candidates is broader—not just strikeout masters or long-ball threats.

But as much as I like many of the Sabermetric tools, we're not really running a math class here. I want to keep it simple and direct. Besides, instead of explaining the process, I'd rather just get down to it.

OK—Deep breath . . . eye on the ball . . . here we go.

Grover Cleveland
Alexander.

Top Fifteen Pitchers in Baseball

Grover Cleveland Alexander (1911–1930)

Born: February 26, 1887   **Died:** November 4, 1950
Bats: Right   **Throws:** Right
Lifetime stats: (22 seasons)—**Wins:** 373 **Losses:** 208
ERA: 2.56 **Ks:** 2,198 **BB:** 951 **SVs:** 32 **WHIP:** 1.121
Best season: 1915—**Wins:** 31 **Losses:** 10 **ERA:** 1.22
Ks: 241 **BB:** 64 **SVs:** 3 **WHIP:** 0.842 **Shutouts:** 12
Complete Games: 36
Honors: Three-time NL Triple Crown **HOF:** 1938

Dennis Eckersley (1975–1998)

Born: October 3, 1954
Bats: Right   **Throws**: Right
Lifetime stats: (24 seasons) —**Wins:** 197 **Losses:** 171
ERA: 3.50 **Ks:** 2401 **BB:** 738 **SVs:** 390 **WHIP:** 1.161
Best season (starter): 1978—**Wins:** 20 **Losses:** 8
ERA: 2.99 **Ks:** 162 **BB:** 71 **SVs:** 0 **WHIP:** 1.226
Shutouts: 3 **Complete Games:** 16
Best season (reliever): 1992—**Wins:** 7 **Losses:** 1
ERA: 1.91 **Ks:** 93 **BB:** 11 **SVs:** 51 **WHIP:** 0.913
Honors: Six-time All-Star, AL Cy Young Award,
AL MVP **HOF:** 2004

Dennis Eckersley.

Bob Gibson (1959–1975)

Born: November 9, 1935
Bats: Right   **Throws**: Right
Lifetime stats: (17 seasons)—**Wins:** 251 **Losses:** 174
ERA: 2.91 **Ks:** 3117 **BB:** 1,336 **SVs:** 6 **WHIP:** 1.188
Best season: 1968—**Wins:** 22 **Losses:** 9 **ERA:** 1.12
Ks: 268 **BB:** 62 **SVs:** 0 **WHIP:** 0.853 **Shutouts:** 13
Complete Games: 28
Honors: Eight-time All-Star, Nine Gold Gloves, NL
Cy Young Award (twice), NL MVP **HOF:** 1981

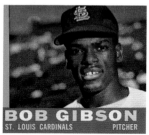

Bob Gibson.

Lefty Grove (1925–1941)

Born: March 6, 1900   **Died**: May 22, 1975
Bats: Left   **Throws**: Left
Lifetime stats: (17 seasons)—**Wins:** 300 **Losses:** 141
ERA: 3.06 **Ks:** 2266 **BB:** 1,187 **SVs:** 54 **WHIP:** 1.278
Best season: 1931—**Wins:** 31 **Losses:** 4 **ERA:** 2.06
Ks: 175 **BB:** 62 **SVs:** 5 **WHIP:** 1.077 **Shutouts:** 4
Complete Games: 27
Honors: Six-time All-Star, AL MVP, Two-time AL
Triple Crown **HOF:** 1947

Lefty Grove.

Randy Johnson (1988–2009)

Born: September 10, 1963
Bats: Right   **Throws**: Left
Lifetime stats: (22 seasons)—**Wins**: 303 **Losses**: 166
ERA: 3.29 **Ks**: 4,875 **BB**: 1,497 **SVs**: 2 **WHIP**: 1.171
Best season: 2002—**Wins**: 24 **Losses**: 5 **ERA**: 2.32 **Ks**: 334
BB: 71 **SVs**: 0 **WHIP**: 1.031 **Shutouts**: 4 **Complete Games**: 8
Honors: Ten-time All-Star, AL Cy Young Award, NL Cy
Young Award (four-times), NL Triple Crown **HOF**: 2015

Walter Johnson (1907–1927)

Born: November 6, 1887   **Died**: December 10, 1946
Bats: Right   **Throws**: Right
Lifetime stats: (21 seasons)—**Wins**: 417 **Losses**: 279
ERA: 2.17 **Ks**: 3,509 **BB**: 1,363 **SVs**: 34 **WHIP**: 1.061
Best season: 1913—**Wins**: 36 **Losses**: 7 **ERA**: 1.14 **Ks**: 243
BB: 38 **SVs**: 2 **WHIP**: 0.780 **Shutouts**: 11
Complete Games: 29
Honors: AL MVP (twice), Three-time AL Triple Crown
HOF: 1936

Randy Johnson.

Sandy Koufax (1955–1966)

Born: December 30, 1935
Bats: Right   **Throws**: Left
Lifetime stats: (12 seasons)—**Wins**: 165 **Losses**: 87
ERA: 2.76 **Ks**: 2,396 **BB**: 817 **SVs**: 9 **WHIP**: 1.106
Best season: 1965—**Wins**: 26 **Losses**: 8 **ERA**: 2.04 **Ks**: 382
BB: 71 **SVs**: 2 **WHIP**: 0.855 **Shutouts**: 8 **Complete Games**: 27
Honors: Six-time All-Star, NL Cy Young Award (three
times), Three-time NL Triple Crown
HOF: 1972

Walter Johnson.

Greg Maddux (1986–2008)

Born: April 14, 1966
Bats: Right   **Throws**: Right
Lifetime stats: (23 seasons)—**Wins**: 355 **Losses**: 227
ERA: 3.16 **Ks**: 3,371 **BB**: 999 **SVs**: 0 **WHIP**: 1.143
Best season: 1995—**Wins**: 19 **Losses**: 2 **ERA**: 1.63 **Ks**: 181
BB: 23 **SVs**: 0 **WHIP**: 0.811 **Shutouts**: 3 **Complete Games**: 10
Honors: Eight-time All-Star, Seventeen Gold Gloves, NL
Cy Young Award (four times) **HOF**: 2014

Sandy Koufax.

Greg Maddux.

Juan Marichal.

Christy Mathewson.

Pedro Martinez.

Mariano Rivera.

Juan Marichal (1960–1975)

Born: October 20, 1937
Bats: Right   **Throws**: Right
Lifetime stats: (16 seasons)—**Wins**: 243 **Losses**: 142
ERA: 2.89 **Ks**: 2,303 **BB**: 709 **SVs**: 2 **WHIP**: 1.101
Best season: 1966—**Wins**: 25 **Losses**: 6 **ERA**: 2.23 **Ks**: 222
BB: 36 **SVs**: 0 **WHIP**: 0.859 **Shutouts**: 4 **Complete Games**: 25
Honors: Nine-time All-Star **HOF**: 1983

Christy Mathewson (1900–1916)

Born: August 12, 1880   **Died**: October 7, 1925
Bats: Right   **Throws**: Right
Lifetime stats: (17 seasons)—**Wins**: 373 **Losses**: 188
ERA: 2.13 **Ks**: 2507 **BB**: 848 **SVs**: 30 **WHIP**: 1.058
Best season: 1908—**Wins**: 37 **Losses**: 11 **ERA**: 1.43 **Ks**: 259
BB: 42 **SVs**: 5 **WHIP**: 0.827 **Shutouts**: 11 **Complete Games**: 34
Honors: Two-time NL Triple Crown **HOF**: 1936

Pedro Martinez (1992–2009)

Born: October 25, 1971
Bats: Right   **Throws**: Right
Lifetime stats: (18 seasons)—**Wins**: 219 **Losses**: 100
ERA: 2.93 **Ks**: 3154 **BB**: 760 **SVs**: 3 **WHIP**: 1.054
Best season: 1999—**Wins**: 23 **Losses**: 4 **ERA**: 2.07 **Ks**: 313
BB: 37 **SVs**: 0 **WHIP**: 0.923 **Shutouts**: 1 **Complete Games**: 5
Honors: Eight-time All-Star, NL Cy Young Award, AL Cy Young Award (twice), AL Triple Crown **HOF**: 2015

Mariano Rivera (1995–2013)

Born: November 29, 1969
Bats: Right   Throws: Right
Lifetime stats: (19 seasons)—**Wins**: 82 **Losses**: 60 **ERA**: 2.21
Ks: 1173 **BB**: 286 **SVs**: 652 **WHIP**: 1.000
Best season: 2008—**Wins**: 6 **Losses**: 5 **ERA**: 1.40 **Ks**: 77 **BB**: 6
SVs: 39 **WHIP**: 0.665
Honors: Thirteen-time All-Star **HOF**: Eligible in 2019

Nolan Ryan (1966–1993)

Born: January 31, 1947
Bats: Right   **Throws**: Right
Lifetime stats: (27 seasons) **Wins**: 324 **Losses**: 292 **ERA**: 3.19
Ks: 5714 **BB**: 2,795 **SVs**: 3 **WHIP**: 1.247
Best season: 1972—**Wins**: 19 **Losses**: 16 **ERA**: 2.28 **Ks**: 329
BB: 157 **SVs**: 0 **WHIP**: 1.137 **Shutouts**: 9 **Complete Games**: 20
Honors: Eight-time All-Star **HOF**: 1999

Tom Seaver (1967–1986)

Born: November 17, 1944
Bats: Right   **Throws**: Right
Lifetime stats: (20 seasons) **Wins**: 311 **Losses**: 205 **ERA**: 2.86
Ks: 3,640 **BB**: 1,390 **SVs**: 1 **WHIP**: 1.121
Best season: 1971—**Wins**: 20 **Losses**: 10 **ERA**: 1.76 **Ks**: 289
BB: 61 **SVs**: 0 **WHIP**: 0.946 **Shutouts**: 4 **Complete Games**: 21
Honors: NL Rookie of the Year, Twelve-time All-Star, NL
Cy Young Award (three-time) **HOF**: 1992

Cy Young (1890–1911)

Born: March 29, 1867   **Died**: November 4, 1955
Bats: Right   **Throws**: Right
Lifetime stats: (22 seasons) **Wins**: 511 **Losses**: 316 **ERA**: 2.63
Ks: 2,803 **BB**: 1,217 **SVs**: 17 **WHIP**: 1.130
Best season: 1901—**Wins**: 33 **Losses**: 10 **ERA**: 1.62 **Ks**: 158
BB: 37 **SVs**: 0 **WHIP**: 0.972 **Shutouts**: 5 **Complete Games**: 38
Honors: AL Triple Crown **HOF**: 1937

Top Fifteen Position Players in Baseball

Henry Aaron (1954–1976) Outfield, First Base, Designated Hitter

Born: February 5, 1934
Bats: Right   **Throws**: Right
Lifetime stats: (23 seasons)—**Average**: .305 **Hits**: 3771
2B: 624 **3B**: 98 **HR**: 755 **RBI**: 2297 **OBP**: .374
Runs Scored: 2,174 **Stolen Bases**: 240 **Fielding**: .982
Best season: 1957—**Average**: .322 **Hits**: 198 **2B**: 27 **3B**: 6
HR: 44 **RBI**: 132 **OBP**: .378 **Runs Scored**: 118 **Stolen Bases**: 1
Fielding: .983
Honors: Twenty-one-time All-Star, Three Gold Gloves, NL
MVP **HOF**: 1982

Ty Cobb (1905–1928) Outfield

Born: December 18, 1886   **Died**: July 17, 1961
Bats: Left   **Throws**: Right
Lifetime stats: (24 seasons)—**Average**: .366 **Hits**: 4189
2B: 724 **3B**: 295 **HR**: 117 **RBI**: 1933 **OBP**: .433
Runs Scored: 2,244 **Stolen Bases**: 897 **Fielding**: .961
Best season: 1911 **Average**: .420 **Hits**: 248 **2B**: 47 **3B**: 24 **HR**: 8
RBI: 127 **OBP**: .467 **Runs Scored**: 147 **Stolen Bases**: 83
Fielding: .957
Honors: AL MVP, AL Triple Crown **HOF**: 1936

Nolan Ryan.

Tom Seaver.

Cy Young.

Hank Aaron.

Ty Cobb.

Jimmie Foxx (1925–1945) First Base, Third Base, Catcher

Born: October 22, 1907   **Died**: July 21, 1967
Bats: Right   **Throws**: Right
Lifetime stats: (20 seasons)—**Average**: .325 **Hits**: 2,646
2B: 458 **3B**: 125 **HR**: 534 **RBI**: 1,922 **OBP**: .428
Runs Scored: 1,751 **Stolen Bases**: 87 **Fielding**: .990
Best season: 1932 **Average**: .364 **Hits**: 213 **2B**: 33 **3B**: 9
HR: 58 **RBI**: 169 **OBP**: .469 **Runs Scored**: 151
Stolen Bases: 3 **Fielding**: .994
Honors: Nine-time All-Star, AL MVP (three-times), AL
Triple Crown **HOF**: 1951

Jimmie Foxx.

Lou Gehrig (1923–1939) First Base

Born: June 19, 1903   **Died**: June 2, 1941
Bats: Left   **Throws**: Left
Lifetime stats: (17 seasons)—**Average**: .340 **Hits**: 2,721
2B: 534 **3B**: 163 **HR**: 493 **RBI**: 1995 **OBP**: .447
Runs Scored: 1,888 **Stolen Bases**: 102,**Fielding**: .991
Best season: 1927—**Average**: .373 **Hits**: 218 **2B**: 52 **3B**: 18
HR: 47 **RBI**: 173 **OBP**: .474 **Runs Scored**: 149
Stolen Bases: 10 **Fielding**: .992
Honors: Seven-time All-Star, AL MVP (twice), AL
Triple Crown **HOF**: 1939

Lou Gehrig.

Ken Griffey Jr. (1989–2010) Outfield

Born: November 21, 1969
Bats: Left   **Throws**: Left
Lifetime stats: (22 seasons)—**Average**: .284 **Hits**: 2,781
2B: 524 **3B**: 38 **HR**: 630 **RBI**: 1836 **OBP**: .370
Runs Scored: 1,662 **Stolen Bases**: 184 **Fielding**: .985
Best season: 1997—**Average**: .304 **Hits**: 185 **2B**: 34 **3B**: 3
HR: 56 **RBI**: 147 **OBP**: .382 **Runs Scored**: 125
Stolen Bases: 15 **Fielding**: .985
Honors: Thirteen-time All-Star, Ten Gold Gloves, AL
MVP **HOF**: Eligible in 2016

Ken Griffey Jr.

Rickey Henderson (1979–2003) Outfield

Born: December 25, 1958
Bats: Right   **Throws**: Left
Lifetime stats: (25 seasons)—**Average**: .279 **Hits**: 3,055
2B: 510 **3B**: 66 **HR**: 297 **RBI**: 1,115 **OBP**: .401
Runs Scored: 2,295 **Stolen Bases**: 1,406 **Fielding**: .979

Best season: 1985—**Average**: .314 **Hits**: 172 **2B**: 28 **3B**: 5 **HR**: 24 **RBI**: 72 **OBP**: .419 **Runs Scored**: 146 **Stolen Bases**: 80 **Fielding**: .980
Honors: Ten -time All-Star, Gold Glove, AL MVP **HOF**: 2009

Rogers Hornsby (1915–1937) Second Base, Shortstop
Born: April 27, 1896   **Died**: January 5, 1963
Bats: Right   **Throws**: Right
Lifetime stats: (23 seasons)—**Average**: .358 **Hits**: 2,930 **2B**: 541 **3B**: 169 **HR**: 301 **RBI**: 1,584 **OBP**: .434
Runs Scored: 1,579 **Stolen Bases**: 135 **Fielding**: .958
Best season: 1922—**Average**: .401 **Hits**: 250 **2B**: 46 **3B**: 14 **HR**: 46 **RBI**: 152 **OBP**: .459 **Runs Scored**: 141
Stolen Bases: 17 **Fielding**: .967
Honors: NL MVP (twice), Two-time NL Triple Crown **HOF**: 1942

Babe Ruth (1914–1935) Outfield, Pitcher
Born: February 6, 1895   **Died**: August 16, 1948
Bats: Left   **Throws**: Left
Lifetime stats: (22 seasons)—**Average**: .342 **Hits**: 2,873 **2B**: 506 **3B**: 136 **HR**: 714 **RBI**: 2,214 **OBP**: .474
Runs Scored: 2,174 **Stolen Bases**: 123 **Fielding**: .968
Best season: 1927—**Average**: .356 **Hits**: 192 **2B**: 29 **3B**: 8 **HR**: 60 **RBI**: 165 **OBP**: .486 **Runs Scored**: 158
Stolen Bases: 7 **Fielding**: .963
Honors: Two-time All-Star, AL MVP **HOF**: 1936

Mickey Mantle (1951–1968) Outfield
Born: October 20, 1931   **Died**: August 13, 1995
Bats: Both   **Throws**: Left
Lifetime stats: (18 seasons)—**Average**: .298 **Hits**: 2,415 **2B**: 344 **3B**: 72 **HR**: 536, **RBI**: 1,509 **OBP**: .421
Runs Scored: 1,676 **Stolen Bases**: 153, **Fielding**: .985
Best season: 1956—**Average**: .353 **Hits**: 188 **2B**: 22 **3B**: 5 **HR**: 52 **RBI**: 130 **OBP**: .464 **Runs Scored**: 132
Stolen Bases: 10 **Fielding**: .990
Honors: Sixteen-time All-Star, Gold Glove, AL MVP (three times), AL Triple Crown **HOF**: 1974

Rickey Henderson.

Rogers Hornsby.

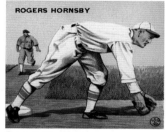
Babe Ruth.

Mickey Mantle.

Willie Mays.

Willie Mays (1951–1973) Outfield

Born: May 6, 1931
Bats: Right   **Throws**: Right
Lifetime stats: (22 seasons)—**Average**: .302 **Hits**: 3,283
2B: 523 **3B**: 140 **HR**: 660 **RBI**: 1903 **OBP**: .384 **Runs Scored**: 2,062 **Stolen Bases**: 338 **Fielding**: .981
Best season: 1927—**Average**: .373, **Hits**: 218, **2B**: 52, **3B**: 18, **HR**: 47, **RBI**: 173, **OBP**: .474, **Runs Scored**: 149 **Stolen Bases**: 10 **Fielding**: .992
Honors: NL Rookie of the Year, Twelve Gold Gloves, Twenty-time All-Star, NL MVP (twice) **HOF**: 1979

Stan Musial.

Stan Musial (1941–1963) Outfield, First Base

Born: November 21, 1920   **Died**: January 19, 2013
Bats: Left   **Throws**: Left
Lifetime stats: (22 seasons)—**Average**: .331 **Hits**: 3,630
2B: 725 **3B**: 177 **HR**: 475 **RBI**: 1,951 **OBP**: .417 **Runs Scored**: 1,949 **Stolen Bases**: 78 **Fielding**: .989
Best season: 1948—**Average**: .376 **Hits**: 230 **2B**: 46 **3B**: 18 **HR**: 39 **RBI**: 131 **OBP**: .450 **Runs Scored**: 135 **Stolen Bases**: 7 **Fielding**: .981
Honors: Twenty-time All-Star, NL MVP (three times) **HOF**: 1969

Frank Robinson.

Frank Robinson (1956–1976) Outfield, First Base

Born: August 31, 1935
Bats: Right   **Throws**: Right
Lifetime stats: (21 seasons)—**Average**: .294 **Hits**: 2,943
2B: 528 **3B**: 72 **HR**: 586, **RBI**: 1,812 **OBP**: .389
Runs Scored: 1,829 **Stolen Bases**: 204 **Fielding**: .984
Best season: 1966—**Average**: .316 **Hits**: 182 **2B**: 34 **3B**: 2 **HR**: 49 **RBI**: 122 **OBP**: .410 **Runs Scored**: 122 **Stolen Bases**: 8 **Fielding**: .985
Honors: NL Rookie of the Year, Gold Glove, Twelve-time All-Star, NL MVP, AL MVP, AL Triple Crown **HOF**: 1982

Tris Speaker.

Tris Speaker (1907–1928) Outfield

Born: April 4, 1888   **Died**: December 8, 1958
Bats: Left   **Throws**: Left
Lifetime stats: (22 seasons)—**Average**: .345 **Hits**: 3,514
2B: 792 **3B**: 222 **HR**: 117 **RBI**: 1,531 **OBP**: .428
Runs Scored: 1,882 **Stolen Bases**: 436 **Fielding**: .971
Best season: 1920—**Average**: .388 **Hits**: 214 **2B**: 50 **3B**: 11 **HR**: 8 **RBI**: 107 **OBP**: .483 **Runs Scored**: 137 **Stolen Bases**: 10 **Fielding**: .975
Honors: AL MVP **HOF**: 1937

Honus Wagner (1897–1917) Shortstop, Outfield

Born: February 24, 1874   **Died**: December 6, 1955
Bats: Right   **Throws**: Right
Lifetime stats: (21 seasons)—**Average**: .328 **Hits**: 3,420 **2B**: 643 **3B**: 252 **HR**: 101 **RBI**: 1,732 **OBP**: .391 **Runs Scored**: 1,739 **Stolen Bases**: 723 **Fielding**: .947
Best season: 1908—**Average**: .354 **Hits**: 201 **2B**: 39 **3B**: 19 **HR**: 10 **RBI**: 109 **OBP**: .415 **Runs Scored**: 100 **Stolen Bases**: 53 **Fielding**: .943
HOF: 1936

Honus Wagner.

Ted Williams (1939–1960) Outfield

Born: August 30, 1918   **Died**: July 5, 2002
Bats: Left   **Throws**: Right
Lifetime stats: (19 seasons)—**Average**: .344 **Hits**: 2,654 **2B**: 525 **3B**: 71 **HR**: 521 **RBI**: 1,839 **OBP**: .482 **Runs Scored**: 1,798 **Stolen Bases**: 24 **Fielding**: .974
Best season: 1941—**Average**: .406, **Hits**: 185, **2B**: 33, **3B**: 3, **HR**: 37, **RBI**: 120, **OBP**: .553, **Runs Scored**: 135, **Stolen Bases**: 2, **Fielding**: .961
Honors: Seventeen-time All-Star, AL MVP (twice), Two-time AL Triple Crown **HOF**: 1966

Ted Williams.

My All-Time Dream Team

The previous list of all-time greats was assembled by reviewing their stats, regardless of their position—at least as far as the nonpitchers were concerned. However, to satisfy those (including myself) who would prefer to see every defensive position accounted for, as well as account for those who didn't make the above cut, the following listing of all-time ballplayers I would want on my team is presented for review (assuming the previously noted players were already taken and not available).

Imagine having a fantasy baseball team with this roster:

1B Eddie Murray

With lots of great first sackers, this choice was tough. But next to the Mick, Eddie Murray was the best switch-hitting power guy ever. In his twenty-one-year career, Murray had more than 3,200 hits, drove in more than 1,900 runs, and had 504 homers. He was

Eddie Murray.

Ryne Sandberg.

Cal Ripken Jr.

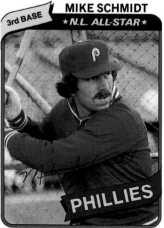

Mike Schmidt.

Rookie of the Year, won three Gold Gloves, was an eight-time All-Star, and entered the HOF in 2003.

2B Ryne Sandberg

After considering Joe Morgan (less range and offense) and Jackie Robinson (only ten MLB seasons), Sandberg got the nod at second. After playing his first full year at third, Sandberg moved to second to take the first of nine consecutive Gold Gloves. The ten-time All-Star won an NL MVP Award, finishing his career with a .285 average, with 282 homers. Sandberg was elected to the Hall in 2005.

SS Cal Ripken Jr.

Establishing a new model for shortstop (tall and powerful instead of small and speedy), Ripken wrote his own story of baseball's "Iron Man." AL Rookie of the Year Ripken played in more than 2,600 consecutive games, ending his twenty-one-year career with more than 3,100 hits, almost 1,700 RBI, and a .977 fielding percentage. The nineteen-time All-Star won the AL MVP Award twice, earned two Gold Gloves, and was inducted in the HOF in 2007.

3B Mike Schmidt

Out of the fifteen third basemen in the Hall of Fame, Schmidt has the best combination of defense and power—with kudos to others like George Brett, Eddie Mathews, and Wade Boggs. The ten-time Gold Glover finished his eighteen-year Phillies career with nearly 550 homers, 1,600 RBI, and just over 1,500 walks. Schmidt was a three-time NL MVP, a twelve-time All-Star, and entered the Hall in 1995.

LF Tony Gwynn

While left-hander Gwynn mostly played right field, he's in left here to make the team. The lifetime Padre studied video long before it was popular, resulting in eight NL batting championships in his twenty-year career. Gwynn finished with over 3,100 hits, more than 300 stolen bases, and a .338 lifetime average. He joined the gang at Cooperstown in 2007.

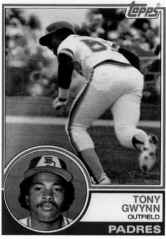

Tony Gwynn.

CF Joe DiMaggio

Clearly one of the all-time greats, Joltin' Joe— The Yankee Clipper—owned the cavernous land of Yankee Stadium's center field long before the fences were brought in. Despite losing three prime years to military service during WWII, DiMaggio posted top-notch stats in just thirteen seasons of play. The three-time AL MVP was an All-Star in every year he played, concluding his career with a .325 lifetime average, 361 homers, and collecting 790 walks against only 369 Ks. DiMaggio went into the Hall in 1955.

Joe DiMaggio.

RF Reggie Jackson

There might be right fielders with better overall stats, but there's no one else I'd want to see at the plate when a big hit was needed. Known as Mr. October for his ability to deliver offense in the postseason, Jackson earned an AL MVP in his twenty-one-year career. He also was a fourteen-time All-Star, closing out his days in the game with 563 homers, more than 1,700 RBI, and over 220 stolen bases. Jackson was inducted into the HOF in 1993.

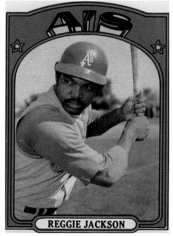

Reggie Jackson.

Johnny Bench.

Frank Thomas.

Bob Feller.

C Johnny Bench

Playing all seventeen years with the Cincinnati Reds, Johnny Bench amassed some great numbers at the catching position. The two-time NL MVP hit 389 homers and drove in more than 1,370 runs. Winner of the NL Rookie of the Year Award, the receiver was a fourteen-time All-Star and a defensive star—earning ten consecutive Gold Gloves. Bench was selected for the Hall of Fame in 1989.

DH Frank Thomas

Known as The Big Hurt, Frank Thomas put the big hurt on many a baseball in his nineteen-year career—playing more than 1,300 games in the designated hitter spot and over 970 at first base. Sixteen of his years were spent with the White Sox, where he twice won the AL MVP Award. The five-time All-Star finished with a .301 average, 521 home runs, more than 1,700 RBI, and over 1,660 walks. Thomas entered the HOF in 2014.

SP—R Bob Feller

Like Joe DiMaggio, Rapid Robert Feller lost three years in the heart of his career by doing his military duty for the war. No matter, he still built an amazing body of work in his eighteen years of baseball. The eight-time All-Star won 266 games, with a 3.25 ERA, almost 2,600 strikeouts, and once threw 104 mph against a speeding motorcycle. Feller pitched all his games for the Cleveland Indians and went into the Hall in 1962.

SP—L Warren Spahn

Left-handed Warren Spahn dominated National League pitching in the '40s, '50s, and early '60s. Spending almost his entire time with the Braves (first Boston, then Milwaukee), the fourteen-time All-Star took the NL Cy Young Award and was feared at the plate as well. Spahn hit 35 homers and drove in nearly 190 runs as a left-handed hitter. He wound up with 363 wins, almost 2,600 Ks, a 3.09 ERA, and had his plaque hung in the Hall in 1973.

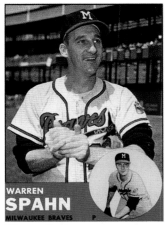

Warren Spahn.

CL Bruce Sutter

Gaining fame with the split-finger pitch, game-finisher Bruce Sutter made great hitters look silly when the ball dropped a foot just as it reached the plate. It left opponents speechless and opposing teams scoreless. In his twelve-year career, he saved 300 games, with a 2.83 ERA. Sutter won the NL Cy Young Award, was a six-time All-Star, and was elected to Cooperstown in 2006.

Any arguments? When you get your own baseball book published, you can pick your own team.

Bruce Sutter.

My View from the Bleachers

Personal Baseball Moments

Your Honor, I'd Like to Approach the Bench . . .

As I mentioned in the introduction, baseball is unique in the vast world of team sports. And, as I also noted, I will not engage in a round of "mine's better than yours," mostly because—it isn't. So the following is merely a personal observation on how the game of baseball differs from all the other wonderful team sports that entertain millions upon millions of fans around the world.

Many years ago, as an eighteen-year-old, I found myself as a truck driver delivering appliances in the Chicago area. While that has no bearing on this writing, one of my former coworkers from then does. He was from Italy, only off the boat a year or so. One day during lunch, he confessed in broken English that he didn't know a thing about baseball and asked me to teach him how it was played (not as a player, but as a fan so he could watch the game).

In view of his request, I found that I was really stumped—how and where would I begin? In many cases, something new can be explained or taught by comparison to something the other person already is familiar with. (I have noted that teaching software often starts with, "if you know 'fill-in-the-blank' program, then you're already halfway there.") But baseball—where would I begin?

The upshot is I never got around to properly conveying the game of baseball to the man, due to its unique components. But someone must have taught him how to bowl, because he would go out, get really blind-drunk, then show up on our company bowling nights and, while stumbling down the alley, consistently throw games over 200—it was amazing. Who knows? He just might have had a no-hitter in him, somewhere.

Consider then, these games—football, basketball, soccer, hockey, and lacrosse (one could also include foosball, but that's really just a combination of soccer and shish kebab). As immensely popular as they are, their structure is essentially the same. Two teams gather on a rectangular area, with a scoring opportunity on either end, be it net, hoop, or end zone. Against the defending team, the offensive team is challenged to take a ball or puck down the field in an effort to score a point or points. Despite the existence of defined segments—whether quarters, halves, or periods—the final closure of the contest is based on a clock, a finite amount of time.

Baseball is nothing like any of those games. The field (while standardized by certain requisites, like distance to the bases and a minimum distance to the outfield wall) is unique in almost every park and stadium. Yes, there is a field of play (called "fair territory"), but even the "out-of-bounds" area—known as "foul territory"—allows the ball to be played upon.

There are defined segments called innings, but there is no clock. As long as the offensive team safely puts the ball in play and scores, the game goes on. Instead of "sudden death" in the other sports, where the first team to break a tie in overtime wins, the home baseball team will always have the chance to settle up if their opponent goes ahead in extra innings.

In terms of time, the longest Major League game played was more than eight hours in twenty-five innings, between the White Sox and Brewers, in 1984. For some, that might seem like a prison sentence, but it's Nirvana to me (without smelling like teen spirit).

As is often noted, no other game begins play with the defensive team controlling the ball. No other game has its manager or coach dressed in the team's uniform, except for the very rare situation of a player-coach. (I'm sure Phil Jackson cut a dashing figure in his day, but would you really want to see him coaching an NBA team in a satiny tank top and shorts? I think not.)

Some believe the leisurely pace of baseball is a negative thing, but I have to disagree. The pace actually varies (except when Rangers/Padres/Indians player Mike Hargrove came to the plate in the 1970s and 1980s. His distracting at bat habits of adjusting his batting gloves, hiking up his pants, knocking the dirt off his cleats, and wiping his brow earned him the moniker of "The Human Rain Delay."). The downtime between pitching and putting the ball in play allows players, coaches, and managers to consider the options and their possible reactions, and prepare accordingly.

While keen physical reflexes are required, the mental portion of baseball challenges other team sports to provide similar and equal opportunities. (That's about as fair, unbiased, and honest as I can be. If you're offended, you can always switch to the FAQ of your choice at any time.)

Mr. Cub

In a former life, I aspired to work behind-the-scenes in the world of television. I hesitate to admit that it was more than forty years ago, but it had to be, because "Mr. Cub" himself, Ernie Banks, had just retired after nineteen years with Chicago's Northside team.

Sitting quietly in the control room of a production facility in downtown Chicago, I watched as Banks did a run-through of a spec commercial for Skil Power Tools. ("Spec" meaning it might never make it to the airwaves, but was a speculative test to see how the ballplayer fared on-camera.)

As for many youngsters growing up—in and out of the Midwest—Banks was one of my heroes. And, finishing his reading of "With a Skil Power Tool—

It's welcome to the pros!" he came into the control room and sat right next to me . . . I almost plotzed right there. I didn't know what say to him, but—good man that he always was—he grabbed my arm, pointed to the video playback on the monitor, and loudly asked me with a big grin, "Who is that good-looking guy up there on the screen?"

Shyly, I responded, "I believe that's you, Mr. Banks." "Ernie, young man," he shouted, "Call me 'Ernie!'" I completed my plotz and thought, "What a great guy." Always was, always will be. May he rest in peace.

The Rebel

In a suburban Chicagoland high school, two young boys were fortunate enough to work for the school's low-powered FM radio station. Every Friday, it offered an interview program with celebrities kind enough to humor the inane questions posed by the teens (even the famed grouchy journalist Mike Royko once sat with them).

The memory of the Chicago Cubs' fall from grace in 1969 was still fresh in the minds of the two young Chicago fans (along with a New York Mets team that was no miracle, but the product of hard work—they won an astounding thirty-nine out of their final forty-nine games of the season). Somehow, the boys finagled an interview with Cubs catcher Randy Hundley, known in those days as "The Rebel," having hailed from Martinsville, Virginia.

In April 1970, the solid defensive catcher found himself in a Chicago hospital bed, recovering from a knee operation. The leg had been injured during a home plate collision with a St. Louis Cardinals player named Carl Taylor only a week earlier.

In the days before handheld digital recorders and portable cassette players, large and cumbersome reel-to-reel tape machines handled the job of capturing an interview for editing and later playback. The two boys dragged the unwieldy device on the local train down into the city, set it up in Hundley's hospital room, and engaged in an interesting and useful sixty-minute discussion.

Upon completion, one of the boys—an avid and rabid Cub fan—sheepishly asked the laid-up catcher for his autograph. But the bone-headed lad carried no pen with him. Randy, clad only in a flimsy hospital gown, also had no writing instrument (nor anywhere from which to pull one). Saddened, the boy went home empty-handed.

Fast-forward more than twenty years and the boy had become a man, still rapt with all things baseball and, specifically, the Cubs. He was fortunate enough to attend a Cubs Fantasy Camp that had been started, coincidentally, by Hundley.

The two met on the infield dirt of Wrigley Field, and the man, still sheepish, said, "Randy, more than twenty years ago, a high school kid interviewed you in your hospital bed and, when he asked for an autograph. . . ."

The Rebel slapped his shoulder and interrupted—"Buddy, did you ever find yourself a pen?"

Randy and I had a great laugh over that.

Pepi

During that same Fantasy Camp, I had the chance to kibbutz with many of my favorite ballplayers from my youth. Among the camp counselors was Cubs and Cardinals infielder Mike Tyson (no, not THAT one), great journeyman catcher J. C. Martin, the infielder Paul Popovich, known to many fans as "Super-Sub," and quite a few others.

For me, though, there was a unique thrill of meeting and playing with Joe Pepitone, formerly of the New York Yankees, Chicago Cubs, Houston Astros, and Atlanta Braves (for three whole games). In the 1960s and early 1970s, Pepitone made his name in the game for his helmet-like hair—much of it a toupee to cover his receding hairline. But I could have cared less—he was Italian, he had been a Cub and Yankee (two of my faves), a multiple All-Star and Gold-Glover, and he hit a bunch of homers.

My first face-to-face with "Pepi" was in the locker room as we prepared for our first day of camp. Joe stomped in, loudly swearing like a sailor that organizer Randy Hundley had mistakenly sent him to somewhere in Indiana and he had to find his own way to the ballpark. I was convinced it was all an act to emphasize the various and larger-than-life personalities found in baseball, but it was still a great scene.

To punctuate his displeasure, Pepitone uttered a final obscenity at Hundley, yanked the toupee from his own head, and hurled it to the floor with great vigor. Feeling suddenly bold, I said, "Joe, you look twenty years younger." He responded with a sexual suggestion that I engage in a physically impossible act with myself.

Later, on the field, I worked out at first base and routinely exchanged the ball from my glove to my throwing hand by flipping the ball about a foot in the air with some flair and grabbing it. Suddenly, Pepitone yelled out to me.

The author with Joe Pepitone, 1992.

"Hey, 44! 44!" (Actually, I had worn Joe's number 8 in college, but had quietly switched to alternate hero Reggie Jackson's 44 a few years later in softball.) He demanded, "Where'd you learn that fancy s%$&?"

"From my hero, Joe," I replied, "You!"

Once more, he responded with the same sexual suggestion that I engage in a physically impossible act with myself. Joe Pepitone—one classy guy.

Mad Dog

Speaking of classy guys, I would be remiss if I didn't share the quick story of my encounter with a truly classy guy—Greg Maddux.

In the summer of 1992—the last year (in the twentieth century) that "Mad Dog" would pitch for the Cubs—the ballplayers' wives had a benefit to collect funds for a charity known as Cubs Care. Part of the event had various players sitting at tables along the outfield warning track, signing autographs for waiting fans.

I attended the evening (with my dear sister-in-law and Cub-fan-in-arms, Nancy—Thanks, Nanc!) and patiently made the rounds, collecting signatures from some of my favorite players—Gary "The Sarge" Matthews, pitcher Danny Jackson, and future Hall of Famer Andre Dawson, among others.

Waiting in line took a fair amount of time for each player, and, finally, I came to Maddux' table. Just as I stepped up, a Cubs handler said, "Sorry, gotta go—no more signing," as he stood Maddux up and prepared to leave.

"Please, Greg," I implored, "Just one more?"

The future four-time Cy Young Award winner and eighteen-time (!) Gold-Glover paused, looked at the assistant, then looked at me, and said, "Sure . . . Of course." And, away he signed.

His Hall of Fame acceptance speech in July 2014 was just as classy.

Sweet Swingin'

While I'm hesitant to add another Cub story, the fact that I'm from the Chicago area naturally leaves me with a plethora of tales from Wrigley Field. One of my favorite memories concerns a great ball player that largely flew under the radar in his career, but he was always visible on mine.

Amid the larger-than-life personalities of Cub greats in the '60s and '70s like Ernie Banks and Ron Santo, left fielder Billy Williams was a quiet presence. Yet, his steady and potent offense at the plate—with, indeed, the sweetest swing you ever saw—thrilled Chicago fans for sixteen of his eighteen-year career in baseball. Plus, manning the ivy-covered well that perilously cut into the left field wall was a tough chore and something Williams took with great pride and importance.

In 1981, a strike stopped the game in mid-June (as noted in another chapter in this book.) By early August, concerns over free agency compensation were somewhat eased and it was announced that baseball would resume.

In an effort to soothe the ruffled feathers of fans, both Chicago teams announced they would feature two Cubs-Sox exhibition games—one each at Comiskey Park and Wrigley Field—before the official season resumed. As an added perk, retired players from both teams would face off in an old-timers game.

The seats were free—a rarity—and I settled into the front-row next to the Cubs dugout on that sunny Saturday afternoon, accompanied by my best baseball buddy, Bruce. We were excited to see many of our favorites—Banks, Santo, and other Cub greats.

In the second inning, Billy Williams stepped into the batter's box. At age 43, and retired since 1976, he still looked great and his swing was as sweet as ever. But the swing got even sweeter as he cranked a long home run out to the right field stands—retired or not. We yelled and hooted as Billy rounded the bases.

Six years later, Williams was honored with induction into the Hall of Fame. He had posted a .290 lifetime average with more

Great memories of the 1971 Cubs team.

than 2,700 hits, accompanied by 426 home runs, nearly 1,500 runs batted in (driving in 90 or more ten times,) and a slugging percentage of almost .500. The 1961 NL Rookie of the Year was also a six-time All Star and twice finished second in the NL MVP voting.

Billy was steady and consistent, playing in every game in a seven-year stretch between 1963 and 1970. His consecutive streak of 1,117 games remains in the Top Ten of the stamina in the game to this day.

The Big Apple (or is there a Missing "C-R"?)

Back in the mid-1990s, I had the chance to work in Northern New Jersey for three months. As my family was back in Chicagoland, I was alone on the weekends and often indulged my love of baseball by making a weekly sojourn to some indoor batting cages where I could work on my swing—and work out the frustrations of the job.

Since I was only a trip over the Tappan Zee Bridge from New York City, I also took the opportunity to attend a game at Shea Stadium, where the Mets were hosting the Chicago Cubs (no coincidence there). It was a clear night in the middle of August, and the Cubs won a close 3–2 game against the Mets. Jose Hernandez and Dave Magadan—hardly household names—hit homers for the Cubs. Mark Grace was hitting his typical .330s average and atypically, Ryne Sandberg was batting a mere .228, having returned to the team after his year-long retirement.

The real things that stay with me from that experience were the garish blue exterior of Shea Stadium and the monotonous drone of a Mets fan who blew a plastic horn (thankfully, many parks ban those kinds of things). What's more, an obviously drunken man in the upper deck on the third base side exercised his First Amendment right by constantly yelling "Meatball!" at the top of his lungs. (As there were no meatball subs being hawked at the game, I don't believe he was craving a sandwich.)

I can still recall that irritating roar, and if I live to be a hundred years old, I will hunt you down, mister, if only to stuff a tasty meatball sandwich down your throat. (Italians from Chicago know how to properly serve a good "sang-witch.")

The Big Apple (Part Two)

Just so you don't think I dislike all New York baseball, I must also relate my experience of visiting the hallowed Yankee Stadium from that same summer. It was a hot Sunday afternoon, and the Bronx Bombers were playing host to the Seattle Mariners.

As for many baseball fans, Yankee Stadium was a mecca for me, and even though the game wouldn't start until 1:30 p.m., I arrived before 11:00 in the morning. Walking around the building, I noted Macombs Dam Park, filled with sandlot-type ball diamonds. I imagined the hundreds or thousands of kids who grew up, playing ball in the shadow of Yankee Stadium. (That area of the park is now gone, becoming the site of the new Yankee Stadium opened in 2009.)

Both teams were filled with top-notch players. Seattle had guys like Joey Cora, Alex Rodriguez, Ken Griffey Jr., Edgar Martinez, and Paul Sorrento—all hitting near or over .300. Likewise, the Yankees started Derek Jeter, Wade Boggs, Bernie Williams, Tino Martinez, Mariano Duncan, Tim Raines, and Joe Girardi, who boasted similar stats. The Yanks had former Met Dwight Gooden starting on the mound, with a young Mariano Rivera waiting in the bullpen. Journeyman lefty Terry Mulholland would go for the Mariners, with a fellow named Randy Johnson ready to provide relief.

I walked inside and there it was—the fence-like façade that ran around the top over the bleachers. As I walked through Monument Park, I marveled at names like Ruth, Gehrig, DiMaggio, Mantle, Maris, and Berra. So far, it was a great day.

I took my seat in the upper deck on the third base side as the Mariners began batting practice. Watching Ken Griffey Jr., with his backwards ballcap, launch ball after ball into the hands of waiting fans in the right field stands, I had to laugh out loud at the consistency of his stroke—and the consistent results.

The game began, and it was obvious this wasn't one of Doc Gooden's good days. He gave up four straight singles and a walk before retiring Sorrento for the first out. The Mariners were up, 4–0, and the Yankees hadn't even batted yet. When they did, only Bernie Williams could muster a lonely single off Mulholland to end the first inning.

It was eighty degrees when the game started, but the humidity was quite high and there was no breeze. Sitting among the 44,000-plus fans, I felt stifled and sweaty. Despite my exciting visit being only one-third over, I decided to the leave the game after three innings. Besides, at that point, the Mariners led the Yanks, 8–0.

But as the great Yankee catcher/outfielder Yogi Berra once noted, "It ain't over 'til it's over" (simplicity at its utmost). By the time I reached my air-conditioned car in the parking building across from the stadium and turned the radio on, it was the end of four innings and the score was now 8–7, with Seattle's 7-run lead cut to just 1. The Yanks had managed 3 singles, 2 walks, 2 ground-rule doubles, and a home run in the bottom of the fourth to score seven times. The Yankees decided to make a game of it.

I sought relief from the heat by enjoying a round of hitting at the indoor batting cages, and when the game at Yankee Stadium finally ended—nearly five hours after it had started—the Yanks suffered a one-run loss in twelve innings. The final score was 13–12.

Considering the weather conditions that day, I didn't regret leaving the game, but it sure turned out to be a wild one. Not surprisingly, the Yankees would go on to win the World Series that year, beating the Atlanta Braves in six games.

And I had a helluva time in the House That Ruth Built.

Mr. Finley, Your Table's Ready

The chapter on the history of the game goes into some depth on the unique, and sometimes alienating, ways of former Oakland A's owner Charlie Finley. While it is my intention to only inform and entertain with the contents of this book, it might seem the stories about Finley there are a bit biased. As they are based on documented facts, I can only contribute this personal observation of the man.

Many years ago, in the late 1970s, I worked in downtown Chicago, just off Lake Shore Drive. Once or twice a week, I would join my friend Russ for lunch at a little restaurant in the area. It was run by an elderly Jewish woman named Ma Sherman and her son. Their daily menu was usually handwritten on a chalkboard in the back of the place.

One day, we're eating lunch, paying no attention to the other patrons (in retrospect, I wish I had looked around). The son approached the table right next to me and loudly said, "Hello, Mr. Finley—we have some very nice short ribs today." One look to my right and it was, indeed, Charles O. Finley, owner of the Oakland A's. Too stunned to say anything, I watched as he ate his lunch (it was the short ribs).

When he finished, a waitress gave him his check. He looked at it, put something on the table, and went up front to pay his bill and leave. I took a quick look at what he'd left and noticed a quarter and a dime.

In those days, the hot lunch might have been six or seven dollars, but I would have thought a multimillion-dollar baseball executive could leave more than a thirty-five-cent tip.

Jody! Jody Davis . . .

While working on the section of the book regarding the art (and science) of seeking autographs, I was reminded of one July Saturday at Wrigley Field. Back in 1983, it happened to be the first date with a very nice gal who eventually became my wonderful wife (the jury is still out as to why). With a pair of tickets that were fortunate enough to be second-row right behind the Cubs dugout, we had a nice afternoon.

But an odd fan grabbed (and continued to grab) our attention throughout the game. At every—I mean every—opportunity, this guy would run to the edge of the railing, slip of paper in hand, and yell whenever Cub catcher Jody Davis moved to or from the dugout. The guy had some rant going on, claiming his wife's aunt's uncle's daughter taught Jody back in grade school (the family members in the story seemed to change, so they may not be accurate; suffice it to say, it was a confusing mess).

Undeterred, Davis moved without acknowledging or reacting to the fellow, which seemed to motivate the jerk to yell louder and in a more animated manner. What occurred to me was, after Davis had just struck out in the fifth inning—in a simple sense, did not fulfill his job at that point—how anyone would expect him to be interested in talking to a fan. Picture it—middle of the game and someone wants an autograph—wrong place at the wrong time.

Imagine that a brain surgeon has just removed a portion of the cranium, exposing the cerebrum at a crucial point of a serious operation. Just then, the cell phone rings, with a telemarketing offer to lower the surgeon's credit card rate. Maybe it's not the same as playing baseball, but, once more—wrong place at the wrong time.

Hey buddy—sit down, be quiet, and watch the game.

Bibliography

Books

Asinof, Eliot. 1963. *Eight Men Out: The Black Sox and the 1919 World Series.* New York. Henry Holt and Company.

Block, David. 2005. *Baseball Before We Knew it: A Search for the Roots of the Game.* Lincoln. University of Nebraska Press.

The Commissioner of Baseball. 2014. *Official Baseball Rules.* New York. Major League Baseball.

Costa, Gabriel B., Michael Huber, and John T. Saccoman. 2008. *Understanding Sabermetrics: An Introduction to the Science of Baseball Statistics.* Jefferson, NC. McFarland and Company.

Dickerson, Gary E. 1991. *The Cinema of Baseball: Images of America, 1929–1989.* Westport, CT. Mecklermedia.

Dickson, Paul. 2009. *The Unwritten Rules of Baseball: The Etiquette, Conventional Wisdom, and Axiomatic Codes of Our National Pastime.* New York. Harper Publishing.

Didinger, Ray, and Glen Macnow. 2009. *The Ultimate Book of Sports Movies.* Philadelphia. Running Press.

Edelman, Rob. 1994. *Great Baseball Films: From Right Off the Bat to a League of Their Own.* New York. Citadel Press.

Erickson, Hal. 2010. *The Baseball Filmography, 1915 through 2001, 2nd Edition.* Jefferson, NC. McFarland and Company.

Feinstein, John. 2014. *Where Nobody Knows Your Name: Life in the Minor Leagues of Baseball.* New York. Doubleday Publishing.

Formosa, Dan, and Paul Hamburger. 2008. *Baseball Field Guide: An In-Depth Illustrated Guide to the Complete Rules of Baseball.* Philadelphia. DaCapo Press.

Foster, Frank. 2012. *The Forgotten League: A History of Negro League Baseball.* Anaheim, CA. BookCaps.

Goldstein Warren. 2009. *Playing for Keeps: A History of Early Baseball.* Ithaca, NY. Cornell University Press.

Green, G. Michael, and Roger D. Launius. 2010. *Charlie Finley: The Outrageous Story of Baseball's Super Showman.* New York. Walker Publishing Company.

Henderson, Robert W. 2001. *Ball, Bat and Bishop: The Origin of Ball Games.* Champaign-Urbana. University of Illinois Press.

Ilson, Carol. 2004. *Harold Prince: A Director's Journey.* Milwaukee, WI. Limelight Editions.

Kirsch, George B. 2003. *Baseball in Blue and Gray: The National Pastime During the Civil War.* Princeton, NJ. Princeton University Press.

Kuenster, John. 2006. *The Best of Baseball Digest: The Greatest Players, The Greatest Games, the Greatest Writers from the Game's Most Exciting Years.* Washington, DC. Ivan R. Dee.

Lowry, Philip J. 2006. *Green Cathedrals: The Ultimate Celebration of Major League and Negro League Ballparks.* New York. Walker and Company.

Lupica, Matt. 2012. *The Baseball Stadium Insider.* Bloomington, IN. iUniverse.

Mahony, Phillip. 2014. *Baseball Explained.* Jefferson, NC. McFarland and Company.

Masterson, Dave, and Timm Boyle. 1985. *Baseball's Best: The MVPs.* Chicago. Contemporary Books.

McBride, Joseph. 2011. *Steven Spielberg: A Biography, 2nd Edition.* Jackson. University Press of Mississippi.

Morris, Peter. 2006. *A Game of Inches: The Stories Behind the Innovations That Shaped Baseball: The Game on the Field (Volume 1).* Washington, DC. Ivan R. Dee.

Neyer, Rob. 2006. *Rob Neyer's Big Book of Baseball Blunders.* New York. Fireside Press.

Pastore, Eric. 2011. *500 Ballparks: From Wooden Seats to Retro Classics.* San Diego. Thunder Bay Press.

Peterson, Robert. 1992. *Only the Ball Was White: A History of Legendary Black Players and All-Black Professional Teams.* New York. Oxford University Press.

Pettis, Eric. 2012. *Just A Minor Perspective: Through the Eyes of a Minor League Rookie.* Seattle. Amazon Digital Services.

Thorn, John, and Pete Palmer, Michael Gershman, and Matthew Silverman. 2001. *Total Baseball: The Official Encyclopedia of Major League Baseball.* Kingston, NY. Total Sports.

Trexler, Phil, and Richard A. Johnson. 2011. *Ballparks, Yesterday & Today.* Lincolnwood, IL. Publications International.

Periodicals

Ashcraft, Jennifer K. and Craig A. Depken II. April 2007. The Introduction of the Reserve Clause in Major League Baseball: Evidence of its Impact on Select Player Salaries During the 1880s. *Working Paper Series, No. 07-10, International Association of Sport Economists.* Limoges, France.

Editors. October 4, 1886. The Western Pennant. *The Sporting News.* St. Louis, Missouri.

Goold, Derrick. October 10, 2014. Warren C. Giles Trophy. *St. Louis Post-Dispatch.* St. Louis, Missouri.

Gromer, Cliff. April 1997. Blue Plate Special. *Popular Mechanics.* New York.

Holtzman, Jerome. July 6, 1933. The First All-Star Game. *Chicago Tribune.* Chicago.

Johnson, John, Editor. July 1976. Bingo Long. *Ebony.* Chicago.

Kaat, Jim. April 1997. Mechanics of a Breaking Pitch. *Popular Mechanics.* New York.

Nathan, Alan M., and Lloyd V. Smith, Warren L. Faber and Daniel A. Russell. June 2011. Corked Bats, Juiced Balls, and Humidors: The Physics of Cheating in Baseball. *American Journal of Physics.* College Park, MD.

Snyder, David L. Spring 2008. Anatomy of an Aberration: An Examination of the Attempts to Apply Antitrust Law to Major League Baseball Through Flood v. Kuhn (1972). *DePaul Journal of Sports Law & Contemporary Problems.* Chicago.

Voelker, Daniel J., and Paul A. Duffy. September 2009. Black Sox: It Ain't So, Kid, It Just Ain't So. *Chicago Lawyer Magazine*. Chicago.

Recordings

Burns, Ken. 1994/2010. *Baseball*. PBS Home Video/DVD.
Savage, Adam., and Jamie Hyneman. August 8, 2007. *Mythbusters: Baseball Myths*. Discovery Channel.
Sweeney, D. B. September 8, 1988. *Late Night with David Letterman: Interview With D. B. Sweeney*. NBC.
Tackett, Mike. November 9, 2014. *Directing The Natural: Interview with Barry Levinson*. Virginia Film Festival.
Tibbetts, John C. February 7, 2011. *Bull Durham: Conversations About the Film*. University of Kansas.

Websites

http://baseballhall.org/
http://baseballjudgments.tripod.com/id45.html
http://bats.blogs.nytimes.com/2008/07/30/a-brief-history-of-the-eephus-pitch/
http://bleacherreport.com/articles/1576321-hardest-autographs-to-snag-in
   -baseball#articles/1576321-hardest-autographs-to-snag-in-baseball
http://chasingmlbdreams.com/about-chasing-the-dream/
http://espn.go.com/mlb/stats/parkfactor/_/year/2001/sort/HRFactor
http://hardballtalk.nbcsports.com/2010/03/17/a-few-words-on-cocaine-in-baseball/
http://law2.umkc.edu/faculty/projects/ftrials/blacksox/blacksoxaccount.html
http://militaryhistory.about.com/od/1800sarmybiographies/p/doubleday.htm
http://mlb.mlb.com/home
http://populous.com/projects/type/ballparks/
http://sabr.org/sabermetrics/statistics
http://www.19cbaseball.com/rules.html
http://www.abbottandcostellofanclub.com/who.html
http://www.ballparks.com/baseball/index.htm
http://www.ballparksofbaseball.com/
http://www.baseball-almanac.com/
http://www.baseballexaminer.com/faqs/scouting_faq.htm
http://www.baseballfieldguide.com/BFG_Judgement.html
http://www.baseballinwartime.com/
http://www.baseball-reference.com/
http://www.brobible.com/sports/article/12-minor-league-baseball-promotions
   -completely-thought/
http://www.ballparkratings.com/articles/n/History_of_Premium_Seating_and_
   Future_Trends
http://www.newsday.com/sports/baseball/a-brief-history-of-baseball-cards-1
   .2227938

http://www.news-herald.com/sports/20140331/baseball247-corbin-bernsen-on
-major-league-25-years-later-it-was-a-lot-of-fun

http://www.nytimes.com/2008/07/27/sports/baseball/27powell.html?_r=0

http://www.nytimes.com/2014/04/09/sports/baseball/30-seconds-with-jim-palmer
.html?_r=1

http://www.qcbaseball.com/pitching/pitching-windup.aspx

http://www.sbnation.com/2012/2/15/2800382/blue-jays-rogers-centre-artificial
-turf-natural-grass

http://www.sportingnews.com/mlb/feed/2011-08/thome-600/story/600-home
-run-club

http://www.statista.com/statistics/201018/purchases-of-baseball-and-softball
-equipment-in-the-us-since-2007/

http://www.statista.com/statistics/202743/hot-dog-prices-in-major-league-baseball
-by-team/

http://www.thisgreatgame.com/1969-baseball-history.html

Index

THE FAQ SERIES

AC/DC FAQ
by Susan Masino
Backbeat Books
978-1-4803-9450-6 .... $24.99

Armageddon Films FAQ
by Dale Sherman
Applause Books
978-1-61713-119-6 .... $24.99

Lucille Ball FAQ
*by James Sheridan
and Barry Monush*
Applause Books
978-1-61774-082-4 .... $19.99

The Beach Boys FAQ
by Jon Stebbins
Backbeat Books
978-0-87930-987-9 .... $22.99

The Beat Generation FAQ
by Rich Weidman
Backbeat Books
978-1-61713-601-6 .... $19.99

Black Sabbath FAQ
by Martin Popoff
Backbeat Books
978-0-87930-957-2 .... $19.99

Johnny Cash FAQ
by C. Eric Banister
Backbeat Books
978-1-4803-8540-5 .... $24.99

A Chorus Line FAQ
by Tom Rowan
Applause Books
978-1-4803-6754-8 .... $19.99

Eric Clapton FAQ
by David Bowling
Backbeat Books
978-1-61713-454-8 .... $22.99

Doctor Who FAQ
by Dave Thompson
Applause Books
978-1-55783-854-4 .... $22.99

The Doors FAQ
by Rich Weidman
Backbeat Books
978-1-61713-017-5 .... $24.99

Dracula FAQ
by Bruce Scivally
Backbeat Books
978-1-61713-600-9 .... $19.99

The Eagles FAQ
by Andrew Vaughan
Backbeat Books
978-1-4803-8541-2 .... $24.99

Fab Four FAQ
*by Stuart Shea and
Robert Rodriguez*
Hal Leonard Books
978-1-4234-2138-2 .... $19.99

Fab Four FAQ 2.0
by Robert Rodriguez
Backbeat Books
978-0-87930-968-8 .... $19.99

Film Noir FAQ
by David J. Hogan
Applause Books
978-1-55783-855-1 .... $22.99

Football FAQ
by Dave Thompson
Backbeat Books
978-1-4950-0748-4 .... $24.99

The Grateful Dead FAQ
by Tony Sclafani
Backbeat Books
978-1-61713-086-1 .... $24.99

Haunted America FAQ
by Dave Thompson
Backbeat Books
978-1-4803-9262-5 .... $19.99

Jimi Hendrix FAQ
by Gary J. Jucha
Backbeat Books
978-1-61713-095-3 .... $22.99

Horror Films FAQ
by John Kenneth Muir
Applause Books
978-1-55783-950-3 .... $22.99

James Bond FAQ
by Tom DeMichael
Applause Books
978-1-55783-856-8 .... $22.99

Stephen King Films FAQ
by Scott Von Doviak
Applause Books
978-1-4803-5551-4 .... $24.99

KISS FAQ
by Dale Sherman
Backbeat Books
978-1-61713-091-5 .... $22.99

Led Zeppelin FAQ
by George Case
Backbeat Books
978-1-61713-025-0 .... $19.99

Modern Sci-Fi Films FAQ
by Tom DeMichael
Applause Books
978-1-4803-5061-8 .... $24.99

Prices, contents, and availability
subject to change without notice.

Morrissey FAQ
by D. McKinney
Backbeat Books
978-1-4803-9448-3............ $24.99

Nirvana FAQ
by John D. Luerssen
Backbeat Books
978-1-61713-450-0............. $24.99

Pink Floyd FAQ
by Stuart Shea
Backbeat Books
978-0-87930-950-3............$19.99

Elvis Films FAQ
by Paul Simpson
Applause Books
978-1-55783-858-2............. $24.99

Elvis Music FAQ
by Mike Eder
Backbeat Books
978-1-61713-049-6............. $24.99

Prog Rock FAQ
by Will Romano
Backbeat Books
978-1-61713-587-3............... $24.99

Pro Wrestling FAQ
by Brian Solomon
Backbeat Books
978-1-61713-599-6.............. $29.99

Rush FAQ
by Max Mobley
Backbeat Books
978-1-61713-451-7................ $24.99

Saturday Night Live FAQ
by Stephen Tropiano
Applause Books
978-1-55783-951-0.............. $24.99

Prices, contents, and availability
subject to change without notice.

Seinfeld FAQ
by Nicholas Nigro
Applause Books
978-1-55783-857-5.............. $24.99

Sherlock Holmes FAQ
by Dave Thompson
Applause Books
978-1-4803-3149-5............. $24.99

The Smiths FAQ
by John D. Luerssen
Backbeat Books
978-1-4803-9449-0........... $24.99

Soccer FAQ
by Dave Thompson
Backbeat Books
978-1-61713-598-9............... $24.99

The Sound of Music FAQ
by Barry Monush
Applause Books
978-1-4803-6043-3............ $27.99

South Park FAQ
by Dave Thompson
Applause Books
978-1-4803-5064-9........... $24.99

Bruce Springsteen FAQ
by John D. Luerssen
Backbeat Books
978-1-61713-093-9................$22.99

Star Trek FAQ
(Unofficial and Unauthorized)
by Mark Clark
Applause Books
978-1-55783-792-9................$19.99

Star Trek FAQ 2.0
(Unofficial and Unauthorized)
by Mark Clark
Applause Books
978-1-55783-793-6................$22.99

Star Wars FAQ
by Mark Clark
Applause Books
978-1-4803-6018-1.............. $24.99

Quentin Tarantino FAQ
by Dale Sherman
Applause Books
978-1-4803-5588-0 .... $24.99

Three Stooges FAQ
by David J. Hogan
Applause Books
978-1-55783-788-2...............$22.99

The Who FAQ
by Mike Segretto
Backbeat Books
978-1-4803-6103-4 .... $24.99

The Wizard of Oz FAQ
by David J. Hogan
Applause Books
978-1-4803-5062-5............ $24.99

The X-Files FAQ
by John Kenneth Muir
Applause Books
978-1-4803-6974-0............ $24.99

Neil Young FAQ
by Glen Boyd
Backbeat Books
978-1-61713-037-3..................$19.99

HAL•LEONARD®
PERFORMING ARTS
PUBLISHING GROUP

FAQ.halleonardbooks.com

0815